2

P9-BYL-411

AMERICAN OPINION AND THE IRISH QUESTION
1910–23

F. M. CARROLL

American Opinion and the Irish Question 1910-23

A study in opinion and policy

GILL AND MACMILLAN
and
ST. MARTIN'S PRESS

First published 1978 by
Gill and Macmillan Ltd
15/17 Eden Quay
Dublin 1
with associated companies in
London, Delhi, Hong Kong,
Johannesburg, Lagos, Melbourne,
Singapore, Tokyo

7171 0822 8

First published
in the United States of America
in 1978 by
St. Martin's Press, Inc.,
175 Fifth Avenue,
New York, N.Y. 10010

Library of Congress Catalog Card Number 78-58897
ISBN 0-312-02890-3

Printed (and bound in Great Britain) by
Bristol Typesetting Co. Ltd., Barton Manor, St. Philip's, Bristol

For
Janet Foster Carroll,
to whom I owe a debt that
cannot be repaid

CONTENTS

Contents, continued

PREFACE

THIS book attempts to define the diverse views held on the Irish question by both Irish-Americans and native Americans from 1910 to 1923, and, in so far as possible, to show how these various opinions influenced the revolution in Ireland and shaped the policies of the American and British governments. It may properly be asked if it is possible to deal in a meaningful way with opinion in so large and heterogeneous a nation as America. Because several distinct groups within the American community were exceptionally conscious of Irish nationalist aspirations and the role played by Ireland in Anglo-American relations this is not an unrealistic proposal; it is upon these groups, rather than the whole of American society, that this study has been focused. Indeed, the Irish-American nationalists (constitutional and revolutionary, and later, republican and pro-Free State), the native Americans (sympathetic and hostile) and the United States government (the several presidential administrations, the State Department and the Congress) can be isolated and analysed, and from the documents now available conclusions and generalisations can be drawn on the degree to which the views of any one of these groups influenced Irish affairs. In attempting to define the various bodies of American opinion considerable emphasis is given to Irish-American nationalism and nationalist organisations and to xenophobic and nativist feelings among native Americans; it should be noted that this volume is not specifically a study of these topics, although from time to time it has been necessary to examine them at some length in order to explain how Irish-American attitudes were translated into political activity or how native Americans reacted to such ethnic nationalism within the United States.

Abbreviations, capitalisation and documentation have been patterned principally after the suggestions set forth by *Irish Historical Studies*, although certain exceptions have been made, especially in footnote citations for manuscript material, where the spelling and coding of the depository have been used. The word 'Republic' has been capitalised when referring specifically to the Irish Republic after 1916, but it has not been capitalised when referring simply to a system of government. However, the capitalised term 'Republican' is used only to designate the American political party of that name: thus 'Republican Party' is capitalised but 'Irish republicans' is not. No suitable term exists to describe accurately in a manner which is not pejorative those native-born Americans of English descent who were largely the founders of the United States and who still in the early twentieth century constituted the establishment. The term 'native Americans', rather than the slang expression WASP, is used here to distinguish this group of people from immigrant groups such as the Irish-Americans.

This book has its origins in a thesis submitted for the degree of Doctor of Philosophy to Trinity College, Dublin, in 1969, and I should like to acknowledge a special debt of thanks to Professor R. B. McDowell, who served as my supervisor. Dr Richard P. Davis of the University of Tasmania and Professor John Kendle of St John's College, The University of Manitoba, both read the manuscript version of this book and gave me their helpful suggestions. For their many kindnesses to me I should like to thank Professor Carleton C. Qualey, now of the Minnesota Historical Society, Professor Robert E. Rhodes of the State University of New York at Cortland, and Professor Joseph P. O'Grady of LaSalle College, Philadelphia, Pennsylvania. I also want to thank The University of Manitoba for grants assisting me in travelling to London and New York in 1970 and 1971 to carry out part of the research for this book. Several of the themes of this volume have been presented as papers or lectures. Parts of Chapter 1 were given in altered form before the Annual Conference of the American Committee for Irish Studies in 1968, and parts of Chapters 6 and 7 served as the basis for one of the Maurice Francis Egan Lectures at LaSalle College in 1971 and a seminar in diplomatic history at the University of Winnipeg in 1976.

The form of research upon which this book is based depended on access to a large number of manuscript libraries on both sides of the Atlantic. It is with great pleasure that I acknowledge my debt for the opportunity to work in the collections of the following libraries and archives and to give my thanks to their staffs: in Ireland, the Friends' Historical Library (and especially Mrs Olive C. Goodbody, the Curator), the National Library of Ireland (and especially Mr Alf Mac Lochlainn, now the Keeper of Books) and Trinity College Library; in Great Britain, the Beaverbrook Library, the Bodleian Library, the British Museum, the Plunkett Foundation and the Public Records Office; and in the United States, the American Irish Historical Society, the Catholic University of America Archives, the Chancery Archives (Archdiocese of Detroit), Harvard University Library, the Library of Congress, Massachusetts Historical Society, the University of Michigan Library, the National Archives of the United States, New York Public Library, Wisconsin State Historical Society and Yale University Library. I particularly want to thank Mr George L. Lodge for permission to use the Henry Cabot Lodge Papers, the Hughes family for permission to use the Charles Evans Hughes Papers, and Miss Kathleen Cohalan for permission to use the Daniel F. Cohalan Papers.

F. M. Carroll
St John's College
The University of Manitoba
8 July 1977

LIST OF ABBREVIATIONS

AARIR	American Association for the Recognition of the Irish Republic
A.I.H.S.	American Irish Historical Society, New York
AOH	Ancient Order of Hibernians
B.M.	British Museum, London
Bodl.	Bodleian Library, Oxford
C.S.M.	*Christian Science Monitor*
F.O.	Foreign Office
FOIF	Friends of Irish Freedom
G.A.	*Gaelic American*
I.H.S.	*Irish Historical Studies*
IPL	Irish Progressive League
IRB	Irish Republican Brotherhood
L.C.	Library of Congress
Lit. Dig.	*Literary Digest*
N.A.	National Archives, Washington, DC
N.L.I.	National Library of Ireland, Dublin
N.Y.P.L.	New York Public Library, New York
N.Y.T.	New York *Times*
P.R.O	Public Record Office, London
UIL	United Irish League of America (founded 1900); associated with the Irish-based United Irish League (founded 1898)

CHAPTER 1
INTRODUCTION: THE IRISH IN AMERICA
1840–1910

I. Prologue

On 7 October 1924 Dr Timothy A. Smiddy, Minister Plenipotentiary of the Irish Free State, presented his credentials to President Calvin Coolidge in the White House. It was a long-awaited moment in Irish and American history. Indeed, as Dr Smiddy said in his address to the President, 'To my country this occasion is of deep and historic interest.'[1] Ostensibly the event marked the culmination of a multitude of aspirations and objectives. In fact at the high point of agitation in the United States six years earlier several bills had been before Congress which were designed to force the President to extend diplomatic recognition to Ireland. Ireland, with diplomatic representation, could now be seen to be 'a nation once again', albeit a dominion as well. The United States, relieved of the interjection of Irish nationalist pleas in its domestic affairs and international relations, could now sympathetically welcome into the family of nations a people with whom it had long and intimate ties. Great Britain, more or less freed from an endemic problem of how to govern Ireland—a problem which seemed to stretch back to at least the reign of Elizabeth—might look forward to a climate sufficiently improved as to remove British domestic affairs from discussion by foreign powers. In particular, she could confidently expect a genuine rapprochement between herself and the one English-speaking country outside the Empire, the United States.

Of course, all of these objectives and aspirations, and more as well, were only partially realised. The irony of the ceremonies in the White House on 7 October was clear. Instead of an extravagant celebration, with hosts of Irish-American dignitaries giving witness to the event and possibly even a benign British Ambassador looking on, an extremely brief and modest ritual took place with the President and the minister giving short and in many ways perfunctory speeches. Outsiders were not invited for the ceremony or after. The British Ambassador, Sir Esmé Howard, thought it better not to accompany Dr Smiddy in order that the new minister not be compromised by too close association with the British Embassy. The newspapers to a large extent ignored it. For example, the New York *Times*, which had a front-page feature story on the fate of the boundary between the Irish Free State and Northern Ireland, described the presentation of credentials in a short, bland article on page twenty-one.[2] The ceremony did indeed mark the end of the most prolonged, intensive and important period of Irish nationalist agitation in all three countries, but it was in truth something of an anticlimax.

II.   *The Irish Question in the United States*

The phrase 'the Irish question', about which arose some dispute and a fair number of quips, became common usage during the nineteenth century as a convenient way of referring to the unresolved problem of how Ireland should be governed. Dating from the great migrations resulting from the famine of the 1840s, the Irish question became a public issue in the United States, particularly by the end of the nineteenth century. Indeed, the discussion of Ireland became an almost permanent feature of both domestic American politics and foreign affairs. British–American diplomatic relations were particularly bedevilled from at least 1860 onwards. The anti-British attitude which many of the Irish immigrants harboured as a result of their migrations and their nationalist political aspirations for Ireland, coincided with a latent anglophobia in the United States which was in part an inheritance of the republican antipathies stretching back to the American Revolution and the war of 1812. This native American anglophobia was partially a response to British supremacy in finance and world trade as it affected United States interests, and partially a reaction to Britain's rather dominant position in world affairs and international relations. Many Americans, because of their own historical experience, republican political institutions, egalitarian ideology and economic tradition, were predisposed to sympathise with the Irish in their anglophobe and nationalist sentiments. The result was that the Irish question was effectively kept before the American people for a longer time, and perhaps on a grander scale, than any other ethnic nationalist movement in the United States before or since.

The attitudes of Irish-Americans and native Americans formed the two significant bodies of opinion on the Irish question, although the former was better organised, more persistently sustained and more important. This book attempts to define the diverse views held on the Irish question by both Irish-Americans and native Americans from 1910 to 1923, and to show as far as possible how these various opinions influenced the revolution in Ireland and shaped the policies of the American and British governments. The study traces American opinion on the Home Rule movement, on the events following the Easter Rising of 1916, on Ireland during the participation of the United States in the First World War and the Peace Conference, on the Anglo-Irish struggle, and on the crisis surrounding the creation of the Irish Free State. Irish-American opinion was extremely complex and often rent by factionalism, although it agreed on the virtues of Irish self-government.[3] In contrast, native American opinion was divided on both the merits and the methods of satisfying Irish nationalist aspirations. After 1916, at least, all these groups articulated more clearly their views on Ireland. The book attempts to demonstrate that the accumulation of this body of opinion was critically important, although not solely decisive, in shaping the policies of the United States and British governments, as well as the plans of the Irish nationalist leaders themselves, during the Irish struggle from 1910 to 1923.

III.   The Growth of Irish-American Nationalism

The full effects of the great Irish migration to the United States which began in the aftermath of the famine of the 1840s were felt from 1870 to 1890, when the number of Irish-born Americans averaged over 1,850,000; by 1900 there were 4,826,904 Americans either born in Ireland or with Irish parents.[4] However, the Census Bureau did not account for the third- or fourth-generation Irish-Americans, who were estimated to number at least 20,000,000 by several Irish-American leaders who claimed to speak on their behalf. Thus, although a minority in the country, Americans of Irish descent may have represented nearly 19 per cent of the entire population by 1920, and they were a very remarkable and powerful element of American society. As an ethnic group, the Irish-Americans seemed unanimous in their support of some kind of self-government for Ireland, although they often disagreed vigorously over the form such self-government should take—Home Rule within the Empire or independence—and the method through which it should be achieved—constitutional reform or revolutionary action. Professor F. S. L. Lyons has argued that it is a mistake to regard these political positions as separate movements, and in fact when circumstances and personalities permitted they coalesced; but broadly speaking these positions represented the two poles of Irish-American nationalism.[5] Furthermore, although it is not yet possible to determine conclusively the causal relationships involved, it is clear that these movements among the Irish in the United States paralleled nationalist affairs in Ireland during the same periods.

Irish-American nationalism was the product of a number of forces. The most obvious, of course, was the response of many immigrants and their descendants to the specific conditions in Ireland that prompted their departure and to the economic and social climate in the homeland generally. These circumstances were seen as the direct result of British rule—or misrule—in Ireland. Only an Ireland governed by Irishmen and answerable to Irishmen would foster Irish interests; only a national government of some kind would create conditions which would allow a prosperous economy to develop and a social system to evolve which would encourage Gaelic Catholic Irishmen to feel fully at home in their own country. Probably in these sentiments the immigrants did not differ very much from Irish nationalists at home. But another force which was at work among the Irish-Americans was their reaction to the social rejection they experienced from many native Americans. Rejected because of their religion, their brogue, their poverty, their ignorance and the comic associations that soon became attached to all things Irish, they fell back upon themselves and indeed upon Ireland. If Ireland could in fact be made 'a nation once again' and the endemic poverty and famine eliminated, if Irish art and literature could be given their true place of standing in the world of culture, if Irishmen could be made masters in their own house, then Irish immigrants abroad could no longer be dismissed as comic figures. In short, if Irishmen could command their own destinies at home, they would command respect abroad as well. One important consequence of this domestic issue was that Irish-American nationalism was often inextricably involved in American politics, to the dismay of purely Irish nationalists. These forces, and others as well, worked to create the Irish-American nationalist movement which carried out an active programme from the 1840s to at least the middle of the 1920s.

Irish-American nationalism has been the subject of several books, the most outstanding of which is a fine study by Thomas N. Brown, and the topic will not in itself be pursued at great length here.[6] It does bear mentioning, however, that one of the most outstanding features of the movement was the high degree of organisation that characterised it. Although specific organisations might decline and become defunct, the energies of Irish-American nationalists were systematically enlisted and put to work by Irish-American societies which were able to institutionalise the process of political activity and fund-raising. To be sure, these organisations were vulnerable to abuse by individuals who hoped to exploit them for their own purposes. But throughout the period under examination there were always several Irish-American organisations on a nation-wide scale that were able to absorb Irish-Americans who wanted to support the cause of Irish self-government. No single scholarly work has yet traced the history of these nationalist organisations from the period of the American Revolution up to the rivalries and court battles between the Friends of Irish Freedom and the American Association for the Recognition of the Irish Republic in the 1920s and 1930s. Working from a variety of secondary sources dealing with various themes or episodes, however, one can form an impression of the activities of the nationalist movement and its failures and successes.

Serious Irish nationalist activities in the United States might be said to date from 1840 with the founding of the Friends of Ireland Society, which worked to support Daniel O'Connell's Repeal movement and which was reorganised as the Confederation of the United Friends of Ireland in order to deal with the crisis of the famine. In the 1850s the political activities of the Irish Immigrant Aid Society kept nationalist efforts alive, but a more formidable organisation was created late in the decade by several of the participants of the 1848 insurrection who were then living in Ireland, France and the United States. The Irish Revolutionary Brotherhood (or the Irish Republican Brotherhood, as it was also known) became the main channel through which both Irish-American and Irish nationalists organised themselves. Through the journalistic efforts of John O'Mahony in the United States this movement became known almost immediately as the Fenian Brotherhood.[7]

Within two years the United States was plunged into the secession crisis and the American Civil War. These events created a set of conditions both within the United States and in international affairs which the Fenians were able to exploit effectively on both sides of the Atlantic. Despite the seemingly international aspect of the movement, historians have increasingly viewed Fenianism as 'a product of the Civil War'.[8] Certainly the war created conditions in which the United States government, and to a lesser extent the Confederate, was prepared to tacitly approve Irish nationalist activities, regardless of the consequences and international implications, in exchange for enthusiastic enlistments in their respective armies by Irishmen. The Fenians, for their part, viewed the war as a training and organising opportunity for the building of a disciplined and combat-experienced military force, and they were also anxious to exploit the ambiguous position of the United States government in order to suggest that their movement had official endorsement. These exceptional circumstances were prolonged during the Reconstruction crisis after the American Civil War until at least the national elections of 1868.[9]

The Fenian movement in the 1860s was, of course, a failure. The attempted insurrection in Ireland in 1867 and the attempted invasions of Canada in 1866 and 1870 and several other projects were all disastrously unsuccessful. Plagued by problems of leadership and command, by effective British intelligence penetration, by over-ambitious plans and by communications difficulties, Fenians in Ireland, England and Canada were easily frustrated by crown forces. But despite their failures, the Fenians had a spark of life which survived. In the United States the movement was reorganised in 1867 into an oath-bound secret society called the Clan na Gael. Cloaking itself in mystery and secrecy, proclaiming fierce Irish-American nationalism, the Clan became the major instrument of revolutionary agitation, and some domestic political activity also, right up to the 1920s. Indeed, the Clan was adaptable enough to work with political programmes such as the 'New Departure' wherein John Devoy, the old Fenian, fostered an uneasy relationship with Charles Stewart Parnell and the Irish parliamentarians in 1878.[10] This facilitated the creation in 1880 of the American Land League, which became a large, successful, and furthermore respectable organisation that was supported by almost all factions of the Irish-American community—the *Irish World*, the Boston *Pilot*, the Irish Catholic Benevolent Union (the largest Irish society in America), the Ancient Order of Hibernians, as well as the Clan na Gael.

By the 1880s the aspirations of the Irish-American nationalists and the necessities of domestic party politics in the United States seemed to coincide once again. Thomas N. Brown suggests that the two political parties, the Democrats and the Republicans, were in a state of 'unstable equilibrium', and that if the Irish-Americans could be welded into a disciplined and independent voting bloc, they could swing the balance of power in the country and thus determine victory or defeat for the two major parties.[11] Through the manipulative skills of an ambitious Chicago lawyer, Alexander Sullivan, the Clan na Gael, the newly formed American National League (the successor to the American Land League) and the Ancient Order of Hibernians were all brought under the nominal control of one man. Sullivan clearly had high hopes that the Irish-American community could be won away from their traditional party, the Democrats, and into the fold of the Republican Party, thus making Sullivan a figure of national political prominence and great power. However, the internal tensions on the Irish-American nationalists became too great. In 1883 trouble developed in the Clan resulting in a split of the organisation into two factions. Rocked by scandal, stunned by the revelations of the British intelligence agent called Major Henri Le Caron at the Parnell Special Commission hearings, and finally placed under critical public scrutiny in a lurid murder trial, in which Sullivan was alleged to have ordered the murder of a Clan member, the organisation was badly crippled. A fight initiated by Sullivan in the Ancient Order of Hibernians over control of that organisation split the society into 'Irish' and 'American' factions, and although Sullivan was ousted during the Cronin murder trial, it took ten years to reunite the AOH. The collapse of the American National League was largely due to the fall of Parnell in Ireland.[12] The result of the collapse of all three organisations as well as the leadership of Parnell in Ireland and Sullivan in the United States was that Irish nationalism, both revolutionary and constitutional, was in a shambles by the 1890s.

The first organisation to rebuild itself was the American wing of the Irish Parliamentary Party, which by May 1891 had established the Irish National Federation of America. The federation was led by Dr Thomas Addis Emmet, the grand-nephew of Robert Emmet and a physician of international distinction, and its functions were similar to the league it replaced—to mould opinion in America in favour of Irish self-government and to raise money for the Irish Party. By 1893 the federation was able to hold large rallies to demonstrate support in America for the approaching fight in parliament over the new Home Rule Bill. Dr Emmet was able to solicit the favourable comments and attendance of a number of state governors, records of which were all sent to Gladstone as an indication of American sympathy for the Irish cause, and John Dillon's appeal for $150,000 to finance the 1892 general election in Ireland was quickly met.[13] But the peak had been reached; the defeat of the Home Rule Bill and the continued disunity in the Irish Party crippled the federation in America.

With the reunion in 1900 of the largest factions of the Irish Parliamentary Party under John Redmond, organised support within the United States grew quickly. The United Irish League of America was founded to replace the defunct federation, and with publicity from the *Irish World* branches sprang up first in the New York area and then throughout the country. By 1901 the league had the endorsement and promise of financial support of the United Irish Societies, a body which co-ordinated activities for small Irish-American clubs throughout the country. Later in 1901 Redmond and Joseph Devlin toured the country to stimulate interest in Home

Rule, and as a result the United Irish League was able to create a national organisation with centres in many major American cities. A national convention was held in Boston in October of 1902 with Redmond, Dillon and Edward Blake as guest speakers, and it was attended by over 700 delegates from throughout the United States and Canada. The Irish leaders later undertook a fund-raising tour throughout the country and collected some $100,000.[14] While all this appeared promising, the league was soon surrounded by scandal as funds destined for Ireland failed to arrive there. When an auditing committee investigated the account books of the New York Municipal Council, which processed all funds from the league branches in the New York area, two conflicting reports were produced. Although the national headquarters supported the report favouring the Municipal Council, the damage was done. The momentum of the league slipped in the middle years of the first decade of the century, and in fact did not revive again until after 1910 when Home Rule appeared to be an immediate prospect.

The discredited and strife-ridden factions of the Clan na Gael were unable to resolve their difficulties until nearly the end of the decade, and until they did the Clan was incapable of exerting significant influence in the United States. The Sullivan wing seemed to be the stronger of the two factions in spite of the charges made against it. Alexander Sullivan was succeeded by William Lyman, who held their organisation together from the Chicago headquarters. But the Sullivan supporters were diverted from effectively forwarding the Irish cause. Even Maude Gonne, who was an admirer of Sullivan, was distressed by how much money the Clan spent on local functions and how little found its way to Ireland to carry on the revolutionary work there. Devoy's years of waiting finally bore fruit in 1899 when Lyman was expelled from the Clan by his own faction at a convention in Buffalo. Lyman proved to be the last major obstacle for a reunion. The Clan was reunited in the following year, 1900, at a joint convention of the two factions at Atlantic City. John Devoy, Daniel F. Cohalan, Joseph McGarrity and John T. Keating emerged as the dominant figures, and they quickly committed the society to a 'physical-force' policy.[15] In 1903 Devoy and his supporters founded the *Gaelic American*, through which the Clan was able to mount a weekly campaign against Home Rule, the Irish Parliamentary Party and the British Empire.

Having broken with Redmond and the Irish politicians, the Clan was left to promote a revolutionary policy during a period when no great reforms were taking place in Ireland and no revolution was possible. Its immediate and natural reaction was to fight the British

Empire in America by opposing the Boer War and by urging the Senate to resist the Anglo-American treaties of 1900, 1904–05 and 1911–12. The policy of the Clan in regard to Ireland was to support those organisations which grew up largely during the 1890s in the wake of the collapse of the Irish Parliamentary Party following the Parnell divorce crisis. Clan na Gael money was found to support Arthur Griffith's newspaper, the *United Irishman*, and by 1906 Bulmer Hobson, who was co-operating with Griffith in Ireland, was invited by Devoy to come to the United States to lecture on the Sinn Féin movement. Hobson was told that the three similar small organisations in Ireland should amalgamate.[16]

The Gaelic League also functioned in the United States from 1899 onwards, and through the efforts of Diarmuid Lynch it won the support of Daniel F. Cohalan and the Clan in 1903. Under the sponsorship of John Quinn and Cohalan, Douglas Hyde toured the United States in 1905–06 lecturing on the Gaelic League. Clan endorsement of the Gaelic League was clear in a circular published during Hyde's visit which said : 'The work of the Gaelic League is in line with the objects of the Clan na Gael. It is preparing the mind of the country for the supreme effort which will lead to the final triumph of the Gael.' Many of the same people—Quinn, Cohalan, W. Bourke Cockran and others—assisted in the tours of W. B. Yeats and other members of the Irish literary movement.

However, all these activities, while perhaps fruitful in the long run, were at the time a most indirect means of forwarding a revolutionary policy in Ireland. Perhaps the most important contribution of the Clan to the possible revolution in Ireland was the continued financial support of about £1,000 a year to the Irish Republican Brotherhood and the regular attendance of IRB representatives at the annual Clan convention. The introduction of such people as Thomas J. Clarke, Dr Patrick McCartan and, to a degree, Diarmuid Lynch to the IRB also contributed greatly to the subsequent rejuvenation of that organisation.[17]

IV. The Native American Response to the Irish Question

Native American attitudes on the Irish question during the nineteenth century turned on a more fundamental issue than did those of Irish-Americans. Native Americans approached the problem by asking whether Irish self-government would be desirable or not, and substantial bodies of opinion developed supporting both positions. Of the two, the hostile opinion was more organised and long-lasting and (for the historians) more accessible and easily recorded. But this is not to say that the Irish cause did not have friends among the native Americans. The American nation was itself an expression of democratic nationalism, and it was regarded also as a monument to the principles of federal home rule. American antipathy towards the British monarchy and aristocracy, and towards colonialism and some forms of imperialism, were part of a long tradition of anti-British feeling in the United States that went back to the War of Independence and George III. Thus many Americans were naturally predisposed to support any nationalist movement such as that in Ireland. Furthermore, native American sympathy for the Irish cause was often motivated by very practical reasons. Some native American public figures made quite insincere statements about Irish nationalism merely in the hope of recruiting Irish-American political support, while others looked genuinely for a solution to the Irish question in a desire to help create more harmonious Anglo-American relations or to eliminate the causes of aggressive Irish-American nationalism in domestic affairs. In any case, in times of opportunity or crisis, such as the periods of the Young Ireland movement or the Fenian movement or the land war, prominent native Americans, from George Washington to Horace Greeley and from Rutherford B. Hayes to Theodore Roosevelt, each in their own way endorsed and supported the Irish cause.

Unfortunately, however, for the Irish movement, favourable native American opinion was not organised to the same extent as either hostile opinion or Irish-American opinion. Those liberal or reform-minded Americans who were the driving force in agitation such as the anti-slavery, temperance, women's suffrage or anti-imperialist campaigns were not moved to marshal their energies in support for Irish self-government, largely because Ireland was too far away and the many social problems at home were all too close. Not until the 1920s were there Irish nationalist organisations which enlisted the support of large numbers of native Americans. The result was that in the nineteenth century no large body of pro-Irish sentiment was developed by native American organisations in an institutional manner. Favourable native American opinion found its expression in editorials and from speakers' platforms at moments of crisis, but often as an adjunct to more organised Irish-American activity.

The unfavourable opinions that many native Americans held on the Irish question were in large part conditioned by at least three factors. Two of these factors, religious bias and racial bias, were a part of the intellectual and cultural climate of opinion in the United States during the late nineteenth and early twentieth centuries. The third factor can be described as the impact made on native Americans by the Irish immigrants themselves.

During the nineteenth century native Americans, Anglo-Saxon Protestants, clearly regarded the United States as a Protestant country, and it is important to keep in mind that much of the force of native American religious heritage came out of the radical wing of the Protestant Reformation. Certainly the power of this movement—as a movement—had largely spent itself by the twentieth century, but nevertheless native Americans still tended to see things from a Protestant bias. Within this framework Catholicism was often seen as a superstitious, idolatrous, oriental religion implemented by a dogmatic, authoritarian, institutional system emanating from Rome. Briefly, many Americans viewed Catholicism as an antichristian conspiracy which threatened political, religious, intellectual and educational freedom. Thomas Nast's provocative cartoons illustrate this point. Furthermore, Ireland was seen as not just another Catholic country, but as one of the principal heirs to the tradition of the Catholic Counter-Reformation. Given the Catholic–Protestant sectarian strife in Ireland, this view, superficially at least, was not altogether mistaken. The resistance of the Ulster Protestants to Repeal and to Home Rule before the First World War tended to convince many Americans that there was something very wrong in Ireland and that the Catholic Church was at the bottom of it.[18] In these circumstances it is not surprising that many Americans had notions of Ireland based on the degree to which Ireland could be made to conform to their own accepted understanding of Catholic–Protestant tension.

A second major bias of native Americans, which during the late nineteenth and early twentieth centuries worked increasingly to shape the image of Ireland, was the concept of Anglo-Saxon racial superiority. Such theorists as George Edward Woodberry, Edward A. Ross, John W. Burgess and Henry Fairfield Osborn had by several tortuous routes arrived at the conclusion that the Anglo-Saxons, or more popularly the English-speaking peoples, were the most highly developed racial or ethnic group in the world. With evidence of the far-flung British Empire, the smooth-running British social and political system and the technical and industrial accomplishments of Britain, Anglo-Saxon superiority was virtually self-evident. Throughout the world the Anglo-Saxons were the most capable, the most technologically competent, the most powerful, the most wealthy and the most enlightened. Paradoxically also, the Anglo-Saxons were both the most democratic and the most fit to govern others. The racial concepts of various other people in Europe were defined in several ways and were vastly modified to conform to the necessities of the First World War. Consistently, however, the Celts were ranked well below the Anglo-Saxons on the scale of civilisation. The very fact that the Celts had obstructed and resisted Anglo-Saxon rule right up to the 1920s and had been unable to comprehend the vital necessity of an Allied victory in the First World War demonstrated for all who had eyes the extent to which they were incapable of good judgment and undeserving of self-government.[19]

While the two factors of religious and racial bias were important in working to shape an image during the early twentieth century, they were probably not conclusive in themselves. Americans were able to form relatively objective opinions about such countries as Belgium and Switzerland which were both non-Anglo-Saxon and very Catholic. The crucial element which dramatised the image of Ireland in the minds of most Americans was the physical presence of large numbers of Irishmen in America—that is, Irish-Americans. To native Americans every Irish immigrant was a virtual ambassador from Ireland. Thus the Irish-Americans formed the basis of the image that many Americans had about Ireland to a far greater degree than, say, the Belgian or Swiss immigrants shaped the view of their homelands. Thus Madison Grant, the socially prominent New York sportsman, geographer and ethnologist, in talking about Irish nationalism, could say: 'An independent Ireland worked out on a Tammany model is not a pleasing prospect,' fully confident that any political institutions controlled by the Irish in Ireland must inevitably copy the pattern of Irish-American politics in his native New York City.[20]

As the Irish-Americans fell prey to American notions about the dangers of Catholicism and about the superiority of Anglo-Saxons several things resulted. Firstly, the Anglo-Saxon Protestants tended to transfer their feelings about the Irish-Americans to Ireland. Moreover, the Irish-Americans, cut off from the mainstream of American culture and rather badly bruised by their contact with the native Americans, fell back on their Catholicism, on Gaelic culture and on Irish nationalism as a means of self-fulfilment. In doing so they continued to reinforce the religious and racial image that the native Americans already had of them and of Ireland. The *Christian Science Monitor*, Senator John Sharp Williams and Madison Grant could dismiss them and Ireland by saying: 'The Irish National movement centers chiefly around religion, reinforced by myths of ancient grandeur.'[21] When the Irish-Americans resorted to history to show that their countrymen had discovered America, won the War of Independence, settled the frontier and saved the Federal Union, the native Americans concluded that in addition to all their other more conspicuous deficiencies the Irish must be mad as well. Of course, there were native Americans who opposed Irish self-government for reasons quite independent of religion, race or contact with Irish-Americans. But organised and articulated opposition to Irish nationalism could generally be traced to at least one of these three factors, if not, as in the case of Madison Grant, all three.

CHAPTER 2
THE CLIMAX OF HOME RULE AND
THE REBIRTH OF REVOLUTION
1910–1916

THE ten years from 1900 to 1910 witnessed the reorganisation of both the constitutional and revolutionary Irish nationalist movements in the United States. Neither was particularly strong, in spite of the potential which was realised between 1910 and 1916, although at the outset the constitutional movement embraced the larger number of both Irish-American and native American sympathisers. To a large extent the momentum of both nationalist movements had been weakened by reforms which improved economic, agricultural and social life in Ireland. Furthermore, the Conservative and even the Liberal governments had been strong enough themselves to resist appeals for Home Rule and to make revolution in Ireland out of the question.

During the period from 1910 to 1916 the fortunes of Irish nationalism took a dramatic turn. The Home Rule or constitutional movement developed fully to a climax and in the minds of many seemed to end the Irish question with a satisfactory nationalist solution. The physical-force or revolutionary movement, weakened initially by the apparent success of Home Rule, found in the discontent of the Ulster Unionists and in the frustrations imposed by the First World War the process through which their own concept of nationalism could be resurrected. In the United States both Irish-American and native American opinion, while a mere shadow of what it would be after the Easter Rising of 1916 and again after the First World War, focused on the Irish question with an intensity which had not been experienced since the high-water mark of the Parnell period. The year 1910 saw the beginning of the last and greatest phase of American opinion on the Irish question.

1. The Home Rule Movement and Constitutional Nationalism

Constitutional Irish-American nationalists recognised immediately the promising implications of the results of the British general election of January 1910. The Liberals held a margin of only two votes over the Unionists in the House of Commons; the Irish Parliamentary Party with 71 seats seemed in a position to make or unmake any government, regardless of the 40 Labour and 11 Independent Nationalists (the O'Brien–Healy group). Home Rule leaders in America, such as Michael J. Ryan, Alexander Sullivan and Patrick Egan, sent their optimistic congratulations. Egan and Sullivan assured Redmond that he was in a strong position, and Ryan wrote confidently: 'Things are better here than I have known them since the organization of the League.' Ryan speculated further that in the event of another general election, which came in December, the party 'could safely count upon a fairly generous remittance from this side'.[1]

Native Americans also observed the improved prospects of Home Rule. The New York *Times* said it was sure that the fullest possible measure of Home Rule within the Union would be in the best interests of Great Britain. When Asquith attempted to delay the reform of the House of Lords the New York *Times* praised Redmond's 'nerve and his power' in forcing the government to 'transform it [the House of Lords] into a practically powerless body'. By May the paper argued that some kind of compromise was necessary because the government did not have a sufficient mandate from the English people to undertake such a fundamental change in the constitution.[2] The *Literary Digest*, more cautious and sceptical, thought that an alliance between the Liberals and the Irish Party might destroy Asquith as it had Gladstone, and it intimated that Asquith might not be altogether serious in supporting Home Rule. However, such papers as the New York *American* continued to see Irish self-government as imminent.[3]

Despite the apparent strength of the Irish Parliamentary Party seen in the opening months of 1910, there was some concern among both Irish and native Americans about the threat presented by the O'Brien–Healy faction, a group of eleven independents who opposed the political methods of the party and favoured a policy orientated towards land and economic reform. Michael J. Ryan saw these factions as a greater problem in the United States, where Irish disunity was often exaggerated. 'The evil about Healy and O'Brien', Ryan wrote to Redmond, 'is not the harm that they may do in Ireland or Great Britain, but their every objectionable utterance is heralded here as evidence of dissension.' Ryan's suggestion to amalgamate all the Irish societies in the United States into a 'federation' which would smother small splinter groups under the weight of the majority was not well received by his fellow officers of the UIL, although the problem of factions was recognised. The

New York *Times* regarded the Healy and O'Brien MPs as a grave danger to the Liberal–Irish coalition, which it felt was already strained by the government's tax proposals, and by November the *Literary Digest* had also drawn attention to the dangers that these splinter groups posed. Even after the Independent Nationalists were reduced to eight by the December election Whitelaw Reid, the American Ambassador to Great Britain, saw them as a grave threat to Irish unity because, he was confident, they were certain to vote with the Unionists on any Irish measure.[4]

Nonetheless, it was into a generally favourable and optimistic climate in the United States that Redmond and Devlin travelled in September 1910 to raise money with which to fight the anticipated election. T. P. O'Connor had made a fund-raising tour of the United States the year before with sometimes discouraging results, but in the autumn of 1910 the leaders of the Irish Party were warmly received by both native and Irish-Americans who were enthusiastic about the party and the Home Rule programme. Within a month's time Redmond and Devlin, as well as O'Connor, who was touring Canada, were able to return to Ireland with $100,000 for the election fund.[5] The results of the December general election were eminently satisfactory to the Irish Party, for it still held the balance of votes in the House of Commons and in fact strengthened its position at the expense of the Independent Nationalists.

There were, however, political problems which Irish nationalists, in both America and Ireland, seemed willing to ignore or disregard. There was the discomfiting fact which Whitelaw Reid pointed out to Secretary of State Philander C. Knox, that the British people were complacently satisfied with the party symmetry determined by the January general election. 'Certainly this gives him [Asquith] no new mandate and no increased power' with which to reform the House of Lords or enact Home Rule, the ambassador observed. Furthermore, he saw clearly what few others recognised as early as 1910—that the Ulster Unionists were willing to risk violence in order to resist Home Rule. While admitting that Irishmen sometimes exaggerated, he observed nevertheless:

> Still, I have been a good deal impressed by the earnest talk of some of the North of Ireland people, who do not deny the fact that they have been taking pains for months past to arm themselves and declare that they intend to meet any demand to set up a Dublin Parliament over them, by an organized armed force.

Reid's concern would have seemed unwarranted by most interested Americans in 1910. The New York *Times*, for example, concluded that the protests of the Ulster Unionists 'were a pretty discreditable piece of party trickery', to be linked with complaints about American money at Westminster, but not to be taken seriously.[6]

The improved prospects of Home Rule in parliament and the corresponding growth of the United Irish League of America were fully understood by American politicians. Although the Republican Party had won the election of 1908, the Democratic Party candidate received an ominously large percentage (45 per cent) of the vote, thereby encouraging the Republicans to look for new sources of support which would allow them to hold their majority and rob the Democrats of their growing strength. It was perhaps with a calculated hope of winning the sympathy of the traditionally Democratic Irish-Americans that President William Howard Taft accepted an invitation to attend the St Patrick's Day celebration of the Irish Fellowship Club, a society of highly successful and respectable Chicago Irish-Americans. For the moderate Irish-American nationalists Taft's presence at the celebration on 17 March 1910 represented official recognition and marked the degree of respectability which the Irish-Americans had achieved. Alexander Sullivan explained to President Taft himself, and later to John Redmond, the importance of the event and the extent to which it demonstrated to both America and Britain 'his [Taft's] respect for our race and his confidence in us'. Patrick Egan was also quick to elaborate on the significance of Taft's endorsement of the Irish movement and cautioned Redmond that the meeting could be carefully exploited later if the State Department were not aroused by too much advanced publicity. Even before St Patrick's Day Egan was working to win the support of former President Theodore Roosevelt for the Home Rule movement. Egan warned Redmond that Roosevelt, travelling through Europe on the way home from his celebrated hunting trip to Africa, should not be left entirely to the British as he passed through England. Egan suggested that official invitations from the Lord Mayor of Dublin would be extended to welcome the former President to Ireland. 'Such a reception would be universally appreciated as a compliment to America', Egan wrote, 'and should greatly help our cause—which even already is becoming fashionable.' Roosevelt did not go to Dublin, although on 1 June 1910 he did have lunch at Westminster with Redmond, T. P. O'Connor and several other Irish MPs.[7] For the first time since the 1880s Irish-Americans merited the attention of national political figures.

President Taft made a second and potentially more dramatic attempt to win Irish-American support in 1911–12 when he responded to public sentiment in favour of a release for Luke Dillon, an Irish-American imprisoned by the Canadian government for his attempt to blow up the Welland Canal in 1900. Successful efforts by the administration to persuade the Canadians to release Dillon would appeal directly to the Irish-American voting bloc and especially to the revolutionary nationalists. As John T. Keating, one of the important members of the Clan, wrote to John Devoy, 'Taft must do something to please somebody and the Anglo Americans are his only friends now.'[8] From the autumn of 1911 until the late summer of 1912 Taft struggled with both the British and Canadian governments to secure Dillon's release, but without success. Whether or not the release of Dillon would have effectively repaired Taft's desperate political fortunes by winning Irish votes for the Republican Party is a matter of some speculation, but what seems to emerge is the apparent rehabilitation of Irish-Americans and the Irish question as a factor in national American politics.

In the presidential election of 1912 Woodrow Wilson, the priggish reform governor of New Jersey and former president of Princeton University, successfully held the Irish vote within the Democratic Party, in spite of the earlier efforts of both Taft and Roosevelt to prove themselves friendly to the Irish cause and attractive to Irish-Americans. How much either Ireland or the Irish-Americans benefited from the new administration has been a source of some controversy. Certainly Wilson seemed cooler to Irish-American politicians, as the British Ambassador noted, than either Taft or Roosevelt, if not to the concept of Irish nationalism. Wilson did retain Maurice Francis Egan, T. St John Gaffney and Nelson O'Shaughnessy in the foreign service and made Joseph P. Tumulty his private secretary, but there were no conspicuous Irish-American nationalists among his appointments or his confidants.[9] Tumulty did not actually promote the Irish question, although he tended to keep Irish matters before the President. In his memoirs Tumulty recorded that Wilson was honestly concerned about Irish self-government. On 10 October 1910, while campaigning for the office of governor of New Jersey, Wilson said that Great Britain would be wise to create a federation that would permit the expression of the national aspirations of the Irish, Welsh and Scots. 'This voice that has been crying in Ireland,' Wilson said, 'this voice for home rule, is a voice which is now supported by the opinion of the world.' While President, however, Wilson was inhibited by diplomatic protocol from speaking out publicly about Ireland, although, as Tumulty rightly acknowledged, Wilson privately urged upon many of the Englishmen he met the necessity of resolving the Irish question. But Wilson, who told Tumulty that 'There never can be real comradeship between America and England until this [Irish] issue is definitely settled and out of the way,' often seemed motivated by a desire to improve Anglo-American relations rather than by a concern for Irish nationalism.[10] Perhaps Wilson's concern for Ireland can best be seen as part of his liberal ideological inheritance from Gladstone, his boyhood hero and political model, but in practical terms Wilson's attitude towards Ireland was characterised by careful correctness.

As Americans increasingly considered the question of Irish self-government within the British Empire they not surprisingly put forward federal solutions drawn from their own political experience. As shown in Chapter 1, native Americans, and especially those who hoped for some kind of Anglo-American union, saw a federal Empire where Ireland could have its proper place as the solution not only to the Irish question but the problem of world stability as well. Early in his political career Woodrow Wilson supported the ideal of a federal solution to the Irish problem. Similarly an American friend of the Rev. Canon James Owen Hannay, the popular Irish novelist who used the pen-name George A. Birmingham, wrote that the world was alive with the ideas of the 'Rights of Man' and that an intellectual revolution was under way. Quite sceptical about Redmond's ability, he told Hannay that 'liberty' for Ireland could best be achieved 'in a Federal Union between the divisions of the United Kingdom'.[11] The Irish-American leader Congressman W. Bourke Cockran maintained a private correspondence with Moreton Frewen, an Anglo-Irish landlord who was related by marriage to Winston Churchill and Shane Leslie as well as to Cockran himself, on the topic of a federal solution to the Irish question, although, as Alan J. Ward has shown, these schemes had the public backing of no Irish-American leaders—even Cockran. However, in spite of the indigenous appeal that federalism had for many Americans, there was some intelligent disagreement also. The New York *Times,* commenting on federalist proposals, stated that the rapid movement of the United States towards centralisation was evidence that federalism was not always suitable for complex government. The problems of the Empire, the paper said, were too diverse to be successfully dealt with in an imperial federation. In fact the paper thought its only virtue was that any solution to the Irish question was worthwhile if it improved Anglo-American diplomatic relations or even American domestic politics.[12]

This view of the New York *Times* was shared by many native Americans; indeed, it occasionally provided the sole source of their interest in Irish nationalism. Early in 1911 Theodore Roosevelt, always a warm supporter of Home Rule, wrote to T. P. Gill of the Department of Agriculture and Technical Instruction in Dublin: 'As I have repeatedly said, I believe that the grant of Home Rule to Ireland would be of very great importance in removing one source of friction between the United States and Great Britain.' Woodrow Wilson expressed the same kind of concern about the unresolved Irish question as an obstacle to harmonious Anglo-American relations.[13] Native Americans also hoped that Home Rule would work to weaken the Irish-American political bloc at home by robbing it of its greatest issue. 'The effect of this [Home Rule] upon our own relations to the reborn Empire would be happy if only because of the pacification of the Irish Americans,' the New York *Times* said. Even Roosevelt, although he phrased it very discreetly, saw that the long-standing Irish question was one reason why the Irish had not assimilated fully into American society. Canon Hannay's American friend put it more bluntly: referring to Mayor John F. ('Honey Fitz') Fitzgerald and Congressman James ('Boss') Curley, both of his native Boston, he wrote: 'I do wish some form of Home Rule could rid us of this group.'[14] Throughout the next ten years many other native Americans felt the same way.

Home Rule made little progress in parliament during 1911, and in fact the Home Rule Bill was not introduced in the House of Commons until 11 April 1912. However, from early 1912 speculation began as to when the British government would act and what the prospects of Home Rule would be under the new constitutional arrangements regarding the House of Lords. In the eyes of the press Ulster presented an obstacle, although the New York *Times* observed that not all of Ulster was anti-Home Rule by any means; however, the fact that there was no real violence done when Churchill spoke on Home Rule in Belfast convinced many that the Ulster resistance movement was entirely bluff. With Asquith's introduction of the Home Rule Bill on 11 April 1912, Irish Party supporters in America cabled their congratulations to Redmond on the 'marvelous success' of the movement and expressed their confidence in the bill.[15] Bourke Cockran wrote to Redmond shortly afterwards extending good wishes and assuring the Irish leader that the destiny of the Irish race was in good hands with him. It was recognised, however, that not all Irishmen in America and Ireland were pleased with the bill; in fact one group of Irish-Americans urged Redmond to reject the measure because it offered Ireland merely 'sham autonomy', the Clan na Gael and the Independent Nationalists presenting the major threat. After the national convention in Dublin in the spring and the second reading of the bill, substantial Irish support was acknowledged. Judge Martin J. Keogh of New York sent Redmond his congratulations on 27 May and gave the assurance that 'You have the race at home and abroad solidly, sincerely, and almost unanimously with you.'[16]

As the Home Rule movement prospered during 1912 the Ulster Unionists correspondingly became more serious and outspoken in their determination to resist. The New York *Times* had not been moved by 'Ulsteria' in January of 1912, and indeed went so far as to call attention to nationalist sympathy in the north of Ireland, but by July the paper began to change its opinion towards the Unionist claims, arguing that the concept of Home Rule, if applicable to the south of Ireland, could be applied to Ulster as well:

> It is not easy to see why Ulster should be denied the degree of independence claimed for the people of Ireland, simply because they wish to use that independence to remain in the British Union, with their rights and powers as British subjects unimpaired.

The *Literary Digest*, which had been reluctant to commit itself to Home Rule, took the Unionist leaders seriously from the first and was outspoken in explaining the conflict in terms of Catholic–Protestant hostilities and ethnic incompatibilities. 'When we look calmly into the Ulster problem,' the *Digest* wrote, 'we find the antagonism between the Home Rulers and Unionism in Ireland is deeply rooted. It is both racial and religious.'[17] This view of the Ulster situation reflected two of the principle biases of middle-class native Americans: a bias towards Anglo-Saxon racial superiority, and a religious bias which prompted a favourable predisposition towards Protestants.

The third reading of the Home Rule Bill in the House of Commons aroused another flurry of congratulations and good wishes from the United States. Congressman Goodwin of Arkansas introduced a resolution on 17 January 1913 'congratulating the people of Ireland on the passage of an Irish home rule bill', although the resolution was never returned from the Committee on Foreign Affairs. The editor of the *Irish World*, Patrick Ford, sent appeals to several American public figures soliciting their favourable comments on 'the heroic fight the people of Ireland are making for the American principle of self government' for eventual publication in his paper.[18] The most important reply came from the Secretary of State elect, William Jennings Bryan, who answered: 'You are right in assuming that I am in sympathy with the fight that is being made to secure Home Rule for Ireland.' Bryan added that he was pleased with the progress of the bill and felt that it was a just settlement in the interests of both the Irish and English peoples. The newspapers, which a few months earlier had speculated that the government might fall, saw the 110-vote majority for the bill as a great triumph for the Liberal–Labour–Irish coalition, and they

B

concurred with Bryan in regarding the Irish Parliamentary Party victory of David C. Hogg in Derry as a vindication of the Home Rule movement. When the Home Rule Bill was reintroduced in the House of Commons on 9 June 1913, after its rejection by the Lords in January, this cycle was to a large extent repeated. Redmond read to the House of Commons a letter to him from Theodore Roosevelt which said that the Home Rule Bill was a just settlement that 'bids fair to establish good will amongst the English-speaking people', and he, like Bryan earlier in the year, stated that 'The measure is as much in the interest of Great Britain as it is of Ireland.'[19]

In the face of these warm comments there was some dissatisfaction or cynicism, even among the moderate constitutionalists. Bourke Cockran wrote uncomfortably to Moreton Frewen: 'The indifference of the country [Ireland] to the Home Rule debate seems to me very significant.' Cockran, along with some others, saw a certain lack of reality about the whole proceedings—a Home Rule measure which gave less than full autonomy to the Irish people and which was resisted by an anachronistic House of Lords in the face of a strong government majority. This indifference had been noted by others as well. Some months earlier the New York *Times* said: 'The issue is not nearly so "live" as it has been,' and the *Living Age* news magazine quoted a Tipperary farmer as saying, in stage-Irish fashion: 'Ah well, now, we're not greatly minding one way or the other,' although he presumably admitted that this could not be said publicly.[20] In order to keep support for Home Rule in America from melting away in apathy the Irish Press Agency in England had leaflets printed during 1913 which illustrated Ireland's political, economic and moral capacities for self-government; these leaflets were distributed in America by the United Irish League to sustain interest in the Home Rule movement.

Increasingly throughout 1913 American newspapers focused their attention on the activities of the Unionists rather than on the progress of the Home Rule Bill. The New York *Times* viewed the Unionists and the Ulster Volunteers as essentially political rather than military, saying: 'It is not likely that "military tactics" will be resorted to,' and later: 'The indications that the whole Ulster situation is a species of political bluff . . . grow plainer from day to day.' On the other hand, the paper increasingly challenged the legitimacy of Asquith's policy because, it said, the British electorate had never specifically approved the Home Rule Bill as then drafted. In a sense the paper saw no way out of the dilemma, but it kept hoping that some kind of compromise—compromise being the genius of British politics—would be worked out for Ireland. Surprisingly the *Living Age* concluded that there was no real problem in Ireland: a businesslike conference between the leaders of Belfast and Dublin, it observed, could save the situation and allow reason to prevail over the seventeenth-century religious antagonisms. The *Literary Digest* found the Ulster situation to be more potentially dangerous and noted in greater detail the growth of the Ulster Volunteer Force and the support it received from highly placed peers and army officers.[21] Actually American newspapers seemed slow to discuss either the Ulster or later the Irish Volunteers, partly because they did not take them seriously, but also perhaps because they did not want to aggravate an already sensitive topic.

Before the Home Rule Bill was given its second reading on its final circuit Michael J. Jordan, secretary of the UIL, asked prominent American politicians for favourable comments which would be cabled to Redmond and printed in the *Irish World*. However, it was difficult to generate the enthusiasm of two years before. On 9 March 1914 the bill was given its second reading, and Asquith offered the Unionists the compromise of the exclusion of Ulster, on the basis of county options, for a period of six years (during which time there would be another general election, perhaps on the issue of Home Rule). Carson rejected the proposals, but he pointed out, what all acknowledged, that the principle of exclusion had been recognised. For the New York *Times* this recognition was a great step forward because it took account of Ulster militancy and also allowed the electorate another opportunity to speak on the matter. Charles McCarthy, a political theorist of the American Progressive movement, wrote to his friend Sir Horace Plunkett to comment favourably on this spirit of compromise, which he wrongly attributed to Plunkett's influence (Plunkett favoured *inclusion* for six years rather than *exclusion*). The historian and Massachusetts politician, Senator Henry Cabot Lodge, explained to Moreton Frewen that the principle of exclusion was perfectly sound. 'I believe and always have believed in Home Rule for Ireland,' Lodge wrote, but he added: 'I also believe in Home Rule for Ulster.' Confessing his preference for American state federalism, Lodge defended Home Rule within Home Rule by the story of the separation of Massachusetts and Maine. 'If you are going to have home rule and local self-government,' Lodge said, 'it must be applied fairly to all.'[22]

To Irish-Americans, even very moderate Home Rulers like W. Bourke Cockran and John Quinn, the proposal of the temporary exclusion of Ulster seemed like a calamitous concession rather than a wise compromise. On 25 March 1914 Cockran sent the first of several worried letters to Frewen specifically discussing the proposed exclusion of Ulster. He was appalled that 'A proposal that the Island be dismembered has not only been considered, but actually accepted by the Irish Nationalist party.' This blow caused irreparable damage to Irish nationalism, Cockran said, because it was authorised by those Irishmen 'acknowledged to be leaders'. Irish-Americans, Cockran insisted, had been 'shocked beyond expression', and in New York large meetings had been held to protest against the 'dismemberment of the Island'. In his disillusion with the Home Rule leaders Cockran could only admire the Ulster Unionists, who at least seemed willing to fight for what they believed. 'I don't think there is a Catholic in any of the four Provinces who does not feel keen admiration for the manner in which these men of the North have made the Government which is supposed to rule them, treat with them—actually capitulate to them,' he wrote to Frewen on 19 May.[23] Similarly John Quinn found himself infuriated with the Irish Parliamentary Party and the Liberal government, while grudgingly admiring the Unionists with whom he violently disagreed on principle. 'I regard English politics and even Irish politics, outside of those few Protestants of the North, as simply beneath contempt, weak, flabby, cowardly,' he wrote to George Russell on 2 July. Quinn hoped that people like Russell, Plunkett, Hyde, Yeats and O'Grady would unite Ireland and make it prosper in defiance of the politicians. Perhaps Cockran was typical of an increasing number of Irish-Americans when he told Frewen: 'If a revolt [against Redmond] were started in Ireland, I think the Irish in America would support it to a man.'[24] Certainly Cockran seemed to anticipate the Irish-American reaction to the Irish Parliamentary Party after the beginning of the First World War and again after the Easter Rising.

To native Americans the so-called 'mutiny' of British army officers at the Curragh overshadowed the subtle complaints of more involved Irish-Americans. The *Literary Digest* said bluntly: 'The old question of who shall rule Great Britain—royalty, aristocracy, or democracy—is reopened by the revolt and resignation of army officers ordered to duty in Ulster, and their reinstatement by the King's influence.' As for Home Rule for all Ireland, the *Digest* observed: 'The attempt to coerce Ulster, if there was one, is at a stand still. . . . Naturally the Unionists are exultant.' The New York *Times* saw the crisis as the result of the government's failure to manage events. Asquith had had two choices, the paper felt: he could have coerced Ulster without concessions, or he could have made concessions and excluded Ulster; he failed to do either. Increasingly critical of the Asquith government, the New York *Times* noted 'weakness in the speeches of the Secretary of War and the Prime Minister' in their explanation of the incident. Nevertheless, during the next few days the paper suggested that the policy of not forcing the issue was gaining time, 'and time makes for peace'. By 29 March the paper felt once again that Home Rule was certain and that Ulster was bluffing. A. Lawrence Lowell, the president of Harvard University, saw in the Curragh incident an indication that the government rather than Ulster was bluffing and that Asquith would not force the Home Rule question. 'I surmise', Lowell said to Lord Bryce, the popular and respected former British Ambassador to the United States, on 22 May, 'that the Government has made up its mind that Ulster cannot be made to submit to Home Rule by force, and that some concessions must be made to conciliate Ulster; or, at least, the Conservatives.' Still Lowell did not rule out the possibility of a civil war, and he asked Bryce if the government had not erred by appearing to make the first move in reinforcing Ulster.[25]

Perhaps some of the most remarkable opinions on the Ulster situation were to be found in the reactions of the American ambassadors to Great Britain and Germany and of President Wilson himself. Walter Hines Page, the American Ambassador in London, candidly admitted to President Wilson that 'If I were an Ulsterman, I fear I, too, should object to being bound to the body of Dublin,' although he considered the Liberal–Conservative political struggle to be more important than Home Rule, Ulster or the Curragh incident and to be the real crux of the problem. 'The Conservatives have used Ulster and its Army', Page wrote, 'as a club to drive the Liberals out of power; and they have gone to the very brink of civil war. They don't really care about Ulster. I doubt whether they care much about Home Rule.' What was really behind the Unionist resistance to the Liberal–Irish coalition, Page believed, was the whole Liberal programme: 'It's the Lloyd George programme that infuriates them, and Ulster and anti-Home Rule are mere weapons to stop the general Liberal revolution, if they can.' The American Ambassador to Germany, James W. Gerard, took a much less serious or even analytical view of the Irish crisis. 'The raising of the Ulster army by Sir Edward Carson', was, he wrote several years later, 'one of the most gigantic political bluffs in all history', and he dismissed it easily by insisting that it 'had no more revolutionary or military significance than a torch-light parade during one of our presidential campaigns'. President Wilson presumably regarded the situation more soberly and perhaps saw more clearly the fundamental threat that the Ulster movement posed to the institutions of democratic government. According to Joseph P. Tumulty, Wilson said of Carson: 'I would show this rebel whether he would recognise the authority of the Government or flaunt it. He ought to be hanged for treason.' Wilson felt that if Asquith did not act 'firmly', the 'unrest and rebellion in Ireland will spread', but that the strong assertion of the government's legitimate power 'would force a settlement of the Irish question right now'. Wilson was certain that Andrew Jackson could have dealt with the situation.[26]

Although the growing tension in Ireland, superimposed upon the Ulster exclusion scheme and the Curragh incident, were the first of several blows for many of the moderate Irish-American nationalists, a certain optimism persisted among native Americans who felt that some kind of satisfactory compromise would most certainly be worked out. By July 1914 the new factor of the Irish Volunteers was recognised but not fully understood. But the news of the gun-running at Howth and the firing of British troops at a Dublin crowd on 26 July was greeted with alarm by the New York *Times* in head-lines, second in size only to the news from Eastern Europe: 'BRITISH TROOPS SHED FIRST BLOOD IN ULSTER WAR'. The papers condemned the Asquith government for allowing such a dangerous predicament to develop.[27] At that point, of course, the First World War intervened, and the attention of American newspapers was largely turned away from Ireland by the events of epic dimension taking place in Europe. Irish politics were not analysed in detail again until the Easter Rising.

II.   The Clan na Gael, the Irish Republican Brotherhood and Revolutionary Nationalism

The rising power and prestige of the Irish Parliamentary Party, following the general elections of 1910, underscored the compara-tive decline of the revolutionary Irish nationalists both at home and in America. The interval between 1900 and 1910, while also one of reconstruction, was a period of anxious waiting for an opportune moment in which to initiate a revolutionary programme in Ireland. The Clan na Gael did not abdicate its role of revolutionary leader-ship among the Irish-Americans, and even among the IRB, but it was forced into a relatively passive position as constitutionalism prospered and living conditions in Ireland slowly improved. The beginning of 1910 found the Clan leaders still waiting for some kind of disaster which would defeat the Liberal government or separate the Liberals from the Irish Parliamentary Party. This anxious hope that something might develop is seen in the letter of John T. Ryan, a leading Clan figure and lawyer from Buffalo, who wrote to John Devoy on the eve of the January election in 1910:

If the results show Conservative gains to such an extent as to forecast the defeat of the Liberals, the policy of the Parliamentary Party will have been proved to be ruinous and will give an excellent opportunity for . . . pointing out the folly of this program, and further calling attention to the fact that under no circumstances was there a chance for Ireland.[28]

The results of the election were not so obliging: the Conservatives did indeed make such gains as to weaken the Liberals, but, of course, this only served to strengthen the power of the Irish Parliamentary Party.

The Clan's problems were a mixture of membership, money and policy, all of which were interrelated. Being oath-bound and secret, the Clan could not make the broadly based appeal for members of the UIL or the AOH. Thus money, most easily raised from members, became difficult to obtain, and indeed, while this situation improved in 1914, the Clan still did not have the operating revenues it wanted by as late as 1916. The most immediately important problem, however, was the creation of a viable programme of action which could compete with the increasingly successful Home Rule programme; without a strongly competitive programme there would be no new members or money. The desperation of the situation was recognised by both Devoy and John T. Keating, two of the three members of the Clan's Revolutionary Directory. 'Nearly ten years of struggle,' Keating wrote Devoy on 22 January 1910, 'and we are reaching what seems to be the end.' They agreed that continued anxious waiting would destroy the Clan. 'You have stated the case very plainly "*another period of mere negative policy*" seems to be before us "*and will kill us if too much prolonged*". Worst of all I can see *no alternative* within our reach.'[29] By 1913 this crisis had still not been overcome. The practice of rejecting the parliamentary solutions while waiting for better times allowed the revolutionary concept of Irish nationalism to drift into obscurity. Dr William Carroll, the old Fenian and Clan leader from Philadelphia, bitterly illuminated the results of this policy to Devoy on 7 February 1913:

The dark side of the prospect here and oversea is not so much what Lloyd George, Redmond and [Michael J.] Ryan propose, but the *fact* that there and here the Irish people accept and applaud their betrayal of everything national they once professed to advocate.

Perhaps in recognition of the undeniable strength and popularity of the prospect of immediate Home Rule, the Clan in March 1913 began shifting its policy to one of partial compromise. While continuing to condemn Home Rule as 'a fraud and a cheat', the Clan published in a circular that it had no objection to the Irish people 'making whatever use they can' of it.[30]

In this situation the Clan and the revolutionary Irish-Americans turned to several activities which they hoped might weaken the constitutional nationalists or the British Empire. Throughout the late nineteenth century the Irish-Americans had been instrumental in obstructing any complete rapprochement between Great Britain and the United States, and during the early twentieth century the revolutionary Irish-Americans rather tentatively joined forces with German-Americans to defeat efforts to establish harmonious Anglo-American relations. The Clan threw itself into the task of defeating the Anglo-American arbitration treaty which came before the United States Senate during 1911 and 1912, and by 11 August 1911 Irish activity was so great that Keating reported to Devoy that in the Chicago area 'all our energies were being used to defeat the treaty'. Such work was perfectly suited to the vigorous anglophobe rhetoric of the Clan, which launched a letter campaign to members of Congress urging the defeat of the treaty because of its threat to America's freedom of action. Devoy also distributed to all the senators reprinted pages from the British Ambassador's book, *American commonwealth*, showing Bryce's critical view of the Senate's control of foreign affairs. The Senate killed the treaty by so amending it that President Taft refused to sign it, and while they had amended it ostensibly to protect America's vital interest, it was felt that the Irish and Germans had encouraged them.[31]

Less successful was the Clan's attempt to defend legislation exempting American merchant ships from the tolls paid for use of the Panama Canal. This law, passed by Congress in 1912 and endorsed by the Democratic Party, was found to be in violation of the Hay–Pauncefote Treaty (1901) between Great Britain and the United States wherein America agreed not to take unfair advantage of her control of the canal. Led by Senator James A. O'Gorman of New York and backed by the Clan, indignant Irish-Americans held large public meetings and sent petitions to Congress; they argued that because America had built the canal American ships should be given free passage, that to charge American ships would put them at a disadvantage to British ships, and that any compromise on the question was 'truckling' to Great Britain. Although Congress was treated to many violent speeches by Irish, German and Tammany Hall politicians, both houses passed the administration's measure in early 1914 making the tolls for American ships equal to those of other nations. The defeat of Irish-American efforts in this instance prompted Sir Cecil Spring Rice, Britain's nervous, Anglo-Irish ambassador in Washington, to observe that the political strength of the Irish in America was declining. 'The Irish vote is not as well organized or as important as it was,' he wrote to Sir William Tyrrell, secretary to the Foreign Secretary, Sir Edward Grey, 'mainly because the immigration has slackened and the Irishman becomes an American after two generations'; in fact, he had noted earlier that the Jewish-Americans were much more powerful. A few weeks later, after the Curragh incident, Spring Rice reported more cautiously that the unresolved Irish question gave American anglophobes a convenient basis for their hostility.

> What I think we ought not to lose sight of [he wrote to Tyrrell] is that speaking generally an unfriendly feeling exists in this country against England, that a great interest is excited by Irish affairs, and that American unfriendliness to England may and most probably will have serious results should affairs in Ireland become worse.[32]

Co-operation between the Irish revolutionaries in America and the German-Americans was the logical by-product of the naval crises of the early twentieth century and of the growing rivalry between Great Britain and Germany. Groups of Germans and Irish had worked together to defeat the Anglo-American arbitration treaties. Moreover, in the face of deteriorating Anglo-German relations the Irish revolutionaries increasingly looked to Germany as that European power, replacing the historical roles of Spain, France, and more recently Russia, which might best secure Irish independence from Great Britain. Irish-American newspapers, led by Devoy's *Gaelic American*, speculated cheerfully about the possibility of Germany's destruction of Britain's world position and the implications that such a German victory would have for Ireland. When the Cunard and White Star steamship lines declared that Queenstown harbour was not safe for their ships Irish-Americans rallied behind Sir Roger Casement's efforts to make Queenstown a regular port-of-call for the German Hamburg–Amerika line. Such a move would not only snub the British lines and open Ireland for German investment, but it would also work to reintegrate Ireland into the European continent, by-passing Great Britain. Irish-American reaction to the final German decision not to send a ship to Ireland, perhaps because of British diplomatic pressure, was expressed in particularly bitter outcries.[33]

Still another area in which the revolutionary Irish-Americans worked is indicated by the support they gave to some of the nationalist groups which had grown up in Ireland since 1890 outside the

Irish Parliamentary Party. The Clan found the Gaelic League a useful medium of expression for revolutionary ideas both in the United States and Ireland, and in fact in 1911 the Gaelic League and the Clan worked so closely together that Devoy complained: 'The time of our men is constantly taken up with raising money for the League, to the neglect of our own work.' The joint membership of many of the revolutionary leaders, such as Bulmer Hobson and Diarmuid Lynch, in the Gaelic League, the Gaelic Athletic Association, Sinn Féin and other nationalist organisations made close relations natural. In late February 1914 Lynch and Thomas Ashe began a successful tour in the United States with the support and co-operation of the Clan to raise money for the league in Ireland. Lynch was also carrying out a mission for the IRB, and Daniel F. Cohalan, then a New York Supreme Court judge and an important Clan leader, presided at one of their important meetings at the Gaelic League headquarters in New York. Bulmer Hobson provided Patrick H. Pearse with introductions to Devoy and Judge Cohalan when Pearse travelled to the United States in 1913–14 to raise money for St Enda's College. Pearse established important contacts with Clan leaders in various parts of the country. Hobson himself came to America in January 1914 to bring Devoy a memorandum on the situation in Ireland to be presented to the German Ambassador. While in the United States Hobson spoke at Clan-sponsored meetings, sometimes accompanying Pearse. The Clan supported other projects meant to benefit Ireland, such as the Gaelic Athletic Association, the Irish Industrial Development Societies and Sir Horace Plunkett's rural co-operative movement. It eventually turned away from Sinn Féin after the adoption of Griffith's 'Hungarian analogy', and, as a result of the American tour of the Abbey Players with their productions of Synge's *Playboy of the western world* and other controversial plays, the Clan was less enthusiastic about the Irish literary movement. According to John B. Yeats, Devoy himself attacked one Irish play by standing up during the performance and shouting: 'Son of a b–tch, that's not Irish!' Both Yeats and John Quinn agreed that Devoy was an 'old fool'.[34]

These various activities—influencing American foreign policy, creating a working relationship with the German-Americans, and supporting Irish cultural movements and minor political organisations—had some moderate success. Indeed, it may be said that such organisations as the Gaelic League and Sinn Féin did in fact create a climate in Ireland in which a revolution could take place, although the German–Irish alliance in America was not effective until the war. On the other hand, in spite of the defeated arbitration treaties, Clan attempts to direct American foreign policy failed to prevent the United States from drifting into closer co-operation and eventually into joint participation in the war. In fact these efforts may well have been counter-productive—alienating native Americans who might have been sympathetic but who felt that the normal course of American foreign policy was being obstructed. None of these activities directly forwarded the revolutionary movement, as the Clan leaders were painfully aware. This declining situation seems to have been very much altered by the creation in Ireland of the Irish Volunteers, and of course still more so by the complicated situation which developed in Ireland after the beginning of the European war.

The founding of the Irish Volunteers on 25 November 1913 seemed to find the leaders of the revolutionary Irish-Americans unprepared, and even the presence in the United States in early 1914 of Patrick Pearse and Bulmer Hobson failed to stimulate the Clan to immediate action. The *Gaelic American* published favourable editorials on the Volunteers as early as 3 January 1914 and also printed news and information about developments in Ireland, but no action seems to have been taken. In April 1914 The O'Rahilly made a direct appeal to Devoy for assistance, explaining the great potential of the situation in Ireland and the need for money from friends in America to exploit it. 'If the sincere Irish in America will not help us in this situation,' he said, 'they will have neglected the greatest opportunity of a century.' O'Rahilly's letter prompted a discussion among the Irish-American leaders as to what should be done, but caution rather than opportunism characterised their reactions. Patrick O'Mara, a New Jersey Clan leader, thought the Irish Volunteers would be under-financed, weakly imitative, victimised by both the British army and the Ulster Volunteers, and that they would obscure the real issue of independence by quarrelling with the Orangemen. John T. Ryan wrote to Devoy from Buffalo saying that he had some reservations about the members of the provisional committee, though he did feel that 'The movement is of a character that should be encouraged.' The old Fenian Colonel Ricard O'Sullivan Burke was the most enthusiastic, although his principal argument was that the Clan should not allow any other Irish-American organisation to become the source of American support.[35]

Months continued to go by and the Clan na Gael leaders still did not make a move to give any direct assistance, despite their talk. Perhaps in this instance Irish-Americans in general were more aggressive than their leaders. In any case, the frustration and anger at the slowness of the organisation to respond can be seen in the letter of a Philadelphia district Clan secretary who wrote to James Reidy, Devoy's assistant at the *Gaelic American*:

> The organization in this dist. feel very much aggrieved at the indifference displayed by the organization in this Country to the exhortations of our brothers in Ireland to supply them with arms to defend their country. It was the consensus of opinion at the meeting that we sell the Irish-American Club and send the proceeds to the men who are willing to do something that will redound to the credit of Irish Nationalists through out the Universe. It was stated by some of the brothers, that if something is not done, and done immediately, the best thing our organization could do, is to disband and let some body of men take our place who are competent of taking advantage of such a condition of affairs as that which exists in Ireland today.

The district threatened to 'act' on its own if the executive of the Clan did not respond to its demands. Effective action was taken by 6 June 1914, when a large meeting was called in New York, drawing participants from as far west as the Dakotas, for the purpose of creating the American Provisional Committee, Irish National Volunteers. They elected Joseph McGarrity, General Denis F. Collins, Denis A. Spellissy and Patrick J. Griffin and established the American Volunteer Fund to buy weapons for Ireland.[36]

Before much work could be done in the United States, however, Redmond forced his nominees upon the Provisional Committee in Dublin. This threw many revolutionary Irish-Americans into considerable confusion. Judge O'Neill Ryan of St Louis lamented to Devoy: 'I do not know where "we are at" on this Volunteer question.' It appeared to him and to many other Irish-American leaders that the revolutionaries in Ireland had lost control of the Volunteers and that Redmond would now be able to divert into the Irish Parliamentary Party the funds intended to arm the Volunteers. Ryan further complained: 'We will be co-operating with the U.I.L.,' which was most unpalatable to physical-force people after a generation of vituperation. Notwithstanding their doubts about the reliability of any organisation associated with Redmond, the committee in New York cabled Eóin Mac Néill $5,000 on 24 June. On 5 July they reassembled to make their committee permanent (rather than provisional) and to send a cable of assurance to Mac Néill. They also sent a very frank cable to Redmond in which they sceptically asked how he could apply to America for arms when he had approved of the British ban on arms importation into Ireland. Perhaps most surprisingly, given the fact that McGarrity was the chairman of the committee and the first signatory of the cable, they counselled Redmond to demand the implementation of Home Rule ('such as it is') to all of Ireland and to make 'any concession to Ulster Protestants which would allay their distrust of an Irish national government'. Thus while obviously not pleased by the situation, the committee revealed its willingness to continue its work with the Irish Volunteers, and it revealed also a degree of moderation that is not generally ascribed to such militants as McGarrity.[37]

Moderation aside, many of the revolutionaries were outraged that the Provisional Committee in Dublin had capitulated to Redmond. After prolonged and worried correspondence with McGarrity, Devoy sent an acrimonious letter to Bulmer Hobson on 3 July stating that by voting for the Irish Party nominees he had weakened the movement in Ireland and America by allowing new factions to develop. Hobson's vote to accept the Redmond candidates, Devoy wrote, 'places us and you on utterly divergent lines of action'.[38] Hobson was dropped as a correspondent in Ireland for the *Gaelic American* despite his own defence. It was the arguments of Sir Roger Casement, who had arrived in the United States on 20 July to raise money for the Volunteers, that finally convinced the Clan leaders of the expediency of the compromise. As Casement wrote to Mrs Alice Stopford Green shortly after his arrival, 'I think I've put it straight now—Devoy admits a change of view.' But the frustration of the revolutionaries was still apparent as illustrated by Peter Golden's poem 'Send us, O God! the revolution'. The Supreme Council of the IRB had never reconciled itself to the compromise of Mac Néill, Hobson, Casement and others, and they sent Dr Patrick McCartan on a mission to the Clan leaders in America to argue their point of view. That McCartan did not arrive in America until after the Howth gun-running, for which Casement claimed full credit, diminished the force of the Supreme Council's protests.[39]

Meanwhile the worst fears of the revolutionaries seemed confirmed when Michael J. Ryan, the national president of the UIL, acting on Redmond's instructions, announced the creation of a new fund-raising drive for the Volunteers, advertised and carried out through the pages of the *Irish World*. On 16 July a UIL national committee meeting was held in New York, and $10,000 was raised and sent to Redmond, a further $100,000 was pledged, and a goal of $1,000,000 was declared. The revolutionary Irish-Americans felt that the UIL fund was established to rival the American Volunteer Fund, with the aim of diminishing the amount of money which could be collected in America to obtain weapons. They further maintained that money sent to the UIL fund would go into the coffers of the Irish Parliamentary Party and not go for arms. Within two weeks a campaign was launched by the UIL and the AOH through the *Irish World* and by the circulation of pledge forms. The fact that these forms—including letters of appeal from Ryan and James J. Regan, the outgoing president of the AOH—indicated that the contribution would be sent to 'the Irish Parliamentary Fund' confirmed their suspicions in the belief that the money would simply go to Redmond and not to purchase rifles. Casement, who had counselled compromise with Redmond's joining the organisation, shrewdly warned his American friends that, in terms of any financial support, 'Please remember that money sent to Redmond for arming Volunteers is money in doubt.'[40]

Although the revolutionaries saw the efforts of the UIL to raise money for the Volunteers as an insidious plan to spread confusion among the serious nationalists in America, the immediate contributions of the constitutional Irish-Americans were deceivingly successful to outside observers. Because of the relative positions of the Clan and the UIL the latter were far better prepared to undertake a national campaign to raise money across the country. Furthermore, the UIL attracted the support of such moderate groups as the AOH which might not have followed the Clan's leadership. The American press tended to see Redmond as giving strength to a previously weak organisation. The new Volunteers with Redmond's patronage were regarded by the New York *Times* as a serious force and every bit as intransigent as the Ulster Volunteers.[41] The *Literary Digest* saw Redmond's joining the Volunteers as another ominous step in the deteriorating situation in Ireland; later it suggested that neither force need be taken altogether seriously, but clearly it was concerned. Certainly the British Embassy found this new situation potentially dangerous. Reports were sent back to the Foreign Office throughout late June and July showing a marked increase in activity among the Irish community. The Pennsylvania Federation of Irish County Societies endorsed Redmond, the Irish Party and the Irish Volunteers; the Philadelphia AOH collected $4,000 for the Volunteers to be added to the $5,000 they had already collected; Michael J. Ryan announced that the UIL planned to raise $1,000,000. This activity called for some reconsideration on the strength of the Irish-American organisations by the Foreign Office. Lord Eustace Percy noted that 'This shows that when the occasion is sensational enough funds can still be raised in America for Ireland,' although he did admit that it did not seem to amount to as much money as in previous years.[42]

The object of Casement's trip to the United States in July had been to obtain assistance for the Volunteers and to explain the compromise with Redmond. While he worked to raise money, he candidly declared that what he wanted were rifles and men rather than cash. As for Redmond, Casement cautioned that there could be no permanent trust but that temporary co-operation was a necessary expediency. This policy was vindicated by the success of the gun-running at Howth Harbour on 26 July 1914. It was a bold step that few Irish nationalists, regardless of their precise sentiments, could fail to support. Devoy told Casement that it was 'the greatest deed done in Ireland for 100 years'.[43] It made the Volunteers, whatever the composition of the Provisional Committee, a serious and popular organisation among the American Irish. Casement's knighthood, reputation and religion were exceptional for an Irish nationalist leader, and perhaps because of this he managed to attract the support of many moderate Irish-Americans for the Volunteers. In New York he stayed with John Quinn, who had access to many levels of public life; and Quinn also arranged for W. Bourke Cockran to go to the national convention of the AOH in Norfolk with Casement, where the two made well-received speeches on the Volunteers. Through the efforts of the Clan Casement also addressed meetings in Philadelphia, Baltimore, Buffalo, Chicago and New York.[44]

If the Irish-Americans needed anything to stimulate their support for the Volunteer movement the shooting by British troops into the crowds at Bachelor's Walk, Dublin, in the immediate aftermath of the Howth gun-running on 26 July 1914 provided it. Large public meetings were held in many Irish-American centres to denounce the incident. In Philadelphia Devoy and Casement were among the principle speakers at a protest meeting. To many Irish-Americans the shootings were simply one more point in a seven-hundred-year-old argument against British rule in Ireland. 'The blood of these murdered people', the *Gaelic American* wrote, 'is the price that Ireland pays for victory in the first skirmish in a war for National Independence which must be fought to the finish.' The Irish people and their kin in America would not forget this 'wanton butchery', the paper went on, even in the moment of joy at having successfully landed German rifles. The *Irish World*, of course, condemned it also and compared this 'massacre' with the Boston Massacre; the issues of liberty and independence were the same as those of the American Revolution. Such native American papers as the New York *Times* were shocked by the shootings:

The first blood has been shed by British soldiers, who fired not on the rebels of the North, but on the loyal upholders of Irish Home Rule, who following the example of Ulster, were providing themselves with arms in case of an emergency.

In comparison with the British government's reaction to the Curragh incident, the Larne gun-running and the inflammatory statements of Carson and his followers, the Bachelor's Walk shootings appeared to both native Americans and Irish-Americans as foolish, incompetent and patently unjust.[45] But the growing war crisis in Europe diverted the attention of American newspapers from further comment or speculation on the events at Howth and Dublin.

III.   The First World War and the Crisis of the Home Rule Movement

The European war drew British attention away from the Irish crisis. Civil war in 1914 was avoided, and superficially it seemed as though the war crisis had created unity in Ireland and England. Parliament appeared to satisfy the Unionists by maintaining the status quo. And indeed, some in the government were moved to support the passage of the bill expressly because of the favourable effect it might have in the United States.[46] While the enactment of Home Rule was a gesture, unconvincing to the cynical, it did allow people to believe what they chose, and its effects were not without some force in America, where many people henceforth spoke of Home Rule as an accomplished fact. Redmond's efforts to demonstrate the loyalty of the nationalists and the unity of the United Kingdom actually resulted in bringing into the open the issue of Ireland's relationship with Britain and the Empire. Redmond, as well as Parnell before him, had often been able to give diverse impressions to various audiences about the nature of the British connection after the enactment of Home Rule. The circumstances of the war, however, forced Redmond to define this relationship immediately by aligning Ireland with Britain. Thus it became increasingly clear to Irish-Americans— certainly to the leaders of moderate groups like the UIL—that the relationship was far closer indeed than had been imagined. Redmond's loyalty to the hated British Empire seemed to many to be a betrayal of the ideals of Irish nationality. In retrospect, the passage of the Home Rule Bill had not solved the Irish question, as many in America had hoped it would; rather it was the beginning of the gradual decline of constitutionalism in Ireland and America.

As native Americans became largely preoccupied with the course of the war the Irish question diminished in importance. Such comment as there was concentrated on the surprising degree to which Ireland loyally supported Great Britain. The extent to which the passions that had created the civil war tensions in Ireland were directed towards the war with Germany was regarded as amazing.

The New York *Times* noted shortly after the war had begun that British fears that 'the union of the kingdom would be imperiled and its strength for defense impaired' by Irish Home Rule were completely unfounded; in fact, 'The Irish, without distinction of party, section, or religion, were absolutely united and were all equally loyal to the national cause.' The Philadelphia *North American* said it now seemed incredible that British Tories could have believed 'that Irishmen were disloyal . . . and that self-government would alienate them from the empire'. The New York *Herald* thought that the Irish were given an opportunity to prove their good faith to the British and that if they kept Redmond's promises they would certainly do so. Theodore Roosevelt, writing to his friend Arthur Hamilton Lee, said: 'The attitude of the Irish in this business [the war] has been fine, and of good omen to the British Empire.' Irishmen were reported by the *Literary Digest* as enthusiastic in support of Redmond and the war effort; the magazine pointed out that the Irish accepted the temporary postponement of Home Rule, but that they regarded Home Rule as a fact.[47]

But it was precisely Redmond's degree of loyalty to Great Britain that many Irish-Americans found difficult to accept and which cost the Irish Parliamentary Party the support of the two pillars of his strength in the United States—the *Irish World* and the UIL. The *Irish World* began to waver as early as mid-August when Redmond and Devlin held talks with Lord Kitchener, Secretary for War, about how the Irish Volunteers could be incorporated into the British army. The paper recognised the magnitude of the war, but it refused to accept the notion that the war, which it saw as one of continental rivalries, in any way affected Ireland's vital interests. For Redmond and Devlin to 'fritter away any part of her [Ireland's] military resources by going to England's defense would be treason of the blackest kind', the *Irish World* thus concluded. This growing discomfort over Redmond's attitude was not forgotten in the joy of royal assent to the Home Rule Bill on 18 September 1914. Although the paper excitedly announced: 'The accursed Union [is] ended' and 'Home Rule is come at last,' it also warned that 'there has arisen a crisis in Irish affairs' which centred on the question of Irishmen in the British army. Home Rule had not been purchased at the price of support during the war, but was merely the grudging restoration of Ireland's natural rights. Ireland, the paper felt, had no obligation to fight for England and Redmond had no power from the Irish people to act as a British recruiting agent. After Redmond's famous speech at Woodenbridge on 20 September the *Irish World* published a long editorial which attacked the speech line by line, challenging Redmond's right to ask Irishmen to fight for England. Irish-Americans had contributed to the Volunteers to give Ireland a means of defending herself against those who would deprive her of her rights, not to train Irishmen in arms so that they could better serve England's interest in a continental war. Breaking with Redmond on this issue, the *Irish World* stated : 'We must part company with him when he asks the Irish Volunteers to help his recruiting campaign for the British army.' For the next several weeks the paper published anti-recruiting editorials and the letters of local Irish-American leaders who supported the paper in breaking with Redmond and in condemning the British for their part in the war.[48]

The national president of the UIL, Michael J. Ryan, also objected to Redmond's decision to lead Ireland in supporting the war effort. On the eve of the king's assent to the Home Rule Bill Redmond wrote to Ryan to explain the importance for the Irish Volunteers to gain military experience at least equivalent to that of the Ulster Volunteers, but this was not an argument destined to win much support among the Irish in America. Ryan replied in early October that in his opinion the UIL was defunct : 'Home Rule has been placed upon the Statute Book, and the work of the League in America can end in honour. Our suggestion would be that you authorize its termination here.' He strongly implied that if the league were to continue, he and several other officers would have to be replaced. While Ryan categorically condemned Redmond's enemies in Ireland and America, 'who talk of revolution and do nothing else', he thought that it was mistaken to ask for assistance from Irish-Americans that would 'even indirectly aid England'.[49] Ryan's disagreement with Redmond was augmented in the pages of the *Irish World*, which published nearly fifteen letters a week from UIL and AOH leaders throughout the country opposing Redmond's efforts to support the war.

It would be mistaken, however, to say that Redmond was without friends in the United States. Patrick Egan, the business manager of the *Irish World*, resigned in protest over the paper's new policy, and he attempted to defend Redmond through a letter to the paper. He also suggested to Redmond that with some financial assistance he could keep the UIL affairs before the American press. Furthermore, he recommended that Ryan be replaced as president of the UIL at the forthcoming convention by Dr John G. Coyle, a leader of the New York Municipal Council of the UIL. By late October William Dillon, the expatriate brother of John Dillon and a lawyer for the city of Chicago, and P. T. Barry, a prominent Chicago Irish-American, attempted to show that the Irish Parliamentary Party still had considerable strength in America by drafting a cable, to be signed by leading Irish-Americans, stating an appreciation of Redmond's actions in supporting the British government. The cable was to acknowledge that Redmond and the party had given Britain a 'solemn promise that, if the Home Rule bill were placed on the statute book, the Irish people would accept it as a settlement of the old quarrel, and would loyally support England in the present war'. Dillon appealed to several noted Irish-Americans, among them W. Bourke Cockran. But Cockran, who had misgivings about the judgment of the Irish leaders since their willingness to consider the exclusion of Ulster from Home Rule, was not enthusiastic and said it was news to him that the Irish people were pledged to unqualified support for Great Britain in the war. The cable was not sent, as the objections to it in New York and Chicago were too great. Many Irish-Americans felt that it would stir up animosity between the Irish and the Germans in the United States, that it would be a breach of American neutrality to support one faction of the belligerents, and that it would be an invitation to those Irish in America who had formed an alliance with the Germans to openly incite rebellion in Ireland. Dillon regretted that a great opportunity had been lost for the loyal Redmondite forces to make their views public.[50] The erosion had begun.

Redmond, however, was not anxious to force any issues with the leadership of the UIL in America. By October and November people still expected a short war in Europe; if this expectation were borne out, the fissures in the moderate Irish-American organisation might easily be plastered over, and the large body of Home Rule support which had existed in July might be maintained. Redmond had no desire, therefore, to see the league split or the leadership shifted. Consequently, Redmond was, according to his biographer, Denis Gwynn, quite relieved when the national officers agreed to continue to serve and when the national convention, scheduled for December, was indefinitely postponed. There was, however, a recognition of the awkwardness of the situation and a resignation that there was little the American Home Rulers could do. As T. B. Fitzpatrick, the national treasurer, told Redmond in early March 1915,

I know you are conversant in the manner in which the European war has interfered with any real activity on the part of the U.I.L. in its ordinary routine of work in this country. The conditions simply impose the practice of waiting, for the time being, and wait I believe we must until the attention of the world is somewhat released from the war tension in which it is held today.[51]

But more waiting meant that the initiative was allowed to slip from the hands of moderates into the hands of the impatient revolutionaries.

Redmond's friends refused to remain altogether passive in the face of the unrest among many of the Irish-Americans. The *Irish World* had not turned over to the UIL all the funds it was in the process of collecting when the split with Redmond occurred. Dr Coyle of New York had threatened to open legal proceedings to recover the money, but was able to intimidate the Fords sufficiently to recover $5,000 without going to court. Further efforts were made, especially by the New York Irish-Americans, to keep the UIL functioning and to contradict publicly the growing assumption that all Irishmen in America were pro-German. The New York Municipal Council of the UIL held a convention, which was well attended but carefully dominated by such friends of Redmond as Stephen McFarland, Dr Coyle, Egan and the national treasurer Fitzpatrick. The convention was held, Dr Coyle reported to Redmond, 'because the noise and clamor made [by the Irish–German groups] were quite capable of making the American public think that all the Irish were pro-German and anti-Redmond'. They sent a cablegram of support to Redmond, denied claims of the Irish–German group to speak for the Irish-American community, and condemned James Larkin and Cornelius Lehane, who had been describing Irish socialist activities on speaking tours. Redmond also received personal assurances that the Irish in America were still loyal to him and the party. P. T. Barry was confident that 'The bulk of our people here are with you and will be to the last.' The UIL treasurer wrote: 'With the rank and file of those who have aided the United Irish League in this country there is, I am satisfied, no defection.' He said also that Redmond and the party were trusted to guard carefully Ireland's interests in the present situation. Much of the criticism of the party was not from new sources, Michael J. Jordan, national secretary of the UIL in New York, told Redmond: 'All of those who have been hostile to us at all times are simply finding increased opportunities at the present moment to vent their spleen.'[52]

The actual strength of Redmond's support in the United States during late 1914 and 1915 is impossible to estimate accurately. Even before the war Casement thought that Redmond's claims for loyalty among the Irish-Americans were exaggerated, as has been shown earlier. However, in late December 1914 John Quinn told Sir Horace Plunkett that the defection of the Irish-Americans was not very large. Quinn, Plunkett recorded in his diary, felt that 'their anti-British influence is now inconsiderable', and Quinn was not contradicted by W. Bourke Cockran, a recognised Irish-American leader who was also present. This was essentially the same view

that Lord Bryce's American friends expressed. In late March 1915
A. E. Pillsbury told Bryce how little impression the German
propaganda had made on the Irish in his own Boston, confirming
Bryce's own view that the passing into law of Home Rule had had
a very favourable effect 'upon opinion in the U.S. as well as in
Ireland'. Almost a year later another friend, Lloyd B. Sanderson of
New York, wrote telling Bryce that Irish and German politicians
would make anglophobe statements but that there would be 'no
real antagonistic sentiment'. That Patrick Egan would call John
Devoy a 'sleepless demon' is not surprising, but the unsolicited
letter of John J. Manning to Devoy which called the old Fenian 'a
rank FAKER, a foul mouthed rat who is in the pay of the Kaisers
agents in this country' and referred to Redmond as 'a gentleman,
a man of honor, a statesman' is perhaps an indication that at least
some of the Irish-Americans resented and resisted the new inroads
made by the Clan.[53] Native American newspapers seemed confused
by the new Irish situation, at least to the extent that they considered
the Irish question at all after the beginning of the war. In December
1914 the *Literary Digest* did note, however, that there was a contradiction between the pro-Ally sentiments of the Irish in Ireland
and the pro-German sentiments of some of the Irish in America.
In late July 1915 the *Digest* again puzzled over the curious contrast
between the conspicuous valour of Irish soldiers, resulting in several
VCs, and the failure of recruiting in Ireland. The Philadelphia *North
American*, in reply to a letter from a German-American reader,
asserted that Redmond, not the late Fenian Jeremiah O'Donovan
Rossa, still characterised the Irish people—although ironically
despite the great funeral given to him by the Irish Volunteers,
Rossa had at the end been supporting Redmond.[54]

Nevertheless, the difficulties of the UIL were soon to be dramatised by the controversy over the attempts to close the national
headquarters office in Boston. Michael J. Jordan, the national
secretary, had promised Redmond at the end of 1914 that 'Our
organization will be preserved here until such time as you consider
there is no longer any need for it.' Thus when Michael J. Ryan and
T. B. Fitzpatrick, the national president and treasurer respectively,
suggested that the national headquarters be closed down, Jordan
objected. He immediately asked Redmond to demand that the
office be maintained, pointing out that its closing would kill the
organisation permanently and would constitute a great triumph for
the enemies of Home Rule. Jordan was supported by Patrick Egan,
who asserted that Ryan's continued relations with the *Irish World*,
not to mention his pro-German statements, 'show that his main
object was to quietly chloroform the League, and put it out of

existence', and the closing of the office would serve as 'a trump card for all the enemies of our cause from Bonar Law and Carson to John Devoy and the Fords'. Redmond's request to keep the office open did not end the matter. Fitzpatrick wrote to Redmond that because of the policy of waiting for the end of the war there was no point in spending $1,500 a year for an office and a stenographer. He also made clear to Jordan that the office would close on 13 March as scheduled and that he would resign if it were kept open.[55]

The New York Municipal Council of the UIL agreed with Jordan and Egan that the closing of the office would be disastrous. It was argued that there was a certain illegality in two officers making such an important decision without the approval or knowledge of the national executive committee or the members of the league. Ryan replied that the council was 'in ignorance of the facts' and that this step had not been taken arbitrarily but was part of a programme of cutting expenses. He and Fitzpatrick agreed to have the clerical work of the UIL done in their own offices for the time being, and Ryan suggested rather facetiously that if the Municipal Council were so anxious to keep the office open, they could raise the money themselves rather than depleting the league funds. After a passionate and bitter meeting the Municipal Council decided they would pay the expenses until more permanent arrangements could be worked out. Jordan was telegraphed on 12 March, the day before the office was to close, with the news that they would guarantee expenses until July 1915. The situation was finally resolved the following month when arrangements were made with the Catholic Federation of the Archdiocese of Boston to share the office and thus reduce the expenses by half.[56]

Ryan and Fitzpatrick had sound reasons for wanting to close the office. Since the beginning of the war no attempts had been made to raise money for the league in the United States; and with no active programme to promote, there was no need, they thought, for the expense of maintaining an office and a full-time stenographer. But there were more considerations than merely conserving financial resources. The constitutional Irish-American nationalists were coming under increasing pressure from their revolutionary counterparts for the leadership of the Irish community in the United States. Dr John G. Coyle of New York outlined the situation to Redmond:

In New York we have felt that the contemplated closing of the Boston office would be heralded far and wide as the practical ending of the League. There is so much anti-English sentiment cultivated by the professional 'Irish' politician here, and readily responded to by the ordinary man of Irish blood, nurtured in hatred of Great Britain, that the closing of the office, following the turnover of the Irish World, the attitude of the National President and other officers of the A.O.H., following the postponement of the Convention last fall, and following the pronouncements of Mr Ryan in his untimely and regrettable attacks upon France, Great Britain and Belgium of several months ago, would, we felt, by widely announced as the ending of the League, the collapse of the Home Rule movement, and [would], in general, be a disaster.

Coyle's description of the pressures on the Home Rule movement by mid-winter 1915 were probably accurate, but it may well have been that the 'disaster' of which he spoke had already struck in spite of the resolves and good intentions of the Municipal Council. Certainly these arguments within the UIL weakened the movement despite Redmond's efforts to avoid open conflict.[57]

In order to express to the UIL leaders his desire to maintain the status quo with as little controversy as possible and to discern the situation, Redmond sent Alderman Daniel Boyle, MP, on a short American tour in May 1915. Boyle travelled to the major Irish-American centres east of Chicago, but talked principally with those UIL leaders who had been involved in the controversy over the Boston office. Boyle reported that the leaders nominally agreed with Redmond's desire to preserve the status quo and not force differences into the open, but he found also that relations among the national officers were very strained. Nevertheless, he was told by Fitzpatrick that the favourable opinion in Boston on Redmond was improving and that pro-German sympathy was not very widespread. Ryan, in spite of his pro-German sympathies, which he himself confessed to Boyle were not representative of Irish-American opinion, would do nothing to damage the league or the prospects of Home Rule. He even said publicly at a dinner for Boyle that he was willing to stand by Redmond whenever he was called. In fact Boyle found Ryan's views similar to Redmond's, and he disregarded Egan's conspiritorial view of the national officers and especially Egan's allegations of Ryan's collusion with the Fords in the defection of the *Irish World*. However, it would appear that Boyle was more sanguine than circumstances warranted, and this, along with Redmond's loyalty to Ryan, which Shane Leslie later noted, led to a continued deterioration of the position of the Home Rule forces.[58]

The creation of the coalition cabinet in late May 1915 further strained Irish-American feeling about the good faith of the British government. Although Redmond could not join the cabinet because of the nature of Irish nationalist politics, Carson did become a member, as did several other Unionists who had been conspicuously anti-nationalist before the war. The imbalance of the situation was immediately apparent both in Ireland and America. The crisis over the nomination of J. H. Campbell, a prominent Irish Unionist, as Lord Chancellor seemed so threatening that Lord Eustace Percy of the Foreign Office, a Conservative and a shrewd observer of American affairs, warned A. J. Balfour, the newly appointed First Lord of the Admiralty, against any ill-considered appointments of Irish Unionists because of the delicate nature of the Irish-American situation. At the beginning of the war many 'responsible' Irish-Americans had supported Redmond's decision on the war or had supported Wilson's appeal for neutrality. The postponement of Home Rule 'shook them a little', Percy said. 'The Coalition Government will inevitably shake them much more.' If these Irish-Americans who had backed Redmond or who had remained neutral were to become too disillusioned, they might 'come off the fence' and join with the revolutionary Irish and the Germans in keeping America out of the war and obstructing the production of munitions. The situation, Percy concluded, 'is really dangerous', and he warned Balfour that the party leaders should consider 'tactics' which would not further alienate moderate Irish nationalists in the United States. Certainly the coalition government invited increased cynicism from Irish nationalists in both America and Ireland.[59]

Many American moderates felt that the Home Rule cause suffered from the loss of a sympathetic newspaper. The defection of the *Irish World* was of genuine importance because it meant that favourable Home Rule news was not distributed and was replaced by the consistently hostile views of the *Gaelic American* and then the *Irish World*. Furthermore, by late 1914 the Chicago *Tribune*, which had regularly published articles by T. P. O'Connor, terminated their contract with him; he later wrote for an American news syndicate, but in the meantime another link had been broken. As early as autumn 1914 suggestions were made to Redmond that several things could be done. Patrick Egan first said that for £25 a month he could keep Home Rule information before the American press, but by December he wrote to Redmond's secretary that what was needed was a newspaper. Others noticed as well: Edward J. Gallagher, editor of the *Lowell Sun*, told Redmond that there was a need to revive the old UIL *Bulletin* in order to respond to the German influence, and Michael J. Jordan, whose views of the problem of trying to hold together the organisation without favourable newspaper coverage were similar to those of Egan and Gallagher, suggested that the *Sacred Heart Review* might be developed as a Home Rule paper. As a temporary measure, Jordan thought articles from the Dublin *Freeman's Journal* might be reprinted and distributed in the United States. At almost the same time William Dillon cautiously inquired of W. Bourke Cockran about the advisability of starting a newspaper to publicise the Home Rule position, although he also queried whether such a publication would be a breach of the neutrality that President Wilson had requested. By spring Egan was fearful that Patrick Ford, who had broken with his brother Robert of the *Irish World*, might start a Home Rule paper backed by Lord Northcliffe, outside the control of the loyal UIL members.[60]

In the autumn of 1915 Redmond was roused to send Alderman Boyle back to the United States for the purpose of raising money for a newspaper sympathetic to the Home Rule cause and the policy of the party. Redmond suggested

> that you ask our leading supporters to provide a moderate sum of money which would be required to start an Irish American weekly paper, produced in high class style, to give the true facts, week by week, with reference to the war, and more particularly, with reference to events in Ireland.

Redmond was certain that such a paper would find a large reading public among the loyal members of the UIL, and would in effect take up Irish affairs where they had been left off in August 1914. If leading Irish-Americans could be convinced that this financial aid might be the 'last and crowning service' to be asked of them, it would go far in countering the effect of the anti-Redmond papers which, it was then widely believed, were being distributed free across the country by German money. Boyle came to the United States and raised money so that, by early 1916, a small paper, *Ireland*, was founded. It was edited by J. C. Walsh, assisted by Shane Leslie. Following Redmond's suggestion, it was produced in a 'high class style' in the hope of appealing to a more respectable class of Irish-Americans than had previous Irish papers in the United States. By March 1916 Leslie was able to report to Redmond that the paper had the approval of Cardinal Gibbons of Baltimore, who had agreed to write an article for it. 'In the growing success of that paper', Leslie confidently asserted, 'you will be able to measure some of the influence and sympathy you still command here.' But the task of rebuilding the position of the constitutional Irish-American nationalists in the United States, after nearly a year and a half of inaction, would take some time, as Leslie himself admitted. Furthermore, the paper, in setting out to be the vehicle of moderate opinion appealing to a sophisticated audience, fell between several stools. It took the unspectacular middle way by supporting Redmond, Home Rule and Irish participation in the war and by opposing Germany in the war and revolutionary tactics in Ireland. Within a few months of the first publication of *Ireland* the Easter Rising drastically altered the Irish political situation and badly compromised the prospects of the constitutional nationalists in cultivating a body of moderate, pro-Ally opinion among the community of Irish-Americans.[61]

IV.   Irish-American Nationalists and the German Connection

The coincidence of the First World War presented the revolutionary Irish-American nationalists with the opportunity to reap the fruits of their labours during the preceding twenty-five years. Through difficult and discouraging times the Clan na Gael had struggled to keep alive the values of revolutionary nationalism in Ireland and America, had worked to create common interests with the German-American pressure groups, and had plotted to prevent the United States from establishing closer relations—not to mention an alliance —with Great Britain. After August 1914 events began to work in favour of the revolutionary nationalists: the United States did not join Britain in the war but declared its neutrality, the German-Americans and the German government were willing to support Irish independence, and the revolutionary factions in Ireland soon broke with Redmond. The revolutionary Irish-American nationalists had only to encourage the growing cynicism of the Irish community in the United States about British good faith towards Ireland and Redmond's competence as an Irish nationalist leader. This was accomplished, in the absence of any effective contradiction from the UIL, through continual public meetings, joint activities with the German-American societies, the publication of anti-British and pro-Entente propaganda, and finally through the founding of a broadly based revolutionary nationalist organisation.

Events moved very swiftly after the war broke out. Initially the revolutionary Irish-American nationalists had two immediate objectives: to dissociate themselves once again from Redmond, and to expand their relationship with the organised German-Americans. Large public meetings were held under the auspices of the Clan na Gael, the Clan-dominated United Irish-American Societies and other anti-Home Rule organisations. At Celtic Park in New York on 9 August 1914 a large group of as many as 10,000 Irish-Americans (according to the *Gaelic American*'s estimate) gathered to hear speeches repudiating Redmond's action regarding the war and denouncing the Irish Parliamentary Party. Cheers were given for the Kaiser and German flags were carried by marching units. John Devoy and Jeremiah A. O'Leary addressed a German meeting in Newark on 14 August, attended by both Irish- and German-Americans, where Irish–German sentiments were expressed. In Washington, DC, a German Irish Committee was formed by the poet Shaemus O'Sheel. On 20 August a New York German meeting vowed itself to an alliance of Germany, Austria and Ireland; and on the following day in Philadelphia Irish-Americans condemned Redmond's pledge to defend Ireland from foreign invaders. On 5 September a meeting of St Louis Irish-Americans repudiated Redmond's leadership. Two days later an Irish-American fair was held at Philadelphia to raise money for the Irish Volunteers; it was attended by Germans, and German and Polish dancers took part in the proceedings. The United Irish-American Societies of New York declared that 'Redmond is a British Imperialist and not an Irish Nationalist.' They also promised to encourage Irish–German relations, to fight British recruiting in Ireland, and to oppose American participation in the war. The national convention of the Clan na Gael, meeting in Atlantic City on 27 September, not only repudiated Redmond but said that 'Ireland must purge herself of the shame and disgrace of Redmond's treason.' It also echoed a viewpoint, recently expressed in the *Gaelic American*, that Ireland's best interests would be served 'by England's defeat in this war'. The New York committee of the Irish National Volunteer Fund held a large public meeting on 9 October to protest against Redmond's treason and to ratify the Irish–German alliance resolution proposed by Jeremiah A. O'Leary. This resolution attempted to define the proper position for Irish-Americans in the new situation: they were to be pro-Irish, pro-American, pro-German, but anti-British.[62]

Similar meetings, devoted to expressions of sympathy for the Germans in the war or to protestations against Redmond and Home Rule in Ireland or to denunciations of British imperialism and militarism, continued at the rate of several a week until the United States entered the war in April 1917. These meetings took place in Irish and German centres throughout the country, although they were largely centred in the major Irish communities of the eastern seaboard. During 1915 and 1916 the emphasis of the meetings shifted slightly to include demands that the United States should not sell arms or make loans to the Allies and that the United States should maintain its foreign policy on the non-interventionist course set by Washington and Jefferson to avoid entangling alliances and European squabbles.[63]

Redmond's speech at Woodenbridge on 20 September 1914

marked a turning-point. Not only did the *Gaelic American* rejoice at the news from The O'Rahilly that the original Irish Volunteers founded by Mac Néill had broken from Redmond's National Volunteers, but the Clan na Gael promised to work for their support in America. Furthermore, Redmond's speech not only cost him the support of the *Irish World*, but it drove many leading Irish-Americans away from constitutionalism. Dr Gertude Kelly, prominent in New York UIL affairs, protested against Redmond's action, and former mayor of Syracuse James K. McGuire resigned from the league. Michael J. Ryan, who refused to say anything against Redmond in public, was reported gleefully in the *Gaelic American* as supporting Germany in the war at a large Philadelphia meeting; and W. Bourke Cockran let it be known that he disagreed with Redmond and that he had not attended any of the recent meetings of the national executive committee of the UIL of which he was a member. The new national president of the AOH, Joseph McLaughlin, published a letter in the *National Hibernian* repudiating Redmond's leadership of the Irish nationalist movement. Certainly Redmond's speech had a demoralising effect on the rank and file, as well as on the leaders. Maurice Donnelly of Indianapolis pointed out to both Joseph McGarrity and W. Bourke Cockran that 'Some of the best men who were with Redmond heretofore, are absolutely disgusted.' In the opinion of Sir Roger Casement, the physical-force people had effectively attracted most of the Irish-Americans: 'fully 85% of them', he wrote to Mrs Alice Stopford Green, were 'dead against Redmond'.[64] The defection of these Irish-Americans was welcomed by the Clan na Gael, which laboured to fill the vacuum created by the UIL's policy of waiting for the end of the war.

There seems to have been some reluctance among Irish-Americans to join forces with the Germans in the United States, with whom there was a history of more bad feeling than co-operation. Even John T. Keating indicated that there was some hesitation in the Chicago Clan organisation to move too quickly; but within a few months, and especially after Redmond's recruiting activities, these misgivings diminished. Eight out of ten Irish-Americans were 'for Germany & against the Crown', Casement told Mrs Green on 14 September, and he further mentioned that the 'good will between Irishmen & Germans in this country has become fact & sure & will bear fruit'. Almost a month later Casement assured Mrs Green that the Irish and the Germans would hold the United States out of the war by forming a new political party to keep the country American and democratic rather than pro-British and imperialistic.[65]

In addition to these overt attempts to shape opinion through large public meetings, the revolutionary leaders in the United States took direct steps to implement a revolutionary policy through co-operation with the German government. Shortly after the opening of the war a special committee of the Clan na Gael met the German Ambassador, Count Johann von Bernstorff, and members of his staff at a reception in the German Club in New York. The committee told the ambassador that their revolutionary counterparts in Ireland intended during the course of the war to free Ireland from Great Britain by force of arms, but that at the moment there were few weapons in Ireland and almost no trained officers. They told von Bernstorff that it would be in Germany's interest to promote such a rebellion in Ireland, by simply providing some arms and officers, because it would weaken Britain and divert troops from France. Von Bernstorff seemed interested and, in fact, on 25 September 1914 cabled the German Foreign Office that if in their opinion there was no possibility of reaching some accommodation with the British, 'I recommend falling in with Irish wishes.' Sir Roger Casement drafted a letter to the Kaiser on behalf of the Clan, outlining the Irish situation, and published a similar letter in both the American and Irish press. Casement reported to Mrs Green: 'We have made a pact of friendship here in America—if Ireland at home will only keep to her own green fields, attend to her own business, keep her volunteers *in Ireland*.'[66] Of course, Casement also negotiated, through the German Embassy, his own clandestine mission to create an Irish brigade from among German prisoners; subsequent news of the brigade and of the attempts by the British Consul in Christiania to capture Casement was fully publicised in the *Gaelic American*.

The Clan as well as the Germans attempted to manipulate the labour situation in the United States. The arrival of James Larkin in America in November 1914 presented both the Clan and the socialists with a dynamic, popular and persuasive figure who travelled throughout much of the country on behalf of those organisations attacking Redmond and Home Rule and preaching revolutionary Irish nationalism and socialism. Although Larkin and Devoy did not agree on socialism, their views on many Irish matters—especially Redmond and the Irish Parliamentary Party—were similar enough to allow them to join forces. Larkin, who opposed the war for socialist reasons, worked to create labour strife among Irish-American workers in the munitions industry and among the stevedores loading ships bound for Allied ports. He was even offered a regular salary from the German agent Captain Boy-Ed, which he turned down. Captain Franz von Rintelen, independent of the German Embassy staff, recruited Irish-American labourers to place bombs on freighters carrying munitions to Britain and paid Irish-American dock-workers handling explosives to strike for higher pay.[67]

As a result of these several Irish-German activities, projects were undertaken to open direct communication with Ireland and Germany. Dr Patrick McCartan was sent back to Ireland in early September with £2,000 for the IRB and with information and documents for Tom Clarke and the Supreme Council about Clan conversations with the Germans and about Casement's plans to create an Irish brigade in Germany. Diarmuid Lynch remained in America as the representative of the IRB to attend the national convention of the Clan na Gael on 27 September at Atlantic City, where he had official meetings with the Revolutionary Directory (Devoy, Keating and McGarrity) and the Committee on Foreign Relations. The people with whom he spoke continued to place their confidence in the Irish organisation and sent Lynch back to Ireland in early November with £2,000 for the IRB, although they were alarmed to learn that the IRB numbered only about 2,000 members. Messages were sent to Germany, elaborating on the talks with von Bernstorff, through Michael Francis Doyle, a Philadelphia lawyer going to Holland for the Department of State, and through John Kenny, who presented documents to the Chancellor and then returned to the United States by way of Ireland, where he informed Tom Clarke of the details on the Irish–German collaboration. In the following year communications with the IRB were maintained through Seán T. O'Kelly and Dr McCartan, who were sent as envoys to work on plans with the Clan for an alliance with Germany, to explain the position of the Supreme Council, and to bring important information back to Ireland. Regular communications and the transportation of funds were carried by Tommy O'Connor, who served as an IRB messenger while working on a British White Star passenger ship.[68]

Shortly after the outbreak of the war the revolutionary Irish-American element in the United States initiated a campaign to influence American opinion in favour of Irish independence or at least in opposition to Great Britain and United States participation in the war. This campaign was undertaken because of the feeling that the American press was generally pro-British and that the British government was spending enormous amounts on propaganda to win neutral American support for their side in the war. Some Irish pamphlets were distributed in the United States: the 'Bodenstown' series and 'Tracts for the times' were given considerable circulation, especially Pearse's *From a hermitage* and *Ghosts* and The O'Rahilly's *The secret history of the Irish Volunteers.*

Casement had several of his newspaper articles collected and published in 1915 as a pamphlet, *The crime against Europe: a possible outcome of the war of 1914.* Such items by Shaemus O'Sheel (published under the name of 'An Irish American') as *The catechism of Balaam, Jr.* and *A trip through headline land* were published in 1915 and used Ireland as an example of British misrule and attacked British diplomacy as the cause of the war. Jeremiah A. O'Leary directed the American Truth Society, the most Irish-orientated of several anti-British organisations to spring up in America in 1915, which carried on a bitter campaign against Great Britain and in favour of Germany. It published *The revelations of an American citizen in the British army*, by Daniel A. Wallace, an account of an American who was tricked into joining the British army, where he was treated very badly, sent to France and Turkey, and finally rescued by the American Consul in Alexandria. O'Leary himself published such items as *The conquest of the United States*, which complained of British propaganda in America, and *The fable of John Bull*, which cast Britain as the villain in American history.[69]

Such books as Frank Koester's *The lies of the Allies* (with an introduction by O'Leary), Edward A. Steiner's *The confession of a hyphenated American*, and S. Ivor Stephen's (Stephen Ivor Szinnyey, pseud.) *Neutrality* all attacked Great Britain in the war and touched on Ireland in some way to show the hypocrisy of Britain's defence of the effect of the Irish question on American life. *British versus German imperialism*, published anonymously, attempted to show how British imperialism, as exemplified in Ireland's case, was crushing and centralised while the German empire was liberal and federal in nature. Two of the most widely read books which dealt with Ireland were those written by the former mayor of Syracuse, New York, James K. McGuire, *The King, the Kaiser and Irish freedom* and *What could Germany do for Ireland?*; McGuire promoted sympathy for Germany among the Irish-Americans and argued that an Irish–German alliance would guarantee successful independence from Great Britain. In spite of these and other similar attempts to woo public opinion in the United States, T. St John Gaffney, former American Consul in Munich, who admittedly was both pro-Irish (he had entertained Casement in Germany) and pro-German, returned to find that 'Popular opinion had become demoralized under the influence of a press corrupted by the munitions traffic and the financial interests which had already begun to realize the gigantic profits to be made out of the war.'[70] In short, the climate of opinion in the United States in late 1915 was pro-Ally.

Nevertheless, it seems clear that by the end of that year a large segment of the Irish-American community had been drawn to revolutionary and pro-German ideas, rejecting their earlier constitutional and Home Rule notions. There was now the tantalising possibility that an independent Ireland might in some way be established as a result of the war through the intervention of Germany. This new concept was juxtaposed to the combined effect of the postponement of Home Rule and the demands made upon Ireland in support of the British war effort, and it worked to create an increasingly attractive alternative to many Irish-Americans. This sentiment was still largely unorganised, although it certainly had ample publicity from the *Gaelic American* and the *Irish World*, and it was, of course, very much nurtured by the Clan na Gael. The Clan, however, was a relatively small secret organisation, and the Irish-American press, while it reached a large audience, was not a systematic means of marshalling popular feelings. What was needed was a new Irish nationalist organisation, with an unmistakable mandate to speak for the Irish in America in order to refute any allegations that most of the Irish-Americans were still loyal to Redmond and Home Rule. After some discussion within the Clan leadership the decision was made to hold an Irish Race Convention in New York on 4 and 5 March 1916. Over the signature of 350 well-known Irish-American leaders an invitation was sent out on 8 February inviting some 2,300 reliable Irish-Americans from all parts of the United States to attend. It stated the general purposes of the convention, and those invited were expected to sign their names in agreement before they were permitted to attend. As Joseph McLaughlin, congressman from New Jersey, president of the AOH and managing editor of the *National Hibernian*, told Devoy,

> Rest assured, I am strongly opposed to admitting any but those whose sentiments are in accord with ours. The Convention will neither be the time nor the place to argue who is right, or who is wrong. We're right, and let the other fellows keep away.[71]

The convention founded the Friends of Irish Freedom, which for the next decade served as one of the leading broadly based, revolutionary Irish-American organisations, whose objective was the fostering of 'any movement that will tend to bring about the National Independence of Ireland'.[72] Victor Herbert, the composer and grandson of Samuel Lover, was elected president, Thomas Hughes Kelly treasurer, and John D. Moore secretary. As C. C. Tansill has pointed out, the organisation was dominated by the Clan, and in fact it could be said that the FOIF was the popular and national auxiliary of the Clan. It was not oath-bound, did not take up clandestine activities, and it did allow women members. In fact it made considerable efforts to include as many members as possible, even to the extent of providing for 'associate' membership for small groups which preferred to maintain their affiliation with some other organisation. The work of creating local chapters and raising of funds began at once. The convention also made a 'Declaration of Principles and Policy' which included demands that America's rights should be preserved against Great Britain, that Irishmen should not be expected to fight for England, and that Ireland should be made independent and be guaranteed a voice in the making of peace at the end of the war. Although the coming rebellion was, according to Devoy, known only to four men in the United States, in retrospect it seems clear that the convention and the creation of the FOIF were attempts to prepare the Irish-American public for the Rising. Certainly, on the strength of the mandate given by the convention, constitutionalism was publicly rejected and a new basis was laid for revolutionary agitation.

Although the Irish Race Convention was applauded by such Irish-American newspapers as the *Irish World* and the *Gaelic American*, as well as the New York *Evening Mail* and William Randolph Hearst's New York *American*, it was not without its critics. The new Redmondite paper *Ireland*, of course, thought that the convention was ill-advised and had been the blatant tool of the Germans inasmuch as it had opposed the policies of all except Germany, and 'It was hostile to the people of Ireland whose deliberate policy was deliberately condemned.' The New York *Herald* observed on the second day of the convention that it was understandable that some Irishmen could be lured by the Germans into thinking that 'Prussian rule would benefit Ireland, but that any sane Irishman should believe such nonsense is incredible'.[73] The Irish people were united behind Redmond in support of the war, maintained the Brooklyn *Citizen*, and the convention was 'at variance with Ireland's elected representatives'. The New York *Tribune* said that the convention was a 'clownish performance' and that most Irishmen were 'humiliated' by this 'impudent set of upstarts who have no authority whatever to express the sentiments of Irishmen at home'. The *Literary Digest* condemned the convention as an embarrassment to American foreign policy at a critical moment, and it quoted Supreme Court Judge John Ford, who refused to attend because he was 'so fully occupied just now trying to be a faithful American citizen' that he had 'no time for consideration of the fortunes of any other country, except to sympathize with the unfortunate peoples afflicted by the unspeakable horrors of the European War'. Needless to say the convention was of some concern to the British Embassy, which sent a full report to London, including news clippings and documents, but the Foreign Office offered no proposals for coping with the situation. As Robert Sperling suggested in a minute written on 24 March 1916, 'When Sinn Féiners are allowed to "practice [sic] street fighting" in Irish towns we can hardly be surprised at proceedings of this sort in the U.S.'[74]

CHAPTER 3
1916 AND ITS AFTERMATH
1916-1917

THE Easter Rising of 1916 caught the American public very much by surprise, as it did almost everyone else, despite the conspicuous activity in early 1916 of the revolutionary Irish-Americans and their co-operation with the German-Americans. Americans in general had been preoccupied with the growing crisis between Mexico and the United States and with the war in Europe—specifically with the exchange of diplomatic notes between Germany and the Wilson administration over the *Sussex* affair and also with the battle of Verdun. Home Rule and Ulster, which had aroused considerable interest in 1914, had been ignored once Ireland seemed to rally behind the war effort and once the crisis of civil war was averted. Although there were exceptions, native American opinion in 1916 was predictable enough: it disliked the rebellion but tended to be shocked by the subsequent executions and disgusted by the British government's blunderings with Home Rule, Casement's execution and the Irish-American relief efforts. Irish-American opinion, of course, was more involved, intense and sustained; and although there was great diversity among the Irish-Americans, they shared a perspective on the Irish question that native Americans did not. Nevertheless, from at least May until August there was a general agreement within the country about the heavy-handedness of the British. This temporary coalition of several elements in American society during 1916 posed a serious threat which the British Ambassador and the Wilson government, for different reasons, recognised, even if the British government did not. The result was that opinion on the Irish question had reached such an intensity that it could no longer be ignored or forgotten.

I. *The Impact of the Easter Rising*

The first reports of any disturbances in Ireland to reach the United States were published in the newspapers of Tuesday 25 April 1916, which noted very briefly that Sir Roger Casement, who had gone from Germany to Ireland in a submarine, had been captured and that a ship carrying arms had been sunk. Papers which went to press later on Tuesday, such as the Chicago *Tribune*, published slightly larger and more speculative articles, although these contained little more information. In fact it appears that so little information reached the United States by the regular channels that the *Christian Science Monitor* speculated on the following day that the cable linking England and America might have been cut. Nonetheless, on Wednesday sufficient details had arrived to enable the Washington *Post* to report that fighting had broken out in Dublin between elements of the 'Sinn Féin Society' and government troops and that serious fighting had centred on St Stephen's Green and the General Post Office.[1] The *Christian Science Monitor* commented that the disturbances were 'little more than a riot', and the New York *World* ran a headline: 'UPRISING IN DUBLIN QUELLED: IRELAND ELSEWHERE IS QUIET'. The deduction seemed to be that Casement had come to Ireland to lead a rebellion, but that he had been captured and an abortive insurrection in Dublin had been successfully suppressed by British forces. By the end of the week American newspapers were able to print considerably fuller stories of what had taken place in Ireland, and some at least admitted that the rebellion was larger than was first reported. Meanwhile, however, in lieu of more concrete information, the New York *World* published an article on Casement written in Berlin by the German-American newspaperman Franz Hugo Krebs (dated 18 March), while the Washington *Post* had several short biographical sketches of some of the known leaders and an analysis of the rebellion by Pádraic Colum. The Chicago *Tribune* published interviews with leading Chicago Irish-Americans, most of whom condemned the Rising as a betrayal.[2]

Initially the major American newspapers denounced the Rising outright in their editorials. Casement was regarded as the leader of the rebellion, and he along with the Germans and Irish-Americans was blamed for all the troubles it brought. While the New York *Times* and the Washington *Post* thought Casement was mad, they agreed with the New York *World* that there was some irony in the situation—that Casement's treason was not markedly different from that of Carson, then a member of the government, or General Sir John French, commander-in-chief in Ireland. The rebellion itself was both foolish and futile, wrote the Chicago *Tribune* and the New York *World*; it weakened John Redmond as the Phoenix Park murders had Parnell and it played into the hands of the Tories and Unionists, noted the *Christian Science Monitor* and the New York

*World.*³ The New York *Times,* although occasionally revealing considerable insight into the situation, did tend to resort to the ethnic bias by suggesting that it was in an Irishman's character to rebel for an ideal, even if he had the substance in the form of Home Rule; indeed, the Irish rebels were 'like forward children, causing untold annoyance to others, but themselves suffering the heavier penalties of misbehaviour'. Broadly speaking, the American papers regarded the Rising as foolish and misguided (and largely inspired by the Germans and the contemptible Irish-American revolutionaries safe in the United States), and they hoped that, in view of the conspicuous loyalty of the majority in Ireland, the British government would heed the lessons of South Africa and deal with both Ireland and the rebels in a lenient and generous manner. The liberal journals, like the *New Republic* and the *Nation,* opposed the Rising and thought it senseless, but were bitter in their condemnation of the British for provoking the Irish into rebellion.⁴

News of the executions of the leaders of the rebellion and the brutal killing of several innocent people provoked strong criticism of the British government by many of the editors of American newspapers which were often regarded as anglophile in policy. Perhaps one of the most critical was the New York *World,* which first commented that the executions served 'no good purpose' and merely created bitterness in Ireland. As the executions continued the *World* appealed to the government to follow Redmond's advice at Westminster and expressed the hope that the 'flurry of British frightfulness is over'. The following day the editors said the rebels should be treated as belligerents as the Confederates had been during the American Civil War and the Boers in the Boer War. The next week the *World* was even more scathing:

> If even now we can be sure what has happened, sixteen men have been killed in cold blood for deeds like those that were forgiven De Wet. One was slain for 'murder' which calls for public trial [Thomas Kent]. The shooting of another seems to Mr Asquith himself 'an inexcusable act' [Sheehy-Skeffington]. Are there to be more? Are the 'rivers of blood' at last dammed?⁵

The Washington *Post* came out strongly against the executions from the beginning, arguing that

> It is no exaggeration to say that a shock went around the civilized world when it was learned that Patrick H. Pearse and the other leaders of the Irish revolt had been tried by drumhead court-martial, found guilty and sentenced in a trice and shot at sunrise against a wall of Dublin castle.

Such action was 'hasty, ill-considered and unstatesmanlike', especially when compared with the action taken against Carson or the Boer leaders or even Colonel Arthur Lynch, who had taken a pro-Boer Irish brigade to South Africa, and it would be a source of future acrimony. The Chicago *Tribune* asserted that the British were within their legal rights in the executions but that they were mistaken to carry out the penalties; really, it said, the rebellion was not as dangerous as the recent labour strikes. The New York *Times* and the Des Moines *Capital* seemed to agree that there was little else the British could do, but it was certain that the executions would create martyrs and win undeserved sympathy. Even the *Christian Science Monitor*, certainly one of the American newspapers least sympathetic to the Rising, thought that the executions were ill-advised because the Irish temperament—unrealistic and provincial at best—would never understand and would subsequently romanticise the rebellion it currently deplored.[6]

The private opinion of native Americans, although less systematic than the press, followed a similar pattern: unsympathetic to the rebellion but startled by the executions. J. H. Kellogg, a close correspondent of Sir Horace Plunkett, wrote on 27 April that he was 'shocked' to learn of the rebellion and thought it pitiful that 'so many people should be willing to accept the guidance of an insane leader [Casement]'. The Wisconsin Progressive, Charles McCarthy, expressed his 'extreme regret' to Plunkett about the Rising and said that he had first concluded that it was the work of Larkin's followers but understood now that there was 'a literati element to it'. McCarthy, however, commented adversely on the executions:

> At the present time there is a great indignation all over America at the killing of so many of the men who are in the rebellion. America, in general, looks upon them as misguided men, and of course you know we have certain traditions here which come down from our own rebellion. Everyone in this country has been glad that Jefferson Davis and other leaders of the rebellion were not killed.

Plunkett was told by the president of Harvard, A. Lawrence Lowell, that the Rising was a 'tragedy' and that Americans could not understand how the British government could have been so ill-informed as to allow it to take place. Both in May and again in July Lowell lamented the executions: 'To us here it seems that the executions of the Sinn Féiners after surrender was a mistake.'[7] Nicholas Murray Butler, a Columbia University don, thought it incomprehensible that the rebels were able to obtain support from German and

American sources, seemingly without the knowledge of the government. Butler wrote to Lord Bryce saying that the rebellion was 'deplorable' and that he was 'only too grateful that it was so speedily suppressed'. Bryce was also told by Seth Low, the New York educationalist and reformer, who was 'distressed' by the rebellion, that his Irish-American informants told him that while the executions had 'disturbed' many Irishmen in New York, the vast majority still supported Redmond and Home Rule. Few were as optimistic as this, although Willard Straight, patron of the *New Republic* magazine and former adviser for the State Department, told Bryce that by 21 June the 'general public' had been distracted by the presidential election in America. Straight commented that in May the executions had excited a considerable amount of criticism: his cautious analysis was that Americans thought 'your authorities had endeavoured to make up for past weakness and incompetence by sudden and unnecessary severity'. But Bryce was further assured by one friend that intelligent Americans were supporting England in spite of the Irish question because Great Britain was fighting America's battle in Europe.[8] Moreton Frewen was told: 'The last Irish outbreak has alienated the sympathies of many people here from the Irish cause.' One of the most moving expressions of private concern was the letter of William Dean Howells, then ageing but still one of the leading literary figures in America, to the New York *Nation*. Howells thought that the executions were acts of 'vengeance' which dramatised England's failure in Ireland and undermined the great cause Britain served in the war. In New York the poet Eleanor Rogers Cox organised a 'Poets' Meeting' in Central Park to express sympathy for Pearse, MacDonagh and Plunkett. It was a successful event which drew the participation of Edwin Markham, Margaret Widdemer, Louis Untermeyer, and many others who recited poems in memory of the Irish leaders.[9]

The role of Germany in the Rising was an explosive issue to native Americans, who were predisposed to support the Allies in the war and feared German intrigue in the United States and Mexico. The New York *World* had observed that 'An Irish rebellion, made in Germany, is not likely to get very far'—certainly not among native Americans. Several newspapers had damned the Germans for assisting the Irish rebels in their folly. Bainbridge Colby, the New York liberal and future Secretary of State, was willing to speak publicly in support of the Irish rebellion, but he disengaged himself from Irish-American organisations when he became suspicious of Irish–German collusion in New York protest meetings.[10] Other native Americans hoped to use the Rising as a weapon with which to weaken the pro-German movement in the

United States. By sheer chance the American journalist and author Arthur Bullard was the guest of Sir Horace Plunkett in Dublin during the Rising. Upon returning to London Bullard, with the assistance of Sir Basil H. Thompson of Scotland Yard, wrote to both E. M. House and Plunkett outlining a plan to reveal how the Germans had 'cynically fooled the Irish' by using the Rising as a trick to 'divert to Ireland British troops which would otherwise have gone to Flanders'. Casement's confession to Thompson that the Germans had 'let him down' led Bullard and Thompson to believe that the Irish had expected greater German assistance. 'If the Clan na Gael could be convinced that the Germans had tricked them this partnership [Irish and German] would be destroyed,' Bullard told House. They also felt that this might prove to be the key to German intrigue in Mexico and India as well. Plunkett joined in enthusiastically, writing letters to his American friends and talking with military leaders in Dublin. The project, though inconclusive, was an indication of the hostility with which some Americans viewed Irish–German co-operation.[11]

Perhaps more important than these comments by leading native Americans were the views of E. M. House and Theodore Roosevelt, who were closer to those in power. House, President Wilson's confidential adviser on foreign affairs, had written to Plunkett on 25 April, although presumably before he learned of the Rising, saying that he had been talking with Lloyd George in early 1916 about the Irish question and had been assured that Lloyd George was 'earnestly trying to work out some solution'. The Irish question 'has now become', House noted significantly, 'almost as much of a political issue in America as in England'. A month and a half after the Rising, on 16 June, House made a more cautious observation at the request of Plunkett:

> The rebellion and its consequences have not made as deep an impression here as they would have otherwise have [*sic*] made if there were not so many momentous events happening from day to day. I think, though, in more peaceful times it may come back to haunt us.[12]

Certainly this analysis hardly confirms his earlier view, although it was perhaps tempered by House's awareness of the certainty that Plunkett would show the letter to political leaders in London as an indication of Wilson's sentiments. Theodore Roosevelt, then out of power but by no means without influence, instructed his friend Arthur Hamilton Lee, then parliamentary secretary to Lloyd George, to tell the minister that because of the activities of Carson and the Ulster Unionists in 1914, 'I wish your people had not shot the leaders of the Irish rebels after they surrendered.' He agreed that it was imperative that the rebellion be put down, but, as he wrote to Plunkett a month later,

> It seemed to me that the extreme leniency with which Carson and the Ulster Unionists had been treated two years previously made it impossible to justify the extreme difference of treatment in the two cases by the far less dissimilarity of offence.[13]

Clearly the British government's handling of the Rising was a trial to its American friends, although this seems not to have influenced British policy.

Quite by accident the United States government became partially involved in one aspect of the Rising, and although its intentions, or those of President Wilson, cannot be precisely defined, it did not initiate action to betray the Rising as was alleged then and subsequently. On 18 April 1916 the United States secret service raided the private offices in New York of Captain Wolf von Igel, a member of the German Embassy staff, because he was suspected of carrying out espionage activities related to the war. Among the papers found in von Igel's possession were eight documents which gave quite detailed information about the time and place of the Irish rebellion and the shipment of arms from Germany and which mentioned the names of John Devoy and Judge Cohalan. Descriptions of the raid were published, filling the newspapers for several days, although the substance of the seized documents was not released.[14] On Tuesday 25 April, four days after the German ship *Aud* had been intercepted by the British navy off Fenit, Walter Hines Page, the American Ambassador in London, cabled to the Secretary of State to ask on behalf of the British for copies of those documents that related to Ireland:

> The Admiralty have received information that among the papers of Von Igel are a number dealing with the proposed smuggling [of] arms into Ireland and with an insurrectionary movement in Ireland. Admiralty would be grateful if photographic copies of these documents might be given to the British Naval Attaché at Washington.

One week later, on 1 May 1916, Secretary Lansing cabled to Page that the 'Charge [has been] made that this Government has already given information in regard to these papers,' and he added that he did 'not believe anything of any value has been discovered here', although he said the department would consider Page's request.[15] Thus whatever the British government knew about the rebellion in Ireland—and clearly it did have some warning in advance—the information came from British intelligence sources and not from the United States government.

The American government was anxious about the extent to which Irish-American revolutionaries might have violated the neutrality laws in the planning of the rebellion. Spring Rice was informed by the Department of State that, in the view of the government, American participation had been minimal. Although money had been collected for clearly revolutionary purposes, the actual planning of the Rising had been done in Ireland and Germany, and in fact few Irish-Americans could have known about it. The report of Wesley Frost, United States Consul in Cork, in October tended to confirm this early conclusion. Indeed, Frost suggested that the complaints about American money financing the Rising were 'absurdly unjustified'.[16] The American government did not want to find itself open to charges similar to those which had been made against Britain during the American Civil War.

Congress was more willing to comment publicly on the Rising than was the Wilson administration. Although events in Ireland were first mentioned in the Senate as early as 5 May 1916, steps were not taken until 12 May when Congressman Leonidas C. Dyer of Missouri introduced a resolution asking that the British government treat the rebels as 'prisoners of war' and not as 'criminals'. Four days later Congressman Jeff McLenmore of Texas, joint author of a recent bill to prevent Americans from travelling on the ships of belligerent countries, made a vigorous speech in Congress supporting the Rising as well as the Irish alliance with Germany and condemning British rule in Ireland and Americans who approved of it. On 17 May 1916 in the Senate William E. Borah of Idaho condemned the British executions. He said that because of the precedents against 'arbitrary power' he had learned with regret of 'these midnight judgements of the court-martial sitting at Dublin'. Such actions were out of character for the British and would cause a strong reaction. Later in the day Senator John W. Kern of Indiana introduced a resolution which asked that the Secretary of State inquire into the cases of American citizens arrested in Ireland during the Rising and that American interests generally be looked after.[17] The resolution was referred to the Senate Foreign Relations Committee and then sent by Chairman William J. Stone, who was a supporter of the administration but was also in favour of an American policy of strict neutrality in the war, to the White House and the State Department for an opinion. Frank L. Polk, Counselor of the State Department, discussed the resolution with President Wilson and reported back to Stone that Wilson 'did not think there was any particular objection to it', although Polk added that both he and the President felt that there was really no need to pass it at all. The resolution was returned to the Senate with a favourable report from the committee, and on 2 June, a date well past the time of effective action, the resolution was unanimously adopted. Wilson sent to the Senate a report from the Secretary of State on the circumstances of American citizens in Ireland in accordance with the Kern resolution.[18]

Meanwhile the Congress, the administration and the consular service had been working to see that due process of law was applied to Americans involved in the Rising. Personal appeals were directed to both the President and the Department of State on behalf of John J. Kilgallon and Jeremiah [Diarmuid] C. Lynch, with the result that some initiative was taken by the government to inquire about these two men. According to the Washington *Post*, Wilson, through a request by Senator James O'Gorman of New York, instructed Lansing to cable to Page 'to make representations in behalf of Lynch in order to save his life, pending an investigation of the facts in his case by the American government'. In Dublin the United States Consul, Edward L. Adams, intervened or inquired about the fate of Kilgallon, Lynch and Edward [Éamon] de Valera, all of whom had American connections which merited American interest if not actual protection (Kilgallon and Lynch were American citizens, while de Valera had been born in the United States). By the time Adams talked with the authorities in Dublin about Kilgallon he had been sent to prison in England, but the consul was instrumental in reversing the death sentence of the court martial in the cases of both de Valera and Lynch.[19]

Irish-American reactions to the Rising, while perhaps less detached or objective than those of native Americans, was also more complex because of the divisions between the constitutionalists and the revolutionaries. The Rising was a grievous, though not mortal, blow to the constitutional Irish-American nationalists which drove home the full implications of the contradictions of the Redmondite position. Ironically the constitutionalists were among the first in the United States to register any opinion on the insurrection when several leading Chicago Irish-Americans were interviewed by enterprising reporters from the Chicago *Tribune* for the Wednesday 26 April edition of the paper. P. T. Barry, president of the Irish Fellowship Club, said that the Rising was not an Irish rebellion at all, that the Irish people were loyal to the Allies, and he added (a bit unfairly) that Casement had never supported Irish nationalism until he lost his job in the consular service. Charles ffrench, a former president of the club, said that the Rising was the worst form of folly and that he had always disliked Casement, the supposed leader. William Dillon, the brother of the parliamentarian John Dillon, who would in a few days come close to championing the rebels at Westminster, said surprisingly that the Rising would not amount to very much. Only one Irish-American interviewed supported the Rising. In various Irish-American centres the United Irish League met to denounce the Rising and make expressions of support for the policy of John Redmond. In New York a meeting held on Friday 28 April was led by Stephen McFarland, John J. O'Connell, Dr John J. Coyle and Patrick Egan, who, after ejecting three disruptive supporters of the rebellion, declared themselves opposed to the Rising and the elements who created it and in favour of Redmond, Home Rule and President Wilson. Resolutions were passed:

> That this meeting express its unqualified sorrow and amazement at the unpardonable wrong now being perpetrated against the whole people of Ireland by the present insane attempt at insurrection—a futile effort instigated solely by the unscrupulous agents of foreign intrigue—participated in by a group of unreasoning enthusiasts, combined with a rank and file made up largely of communistic disciples of the unspeakable Jim Larkin and financed by foreign funds.[20]

The UIL in Boston sent Redmond a cable expressing their confidence in him and assuring him of the loyal sentiments of the Boston Irish for the party. In Dorchester, Massachusetts, Judge Thomas P. Riley spoke out in enthusiastic support of Redmond at a public meeting: Redmond and not the Sinn Féiners spoke for Ireland. Even Cardinal Gibbons expressed his disapproval of the Rising to the British Ambassador: 'At the present he said that all respectable Irishmen condemned [the] revolt in unqualified terms, but there was a danger of "manufacturing martyrs" for American use.' John Quinn, certainly a moderate without any organisational connections, wrote on 1 May to his friend the writer Joseph Conrad that he had been 'disgusted and depressed by the horrible fiasco in Ireland'. Quinn thought that if anything the rebellion typified the worst aspects of Irish romanticism and the 'refusal to face facts'. Nonetheless, he sent his friends gift copies of Pearse's writings.[21]

The executions of the leaders of the Rising caught the Irish-American moderates off guard. Stephen McFarland cabled to Redmond on 4 May: 'Irish in America contrasting execution of Dublin leaders with treatment in Ulster and South Africa are revolted by this sign of reversion to savage repression.' The constitutionalist weekly *Ireland* tried to explain the difficulty of the new situation. It questioned the necessity of the executions and said that they would be interpreted as a racial outburst by the British. More importantly, however, *Ireland* said that while Irishmen had committed themselves to the Home Rule policies of the pre-war government, 'No Irishman has wholly renounced the idea of being willing to fight for freedom if pushed to the extremity. The rashness of the idealists who have done this thing does not impair the universal sympathy of their ideal.' On 15 May Michael J. Ryan sent a gloomy cablegram to Redmond implying that Redmond was undone:

> Irish executions have alienated every American friend and caused resurgence of ancient enmities. Your life work destroyed by English brutality. Opinion widespread that promise or [*sic*] Home Rule was mockery.

Shane Leslie wrote from the home of W. Bourke Cockran to Redmond the following day of the deterioration of the prospects for moderate policy:

> The present wave of fury sweeping through Irish America originated with the executions and not with the rising. The rising only called out sympathy for you, except in a small circle. The executions enabled that circle to spread their ripple further than they had hoped or dreamed.[22]

Leslie said that Irish-Americans who had taken the news of the Rising quite calmly had become 'hysterical' during the extended executions, and he concluded that until Redmond was 'in charge of a provisional Government, Irish America would prove intractable to all except German agents'. A few days later he wrote that the situation was even more 'desperate'. P. T. Barry said much the same thing: the rebellion won condemnation, the executions sympathy, even among the native Americans. Despite the large meetings held by Devoy and his followers, Barry, like Leslie, felt that the whole thing would 'blow over' if the British government resolved the Irish question, and he urged that the 'final settlement should not be longer delayed'. The only effective defender of Redmond's policies and Home Rule after the executions seemed to be Lawrence Godkin, a New York lawyer whose Irish-American father had edited the *Evening Post*, who told the American Rights Committee (meeting in Carnegie Hall on 19 May to condemn the sinking of the *Lusitania*) that Redmond was correct on the issue of Irish participation in the war. Godkin spoke out because he thought there 'ought to be some expression of the point of view of the right-minded Irish of this country—who were many'. Joyce Kilmer, a romantic second-generation Irish-American, wrote several poems for the Central Park

'Poets' Meeting' in which he exalted the notions of freedom for
which the Irish rebels had died:

> Lord Byron and Shelley and Plunkett,
>   McDonough [sic] and Hunt and Pearse
> See now how their hatred of tyrants
>   Was so insistantly fierce.

Kilmer, who asserted that romantic Ireland was not dead as Yeats
had written, also praised the English libertarian tradition.[23] But even
moderate Irish-Americans like Kilmer and Godkin were then joining with Irish revolutionary nationalists.

The revolutionary Irish-American nationalists, while no doubt
more closely concerned with the events in Ireland, did not successfully make a public impression until the end of Easter Week. The
Gaelic American arrived on the newsstands on Saturday 29 April,
but it gave a report of events in Ireland that differed considerably
from the accounts in the large daily newspapers. Devoy, clearly
writing without any detailed information from Ireland, described in
fairly general terms what he thought was happening according to
the original plans: the Irish Volunteers had started an insurrection
on Saturday and Sunday, a cipher message told Devoy, and Ireland
was 'fighting gallantly for her Independence'. The British censor
and the slave-minded American newspapers had misrepresented and
minimised the significance of this major event by asserting that the
Rising was a 'riot' started by the 'Sinn Féiners'. Ireland had
changed the war situation by becoming one of the 'belligerents' and
by disproving England's claim to be fighting for the rights of small
nations. Ireland's position, the *Gaelic American* wrote confidently,
was good, although the betrayal to the British of the von Igel
papers by the Wilson government deprived the rebellion in the
west of the arms necessary to spread the Rising throughout the
island. The paper denied that the Rising was planned in Germany,
although German help had been requested and the Germans had
complied. The *Irish World* saw the Rising in much the same context. Picking up the issue over which the paper had broken with
Redmond, it stated that the Rising showed that 'Loyalty to the
British Government is not so universal in Ireland as Mr John
Redmond and his fellow recruiting-sergeants would have us believe.'
For the *Irish World* the Rising had redeemed Ireland's soul and
had asserted Ireland's nationality in the eyes of the world. On the
following day, Sunday 30 April, large meetings were held in several
cities on the east coast supporting the Rising. In New York the
United Irish Societies, an organisation dominated by the Clan na
Gael, held a large public meeting at the Cohan Theatre under the

chairmanship of Denis A. Spellissy and Judge John Jerome Rooney. The crowd consisted of Germans as well as Irish-Americans, and together they denounced Redmond and England while cheering Ireland, Casement and the Central European powers. A band played 'Deutschland über Alles' and 'The Watch on the Rhine', as well as several Irish and American songs and marches. The speakers emphasised the 'Americanism' of the meeting, the similarity of the Irish rebellion to the American Revolution, and demanded American support for Ireland; resolutions were passed pledging sympathy for the rebellion and praising the Irish efforts while also cursing England and thanking Germany. Similar meetings were held in the Boston area by the Gaelic School Society and by the Friends of Irish Freedom, and in Pittsfield Judge Cohalan and John F. Kelly led a separate rally. Dr Gertrude B. Kelly, the New York president of Cumann na mBan, told reporters of the New York *World* that there were 100,000 American volunteers ready to fight for Ireland, while Devoy's newspaper put the number at 500,000 and said that these would be led by German officers.[24]

When it was clear that the British had successfully crushed the rebellion, but before the impact of the executions had made itself felt, and most recorded reactions to the Rising were asserting that it was a most foolish and mischievous attempt, the *Gaelic American* published a vigorous defence insisting on the wisdom of the whole affair. Although Redmond had got the Home Rule Bill 'on the statute books', the *Gaelic American* argued that there was little chance of its actual implementation. Furthermore, the soldiers that Redmond recruited for the British army to fight in Europe were men lost to Ireland. On the other hand, the paper went on to say, the few men who fought in the rebellion, and the fewer who were killed, asserted the nationality of Ireland more effectively than anyone in recent years. The Rising, the *Gaelic American* proclaimed, 'notified the world that Ireland still demands National Independence and that her young men are ready to give their lives for it'. The lives lost were not squandered: 'It was a small price to pay for the advantage gained.' Although the Irish people had suffered a momentary reversal, there would be another rebellion on the verge of England's collapse, which through the alliance with the Germans would be complete and successful.[25]

The news of the continued executions evoked a more outraged burst of protest from the revolutionary Irish-Americans than they had made previously. On 6 May the *Gaelic American* called the executions simple 'murders' and promised that before the war was over Irishmen would court-martial British officers and execute them. A week later it bore down fully on the 'Military Massacre in

Dublin'. Meetings were held in various parts of the country on 8 May under the direction of Clan and FOIF leaders. Judges Cohalan and Rooney and Francis S. Clark presided at a meeting in Philadelphia where Cohalan explained the importance of the Rising, Rooney attacked Redmond and praised the executed leaders, and Joseph McGarrity appealed for funds ($5,000 were collected). In Boston the Clan sponsored pledges to support Ireland to the end of its struggle; Robert Sturn, president of the German Alliance, spoke at the meeting along with John Devoy and William Larkin. Former Congressman Joseph F. O'Connell told a meeting in Springfield that it was better for Irishmen to die by the thousand fighting for independence in Ireland than to be killed in Flanders fighting for England. In San Francisco Father Peter C. Yorke presided over a mass meeting addressed by John J. Cox, the state president of the AOH, and Major Lawrence O'Toole. Resolutions sent from the meeting to President Wilson condemned the executions as contrary to the laws of warfare and humanity and exhorted the United States government to protest then as it had during the Armenian massacres. That the executions would jolt many Irishmen into a new appreciation of the concept of nationalism was not lost on revolutionary American leaders. Joseph McGarrity, better known as a leader of the Clan na Gael than as a poet, wrote after the executions :

> See her evil hand once more
>   Hang on a tree such gallant fruit,
> See the sacred tree has bore
>   A seed that's found a lasting root.[26]

The dead men, McGarrity foresaw, would create a new spirit in Ireland.

Probably the largest and most important mass meeting condemning the executions was that held in Carnegie Hall in New York on the evening of Sunday 14 May. Several thousands stood outside while Judge Edward J. Gavegan, W. Bourke Cockran, Father Francis P. Duffy, Bainbridge Colby and several others addressed the 5,000 people in the audience. Perhaps the most significant speaker was Bainbridge Colby, who said that British rule in Ireland was based on ancient conquests and was every bit as bad as German rule in Belgium; Britain's treatment of the rebel leaders betrayed her position as the defender of small nationalities. Cockran said Ireland demanded and deserved 'her own sovereignty', and Father Duffy observed that 'England's friends were sickened' by the executions. Duffy further pointed out that had the Rising taken place in Warsaw, the British would have been the first to applaud it and the first to protest against the executions. Michael J. Ryan of the UIL telegraphed his support to the meeting and asked to join 'in denouncing the latest evidence of British barbarity'. Resolutions were passed condemning the executions, demanding that the present government in Ireland be changed, and damning the British government for allowing Sir Edward Carson and his followers to rebel without punishment. Although the meeting was dominated by revolutionaries—leaders of the FOIF, if not actually the Clan—it had attracted sincere constitutionalists and interested native Americans. Because of this the separatist tone of the meeting was a telling indication of an important shift in Irish-American thinking. As Shane Leslie wrote in 1917, after the executions the Irish 'remembered Robert Emmet and knew where they stood'.[27] Perhaps not since the 1880s were the two nationalist traditions in America so close together.

II. The Execution of Sir Roger Casement and the Problems of Politics

By the early summer of 1916 the powerful effect of the Rising and the executions had begun to diminish. American editors turned increasingly to American domestic affairs and to the international situation, and even the *Gaelic American* featured headlines dealing with American political news by 24 June. Nevertheless, the Irish question was kept before the American public until early autumn because of three simultaneous activities: the British government's new Home Rule proposals, the trial and execution of Sir Roger Casement, and the relief operations financed and partially administered by Irish-Americans. Great Britain had lost goodwill through the handling of the Irish rebellion; and in fact the whole list of failures, hesitations and mistakes of the past few years coloured the view of many observers of the Irish situation.

On 25 May 1916 Asquith announced that Lloyd George would attempt to settle the Irish crisis. Although American newspaper editors felt an urgency in resolving the situation, few had confidence in the strength of the Asquith government to deal boldly with the situation. The New York *World*, which on 17 May had suggested that Home Rule be implemented immediately, was on 26 May sceptical of the government's ability to act and of the good intentions of Carson and the Unionists. The *World* said that Carson was still master of the Irish crisis and that he had 'once before plotted rebellion and intimidated the Government by threats of forcible resistance'. *The Christian Science Monitor* thought that Lloyd George had great ability, but questioned whether he could get

Redmond, Carson and O'Brien to agree on any meaningful Home Rule programme. When the Home Rule proposals were made public in early June the New York *World* lamented that they represented one of those typical British compromises which 'satisfy no one and settle nothing'; in fact they meant 'a continuance for years to come of dangerous agitation'. Nonetheless, the *World* praised Redmond and Devlin for making statesmanlike sacrifices.[28] In early July the New York *Times* was moderately optimistic about what Lloyd George had accomplished, although it was concerned that earlier the 'Asquith Ministry bungled the home rule matter', and the paper was not so certain that it would not do so again. A few days later the New York *Times* said that any solution of the Home Rule question which excluded part of Ulster was not a complete settlement at all and would lead to further complications.

When it became clear in late July that there had been a fundamental misunderstanding about the position of Ulster in the proposals, and that the prospects for any kind of settlement had been jeopardised, the American press reacted bitterly. Lord Lansdowne was condemned for rocking the boat, the Irish Party for not agreeing to the 'permanent' exclusion of Ulster on a 'temporary' basis; as the New York *Times* argued in an extremely facile way, 'There can be no permanence in an avowedly temporary arrangement.' Indeed, the *Times* felt that the Home Rulers should take Carson's advice of accepting the exclusion of Ulster but winning it back with exemplary good government. The New York *World* condemned the Asquith government for being guilty of either 'trickery' or 'muddling', and concluded that the government had to choose between its friends or its enemies, the Irish Party or the Unionists. The *Literary Digest* also attacked the government for not acting quickly or firmly: 'The extraordinary vacillation of the British Government in dealing with the Irish question is one of the most curious political puzzles of modern times.' Of the Irish-Americans, perhaps diverted by the Casement trial and the relief fund activities, the *Gaelic American* expressed the most consistent opinion on the Lloyd George proposals; predictably, it attacked Redmond as a 'traitor' to Ireland and the proposals as a worthless 'emergency war measure'. When the efforts failed the *Gaelic American* said the failure was evidence of Redmond's incompetence; only the Rising would save Ireland.[29]

While the Home Rule proposals were being discussed attention in the United States was focused much more intensely on the fate of Sir Roger Casement and the prisoners arrested in the wake of the Rising. Casement had received disproportionate newspaper attention in the early days of the Rising, perhaps as much because more was known about him in America, through his humanitarian efforts in Africa and South America, than because he was regarded as the leader of the rebellion. The irony of Casement's position was continually mentioned by the press, which saw little actual difference between the acts of Carson and his followers before August 1914 and Casement's after 1914. The American newspapers also agreed that he was insane. They felt that Casement should not be executed, in spite of the results of his trial. The *Christian Science Monitor*, which was still one of the strongest critics of the Rising, argued that a live fool was better for the British government than a dead hero. The New York *Times* and the New York *Evening Mail* seemed to agree that his execution would stimulate unrest and needlessly make him a martyr.[30] Native Americans differed privately on what should be done about Casement. A. Lawrence Lowell thought that Casement's excellent earlier service to Britain and to humanity ought not be forgotten in spite of the seriousness of the charges against him. Nonetheless, Lowell feared that the Irish-Americans would think that if he were spared, it would be 'because he is a Protestant'. Willard Straight hoped that the Casement trial would be handled in such a way as to not 'open up sores which are now healing', although he did not suggest mercy. On the other hand, Theodore Roosevelt, who thought the Dublin leaders should have been spared, felt that Casement could not be excused from the penalties of his treason. The notorious anti-Irish New Haven schoolmaster George L. Fox also thought Casement should be executed and attacked him violently in a pamphlet.[31]

President Wilson became the object of an intense campaign on the part of both Irish-Americans and native Americans to enlist the support of the United States government in an appeal for clemency for Casement and the remaining prisoners arrested in the wake of the Rising. A large number of appeals and petitions were sent to Wilson and to members of Congress asking that the government do something. One such group was the Knights of St Patrick from San Francisco, who requested Wilson to use his good offices to influence the British government to exercise clemency towards the Irish prisoners. They asserted that every people had the 'divine right of revolution' and that Americans of an earlier generation had done what the Irish had done during the Rising and that they ought to be regarded in similar terms. They asked that secret trials and executions be stopped and civil law re-established, and they referred to earlier instances when the American government had sent appeals on behalf of Lafayette, Kossuth, Maximilian and others. They also sent a copy of the letter to their senator, James D. Phelan, who wrote to Wilson endorsing their appeal and had a copy of their letter read into the *Congressional Record*. Wilson's secretary, Joseph P. Tumulty, asked Frank L. Polk what the President could do, and he was informed that, although the State Department had protected American citizens who were involved, as to the fate of Irish subjects the American government 'would not be in a position to make any protest'. Tumulty, undiscouraged, wrote back to Polk that he would like to discuss the letter with him as soon as possible. Conscious of the political effect of such letters on Irish-American voters, Tumulty replied: 'There is so much dynamite in it [the appeal on behalf of the prisoners] that we ought to proceed with care.'[32] After an interval of about a month Wilson sent a reply to the Knights of St Patrick in regard to Irish prisoners in which he said: 'I have done everything, so far as representations go, to provide for their humane and just treatment.' Wilson also wrote: 'My natural sympathies are with men struggling for freedom, and concerning whose sincerity as patriots, seeking solely the welfare of their country, can not be questioned.' It cannot be known how specifically Wilson was referring to Irishmen struggling for freedom or men in general, nor can it be known the extent to which this statement, with its strong pro-Irish implications, was motivated by purely political reasons; certainly it manifests as much warmth for the Irish cause as his statements in his early career. To deal with more pressing appeals from powerful sources—such as the telegram from Congressmen London of New York, Carey of Wisconsin, Ligoe and Dyer of Missouri, Gallivan of Massachusetts, Roddenberg of Illinois and Keating of Colorado—Tumulty drafted a noncommittal form letter which said that Wilson would 'seek the earliest opportunity to discuss this matter with the Secretary of State' and that he would give the matter 'the consideration its great importance merits'.[33]

The support of President Wilson and the government was also sought by Michael Francis Doyle, who, although an American, was to assist at Casement's trial in London. Doyle, a Philadelphia lawyer with a reputation in labour law and Democratic Party politics, cabled to Tumulty on 28 April asking for an interview with him in order to discuss the request of Mrs Agnes Newman, Casement's widowed sister living in the United States, that he assist in Casement's defence. In a letter written on the following day Doyle told Tumulty that he wanted Wilson to understand what he hoped to do at the trial and that he did not want to embarrass the administration. Tumulty sought the advice of the State Department and was cautioned by L. H. Woolsey, Assistant Solicitor of the department, that the United States would have no authority to use its offices on behalf of a British subject charged by his own government. Simultaneously Mrs Newman wrote to President Wilson asking his help in view of Casement's work in Africa and South America. Wilson, however, refused to be drawn out by either Mrs Newman or Doyle. 'We have no choice in a matter of this sort,' he told Tumulty. 'It is absolutely necessary to say that I could take no action of any kind regarding it.' However, while Wilson himself was unwilling to speak for Casement either publicly or privately, the State Department did agree to secure the nominal co-operation of Ambassador Page in London. Frank L. Polk wrote to Doyle: 'I regret that we cannot write to the British Foreign Office,' and he assured him: 'Mr Page undoubtedly will notify the authorities of your relation to the case.'[34] This was not the kind of government assistance Doyle wanted.

Doyle proceeded on Casement's defence as if he had the full endorsement of the administration, and he told British authorities of his 'acquaintance with President Wilson and other circumstances tending to give him influence in the United States'. In fact Doyle went so far as to 'imply that if he were given full facilities here he might exercise an influence in the United States favourable to the action of the British Government'. Doyle was certainly bluffing about his intimacy with the Wilson government, but his posture was credible enough to move Grey to request Sir Herbert Samuel, the Home Secretary, to allow Doyle to join George Gavan Duffy in preparing the brief for Casement's defence. Furthermore, Doyle was recognisably in a position to influence public opinion if he were later to spread stories that Casement 'had not been allowed full facilities for preparing his defence'. Grey concluded that were any such statements made in the United States, 'the effect will be very undesirable'. Doyle's contribution to the case was probably minimal, inasmuch as Serjeant A. M. Sullivan's brief depended on points of English law. However, he claimed to have more contact with Casement than either Duffy or Sullivan (it was Doyle who told Casement of circulation of passages of a diary, allegedly written by him, in order to damp public support). Later it was Doyle's idea to go to Germany to obtain new evidence to prove Casement's innocence.[35]

When Casement was found guilty and sentenced on 29 June efforts were renewed in the United States to wring some support of favourable comment from Wilson. On 30 June a Boston lawyer, Josiah Quincy, asked Tumulty to talk with Franz Hugo Krebs, a journalist, who since the outbreak of war had paid several visits to Germany, where he had met Casement. Tumulty agreed to see Krebs on 3 July and not only introduced him to Frank L. Polk but also arranged for him to talk with President Wilson as well. Krebs

later recorded in a memorandum that all three were very well informed about Casement and that Wilson was particularly interested
to learn about Casement's mental condition when Krebs had last
seen him in February 1916. Krebs wrote that while Wilson had
given him 'a most sympathetic hearing', he recorded no opinion
about Casement. Krebs also surmised that although the United
States government would make no statements in the matter, 'indirectly and unofficially' the British were aware of the interest of
the administration. In fact shortly after the sentencing in London
the Department of State cabled a personal message from Mrs
Newman to Casement. Page, however, was unwilling to allow any
message to Casement to pass through American diplomatic channels. In a letter circulated among the White House and State Department staffs Page stiffly recorded: 'Not only does Casement, a
British subject, stand convicted of treason but I am privately informed that much information about him of an unspeakably filthy
character was withheld from publicity.' He suggested that the cable
be delivered to Doyle, who could see that it reached Casement
without its passing through government hands. 'If all the facts about
Casement ever become public,' Page warned finally, 'it will be well
that our Government had nothing to do with him or his case even
indirectly.'[36]

Doyle was quick to write to Tumulty describing the unfairness of
the British government in not allowing any evidence from Germany
and in circulating stories which defamed Casement's character.
Doyle argued, quite correctly, that Casement had been on trial for
treason and nothing else. Both Redmond and Lord Northcliffe,
Doyle said, had told him that a word to the British government from
Wilson would save Casement. When shown this and later requests
from Doyle, however, Wilson replied to Tumulty: 'It would be in-
excusable for me to touch this. It would involve serious international embarrassment.' Wilson thus refused to be drawn into the
Casement affair. As Alan J. Ward has pointed out, because Casement was a British subject properly tried in the courts and because
Wilson had refused to intervene in similar circumstances in Central
Europe, Wilson had solid reasons for refusing to act, despite the
mitigating circumstances.[37]

Congress, on the other hand, was much more willing to debate
the merits of the Rising, Casement and the prisoners. Indeed, by
the conclusion of Casement's trial in late June several Irish resolutions had been introduced in both houses and the Irish crisis had
been repeatedly discussed. These gestures became considerably
more meaningful on 20 June when Senator James E. Martine of
New Jersey introduced a resolution which proposed that President

Wilson ask the British government for 'a stay of execution of said sentence [passed on Casement], in order that new facts may be introduced'. The resolution was sent to the Senate Foreign Relations Committee for consideration, over the objections of Senator Martine, who demanded that it be adopted immediately because he feared that otherwise it would 'sleep the sleep of the righteous and just never come out of committee'. Martine was assured that the committee would deal promptly with the resolution. However, after being told by the chairman two weeks later that the committee had decided not to report the resolution at all, Martine moved that the committee be discharged of his resolution. He argued, on the very day that Casement's appeal was being heard in London, that British public opinion had discouraged the American government from executing Jefferson Davis after the American Civil War and that in this instance, through the 'kindly intercession' of the President, America could similarly speak for humanity in the Casement matter.[38]

At the request of the committee chairman, Senator William J. Stone, Martine agreed to postpone the vote on the resolution until the following day, but when there was no further response he restated his motion in the Senate on 22 July. Again Senator Stone said that the committee voted not to report the resolution, noting that the committee had agreed that the language of the appeal 'would be offensive to the Government of Great Britain' and that it 'would not tend to promote the end it sought to be accomplished'. The Department of State had already transmitted an appeal from Mrs Newman to the British government and had intervened to save the lives of American subjects involved in the Rising; the department had in addition been informed 'that official representations to the British Government touching on this case would not be received in a kindly spirit'. Senators Nelson, Borah and Williams all objected to Martine's resolution, as did Senator James D. Phelan, who introduced a more mildly worded resolution which asked for 'clemency in the treatment of Irish political prisoners'. This prompted Martine to introduce also a less provocative resolution. Debate erupted in the Senate again on 25 July, when Senator Martine argued that it was important to include Casement's name in the resolution inasmuch as he was the only Irish prisoner in any immediate danger. The Foreign Relations Committee considered the resolutions the following day, but again they felt it 'inexpedient' to recommend the adoption of any of them.[39]

The issue was not closed, however. On Saturday 29 July, after the Casement resolutions had been brought into discussion on the Senate floor by Chairman Stone, Senator Key Pittman said that a minority of the committee felt that once the resolutions had been introduced some version should be adopted. Pittman therefore proposed a minority report in the form of a resolution:

> That the Senate expresses the hope that the British Government may exercise clemency in the treatment of Irish political prisoners, and that the President be requested to transmit this resolution to that Government.

Martine scoffed at the cautious phrasing of the resolution and said that the United States Senate was quivering before the prospect of a growl from the British lion. Senator Pomerene replied that he hoped Casement would be spared, but he added pointedly:

> While seeking to secure clemency, Senators on the floor insist all the while upon twisting the lion's tail. How much do we expect to gain by this? 'Not everyone who cries unto me, Lord, Lord, shall enter the kingdom of heaven,' and it is not everyone who professes friendship for Sir Roger Casement who is doing him a real act of kindness.

This was much the same view as that of Senator Henry Cabot Lodge, a leading member of the committee who had voted against the resolutions. He felt that such resolutions would not accomplish their objective and 'would do harm to the very purpose we all had at heart'. Lodge said he had been working on Casement's behalf through private channels, as indeed he had. Finally, the Senate voted to adopt the resolution proposed by Senator Pittman by a margin of 49 to 19 (with 30 abstaining from voting).[40]

The results of the Senate appeal were unspectacular and indeed somewhat anticlimactic. The official copy of the resolution was sent from the White House to the Department of State at 11 a.m. on 2 August and was cabled to the London embassy by 1 p.m. Because of the time difference between London and Washington the cable was not ready for delivery until the morning of 3 August, the day Casement was to be executed. In the absence of Page, the Chargé d'Affaires, Irwin B. Laughlin, took the resolution to the Foreign Office and, in as discreet a manner as possible, presented a copy to Sir Edward Grey. Unfortunately, however, this was done either at the same time or slightly after Casement was to be hanged, rendering the appeal, technically at least, futile.[41] This delay would later create considerable animosity in American domestic politics during the 1916 election, although it in no way diminished the significance of the Senate's action. Thanks to Spring Rice and the newspapers, the British government was fully informed about the resolution and had already taken it into consideration in reaching its decision about Casement—in fact it was Grey who actually raised the issue in his conversation with Laughlin. The British government, however, made no direct reply to either the State Department or the Senate, although Grey did write unofficially with cabinet approval to E. M. House on 28 August saying: 'We are not favourably impressed by the action of the Senate in having passed a resolution about the Irish prisoners, though they have taken no notice of outrages in Belgium and massacres of Armenians.'[42] This was certainly the impression the British gave to the American public, but fortunately for Anglo-American relations these views were not publicly expressed.

Private efforts were also made directly to the British government to try to save Casement's life. In early May several people, including Cardinal Gibbons, expressed to Spring Rice the hope that Casement would be spared. As the date of the execution approached more concerted efforts were made. John Quinn, working with James Byrne, William D. Guthrie and former United States Attorney-General George D. Wickersham, drafted a cable to Sir Edward Grey asking that the British government exercise 'clemency' in dealing with Casement. The cable was signed and sent to Grey by twenty-five distinguished Americans including ten lawyers, four editors, a former cabinet member, a New York State Supreme Court judge, a former consular officer in England, a Columbia University professor, a leading American artist and a corporation executive. Spring Rice was fully informed and indeed sent all the background information to Grey, pointing out that the signatories were 'important men all pro-Ally'. In addition, several groups of American Negroes asked that Casement's services to humanity be taken into consideration. Perhaps more important was the private appeal from Senator Henry Cabot Lodge who, noting that the Casement resolution was before the Senate, told Grey that it would be a mistake to execute Casement, that England's enemies hoped he would be executed while her friends hoped he would be spared. Finally, on the eve of the execution, Spring Rice cabled to Grey: 'Suggest that as a personal favour to President Casement may be reprieved with understanding that we may count on him on behalf of our prisoners.' Such a reprieve, Spring Rice advised, would assist Wilson in dealing with his own party and put him in debt to the British. But these appeals, like that of the Senate, were without effect. On 2 August the cabinet made its final decision that Casement must be hanged despite 'the urgent appeals for mercy from authoritative & friendly quarters in the United States'. Page had already been given that impression from Asquith himself the previous day, and Spring Rice told Polk of the decision on the evening of 2 August.[43]

Casement's execution created a profound impression in the United States. Newspapers which had been critical of him earlier seemed to moderate their indictments. The Washington *Post* thought the execution was a 'colossal blunder', and the New York *World* linked the execution to the failure of the Home Rule proposals and also called it a 'blunder'. The Chicago *Tribune*, condemning the 'Tory English mind' that attempted to rule in Ireland, said that British policy was responsible for Casement's action: 'England made him; England unmade him.' The *Gaelic American*, of course, deplored the execution, but pointed out its irony, inasmuch as from the information that it had Casement had come to Ireland to stop the Rising.[44] Perhaps the most outraged, and the most effective, comment came from John Quinn in an essay for the magazine section of the New York *Times* of Sunday 13 August. Quinn conceded Casement's probable legal guilt, but he stressed, as several other newspapers had attempted to do, the extenuating circumstances and ironies of Casement's situation—Casement's humanitarian achievements, British generosity in dealing with South African rebels, Unionist treason and flirtations with Germany, the failure of the government to implement Home Rule fairly won in parliament, and the reward for Ulster treason with cabinet posts.

> Fair-minded people [Quinn wrote] generally feel that the motives which actuated Casement were the thing by which he should be judged. However technically his offense may be phrased, his actual offense, if any, was that he put the cause of Ireland before that of England or even the Allies.

Quinn's article was reprinted in the Philadelphia *Ledger* and the Boston *Herald* and made a forceful impact on such diverse readers as the New York lawyer James Byrne and the conservative Alabama senator Oscar W. Underwood.[45]

One immediate result of the Rising and the executions was a dedicated commitment on the part of Irish-Americans to extend relief assistance to the Irish people. As early as 12 May the famous Irish singer John McCormack was writing to the leaders of New York public life, such as Mayor John Purroy Mitchel, soliciting their assistance and patronage in a benefit concert he had arranged to give for the cause of Irish relief. The financier and art collector Otto H. Kahn had donated the use of the Century Theatre; Cardinal Farley of New York and the Lord Mayor of Dublin had agreed to act as patrons. 'Apart from whatever may be our individual opinions regarding the recent rebellion in Dublin,' McCormack told his potential contributors, 'the heart of every man with a drop of Irish blood in his veins, goes out in deep sympathy

to the families and relatives of those who lost their lives.' Further-
more, he said, the Rising had caused great suffering through the
loss of income and the destruction of property. The concert, held
23 May, was a success (between $8,000 and $9,000 was raised and
cabled to Ireland) and drew the attendance of Miss Margaret
Wilson, the President's daughter, and his private adviser E. M.
House. Other efforts were also under way. On 20 May the Irish
Relief Fund Committee was established in New York with
Cardinals Farley, Gibbon and O'Connell and Archbishop Walsh of
Dublin as honorary officers, Dr Thomas Addis Emmet president,
George G. Gillespie chairman, Thomas Hughes Kelly treasurer,
and John D. Moore secretary. An appeal for funds was announced
because, the announcement went on, the economic life of the
country had been paralysed by the fighting and by the military rule
that followed. While certainly a gross exaggeration of the condition
of Ireland, if not parts of Dublin, this appeal had its effect: a large
fund-raising concert was held on 27 May in Carnegie Hall, Victor
Herbert donated the services of his band, several people sang,
Pádraic Colum read some poems, and various German-Americans
contributed.[46]

Supported by the Irish-American newspapers the Irish Relief
Fund Committee was able to direct its appeals to a large audience
and to attach its cause to other activities. By the end of June a
national organisation was assembled to collect money for Irish relief
throughout the United States. Peter Golden, a poet and Gaelic
singer well known in Irish-American circles, was recruited to travel
throughout the country making clear to people the 'pressing and
urgent need for assistance' which had been created by the Rising.
Simultaneously formal appeals for contributions, referring to the
'unspeakable want and distress' that existed in Ireland, were published by the committee in the Irish-American press. By mid-July
$100,000 had been raised by the committee. Ironically, at approxi-
mately the same time Robert J. Waddell of the United Irish League
wrote to Redmond to ask if there was any need for relief money in
Ireland. The UIL, he said, had refrained from taking any initiative
in the matter on the assumption that they would have been instructed by the party had Redmond so desired. Regardless of the
situation in Ireland, the call for relief funds made a powerful impression on moderate nationalists in the United States, which the
UIL might possibly have been able to exploit. On 8 July John A.
Murphy of Buffalo and John Gill of New York sailed for Ireland,
representing the committee, with a substantial amount of money
with which to begin relief operations. Once established they were
able to effect an amalgamation of the Irish National Aid Associ-

ation and the Irish Volunteer Dependants' Fund, which created conditions that allowed for the rational distribution of relief funds.[47]

Thomas Hughes Kelly, treasurer of the committee and a New York banker, and Joseph Smith, a Massachusetts journalist and labour leader, were to have followed Murphy and Gill to Ireland a week later with a second instalment of money. However, they were stopped in Liverpool by British authorities and denied permission to proceed to Dublin. Before any of the committee had left the United States they had understood from the British Ambassador that there would be no objection to their travelling to Ireland; indeed, Spring Rice had advised Grey: 'I think we might adopt a benevolent attitude towards the distribution of funds for the sufferers by the revolt,' in the hope that it would appease moderate Irish-Americans. Furthermore, they were armed with a letter of introduction from Secretary of State Lansing to Ambassador Page in London. This letter was immediately put to use in the hope that it would open some doors. On 26 July Frank L. Polk, then Acting Secretary of State, instructed Page to request the British government to reconsider its decision to prevent Kelly and Smith from going to Ireland. They were 'very prominent in Catholic circles', Polk cabled, and not politicians. Spring Rice was writing to his government, and Polk hoped Page would also 'do everything possible to assist these persons'. Page was not inclined to meddle in any Irish affairs. He reported that the British had no objection to Kelly personally, although they disliked the idea of foreigners distributing money in unsettled areas of Ireland, but they regarded Smith as a Sinn Féin 'agitator' and 'an agent of the German Government'. Tumulty assured several Irish-American leaders that the President himself had instructed Polk to take up the matter with both Page and Spring Rice and that the government had done all it could. While this effort was considered insufficient by John D. Moore, the national secretary of the FOIF, who demanded that the State Department get the matter settled without further delay, Cardinal Farley two days later wrote a gracious letter to Wilson thanking him for his efforts and assuring him that Kelly and his friends 'will be pleased to learn how deeply you have interested yourself in his case'.[48]

Americans who had contributed to the fund which Kelly and Smith were to distribute were outraged at the capriciousness of British action. The *Gaelic American* claimed, perhaps correctly, that this 'personal insult' had won the sympathy of many Irish-Americans who had previously been indifferent to the revolutionary cause, and that furthermore British policy stimulated financial contributions. When Murphy and Gill returned to the United States in

late August they further promoted anti-British feeling by their reports of conditions in Ireland and the growth of nationalist feelings. Indeed, Murphy reported that he had never seen 'so much
misery and destitution' and that both the government and Unionist
businessmen had conspired to create such dire social and economic
conditions in Ireland as to 'force recruiting [of Irishmen into the
British army] by the starvation process'. By early 1917 the Foreign
Office was still attempting to deal with the appeals of the Irish Relief Fund.[49] The British were thus embarrassed by the contradictions of a policy which on the one hand admitted suffering of such
dimensions as to need large-scale relief operations (in the minds
of Irish-Americans as great as those in Belgium or Armenia) and
on the other hand arbitrarily refused to permit certain members of
the relief committee to carry out their functions.

III. Rumours of War

From the autumn of 1916 until America's entry into the First World
War in the spring of 1917 American interest in Ireland expressed
itself principally through the presidential election campaign of 1916
and in the reception provided for Irish exiles who made their way
to the United States. To a lesser extent the continued appeals for
the Irish Relief Fund and Redmond's attempt to invite the intervention of President Wilson in a settlement of the Irish question also
kept nationalist concerns before the public. By all rights the election
should not have been clouded by issues concerning Ireland at all.
As has been shown earlier, the Democratic Party had traditionally
been the political home for the Irish in America, and Wilson should
normally have commanded their loyalty without much question in
his efforts to secure a second term of office. There were, however,
several disconcerting facts which tended to challenge these normal
assumptions. Since the outbreak of the war there had been a growing feeling, at least among the Irish-American leaders, that Wilson's
neutrality policies were definitely pro-British. Wilson's Mexican
policy, at its low point during the second half of 1916, annoyed
Catholics generally. During the summer Wilson had spoken out
against the increasing influence of 'hyphenate' groups, such as
Irish-Americans or German-Americans; and furthermore, many
Irish-Americans resented Wilson's refusal to make a public declaration about the Rising, the executions or Casement's hanging
when it was felt that any statement by him would be of some force
in determining British policy. On the other hand, the Wilson administration had not been indifferent to the Irish situation. There
had been White House intervention concerning prisoners in Ireland

of American nationality; the State Department cables had been used by Casement's American lawyer and by his sister; moreover, Wilson had used his influence to persuade the British government to allow Kelly and Smith to carry out their relief operations. William M. Leary, Jr, has also suggested that Wilson had appealed to the Irish-American labourers with his reform legislation and that the Republican candidate, Charles Evans Hughes, had little to offer the Irish-Americans on either the Irish question or the war question.[50] Indeed, Hughes was probably hindered by the return to the Republican Party of Theodore Roosevelt, who, although in favour of Home Rule, campaigned vigorously for American intervention in the war on the side of the Allies, thus alienating the Irish and several other ethnic groups.

By the end of the Casement affair Wilson, especially because he had made no direct appeal himself, was vulnerable to the criticism that he had deliberately delayed the sending of the Senate resolution until it was too late to save Casement. The fact that the resolution had not reached the Foreign Office until it was too late was revealed on 3 August when Lord Robert Cecil, in explaining why the government had carried out the execution, mentioned that no appeal had been received by the British government from the State Department. This information, subsequently published in American papers, brought an immediate protest from such people as Senator Phelan, who angrily told Tumulty that he had vigorously supported the resolution 'for the purpose of doing some good'. Congressman Peter F. Tague of Boston introduced a resolution in the House of Representatives calling for a committee to 'investigate the delay in delivery of certain cablegrams'—namely the Casement resolution. The chairman of the executive committee of the FOIF, James K. McGuire, also wrote to the White House condemning the delay. Tumulty referred these inquiries to Polk at the State Department for an explanation. Polk replied that 'there was no delay in this Department' and suggested that there was no effective statement that he could make about the matter.[51]

The matter was not allowed to drop, however, because of the growing tensions about the election. In late August Lansing received inquiries from Senator Henry F. Ashurst, and Tumulty a letter from Michael Francis Doyle, asking what reply the British government had made to the Senate appeal. Lansing repeated Polk's observations that the State Department had expedited matters and that the British had sent no reply. This in no way solved the delicate political situation of the moment, so Tumulty asked for an explanation of the Casement resolution difficulty 'which in diplomatic language would set forth our position with regard to this case' and which would also emphasise what the administration had done for the Irish. Lansing refused to comment until Polk returned from his vacation. In the meantime Doyle again appealed to Tumulty to provide him with information which would exonerate the Wilson administration, warning that the Republican Party's national committee was attempting to persuade Casement's sister, Mrs Newman, to state publicly that earlier delivery of the resolution would have saved her brother. To these appeals the Secretary of State replied that Tumulty already had all the facts in the case and that he himself could not make an 'incorrect statement' about it. When Polk returned to Washington he drafted a letter for Tumulty which attempted to save the situation by drawing attention to his conversations with Spring Rice before the execution which showed that the British government had been fully informed about the Senate appeal through its representative and that they had nevertheless made the decision to hang Casement regardless. After some discussion between Polk and Tumulty a press release to this effect was drafted in such a way as to avoid too precise an account of the time schedule of the Casement resolution. A suitable letter was sent to Doyle to help support the Democratic Party in the face of its Irish-American opponents and was later released to the press. Doyle himself had the letter sent to both *Ireland* and the *Irish World*, and other newspapers published it as well.[52]

While the Casement resolution crisis was being met the administration was beset by other Irish-American attacks as well. The *Irish World* and the *Gaelic American* became increasingly hostile to Wilson during the election campaign, and such Clan na Gael leaders as Devoy and Cohalan were outspoken in their criticism of the President. The Republican presidential candidate, Hughes, had encouraged the impression that he was sympathetic to the Irish and German causes in order to win the 'hyphenate' vote away from the Democratic Party. Wilson met this challenge by his response to a telegram on 29 September from Jeremiah A. O'Leary, a well-known New York Irish-American and anglophobe (he was president of the American Truth Society and editor of the anti-British periodical *Bull*). O'Leary wrote to Wilson: 'Your foreign policies, your failure to secure compliance with all American rights, your leniency with the British Empire, your approval of war loans, the ammunition traffic, are issues in this campaign.' According to O'Leary, the victory of Congressman William S. Bennet of New York and Senator James E. Martine of New Jersey, both of whom had opposed Wilson's policies in the primary elections, was a repudiation of the administration by the Irish-American voters. 'When, sir,' O'Leary concluded, 'will you respond to these evidences of popular disapproval of your policies by action?' Wilson responded immediately and vigorously by reading his reply to O'Leary in a press conference that same day:

> Your telegram received. I would feel deeply mortified to have you or anybody like you vote for me. Since you have access to many disloyal Americans and I have not, I will ask you to convey this message to them.[53]

As O'Leary later pointed out, this reply was a personal attack which avoided the issues, but it said by implication what a great many Americans were delighted to hear. In fact the telegram was felt by Tumulty and House to be the turning-point in the election campaign. Many of the leading eastern newspapers and even several Republican papers strongly supported Wilson's repudiation of any election support from what were understood to be pro-German groups in the United States. Even the liberal journals, which might have been expected to demand a fuller argument from Wilson, commended the President's rejection of O'Leary and other 'disloyal Americans'.[54]

The election of 1916 was an extremely complex one. Progressivism and prosperity were two issues which determined the minds of many voters, but undeniably the single most important question before the public was peace. 'He kept us out of war' became the not altogether deserved rallying cry of the Wilsonians, and it referred not only to the European war but also to the full-scale intervention in Mexico as well. Despite Wilson's most vociferous critics, who accused him of being shamelessly pro-British, it became clear throughout the campaign that a Republican administration would be even more inclined towards intervention than the Democrats. The result of the election, therefore, was a solid victory for Wilson. However, of the nine states with large Irish-American populations, only two—California and Ohio—went for Wilson. The *Gaelic American* claimed, and apparently Wilson believed, that the Irish-American vote in New York, Massachusetts, Pennsylvania, Illinois, New Jersey and Connecticut had been against him. William M. Leary, Jr, has argued convincingly that, as far as can be calculated, the Irish in America did tend to vote for Wilson and the Democratic Party rather than for Hughes; indeed, despite his repudiation of 'disloyal Americans', Wilson probably won the German-American vote and the 'hyphenate' vote generally.[55] The several states listed above were traditionally won by the Republicans rather than the Democrats, but Wilson may not have accepted that fact.

Meanwhile by mid-October the Irish-Americans in New York

opened an 'Irish Bazaar' to raise more money for relief operations. The bazaar was significant because it represented the continued effort on the part of revolutionary nationalists to keep the emotions of Irish-Americans at the high pitch of the previous summer and because it involved the active participation in Irish-American life of the first of the new exiles to arrive in the United States in the wake of the Rising. The bazaar ran for three weeks and was considered to be a great success. It was opened by Nora Connolly, the daughter of James Connolly, who raised the republican flag, and it featured Irish art works (some paintings by Constance Markievicz and a statue of Emmet by Jerome Connor) and handicrafts; Mrs Agnes Newman, Casement's sister, ran a booth which drew large crowds of people. Significantly, one of the principal exhibits was one of the submarines invented by the Irish-American John P. Holland, which must have pleased the Germans. German-Americans participated actively to promote goodwill and cement their alliance with the Irish by operating booths and making conspicuous purchases. In Chicago a flag-day was used, among other activities, to raise funds for Irish relief. How much money was collected by all these measures is not certain, but by August at least the *Gaelic American* reported that some $140,000 had been sent to Ireland. Renewed efforts were made on the part of the Department of State and the White House to persuade the British government to allow selected Irish-Americans to travel to Ireland to distribute these funds, but the British, having burned their fingers with both Murphy and Gill as well as Kelly and Smith, refused to permit any Americans, no matter how highly recommended, to carry out such a mission.[56]

The appearance of Nora Connolly at the bazaar, although contrary to the understanding worked out by Sir Horace Plunkett with the military in Dublin permitting Connolly's family to go to America, marked the first of a number of refugees from Ireland. Outstanding among these people were Nora Connolly herself, Margaret Skinnider, Mrs Hannah Sheehy-Skeffington, Liam Mellows, Captain Robert Monteith and, some time later, Dr Patrick McCartan and Diarmuid Lynch; indeed, according to Captain Monteith, in New York they formed the 'Easter Week Exiles' Association'. Once in America many of these refugees joined forces with the Clan na Gael and the Friends of Irish Freedom, and they were warmly received by such Irish expatriates as Pádraic and Mary Colum, Peter Golden, James Larkin and Cornelius Lehane. Almost all of them worked in some way to forward the revolutionary Irish nationalist cause: Monteith and Mellows went on speaking tours (Mellows in fact accompanied the old saboteur Luke

D

Dillon in his travels up and down the east coast as an 'organiser' for the Clan); Margaret Skinnider and Nora Connolly lectured and published books (*Doing my bit for Ireland* in June 1917, and *The unbroken tradition* in 1918 respectively); Lynch became the national secretary of the FOIF; and Dr McCartan, representing the Supreme Council of the IRB, attempted to serve as 'Envoy of the Provisional Government of Ireland' to the United States throughout 1917 and 1918. The Colums had already contributed substantially to a book of short portraits of the leaders of the Rising (*The Irish rebellion of 1916 and its martyrs*), as well as their articles for the American press, and they would join Peter Golden in the autumn of 1917 in creating the Irish Progressive League (Golden was then prominent in the Irish Relief Fund organisation). Larkin and Lehane were working among the Irish-American labourers.[57]

Perhaps the most effective propagandist of these exiles was Mrs Sheehy-Skeffington. Americans had learned about the murder of her husband through the newspaper reports of the summer, but her trip to the United States in December brought the whole matter up once again. Her illegal arrival with her small son was an event reported by the major American dailies and the Irish-American newspapers. She told the New York *Times* that she had come to inform the American people about the methods of British rule in Ireland. This she proceeded to do in a long speaking tour of the United States wherein she delivered a lecture entitled 'British militarism as I have known it'. The fact that she had been forbidden to leave the British Isles and had escaped with her seven-year-old son, in addition to the actual story of her husband's demise, made her an appealing figure who could win sympathy and support in quarters where other more typical Irish refugees could not. Mrs Sheehy-Skeffington held a successful meeting in Carnegie Hall in New York on 6 January 1917; her lecture was presided over by Bainbridge Colby and her speech enthusiastically received. She also met E. M. House and Theodore Roosevelt and told them of conditions in Dublin during the Rising and of her own experiences. Roosevelt, true to his limitless interests and sense of fair play, asked Mrs Sheehy-Skeffington to write up what she had told him, after which he himself wrote to Sir Francis Fletcher Vane, a participant in the Sheehy-Skeffington affair, to ask if what he had been told was true.[58] During the year and a half that Mrs Sheehy-Skeffington was in the United States she travelled across the country speaking at universities, civic groups, women's societies, Irish-American, pacifist and suffragette meetings. She was especially effective because she went beyond merely Irish groups. Once America entered the war her relationships with socialists, pacifists, feminists and Irish revolutionaries—in short those Americans who opposed the war—partially compromised her position and appeal.

Throughout the winter and spring of 1917, while the United States was moving closer to war with Germany, the Irish question was reaching a new crisis at Westminster. In the House of Commons on 9 March 1917 T. P. O'Connor moved that Home Rule be extended to Ireland immediately, and after a bitter debate, when it was clear that Home Rule for the whole island was not to be carried, Redmond and many of the Irish Nationalists stalked out of the House. On the following day they issued a manifesto declaring their position and appealing to the colonial premiers and also to President Wilson to intervene and resolve the Irish question fairly. Wilson, refusing to be drawn into this controversy, said nothing, but the general reception of these remarks in America was not favourable. The New York *Times* thought that the Irish members had a just grievance, but that this outburst was futile and could only create difficulties for the Lloyd George government. The *Christian Science Monitor*, while first saying coldly that the Southern Irish could have Home Rule any time they wanted it if they did not insist on coercing Ulster, later suggested that the government might have to make some accommodations. The Springfield *Republican* thought that Redmond's appeal was a mistake, 'managed and timed as if Herr Zimmermann had arranged it'. The St Louis *Republic* was concerned that the Irish members might break up the government; and contrary to its editorial procedure the *Literary Digest* observed that none of Ireland's many appeals to America had ever come at 'so ominous a moment'. For understandably different reasons the leading Irish-American papers also scorned Redmond's appeal. The *Irish World* said that Redmond's position had been steadily declining since his first recruiting speech and that his current treatment by Lloyd George was evidence of British regard for him. This was just another public gesture, the *Gaelic American* declared; Redmond did not have Ireland's interests in mind at all. *Ireland*, the Home Rule weekly, supported Redmond's appeal, however, suggesting that with Britain looking for an ally in the United States a body of organised Irish-Americans might be in a position to dictate terms to England that would be better than those Redmond could himself obtain from Lloyd George. According to *Ireland*, conditions had never been so good for agreement between Irishmen.[59]

Shane Leslie, one of the editors of *Ireland*, wrote to Redmond on 9 March suggesting that the appeal should find many supporters in the United States. He was planning to enlist the support of the American cardinals, but he also feared that it would be difficult to exert much pressure on the United States government because there was no strong moderate organisation (the United Irish League being almost moribund) to capitalise on such a situation. A few weeks later he wrote again that the lack of a reliable organisation prevented the Irish-Americans from doing anything genuinely effective in Washington, but that the situation was improving for the moderates. 'The extremists have long shot their bolt,' he said. 'The moderates have certainly a game to play if the pieces on the board can be reached.' Certainly there was some basis for Leslie's optimism. Dr John C. Glennon, Archbishop of St Louis, sent Redmond a copy of a speech he had made and several resolutions passed by Irish-American groups which expressed the hopes of both Irish-Americans and native Americans that a moderate Home Rule Bill would be implemented.[60] The next few months saw what pressures moderate Irish-American nationalists could exert on both the American and the British governments.

Throughout the winter and early spring of 1917 conditions changed rapidly in the United States. The summer and autumn of 1916 provided the last opportunity for the revolutionary Irish-Americans until well into 1919. With America about to enter the war against Germany the alliance between the Irish-Americans and the German-Americans which since 1914 had seemed so formidable and so filled with potential for Ireland suddenly became an enormous liability. President Wilson's violent repudiation of Jeremiah A. O'Leary was a harbinger of events to come, not only for O'Leary, but to a great extent for the whole revolutionary wing of the Irish nationalist movement in the United States which O'Leary typified. The moderates who had seemed badly weakened by the Rising and the executions appeared to have another opportunity because of the restrictions that the war imposed on America. The Irish question took on a new dimension in America, in no small part because of the obligations of self-determination that Americans incorporated into their war goals.

CHAPTER 4
IRELAND AND THE AMERICAN WAR CRISIS
1917-1918

AMERICA'S entry into the war gave the Irish question a new significance for Anglo-American relations. For the first time President Wilson and the Secretary of State requested the British government, albeit cautiously, to resolve the Irish situation. Furthermore, Congress, always pro-Irish in its expressions, then held the power to supply Britain's needs in the war. As a result United States approval of British policy in Ireland became crucially important. For Irish-Americans also the entry of the United States into the war had profound implications. To the constitutionalists it meant the slim chance that the necessities of Anglo-American co-operation in the war might prove to be the means through which Home Rule could be enacted. To the revolutionary Irish-American nationalists United States participation in the conflict marked the collapse of a policy which hoped to link Ireland with a possible German victory in the war. But the position of the constitutionalists, which might have been salvaged by the Irish Convention, was turned upside down by the conscription crisis: the constitutional movement disintegrated, while the revolutionaries were heartened and driven together, despite their harassment by the government. The war crisis shaped the character of the Irish struggle in America for the next four years, largely determining both the arguments in favour of Irish nationalism and those against.

I.   The Irish Crisis in Wartime Diplomacy

The United States declared war on Germany on 6 April 1917. Wilson's policy of neutrality, his desire to allow Americans to travel freely and to trade with whom they pleased, and his ambition of being the mediator between the warring parties, were defeated with the resumption of unrestricted submarine warfare by the Germans in early 1917.[1] During February and March, while the United States government waited for the Germans to commence sinking American ships, steps were taken in the United States and Great Britain to discuss those problems which obstructed closer relations between the two countries. E. M. House and Sir William Wiseman, a British intelligence officer assigned to work directly with House, prepared a memorandum on Anglo-American relations to be presented at the Imperial Conference, meeting in London in March. The Irish question was an important item discussed, and it was asserted to be 'one of the greatest obstacles to a good understanding' between Britain and the United States. The memorandum went on to state:

> The Unionist side of the question is little understood and never presented. The only arguments heard are the stock-in-trade of the discontented Nationalists. There are, however, many reasonable and intelligent Americans of Irish extraction who feel very strongly on this subject, and who might be persuaded to lend their assistance with all honesty to the settlement of this question at the end of the war. Sensible opinion in the States would not expect the British to listen to Irishmen of the type of Devoy and [Jeremiah A.] O'Leary; but the movement is given its greatest strength by the fact that reasonable honest citizens of the type of John Quinn feel so strongly about it.

This analysis of both the Irish political situation and the principal groups of Irish-Americans was given added significance by House's comment that President Wilson 'had read it and thought it a just statement'.[2] This modest endorsement by Wilson was important not only because it represented a fairly sound understanding of the complexities of the Irish situation but also because Wilson was at the time attempting to keep his involvement with Allied powers at a bare minimum.

Within a few days after the United States went to war, however, Wilson took further steps to inform the British government of the importance of the Irish question to harmonious relations between the two countries and for the successful prosecution of the war. Lansing was instructed on 10 April to inform Page in London to tell Lloyd George confidentially:

> The only circumstance which seems now to stand in the way of an absolutely cordial cooperation with Great Britain by practically all Americans who are not influenced by ties of blood directly associating them with Germany is the failure so far to find a satisfactory method of self-government for Ireland.

Wilson noted that the Irish question had been a matter of some concern among congressmen before voting for war and he felt that Americans generally would more willingly support the alliance with Britain if they were confident that self-government for Ireland were implemented. Actually Wilson saw Ireland as an embarrass-ment to the Allied powers, and he asked that Page tell Lloyd George:

> If a way could be found now to grant Ireland what she has so often been promised, it would be felt that the real programme of government by the consent of the governed had been adopted everywhere in the anti-Prussian world.[3]

In short, Wilson saw Ireland as the one area in Europe outside the Austrian-German territories which was deprived of democratic government.

Page replied on 18 April that he had talked with Lloyd George, who understood perfectly and was 'glad that the President had instructed me to bring the subject up'. But Lloyd George's answer to the President's request was the suggestion that Wilson himself talk with A. J. Balfour, due to arrive shortly in the United States. Balfour was then the Foreign Secretary, but he was also a prominent figure in the Unionist Party, and the Prime Minister felt that if Wilson could convince him of the importance of the Irish question in America, it would be of great assistance in winning the support of the Unionists in England for the implementation of Home Rule.[4] Lloyd George pointed out to Page that he was trying to settle the Irish question but that the Ulster leaders had been implacable. Page reported that he would attempt to point out the importance of a settlement to other members of the government when the opportunities presented themselves. Wilson was advised to talk with Balfour about the Irish question by several other people as well as Lloyd George. Through the press Lord Northcliffe claimed that 'The happiness of Ireland is entirely in the hands of Mr Balfour and the British mission to the United States.'[5] Wilson was also receiving private appeals from Americans asking that he impress upon the British delegation the importance of a settlement of the Irish situation as an act of good faith to the Allied cause.[6]

The Balfour mission was one of three official delegations from the Allied powers sent to the United States to confer with the gov-ernment about the successful integration of resources in the war effort. Balfour was also instructed to learn for himself the import-ance of the Irish question in America. Indeed, it had been under-stood by Spring Rice that Balfour would be confronted with the Irish question on his mission to America, and he proceeded to draft a memorandum for the Foreign Office which attempted to anticipate the several issues that would come under discussion. In the ambassador's view,

> The [Irish] question is one which is at the root of most of our troubles with the United States. The fact that the Irish question is still unsettled is continually quoted against us, as a proof that it is not wholly true that the fight is one for the sanctity of engagements or the independence of small nations.

Spring Rice was certain that at the least Wilson would have to make some demands to satisfy the Irish-Americans in his party, and that the success of Balfour's mission would to some extent depend on how convincingly he could talk about a solution to the Irish problem.[7] The Secretary of State, whom Tumulty had personally informed of the importance of the Irish question, presented the problem forcefully at a private conference with Balfour and his secretary, Sir Eric Drummond, on 6 May. After telling Balfour that one of the reasons why the American people had greater sympathy for the French than for the British was the failure of the British government to satisfy Irish national aspirations, Lansing further said that the British government's inability 'to respond to the intense longing of the Irish for the freedom of Ireland from British rule by conceding to them a measure of independence made thousands of Irish-Americans bitter enemies of Great Britain'. Lansing emphasised the point that these circumstances created a 'situation with which our government found it difficult to cope'. A solution of the Irish problem would end the antagonism of the Irish-Americans and their friends towards Great Britain and would generally strengthen the war effort in both America and Ireland. Balfour, Lansing wrote later, 'promised to lay the matter before his government when he returned to England'.[8] However, in his report to the cabinet Balfour minimised the importance of the Irish question in America, pointing out that among government officials he had 'fewer conversations on it than might have been supposed' and that 'The President never referred to it at all; the Secretary of State never referred to it officially.'[9]

Congress, during the opening days of America's involvement in the war, attempted to exert pressure on both the Wilson administration and the British government to deal with the Irish question and to give some expression to the pro-Irish sympathies in the country. Just a little over a week after the declaration of war Congressman Gallagher introduced a resolution which advocated a 'free government for Ireland and Poland', and on 28 April Congressman Cary introduced a resolution which called for 'the freedom of Ireland'. Congressman Mason, who ten days before had spoken passionately about an Irish republic as the wish of 'every lover of liberty all over the world', introduced a resolution on 14 May 'to declare the liberation of Ireland one of the purposes of the present war'. In late July Congressmen McLaughlin, Kennedy and Morin each introduced resolutions asking that the issue be terminated immediately by implementation of dominion status, plebiscite or Home Rule.[10] On 28 April Speaker of the House Champ Clark and 140 congressmen signed and sent a cable to Lloyd George asking that the Irish question be quickly resolved in accordance with President Wilson's recent pronouncements on self-government and self-determination for all nations. Congressman Gallivan, who in January had introduced a resolution saying that Congress acknowledged that there would be no peace in the world until self-determination was recognised by the great powers, spoke to the House about the cable and said that the solution to the Irish problem was 'to put the home rule bill into operation at once, even persuading or compelling a few counties that oppose it to yield to the will of the majority'. Ireland could be won over if the British government were strong enough to act firmly and immediately.[11] In addition to these efforts, a substantial number of senators and representatives made speeches on the Irish question or had petitions and memorials from their constituents printed in the *Congressional Record*. But Congress, with the support of the Irish-American members, also asked Balfour to address them. Significantly, perhaps, he was the first foreigner since Parnell to do so.

To be sure, constitutional Irish-American nationalists saw America's entry into the war as an opportunity which could be turned to Ireland's advantage. Perhaps as their price for full participation in the war effort Ireland might be given some form of immediate self-government in a British gesture to cement harmonious Anglo-American relations. Certainly, as Shane Leslie had told Redmond in March, the moderates had 'a game to play'.[12] Among the first efforts to investigate American opinion was that initiated by the British newspaper tycoon Lord Northcliffe, who appealed through the New York *World* for the views of influential Americans on the importance of the Irish question on the new war situation. Through his representatives in New York and Washington, W. F. Bullock and Arthur Willert, and the assistance of John Quinn and Shane Leslie, Northcliffe solicited letters on the Irish question from highly placed Americans to be published in the New York *World* and the London *Times* in the hope of moving the British government to implement some kind of Home Rule in Ireland.[13] Such distinguished native Americans as Theodore Roosevelt and William Howard Taft responded that an immediate settlement which would place Ireland in a relationship to Westminster similar to that of the state of Maine to Washington was important for a successful prosecution of the war.

Several outstanding Irish-Americans also contributed statements, which, although perhaps more attentive to the details of Home Rule, were essentially similar to the suggestions of Roosevelt and Taft. Cardinal Gibbons of Baltimore favoured immediate Home Rule but emphasised the importance of a unified Ireland with guarantees and concessions for minorities and interest groups. 'Ireland cannot be sacrificed to a few counties in Ulster,' the cardinal wrote; but he added: 'These few counties cannot be sacrificed to the rest of Ireland.' Mayor John Purroy Mitchel of New York hoped that Home Rule would be implemented but that it would not be on the basis of 'county options' which the government had just suggested. New York Supreme Court Judge Victor J. Dowling thought that Ireland was the test of England's war aims, as did John F. ('Honey Fitz') Fitzgerald, the former mayor of Boston. Colonel Robert Temple Emmet and Robert E. Dowling, former chairman of the State Workmen's Compensation Commission, both wrote that minority rights in Ireland could be protected by constitutional guarantees. Archbishop Ireland of St Paul said that Great Britain needed Ireland's support in the war but would get it only by extending Home Rule; once this was done, American support would be more enthusiastic also. The effect of these letters, both in England and in America, was to re-emphasise the importance of the Irish question to the creation of a working alliance between Britain and the United States. They were important also in that they demonstrated the rather remarkable agreement among important and influential native Americans and Irish-Americans on the merits of immediate Home Rule for an undivided Ireland, for political and ideological reasons.[14]

Moderate Irish-Americans began working to encourage the best possible terms for a Home Rule settlement—one which would pacify nationalists and also make Ireland a willing partner in the war. Twenty-seven distinguished Irish-Americans cabled to Redmond on 22 April saying that the partition of Ulster or exclusion by county options would not be an acceptable settlement in either America or Ireland. 'Americans refuse to believe', they asserted, 'that every legitimate right of a minority cannot be made absolutely secure, as in this country, without impairing in any way the unity of the Irish nation.' And to make the point about the war they closed by saying: 'No settlement of the Irish question will be final unless it is based upon that justice which this country has entered the war to make universal.'[15] At the same time a similar group of

Irish-Americans, this time inspired by John Quinn, who had learned in 'high official quarters' that an appeal would be welcomed by the British government, sent a cable to Lloyd George emphasising the importance of a satisfactory early resolution of the Irish question because of its vital relationship to the war effort.[16] The national executive committee of the UIL met in Washington on 3 May to plan strategy and to cable support and encouragement to Redmond. Several days later M. J. Jordan wrote Redmond telling him of the enthusiasm and determination of the meeting. Furthermore, he found Ireland and Home Rule the main topic of conversation in Washington; he was told by someone of authority that President Wilson was 'straining every nerve to see that the Home Rule Bill goes into effect'. John Quinn, Shane Leslie and Judges Keogh, O'Brien and Dowling also cabled to Redmond telling him that they had been in consultation with Plunkett and that they thought Redmond could profit by discussing the attitude of Americans and the new prospects of Home Rule with him.[17]

All these appeals, resolutions and public declarations were designed to exert such pressure on the British and American governments that Home Rule would be put into operation immediately. To those Irish-Americans as impatient as John Quinn the efficient way to get things done was to work personally at the highest possible level. Thus when Plunkett and Leslie, equally impatient Irishmen, explored the possibility of a delegation of Irish-Americans meeting Balfour in order to explain the importance of the Irish question in the United States, Quinn was anxious to organise such a group.[18] On 24 April Plunkett met Balfour and advised him of the extreme importance of a quick resolution of the Irish question for the establishment of harmonious Anglo-American war co-operation. Balfour, Plunkett wrote in his diary, agreed that this was true, and at Plunkett's suggestion agreed also to see any small group of Irish-Americans that Plunkett might recommend to him. The following day Plunkett talked with Quinn and House and wrote to Balfour that he thought his own proposed solution to the Irish question would be most appealing to American opinion. Quinn organised a delegation made up of himself, New York Supreme Court Judge Morgan J. O'Brien, Colonel Robert Temple Emmet, Lawrence Godkin and John F. Fitzgerald. Quinn explained to Theodore Roosevelt that Emmet and Godkin represented Protestant Irish-Americans and the rest moderate Catholic opinion, and that America's entry into the war provided 'a great chance for England to make a generous settlement'. To another friend Quinn pointed out that the deputation did not want to 'embarrass' Balfour or to browbeat him, but rather to have an earnest talk with him to try to impress upon him the fact that the way to take the wind out of the sails of the irreconcilables, the way to put them out of business, is to have Home Rule be given to an undivided Ireland. That will settle the Irish question, and it is the only thing that can settle it.[19]

The meeting was held in Washington on 4 May 1917 and lasted for two hours. The delegation told Balfour that Americans felt that Ireland had won Home Rule constitutionally and in all fairness should not be denied this measure of self-government. Partition would be as unacceptable in America as in Ireland; such a concession to Carson would be considered a 'betrayal' and would, like much of Britain's current Irish policy, play into the hands of extremists. On the contrary, a generous policy would be welcomed and endorsed in both Ireland and America by all right-thinking people. The Ulster Unionists would have to compromise for the good of the majority and for the war effort; they would be protected by adequate written guarantees and could look forward to good government, not Tammany Hall politics, with the Southern Irish. The delegates spoke out because they felt the Irish question had become an American political issue and because, owing to the collusion between revolutionary Irish-Americans and German-Americans, the continued instability in Ireland was as much a danger to America as it was to Britain and the war effort.

Balfour agreed that the Irish question was a source of irritation in the relations between America and Britain and that it was also a source of exasperation to Englishmen. He wanted to make clear that Ireland was already free and that, in fact, because of the land acts, the availability of Catholic university education, and the absence of conscription, Irishmen might be said to have more rights than Englishmen. A great deal had changed in Ireland in the past hundred years. The real problem, Balfour said, was in obtaining a settlement which would be satisfactory to all parties in Ireland. The fears of the Ulstermen were real and had to be respected, and to force them out of the United Kingdom would not be acceptable. In closing he said he thought a solution was imminent—that the postponement of debates on Ireland in the Commons was an indication that Redmond and Lloyd George were probably having discussions. Furthermore, Balfour promised to report faithfully the views that the deputation had put before him.[20]

Balfour cabled Lloyd George the following day that he had received a deputation of Irish-Americans 'of high standing' and that they had in very moderate terms emphasised how much an Irish settlement would 'promote unity in the United States'. He said that the group had supported Plunkett's proposals and rejected any scheme of partition, although Shane Leslie had told him confidentially that should partition be the only means to a settlement, 'a considerable portion of Irish moderate opinion here would rally to it'. Balfour endorsed the view of the delegation that the Irish question was 'the only difficulty we have to face here and its settlement would no doubt greatly facilitate [the] vigorous and lasting co-operation of [the] United States Government in the war'.[21] A day later Secretary of State Lansing told Balfour much the same thing.

The effect of the meeting with Balfour was felt quickly in the United States. The members of the delegation were pleased. Godkin told Plunkett—whose scheme for Home Rule he had promoted—that Balfour had been 'delightful', and Quinn also reported that the meeting had been 'very satisfactory'. In fact Quinn was told by Spring Rice and General G. T. M. Bridges, Balfour's aide, how convincing they had been. Plunkett himself understood from Leslie that the meeting 'did great good'. Some time later Leslie wrote to Mrs Alice Stopford Green that part of the good that had come from the meeting had been brought about by Balfour's cordial reception of the Irish-Americans and also because the meeting had acted as a 'lightning conductor to Irish feeling in New York'.[22] Thus whatever the effect of the meeting on British policy, its immediate result was to assist in smoothing American opinion on Ireland.

In the meantime, however, the revolutionary Irish-American nationalists found themselves on the defensive, having fought American intervention right up to the declaration of war on 6 April 1917. The war meant the end of the German–Irish alliance in America and the collapse of the policy of the past four years. A new programme had to be created which would still promote revolutionary separatism for Ireland but which would not jeopardise the security of the United States. On 8 April, two days after the country went to war, Judge Cohalan told Irish-Americans at a large meeting in Carnegie Hall to be loyal Americans during the war, but also to hold the United States to its war aims so that Ireland would be included among the nations to be given freedom. By the end of the month these sentiments became the official policy of the revolutionaries. A Clan na Gael circular sent to officers and members on 28 April 1917 instructed that 'The efforts of the Organization shall be devoted to securing intervention by the United States in favour of the National Independence of Ireland.' The letter carefully explained the delicacy of the situation but insisted on the correctness of the Clan position:

That work is entirely within the law and consistent with loyalty to the United States, in which we yield to no class of citizens in this Republic, to which our race has rendered valiant service in every crisis of its history from the Revolution to the present day. Our previous activities were always perfectly legal and legitimate, and we have never violated American law, in letter or spirit. But the new situation developed by the entry of the United States into the European war renders necessary the adoption of new methods for the achievement of the same object—the complete emancipation of the land of our fathers.[23]

Although clearly alarmed, the Clan suggested that work begin immediately to undertake a national campaign to hold the Wilson administration and the British government to the pious pronouncements about the rights of small nations. The *Gaelic American,* which grudgingly reconciled itself to the war, emphasised this point also, but further argued that the war situation was such that America had the power to compel Britain to grant independence to Ireland because American troops were about to win the war for the British.

Thus the revolutionary Irish-American nationalists began a campaign which was to continue through 1919. The United Irish Societies of Chicago, Illinois, demanded Irish representation at the Peace Conference and a congressional pronouncement on Irish autonomy from Senator J. Hamilton Lewis of Illinois. The San Francisco FOIF cabled to President Wilson saying that Ireland must have 'complete separation' from Britain and that Home Rule would not suffice. Congressman McLaughlin, who was also national president of the AOH, told Congress that his organisation was asking Wilson to secure Irish independence and was calling on the nation to support Ireland at the Peace Conference. Constituents of Senator Wesley J. Jones of Washington sent resolutions calling for Irish independence.[24] Séamas MacManus published a thick little paper-covered volume, *Ireland's case,* which gave a long nativist history of Ireland and argued for complete independence. The revolutionaries expressed contempt for the efforts of moderates to bring Home Rule into force, labelling such proposals as attempts to keep Ireland tied to British control. The publication of Tumulty's reply to John D. Crimmins, which said that Wilson showed sympathy for Ireland's claim for Home Rule, brought a strong protest to the White House from the national secretary of the FOIF.[25] The *Gaelic American* and the *Irish World* attacked the Balfour mission, upon which the government and the moderates had placed so much hope. Devoy's paper said that British insincerity about the war and small nations could be seen in the choice of Balfour to lead the mission to America. Balfour was denounced as one of the 'dyed-in-the wool Tories', one of the 'Big Chiefs of the Oligarchy' which held millions of people in oppression across the world. The *Gaelic American* also condemned the delegation led by John Quinn to see Balfour, and said that they had authority to speak only for John Quinn.[26]

II. The Struggle of the Moderates

During the twelve months after the United States entered the war the Irish question steadily declined in importance as both native Americans and Irish-Americans were diverted by the new demands made upon them. As a result the Irish Convention, for whose creation American opinion was in part responsible, aroused surprisingly little interest, given the fears of British and American political leaders in April and May 1917. This decline in interest was all the more surprising because of the degree to which the survival of the moderate nationalist movement in the United States and at home depended on a successful Irish settlement, such as was promised by the Irish Convention with its avowed purpose of drafting an all-Ireland constitution. Many Americans were pleased at the selection of Sir Horace Plunkett as chairman and regarded this as a good omen. However, the newspapers, inasmuch as they discussed it at all, remained somewhat sceptical about the possible prospects of a settlement. President Wilson was himself particularly interested in the Convention and went so far as to open correspondence with Plunkett through E. M. House, ignoring Ambassador Page in London, who was often unreliable in reporting the intricacies of the Irish situation. And indeed in February, when the Convention seemed in America to have lost its momentum, Wilson let it be known to the British Ambassador that he regarded the unresolved Irish question as 'a millstone' around his neck.[27]

The apparent lack of interest of Americans in the Irish Convention was noted by many, and elaborate steps were taken to make the public more aware of the efforts being made and the dimensions of the Irish problem. John Quinn published a little book in September 1917 entitled *The Irish Home-Rule Convention* which was a composite of the pamphlets by George Russell, *Thoughts for a convention,* and Plunkett, *A defence of the Convention,* along with an introduction of his own and two anonymous chapters which drew heavily on a letter from Theodore Roosevelt to Russell.[28] The book asserted that the British administration in Ireland had been a failure; that the insurrection had been wrong but the suppression of it worse; that the Convention offered the only realistic hope of a settlement; and that the war crisis made an immediate settlement imperative. A month later Shane Leslie published his *The Irish question in its American aspect* which attempted to analyse the triangular relationship between the United States, Great Britain and Ireland and the importance of a settlement for normal relations between the three countries.[29] Plunkett himself took great pains, even before he was selected as chairman, to see that Americans he talked to or corresponded with were given information about the possibilities of the Convention.

If the Irish Convention did not arouse great interest or support in the United States, it did serve a practical function which many interested observers were quick to notice. The Convention appeared as visible proof that the British government was attempting to resolve the Irish question and therefore was working in harmony with the American war aims of self-determination and the rights of small nations. Karl Walter, director of the Reciprocal News Service, told Plunkett: 'While the Irish Convention is sitting the British Government is safeguarded from hostile opinion in America based on the Irish question.' By early 1918 British observers in America had come to the same conclusion, and they advised the government that the Convention should be kept in session as long as possible, even if there were no prospects for a settlement, because the actual meeting of the Convention served as a shield against criticism on the Irish question. The Foreign Office seemed to agree that the deeper the United States got into the war the less likely it was to be concerned about Ireland.[30] When the results of the Convention were submitted to the House of Commons the British analysis was borne out: American opinion was largely unperturbed by the failure to implement Home Rule and by the conscription crisis, although the Irish-American reaction was more complex.

The Irish nationalist movement in the United States passed through an extremely critical period during the twelve months between America's entry into the war and the conclusion of the Irish Convention. For the constitutionalists the Convention offered something of a reprieve from the disasters of 1916, but a reprieve dependent on the success of the Convention. The interest shown by the American and British governments, in April and May of 1917, in pacifying the Irish in America in order to strengthen the war effort, and the general goodwill fostered by the letters to the New York *World* and London *Times,* created an atmosphere which held some promise for the failing UIL—especially if working to solve the

Irish question could be seen as congruent with American war aims. Letters by prominent Irish-Americans expressing views on the Convention were published in the New York *Evening Post* through the efforts of Dr W. J. M. A. Maloney, a discharged British army medical officer, for the purpose of creating the kind of dialogue similar to those in the New York *World* several weeks earlier. These letters, however, revealed a wide divergence of opinion about the prospects of the Convention. Shane Leslie attempted to analyse the Irish-American situation for Redmond, and indeed admitted realistically that feeling was very mixed at the moment, but he was confident that the Irish in America would willingly accept a Home Rule settlement. Redmond's response was an appeal for money from the leading members of the UIL and prominent Irish-Americans to support the party and to meet the growing election threat posed by the new Sinn Féin party. A special meeting of the recipients of Redmond's appeal met in New York and rather than make a flat refusal suggested that an Irish delegation, perhaps led by John Dillon or Joe Devlin, be sent to the United States to join the various other 'missions' touring the country for reasons connected with the war.[31]

An Irish mission made up of T. P. O'Connor and Richard Hazleton, one of the promising younger members of the Irish Parliamentary Party, was sent to America in late June 1917 to raise the money needed to keep the party operating and to try to breathe life into the Home Rule movement in the United States. As Leslie had promised, O'Connor and Hazleton met President Wilson, despite Ambassador Page's disapproval and Wilson's own reluctance to meet them without British Embassy introductions (they were presented by Senator James D. Phelan), although this official endorsement did not launch them on an easy or successful trip.[32] Within a week after the two arrived Leslie reported back to Redmond that unforeseen problems had developed. 'The difficulties are chiefly with our own people as I realized when I went to Boston to arrange a visit for the Irish envoys,' Leslie said, while informing Redmond that Irish-American hostility was so great that no large public meetings could be held for fear of disagreeable public demonstrations. By late August Leslie, who had suggested the Irish mission, told Dillon that it might be 'wise' for O'Connor to leave 'without raising up too many hornets'. Even John Quinn, who gave O'Connor what assistance he could, thought the trip 'ill-advised' and foredoomed to 'failure'.[33]

O'Connor soon realised that the constitutionalists were diverted by the war, the revolutionaries still implacable, and that he would find little popular support in America. He had hoped that the bitterness of the Irish-Americans towards the Irish Parliamentary Party would have diminished after America's entry into the war, but it had not. Moreover, the argument on which O'Connor and Hazleton attempted to tour the country was too negative to arouse much interest. Because of the war they could not make their customary anti-British statements which had always delighted audiences; yet, Hazleton complained to Shane Leslie, 'To be for England looks as if we were against Ireland.' By early December Hazleton concluded that the Irish-Americans had given way in the United States to the priorities of the war and that the Sinn Féiners were 'dropping all Irish work till after the end of the war'; the idea that the entry of America into the war 'would bring a great reaction in our favour' had not materialised. The result in both cases was that there was no money to be found among the grassroots Irish-Americans. O'Connor wrote to Dillon that 'Most of the money would have to come from native Americans.'[34] In fact he found the National Security League and the Armenian Committee more congenial than the Irish-American organisations, and Samuel Insull, a public utilities millionaire originally from England, was his most generous contributor. The situation was clear to Hazleton: everything in America and Ireland hinged on the Irish Convention. If the Convention were successful, the party could 'carry Ireland for [a] settlement', he thought. If the Convention failed, the party would be a dead letter both in America and Ireland and all honest men would have to support Sinn Féin. In the meantime, however, Hazleton felt that it was useless to attempt to rebuild the movement in the United States 'until England shows she is willing to deliver the goods'. Many in America felt by late 1917 and 1918 that only the actual implementation of Home Rule would show Britain's good faith, and some no longer considered that event likely. Cardinal Gibbons told O'Connor in the autumn of 1917 that he saw no chance for either the Convention or the party. 'It is reasoned,' the cardinal said, 'that, since Ireland has not received, in this crisis of the English Government, the Home Rule which she has been contending for, she has practically no hope in the future.'[35]

For the revolutionary Irish-American nationalists the twelve months from America's entry into the war until the conscription crisis was marked not only by the collapse of the 1914–17 policy of a German–Irish alliance; it also saw the beginning of a period of some persecution by the federal government because of Irish collusion with German agents during the several preceding years. The government, in fact, employed a dual policy of repression and conciliation in dealing with the Irish extremists in the United States

—attempting perhaps to separate nationalist activities which were merely concerned with Irish independence or an Irish republic from nationalist activities which were tied to Germany or to efforts which weakened the British ally or the recruiting drive. In July the United States Attorney in San Francisco, John W. Preston, attempted to suppress Irish meetings. In New York in late August police broke up a FOIF meeting near Herald Square where England and Mayor Mitchel were condemned; six people, including the sister of the mayor of Boston, were arrested. Patrick McCartan recorded similar instances of police efforts to prevent Jeremiah A. O'Leary's 'soap box orators' from making anti-British speeches on behalf of the American Truth Society.[36] John D. Moore, the national secretary of the FOIF, was interrogated by secret service agents about the finances of his organisation, and Mrs Sheehy-Skeffington was obstructed in her speaking tour across the United States. Judge Cohalan and Devoy were deeply implicated in German espionage before 1916 by the publication of the Wolf von Igel papers in the press on 23 September 1917. The government took no legal action against Cohalan or Devoy, but the insinuation was that their activities had been treasonable, although Cohalan successfully fought a libel case on that allegation against the Mail and Express Company of New York. On 10 October the government released additional documents which linked Joseph McGarrity, John T. Keating and Jeremiah A. O'Leary with possible German sabotage. McGarrity and O'Leary fought back in the papers (Keating having died in 1915) and successfully stated their case. O'Leary's paper, *Bull*, was suppressed on 8 October, and after a chase across the country he was arrested and prepared for trial. A warrant was put out for the arrest of John T. Ryan, an Irish-American leader from Buffalo, who fled the country. Patrick McCartan and Liam Mellows were arrested and prevented from travelling to Germany and Russia to attempt to gain recognition for Irish independence. And, as a final blow, from 19 January 1918 onwards the United States Post Office refused to allow the *Gaelic American,* the *Irish World* and the New York *Freeman's Journal* to pass through the mails.[37]

The climate of opinion in the United States had shifted. Revolutionary Irish-American nationalists could no longer carry out their plans without regard for the almost hysterical emotions created by the war. When Pádraic Colum published a letter in the *New Republic* protesting against the irrationality of the war fever in America, John Quinn sent him what his (Quinn's) biographer called a 'bitter and insulting letter' condemning pleas for moderation as essentially pro-German. Senator William H. King wrote to Senator John Sharp Williams on 13 February 1918: 'The time for hyphenated Americans is over and the cowards and disloyalists in our country have got to be weeded out and held up to the execration which they deserve.' These sentiments were repeated at the Senate hearings on the National German–American Alliance on 26 February by Senator McCumber of South Dakota, who also condemned the 'hyphen' in America. As he put it,

> The time is past for German-American, Irish-American, Bolshevist-American and every other type of alias citizen. We want no more fooling with those few Irish agitators, reared on traditional hatred, who would line themselves with Germany against our ally, who is doing the real fighting in this war. Whoever attacks Great Britain attacks us, anything calculated to increase her troubles at home is postponing the ultimate victory.[38]

The Senate hearings revealed that there had been some collusion between the German-American organisations and at least the leaders of some Irish-American organisations, Jeremiah A. O'Leary and Daniel O'Connell of the Independence Union specifically. Gustavus Ohlinger, a lawyer from Toledo who had been associated with the National German–American Alliance, asserted in his testimony that it was 'significant' that the alliance between Germany and the Irish rebels, which led to the rebellion in Dublin in 1916, had its corresponding counterpart in the United States in the coordination of Irish and German activities to resist the government's policies towards the belligerents. Although one witness said that the actual number of Irish-Americans who worked with the Germans or who even were pro-German was very small, this could not undo the damage that had been done to the reputation of the revolutionary movement. The revolutionary nationalists in Ireland were also increasingly condemned. In his book on the current international situation, *The world's debate*, William Barry called attention to the material and political destruction resulting from the Easter Rising; and Elmer T. Clark, a journalist who travelled through Ireland after American sailors had been stationed at Queenstown, wrote that he found the attitude of Southern Irishmen 'impossible, deplorable, and unworthy', and he thought Sinn Féin claims were based on a foolish interpretation of history and their arguments and were so impractical that they would reduce Ireland to ruin if implemented.[39]

Conciliatory gestures towards the revolutionaries were also made by the government simultaneously with the arrests and intimidations, and in some cases involved the same people. Dr Patrick McCartan, along with Clan and FOIF leaders James K. McGuire and John D. Moore, presented a statement signed by the twenty-six Irish leaders who had just been released from prison in England and a long memorandum to Joseph Tumulty in the White House offices on 23 July, in somewhat the same manner that O'Connor and Hazleton had done less than three weeks earlier. McCartan, who had crossed the Atlantic under false pretences as a sailor and then jumped ship in New York, could as easily have been deported as received by President Wilson's secretary. More important, however, was Mrs Sheehy-Skeffington's meeting with President Wilson on 11 January 1918.[40] Through the efforts of Shaemus O'Sheel and Bainbridge Colby, then working for the Wilson administration, Mrs Sheehy-Skeffington had a short meeting with the President, during which she presented him with a petition and asked him 'to consider our claims as a small nation governed without consent'. Wilson seemed 'courteous' and 'interested' and 'acknowledged smilingly his Irish blood'. Wilson, of course, made no commitments, but Mrs Sheehy-Skeffington told Peter Golden that people had been 'stirred' by her visit with the President and that it was 'considered a *sign* of the times and so it is'.[41] During the same week Senators Phelan and O'Gorman ceremoniously presented President Wilson a statue of Robert Emmet in the White House, along with a strong plea for Irish self-government. The significance of these various gestures was not altogether clear. Mrs Sheehy-Skeffington pointed out to Devoy that 'It is apparently no treason to the U.S. to plead for Ireland, otherwise assuredly the President would not receive me or the petition.'[42] On the contrary, Wilson may have been trying to give the British government a tacit warning of the dangers for Anglo-American relations if a settlement were not reached.

Congressional activity tended to encompass both aspects of the President's policy. The anti-Irish and almost xenophobic responses of the senators investigating the National German–American Alliance certainly typified a desire to stamp out ethnic nationalism as fully as possible. However, at approximately the same time more conciliatory gestures were also being made. On 4 January 1918 Congresswoman Jeanette Rankin introduced a resolution 'proposing recognition by the Congress of the United States of the right of Irish independence', and two months later Senator Gallinger proposed that a plebiscite be held in Ireland to allow the Irish people to enjoy 'the great principle of self-determination, as interpreted by the President of the United States in his discussion of the fundamental and indispensable conditions of a lasting peace'.[43] Both McCartan and Mrs Sheehy-Skeffington, unabashed 'Sinn Féiners', were given warm welcomes by politicians and civil servants throughout Washington. But, of course, these individual acts did not compensate for the indictments, suppressions and insinuations for which the Irish-American nationalists felt the government to be responsible.

In the face of governmental harassments and arrests and growing public hostility, many leaders of the revolutionary Irish-Americans, having exclaimed their loyalty to the United States and identified Ireland's cause with the American war effort, were understandably reluctant to pursue an active policy until the climate began to change. The Irish Race Convention which had been planned for the late autumn of 1917 was never called; and McCartan records that the AOH not only postponed their national convention but also arbitrarily suspended publication of the *Hibernian*. The consequences of this policy produced a reaction not unlike that which had afflicted the constitutional nationalists in 1914: rather than comply with a *de facto* suspension of activity for the duration of the war, the more radical elements found new machinery with which to maintain agitation. For the Home Rulers this had been the gradual erosion of the UIL as members joined the FOIF; for the Clan and the FOIF in 1917 and 1918 a similar pattern of erosion began to develop.

The organisation which now began to attract revolutionary nationalists was the somewhat left-wing Irish Progressive League, which was organised in the autumn of 1917 and made its first public appearance supporting Morris Hillquit, the socialist candidate for mayor of New York.[44] The IPL was open to 'all men and women subscribing to the principle of complete Independence for Ireland', and at its first meeting it elected Peter Golden, then an assistant to Devoy on the *Gaelic American*, general secretary, and Mrs Margaret E. Hickey treasurer. Its initial programme was to insist on Irish representation at the Peace Conference, but stimulated by the indefatigable and fearless Mrs Sheehy-Skeffington, the league began a campaign to raise money to establish an 'Irish National Bureau' in Washington through which propaganda about Ireland could be disseminated and through which political pressure could be organised and applied to American politicians in order to place Ireland within the objectives of the war effort.[45] In advance of the Irish National Bureau Mrs Sheehy-Skeffington canvassed politicians and lobbied at Congress, making plans to 'blacklist' people like Senators Kenyon and McCumber for their anti-Irish statements and complaining bitterly at the failure of many Irish-Americans to rally behind her efforts. 'Most of my support', she told Peter Golden, 'has been from suffs [suffragettes], radicals and progressives—and very little from the Irish.'[46] On the eve of the conscription crisis

Mrs Hickey led a group of thirty-four IPL members from ten cities, including Pádraic Colum and Nora Connolly, to the White House to deliver a petition for Irish independence.

This activity was effective in keeping the Irish revolutionary cause before the public, and especially the government, during a period when the cause was no longer easily promoted with impunity, but it was also a direct challenge to the old leadership of the revolutionary movement in the United States. Indeed, the Irish Progressive League was accused of 'butting in' by Devoy, and Mrs Sheehy-Skeffington was warned that she was working with unapproved groups of Irish-Americans. Mrs Sheehy-Skeffington's co-operation with the National Women's Party in Washington (a suffragette group) and with socialists and radicals was a matter of grave concern for some Irish-American leaders, and in fact the left-wing tone of the IPL, beginning with its support of the socialist candidate mayor of New York, was resented. Captain Robert Monteith found Devoy and the Clan na Gael unwilling to tolerate his independent Irish agitation, and Devoy was not pleased either with the founding in Philadelphia by Joseph McGarrity of the *Irish Press,* although after eight issues it, like the *Gaelic American,* was refused by the Post Office.[47] On being criticised by Devoy for 'butting in', Golden made a firm defence of his actions and those of the IPL, pointing out that all too few Irish-Americans were willing to risk anything at that time, although something had to be done if the cause were to be maintained. He later argued that he appreciated Devoy's position because of the war, but that there was among the revolutionary Irish-Americans a 'great feeling of dissatisfaction' and the conclusion was that the *Gaelic American* and the Irish-American leaders were 'lying down'. Golden thought that they must be firm in their action and constant to their principles. He queried:

> If the Government would resort to such measures as making arrests etc., would it not be as well to have them do that so that we and the entire world may know where we stand and what all their fine phrases amount to.[48]

To openly court arrest to test the government's sincerity about the national aspirations of small nations was a project upon which the older Irish-American leaders were most reluctant to embark. The Irish Progressive League, however, was unintimidated by Devoy, the Clan, or the United States government.

III.   The Conscription Crisis, the Collapse of Moderation, and the Irish as Enemies

The attempt of the British government to extend conscription to Ireland in April 1918 in an effort to meet the manpower problem imposed by the new German offensive provoked a crisis in Ireland and America which ended the uneasy calm that had been the product of the Irish Convention. Actually the American government was consulted in the cabinet's decision to extend conscription to Ireland. After a warning from Lord Reading, the new British Ambassador, that conscription in Ireland would have a bad effect in America, Balfour cabled E. M. House on 2 April outlining the government's problems in increasing conscription in England without introducing it in Ireland as well. Balfour admitted that the government expected 'serious disorder and possibly, even, bloodshed', that the troops raised might not be 'reliable', and that the 'priests, Parliament, the Nationalists, and Sinn Féiners will unite to oppose conscription'. These events might be averted by the immediate implementation of Home Rule, but that in turn might cause equal disruption in Ulster. Confessing that he was unable to 'gauge the exact part that [the] Irish question takes in American politics', Balfour asked that House openly and freely 'inform me of your opinion of the policy which I have outlined above and of its effect on the conduct of the war viewed from America'.[49] House showed the letter to President Wilson, who replied that conscription in Ireland would 'accentuate the whole Irish and Catholic intrigue which has gone hand in hand in some quarters in the country with German intrigue'. Thus House responded immediately to Balfour advising that the American government viewed Irish conscription as a source of domestic difficulty which would aggravate the war situation.[50] Nevertheless, according to Alan J. Ward, Sir William Wiseman later reported Wilson's views in such a way that the British government understood that there would be no objection to conscription if a solution to the Irish question could be worked out immediately.[51]

It became obvious that the British decision to extend conscription to Ireland would have serious repercussions in the United States, and that President Wilson would become the centre of a struggle to save the situation. Among the first to attempt to influence the President were Shane Leslie and Maurice Francis Egan, the former United States Ambassador to Denmark, both of whom had attended a meeting with the three American cardinals and several bishops at the Catholic University at which grave concern had been expressed about conscription in Ireland. Egan wrote to

Wilson: 'If conscription is applied by force—without Home Rule—there will be terrible resistance,' and he went on to add: 'The effect on the Irish in this country will be bad; it will embarrass the great [war] movement.' Wilson replied: 'I realize the critical significance of the matter to which you call my attention . . . and [I] wish there were some proper way in which I could help to guide matters, but so far, unfortunately, none has opened before me.'[52] Certainly Wilson's hint to Balfour through House had not been acted upon.

Later in the month Sir William Wiseman, then in London, attempted to explain the situation to House. The government had had no alternative, but it did not 'intend to put conscription into operation until the new Home Rule bill is passed, based on Sir Horace Plunkett's report'. Wiseman added that he thought the government's critics could be partially forestalled if President Wilson could make some public statement 'expressing his view along the line that he is glad that Sir Horace Plunkett's conference has recommended a form of Home Rule that H.M. Government intends to legislate accordingly, and feels sure now that her national aspirations have been satisfied Ireland will not fail to do her part with the other democracies'.[53] Wilson, while possibly encouraged that Home Rule might end the Irish question for all but the most militant, was most unlikely to make the kind of statement suggested by Wiseman, and indeed Wilson scrupulously avoided any public statements about Ireland. In any case, on the following day Wiseman counselled against any statement by the President on the Irish question. He said it was no longer 'absolutely certain that H.M. Government will legislate on Sir Horace Plunkett's recommendation', and he further warned that 'both sides intend to try to bring him [Wilson] into the controversy'.[54] Shane Leslie also conveyed messages between Wilson and Lord Reading. After Leslie had expressed Tumulty's view that it was a mistake to press conscription before Home Rule, Lord Reading assured him that Lloyd George had 'given his word' that Home Rule was 'certain and immediate'.[55] Leslie seemed sceptical, and the American government must by this time have been even more so.

By mid-April an appeal to President Wilson was being prepared from Ireland where, as a result of the great anti-conscription meeting in the Mansion House in Dublin on 18 April, Laurence O'Neill, the Lord Mayor of Dublin, had been commissioned to go to America to explain to Wilson and the American people why Ireland would resist conscription. Both Wiseman and Leslie wished that the President were in a position to make some public announcement about the implementation of Home Rule which would, in Leslie's words, 'rally the whole Irish race'. Page in London reported that the British government was inclined to grant the Lord Mayor a passport when he applied for it on the assumption that his reception in the United States would be so hostile that it would be a good lesson to the Irish as to just what Americans thought about resistance to conscription. Because of the possible repercussions of such a visitor, the State Department asked for instructions from Wilson.[56] Wilson replied: 'It is plain to me that there is no way in which we can head off the Lord Mayor of Dublin, though I think his visit is most unwise from every point of view.' The President thought that they would have to deal with O'Neill as best they could when he arrived, and he closed by saying: 'If he knew how little he was going to get out of the trip, he would stay at home!'[57] Page was instructed to issue a visa to O'Neill. Lord Mayor O'Neill eventually decided to stay in Dublin rather than submit to Lord French, the new Lord Lieutenant, the documents he had planned to take to Washington.[58] Certainly the war and conscription in America gave Wilson little alternative in the matter, so that O'Neill's decision to stay home spared all parties a difficult situation.

In order to ascertain the possible effects of the Military Service Bill, which contained a provision for Irish conscription, Wilson sent an observer to Ireland on 29 April. This was Ray Stannard Baker, a journalist in whom he had great personal confidence and who was then in Europe on behalf of the government to investigate political unrest among the Allies. Baker travelled throughout the country, talking with such leaders as Plunkett, Russell, Dillon, Devlin and Gwynn in the South and Sir George Clark and several Ulster leaders in the North. He attended the famous anti-conscription meeting at Ballaghaderreen, Co. Roscommon, where he saw de Valera and heard the crowd shout: 'God save the Kaiser!' By 16 May he was able to report to the State Department that the gravity of the situation was appreciated throughout Ireland but that the British were increasing their troops in Ireland and the Irish people were certain that the government would attempt to use force. The Irish leaders were convinced, Baker said, that the enforcement of conscription would result in 'desperate resistance and bloodshed in southern Ireland, requiring large forces to secure few unwilling recruits, with [the] complete paralysis of food production in the island'.[59] Baker thought that it was unlikely that Ireland would accept any form of Home Rule proposed by the government while the conscription issue threatened. Plunkett and Dillon felt that the government would have to abandon conscription, allow the situation to ease, grant some kind of self-government, and hope for some voluntary recruiting. Baker viewed the situation as very dangerous both for the war effort and for the future of the British Empire.

While Baker's report was being cabled to Washington the British government was working to enlist the assistance of the United States government in the arrest of the leaders of Sinn Féin and the suppression of the anti-conscription movement. Documents showing Irish–German collusion were sent to the State Department. Ostensibly for intelligence reasons the British thought it essential that the documents be released in the United States rather than in Britain, and Reading was instructed to use all his influence to see that the documents got the widest possible publicity.[60] When the documents arrived at the State Department, however, Lansing was unwilling to comply with the British request. He told the President that the documents were 'translations of decoded German messages relating to the Sinn Féiners' intercourse with the German Government through Sinn Féin agents in this country prior and subsequent to the rebellious outbreak at Dublin at Easter time in 1916'. Lansing noted that it would be advantageous for British security reasons to have the documents published in America, but he regarded it as 'impolitic' and advised against it. 'The Irish situation is very delicate,' the Secretary told Wilson, 'and anything which we might do to aid either side in the controversy would, I fear, involve us in all sorts of difficulties with the Irish in this country.' He was certain that such action would be 'construed as a direct assistance to Great Britain in the matter of conscription in Ireland,' and he was 'loath to involve this country in the quarrel'.[61] The following day Page was given the President's instructions to inform the British government that the State Department would not release the documents.

Lord Reading informed his government that the handling of the whole affair had caused 'annoyance' in high circles in Washington, although Lansing had said that the fact that the documents dealt with Irish–German activities before the United States entered the war made it 'impossible for them to act'.[62] President Wilson had been reluctant to intervene in the conscription crisis to come to the assistance of either the British government or Lord Mayor O'Neill. Indeed, Sir William Wiseman reported to Sir Eric Drummond that Wilson told him that he 'hoped the Government would not force Conscription without Home Rule'. When Wiseman suggested that they were separate problems Wilson replied that this would not be appreciated throughout the United States.[63] Wilson made it clear that he wished the British government would solve the Irish question, although he himself felt that he could play no part in its solution.

The Irish-American reaction to the conscription crisis was mixed and complex. A number of prominent Irish-Americans from the Boston area, interviewed by the *Christian Science Monitor*, revealed diverse attitudes towards conscription although they agreed on the necessity of Home Rule. A former governor of Massachusetts, David I. Walsh, then standing as a candidate for the United States Senate, observed: 'A people that have no rights in time of peace, have no responsibilities in time of war'—although once given Home Rule the Irish would fight for freedom as they had always done. Daniel J. Gallagher, assistant district attorney for Suffolk County, Edward F. McLaughlin, state senator from Boston, Michael J. Jordan, national secretary of the UIL, and John F. Dever of the Charitable Irish Society of Boston all took a cautious and moderate view—that the war must be won, that Ireland must support it, but that England must grant Home Rule first. On the other hand, some Irish-Americans insisted that to support Sinn Féin in Ireland—with its pro-German and anti-war attitudes—in its efforts to resist conscription was to betray one's loyalty to the United States. Patrick Ford, Jr, denounced the treachery of his brother Robert E. Ford, editor of the *Irish World*, to Tumulty, exclaiming that 'the independence of Ireland would not be worth purchasing by a disloyal act toward' the United States. Similarly the editor of the Boston *Post*, P. J. Lynch, reported to Tumulty his scolding of Séamas MacManus for the latter's continued obsession with Ireland in the midst of the war. Major Eugene F. Kinkead, who later took an active part in Irish-American agitation himself, wrote to President Wilson that the FOIF were expected to be of service to America rather than disruptive.[64] In San Francisco Garret W. McEnerney, a leading lawyer, speaking at a testimonial dinner for T. P. O'Connor, said that support for any movement in Ireland that sought to weaken England was now 'treasonable to the people and to the government of this country'. Senator Thomas of Colorado reported in the Senate that Irish-American meetings in Chattanooga and St Louis had endorsed conscription for Ireland. Senator Phelan of California attempted to keep the views of Home Rulers such as O'Connor before both Wilson and Lansing throughout the summer of 1918. More actively moderating influences were to be found in the efforts of Senator Thomas J. Walsh of Montana, who attempted to convince his constituents of the importance of the war effort and the virtues of Irish self-government within the British Empire.[65]

The revolutionary Irish-American nationalists found in conscription, which was resisted by a substantially united Ireland, an issue they would vigorously assault. The *Gaelic American*, the

Irish World and the *Irish Press,* though barred from the mails, be-
gan immediately to inform the Irish-American community of the
infamy of conscription without consent. Through Dr W. J. M. A.
Maloney, Joseph McGarrity and Dr Patrick McCartan, articles
explaining the Irish point of view were published in the New York
Evening Post, the New York *Globe* and the Philadelphia *Public
Ledger.*[66] On 4 May some 15,000 Irish-Americans met in Madison
Square Garden in New York to hear speeches by the Rev. A. A.
Berle and Congressmen W. Bourke Cockran and John J. Fitzgerald.
Peter Golden sent a telegram to President Wilson on behalf of the
meeting asking him to intercede in order to save the Irish people
from the extermination which would be the result of conscription
forced by Britain. Mrs Sheehy-Skeffington, then touring the country,
spoke out against conscription in Ireland, although she was tem-
porarily incapacitated by her arrest in San Francisco on 28 April.
To register an official protest against conscription, Dr McCartan,
acting in his capacity as the IRB-sponsored 'Envoy of the Provisional Government of Ireland', presented a long memorandum
to the Department of State, denying the right of the British to draft
Irishmen into their army and pointing out both the burden such
a cruel device would be on the Irish people and the inconsistency
it posed to the war aims of the Allies.[67]

Largely through the efforts of the aggressive leaders of the IPL,
the FOIF called an Irish Race Convention, to be held in New York
on 18 and 19 May 1918. Its purposes were to endorse President
Wilson's war aims, to assert that there was no conceivable way in
which the claim for Irish independence could be excluded from the
objectives of the war, to state clearly that England would be
expected to honour the rights of small nations after the war, and to
protest against the anti-Irish campaign being carried on in the
United States. The convention was addressed by Mrs Sheehy-
Skeffington, James Larkin, Dr Patrick McCartan, Diarmuid Lynch,
Liam Mellows, Pádraic Colum, John Devoy, Judge Cohalan and
several Irish-American leaders; Father Thomas J. Hurton served
as chairman. The Very Rev. Peter E. Magennis was elected national
president of the FOIF, and Diarmuid Lynch national secretary.
Speeches were made supporting self-determination for Ireland,
condemning conscription and the alleged 'German plot', and denouncing England as the 'single enemy' of Ireland. A petition was
proposed by Judge Goff supporting Ireland's case for independence,
and it was later presented to President Wilson's secretary.[68] The
convention closed with a careful speech by Judge Cohalan asking
the audience 'not to lose their heads' and stressing the importance
of 'Americanism' during the war.[69] The importance of the 1918

Irish Race Convention was that it rallied the revolutionary Irish-American nationalists around an active programme after a very demoralising year.

Although there was still a reluctance on the part of many to be too bold in advocating the Irish cause, some steps were taken. Under the effective leadership of Diarmuid Lynch the FOIF began to reassert itself more fully in Irish agitation. By late August Mellows wrote to Golden that Lynch 'appears to be doing well' at strengthening the organisation. The FOIF and the Irish Progressive League kept up their campaigns of letters and memorials to politicians.[70] One of the projects begun at the convention was the attempt of Mrs Mary F. McWhorter, president of the Ladies' Auxiliary of the AOH, to lead a group of Irish-American mothers who had sons in the war to see President Wilson in order to ask him to oppose Irish conscription. Mrs McWhorter's 'Mothers' Mission' was successfully put off by the President, although she finally met Tumulty and presented him with a petition with 600,000 signatures and an eight-page letter reviewing the course of English misrule in Ireland and the injustices of conscription authorised by a foreign government. The IPL continued to labour throughout the summer of 1918 to raise money for an information bureau in Washington in order to establish an effective lobby which could bring sustained pressure to bear on the government.[71] By late September, when it was certain that the war was drawing to a close, the Clan na Gael held its national conference to draft its future programme. The Clan re-emphasised the determination of the Irish in America to see that Wilson apply to Ireland at the Peace Conference those principles of self-determination which he had so bravely proclaimed during the war. But the revolutionary nationalist movement still functioned on the edge of the law. In October and November the eminently respectable Jesuit weekly *America* was barred from the mails by the Postmaster-General for the publication of a series of articles on the Irish question by Dr Maloney.[72]

Nearer to home Irish nationalists in the United States found there were really two conscription crises. The more prominent crisis resulted, of course, from the British government's attempts to extend conscription to Ireland. But there was another, less obvious crisis which was brought about by the measures taken by the United States government to bring into military service the resident nationals of co-belligerent countries. The United States had introduced conscription shortly after it entered the war, and by early 1918 the British and American governments had negotiated a reciprocal agreement whereby aliens either had to return home or submit to the draft in the country in which they were then residing. The FOIF had attempted to defend Irish expatriates living in the United States in 1917 from the normal conscription procedures, but their position would be less secure from 1918 on. This presented a predicament to political exiles such as Dr McCartan or Liam Mellows, so McCartan wrote to the Secretary of State on 17 February outlining the problems of Irish exiles, exempt from conscription in Ireland, who might be forced to fight in alliance with Great Britain. Although Lansing made no comment on the letter, Congressman Mason read McCartan's objections in Congress and argued that the conscription of Irishmen in the United States was wrong, and Congressmen McCormick, Gallagher, Mason, McLaughlin, Morin, Kennedy and Cary and Congresswoman Rankin all attempted to block the treaty which would make Irishmen in America eligible for the draft, but were unsuccessful in doing so. Although Dr McCartan wrote letters to Irish nationals living in the United States telling them that because the 'Provisional Government' of Ireland was not at war they were exempt from military service in America, by the late summer of 1918 they had begun to register. But to make things as painless as possible it was decreed by the Director of the Draft in New York, Martin Conboy, that aliens registering for conscription could list the 'Republic of Ireland' as their native country if they wished.[73]

American newspapers condemned Irish resistance to conscription outright. The Buffalo *Express* and the *Ohio State Journal* felt that Ireland was making a stand at the wrong time over the wrong issue; in the war crisis there could be no room for such domestic problems. American support for Ireland would be greater after the war, said the Kansas City *Times*, if Ireland accepted conscription and fought. The St Louis *Post-Dispatch* asked why Irishmen in the United States had to accept conscription if Irishmen in Ireland be permitted to resist it. More passionate criticism came from the New York *Herald*, which said that if the Irish did not have the intelligence to understand that the defeat of Britain in the war would mean the subjugation of Ireland, they did not have the intelligence to be given Home Rule. The New York *World* carried this argument further by saying: 'In lending aid and comfort, for their own mistaken purposes to the enemy of England, they were not restrained by the knowledge that they were lending aid and comfort to the enemy of France and the United States.'[74] The *Christian Science Monitor* asserted that the Catholic conspiracy was behind the crisis and, indeed, pointed to Cardinal Logue in Ireland, Cardinal Begin of Quebec and Archbishop Mannix of Australia as the sources of resistance to conscription throughout the British Empire. The projected visit of the Lord Mayor of Dublin provoked an equally hostile reaction. The New York *Times* felt the visit was impudent and that O'Neill would be as welcome in the United States as the 'Chief Burgomaster of Berlin'. The *Christian Science Monitor* said that the Lord Mayor was 'likely to find Mr Wilson extremely un-sympathetic on the subject of Professor DeValera's German ally'. If the Irish did not like conscription, they could appeal to their friends in Germany, said the Detroit *Free Press*.[75]

If not general throughout the press, there was some sympathy or understanding of the Irish nationalist point of view, but even that in many cases was qualified. The New York *Evening Post* warned against any attempt to force conscription on the people and lamented that there had not been better communications between the British government and the Irish leaders. The alternative to conscription of allowing Irishmen to volunteer in the American army was suggested by the New York *Commercial*, and the Chicago *Daily News* thought that opposition to conscription was not neces-sarily opposition to the war. The Brooklyn *Eagle*, however, ques-tioned whether there was anything to the 'German plot' or if it were all just talk.[76]

The attitude of native Americans to the rejection of conscription by the Irish was inevitable in the context of the war. Certainly the tensions and the psychology of the war made objective considera-tions of the peculiarities of the Irish situation difficult for those Americans without a detailed knowledge of the circumstances. On 18 April Peter Golden wrote to a number of senators and repre-sentatives telling them that the conscription bill had been passed 'without asking the consent of a single Irish man or woman' and noting that such an act was contrary to the principles for which President Wilson had said the United States was fighting. He added that he did not think the congressmen would allow the country to become a 'partner in such infamy as the English Government seems determined to carry out in Ireland'.[77] The replies were in large part indignant and self-righteous. Senator William H. King of Utah, who had attacked the Irish earlier in the Senate, said that the United States was fighting for 'liberty and civilization' and that if Golden was 'trying to stir up rebellion in Ireland you are an enemy to this Country and to civilization'. King thought the IPL ought to disband and its members 'learn something of Americanism and their duty to America'. Senator Asle J. Gronna of North Dakota answered that Americans had made the supreme sacrifice in joining the war and that everyone must work for victory; after the war there would be 'liberty of every nation and every land—for all humanity'. Golden did receive some consolation from Congressmen H. C.

Claypool and Denver S. Church, both of whom objected to conscription of any kind. But the situation was more realistically
appraised by Senator William L. LaFollette, who said that he had
noted that President Wilson had not included Ireland in his speeches
about the small nations of Europe because Ireland was part of one
of America's allies in the war. LaFollette thought Golden could
hardly expect the government to challenge Britain about the conscription of Irishmen when the United States itself was conscripting
the former citizens of the Central European powers.[78]

Private opinion seemed largely to reflect that of the politicians.
A group of indignant citizens from Fort Morgan, Colorado, sent a
telegram to President Wilson insisting: 'All loyal Americans have
accepted the draft. Why shouldn't Ireland accept it?' They protested against the Lord Mayor's proposed trip to Washington and
asked that he be denied permission to enter the United States. That
a shift in American opinion was taking place was certain. Charles
McCarthy commented to Plunkett that there was a reversion to the
nativist, anti-Irish and anti-Catholic passions of the nineteenth
century:

> I find that there is a great anger in America against the Irish, and
> many old class prejudices are being aroused. There is a good deal
> of an anti-Catholic movment [sic], as I judge it, based upon the
> idea that priests are dictating policies in Ireland. . . . I do hope
> that something can be done to bring them into the war very
> soon.[79]

Indeed, the rising white Anglo-Saxon Protestant hostility that
McCarthy observed was to help shape native American attitudes
towards Ireland for the next few years. Shane Leslie reported to
John Dillon that the arrests and the 'German plot' had been very
damaging to the American image of Ireland. 'The unthinking and,
unfortunately, the patriotic American, has swallowed it whole,' he
said regretfully.[80] A growing consensus in America held that the
Irish were expected to step forward and do their duty to the cause
of world freedom just as Americans and others were doing. To
argue or object or refuse, either in Ireland or the United States, was
treasonable.

To a number of people in the United States and Ireland who
shared an interest in the satisfactory resolution of the Irish question
the refusal of the Irish people to accept conscription, or after 1916
to volunteer in any great numbers, seemed a disaster which would
prejudice Ireland's case either with Great Britain or with the
anticipated Peace Conference. In fact the Irish refusal to join
enthusiastically in the war created suspicions in Britain and the

E

United States that Ireland could not be trusted with self-government or that Ireland did not deserve it. To forestall these suspicions and to rehabilitate Ireland in the eyes of the Allied powers, as well as to augment the war effort, several plans were proposed to enable Irishmen to join the American army or for Irish nurses to serve in American hospitals. Such solutions, it was hoped, would utilise Irish manpower but would avoid the psychological impasse of forcing Irishmen to fight 'England's war'.

The first suggestions were mooted before the conscription crisis when a retired colonel of the 18th Royal Irish Regiment, J. Eustace Jameson, then an organiser of the Territorial Association of Ireland, offered to raise an 'Irish American Foreign Legion' in Ireland. Discussions were begun as early as June 1917 with General Pershing's *aide-de-camp* and were carried on both in England and America with E. M. House and Tumulty. Colonel Jameson's plans varied, but essentially the legion was seen as consisting of both Irishmen and Americans who would train in Ireland and fight under the American flag. Tumulty had Jameson's proposal appraised by several people in the War Department, who saw considerable difficulties but who felt that the British government would have to give its approval before serious consideration could begin. The British government had already considered Jameson's ideas and rejected them; the Army Council decided that no such scheme involving the training of American troops on Irish soil could be approved until the United States government agreed to train troops throughout the United Kingdom; furthermore, it was felt that Jameson 'should not be employed for recruiting of any kind in connection with this country'.[81]

A similar sort of plan was proposed to Tumulty in June by Charles McCarthy, who was in England on behalf of the government during the summer of 1918. He was invited to Ireland by Lord French, the Lord Lieutenant, where he developed his idea that if Irishmen could be induced to join Irish-American regiments in the American army or if Irishwomen could be employed to work in American hospitals or if wounded Americans could be sent to Ireland to convalesce, the 'bitterly anti-Irish' feeling in the United States might be reversed. He discussed his ideas with George Russell and Sir Horace Plunkett, the latter of whom thought that Irishmen in the American army would help to drive the North and South further apart by strengthening republican sympathies and encouraging sentiments hostile to Britain and the Empire, and this might in the future involve the United States in Anglo-Irish quarrels. Back again in the United States, McCarthy sent his recommendations to the Secretary of State and subsequently to E. M. House, who forwarded them to the President. Wilson did not think much of either McCarthy or his recommendations for recruiting Irish troops or Irish nurses. McCarthy's proposals, like those of Colonel Jameson, were allowed to drop. What sort of influence an Irish legion would have had in the war is, of course, impossible to say, but at a time when the United States was assembling Polish and Czechoslovak legions it was not an outlandish idea.[82]

Less complicated or controversial plans were also rejected. Colonel Arthur Murray, Assistant Military Attaché at the British Embassy in Washington, worked out a scheme in early 1918 to have various Irish-American regiments simply land at Cork and march through Ireland on their way to France. This met the approval of the American War Department and the General Staff, and the *Mauretania* was actually scheduled to transport the selected regiments, but the British government refused to give its permission. Walter I. Austin of Dorchester, Massachusetts, wrote to Wilson that American troops might be allowed to garrison Ireland in order to relieve British troops for the front lines. Tumulty, although he told Wilson that the letter might be a trick to draw the President out on the Irish question, replied that the suggestion would be brought to Wilson's attention. In late August 1918 Plunkett talked with Lord French about how to deal with the problem, and as a result began work on the idea first raised by Charles McCarthy to get Irish nurses to serve in American hospitals. Plunkett went to France where the American Army Medical Service flatly rejected the offer, but through Lord French he obtained General Pershing's qualified approval. The British government and the Irish Office, however, were concerned that the Irish nurses might use the opportunity to spread anti-British propaganda among the American troops.[83] In the end no special units were created.

American intervention in the war placed the Irish question in a critical position in the minds of many Americans, but the priorities of the war itself made any political solution to the Irish question— certainly any solution emanating from the United States—almost impossible. Indeed, as United States involvement increased, the climate for revolutionary Irish-American nationalists deteriorated to the extent that many felt themselves to be persecuted, while the remaining moderate constitutionalists were fatally undercut by the failure of the Irish Convention, the conscription crisis, and the unwillingness of either the British or the United States governments to form any special military units which might have attracted public sympathy. Thus, despite the recognised merits of Irish nationalist claims, despite the participation of thousands of Irishmen and Irish-Americans in the British and American armies, despite the endlessly repeated war aims of the Allied powers concerning the rights of small nations and making the world safe for democracy, the end of the war found the Irish nationalist cause in serious difficulties with the authorities at home, in Britain and in the United States.

CHAPTER 5
IRELAND AND THE PARIS PEACE CONFERENCE
1919

THE Peace Conference was the final phase of the war crisis, and the Irish-American nationalists understood full well, as did many similar nationalist groups in the United States, that if their war goals were to be achieved at all, it would have to be through the machinery of the conference. Not surprisingly, President Wilson, who of all the leaders of the Allied powers had been the foremost spokesman for the principle of self-determination, became the focal point of the Irish nationalist movement, along with many other nationalist movements as well. In the United States enormous efforts—direct and indirect, congressional and diplomatic, public and private—were expended to win Wilson's open support at the conference for the Irish cause as it had been won for the Polish nationalist movement.[1] The President's preference to work unofficially or to rely on the League of Nations to solve the Irish and other problems, rather than to challenge the British openly on the Irish issue, sharpened antagonisms between Wilson and the Irish-American leaders which pre-dated the war. Even before the details of the league and the Versailles Treaty were fully announced the reaction, bitter and destructive, had begun. The Irish-American nationalist leaders joined forces with Wilson's opponents in the Senate and throughout the country to co-operate in a campaign presumably to save both the United States and Ireland from the pitfalls of the league.

Indeed, quite apart from the Irish question, the league and the treaty stirred up a whirlwind of controversy within the United States. Not only had Wilson made some serious political blunders in the congressional elections of 1918, having refused to recognise that the balance of power in the Senate had shifted to the Republicans, but he also committed the country to several obligations which the Senate and the people of the United States had never previously found to be acceptable. One such obligation was imposed by Article X of the league covenant, which was thought to commit the United States to defend the territorial status quo of its fellow league members, many of whom were imperialist powers who might be expected to be faced with insurrections. Furthermore, Article XI and several other articles were understood to commit the United States to military action by the orders of the league, thereby disregarding the constitution of the United States, which stated that only Congress could declare war and commit troops. Irish-American nationalists were able to mount a very large and effective campaign which successfully exploited these fears which genuinely existed in Congress and in the country. However, these activities, carried out on blatantly ethnic lines, provoked a reaction of their own among native Americans who felt that the interests of the United States were being subordinated to those of foreign interests.

I.   The Mobilisation of Irish-American Opinion

The end of the war allowed the Irish-American nationalists to resume their energetic efforts in promoting the Irish cause without the stigma of weakening the war effort or the insinuation that they were disloyal to the United States. President Wilson's idealistic pronouncements during the war had encouraged them to view the Peace Conference as a congress of the great powers to create a new world order rather than as a diplomatic meeting of the Allied victors to draft a peace treaty for the defeated countries. Thus their primary object was to enlist the support of President Wilson in making Irish self-determination one of the items of the Paris Peace Conference, and indeed throughout most of 1919 Wilson was at the centre of Irish-American agitation. In addition to presenting direct personal appeals to the President, the Irish-American nationalist leaders worked to create nation-wide agitation which would compel Wilson to lend his support to Ireland, and to carry out part of this goal they made substantial efforts to enlist congressional support to attempt to force the President to intercede for Ireland. However, to do all these things systematically the nationalist movement in the United States, having suffered a considerable blow during the war, had to be rebuilt and new funds raised.

Appeals directly to Wilson and other leading politicians began almost within hours of the armistice. As the result of a mass meeting held by the IPL in New York on 12 November 1918 to demand that the United States recognise the Irish Republic and to protest against the imprisonment in Britain of Sinn Féin leaders, Pádraic Colum attempted to lead a delegation to see President Wilson to make their appeal in person. By the end of November the FOIF delivered a memorial to the White House asking that Ireland be dealt with favourably at the Peace Conference. Congressman Joseph McLaughlin, as national president of the AOH, sent President Wilson resolutions endorsing 'self-determination' for Ireland and he urged that the Peace Conference consider the Irish question. A more successful appeal was sent by Senator Thomas J. Walsh of Montana, who gave Wilson copies of several letters on the Irish question along with one signed by the Lieutenant-Governor of Montana and fifty-four other civic leaders. He also expressed his own view that Britain's Home Rule policy and capitulation to the Ulster extremists had been 'discreditable', and he urged Wilson, once he reached the conference, to 'impress upon them [the British government] the necessity for a speedy solution of the question of self-government for Ireland'. If Ireland were ignored at the Peace Conference, Walsh wrote, Anglo-American relations would be jeopardised by disgruntled Americans.[2]

President Wilson's attitude after the armistice towards Irish nationalism was still one of sympathy. He replied to Senator Walsh on 3 December 1918, shortly before he left for Paris:

> I appreciate the importance of a proper solution of the Irish question and thank you for the suggestions of your letter of yesterday. Until I get on the other side and find my footing in delicate matters of this sort I cannot forecast with any degree of confidence what influence I can exercise, but you may be sure that I shall keep this important interest in mind and shall use my influence at every opportunity to bring about a just and satis-factory solution.[3]

Wilson also told Bishop Shahan of the Catholic University of America that he would use every opportunity he found to bring about a resolution of the Irish question according to the principles for which the war had been fought. But while sympathetic and willing to make the best of any opportunity that presented itself, Wilson was not, according to Tumulty, willing to imperil the work of the entire conference or Anglo-American co-operation in order to force an Irish settlement. In short, in Tumulty's opinion Wilson was not willing, as the Irish-American nationalists increasingly insisted he must be, to make the Irish question the '*sine qua non*' of the Peace Conference. In lieu of some immediate British initiative in which he might give assistance Wilson saw the League of Nations as the ultimate instrument by which he could induce the British to satisfy Irish aspirations. Largely on this issue Wilson's relations with the Irish-American leaders deteriorated. Actually by late December, perhaps increasingly aware of the many requests that were being put upon the President, Secretary Lansing began to have some misgivings about the implications of Wilson's use of the term 'self-determination'. Querying its effect on the nationalist movements in Ireland, India and Egypt, he confided to his diary on 30 December that the phrase was 'loaded with dynamite', that it would 'raise hopes which can never be realized', and that, indeed, it was certain to discredit the President.[4] But, as Lansing began to perceive, it was too late for second thoughts about self-determination.

In addition to the agitation and demands of the Irish-Americans, Wilson also had to take account of the changed circumstances in Ireland after the 'khaki' election of December 1918, which resulted in an overwhelming Sinn Féin victory and the first sitting of Dáil Éireann, which immediately declared its independence from Great Britain. As a result of these developments, Wilson sent George Creel, formerly head of the War Information Bureau and currently Wilson's roving trouble-shooter in Europe, to Ireland to investigate the political situation there. Creel talked with a number of Irish leaders, including Collins and Boland, and he found them to be more flexible in their demands than the Irish-Americans. He sent a report to Wilson on 1 March 1919 in which he said that the Sinn Féin victory in Ireland had been extensive except in four Ulster counties. Home Rule was 'discredited' and a republic was being demanded, although few seriously thought they would get a republic. Creel believed that if the British government gave Ireland dominion status immediately, it would be accepted, but if the government delayed, 'sentiment in Ireland and America will harden in favor of an Irish republic'. He warned of Lloyd George's duplicity in the Irish matter and stressed the vital importance of a settlement in order for Wilson to placate the aggressive Irish-American nationalists.[5]

Irish-American nationalists exerted large-scale efforts to extract from Congress statements expressing sympathy for Irish self-government and instructions to Wilson to raise the Irish matter at the Peace Conference. In early December 1918 several resolutions were introduced in Congress calling for the assistance of President Wilson and the American delegation at the Peace Conference in obtaining self-determination or independence for Ireland.[6] Resolutions had often been introduced in Congress dealing with the Irish question, but they had normally been sent to the House of Representatives Foreign Affairs Committee, where they were forgotten. However, on this occasion public congressional hearings on the Gallagher resolution, asking that the American Commission to Negotiate Peace present to the conference 'the right of Ireland to freedom, independence and self-determination', were scheduled by the committee for 12 and 13 December. Over sixty sympathetic witnesses from the major Irish-American centres in the country came to testify in favour of Ireland's claim to self-government. Twelve congressmen, three state legislators, several union leaders, two college presidents and a large number of official representatives of Irish nationalist organisations attended. These witnesses argued that the resolution should be adopted because the United States owed Ireland support in 1918 for the Irish aid during the American Revolution of the 1770s, because Allied war declarations to permit suppressed nationalities governments of their choice should be applied to Ireland, and because the Ulster question was an artificial one created by the British. The House committee also received almost two hundred letters, telegrams, petitions, memorials and resolutions, and it accepted from the witnesses large amounts of printed material, including, ironically, Dr Maloney's 'Ireland's plea for freedom', which had caused the Jesuit magazine *America* to be banned from the mails a few months earlier, and an important speech on Ireland by Cardinal O'Connell. All these items, as well as the testimony given at the hearings, were specially printed as a separate volume by the government as a House document, and 5,000 copies were distributed.[7] One hostile witness, George L. Fox, the indefatigable anti-Irish propagandist from New Haven, attempted to refute the assertions of the Irish-Americans, but of the two days' hearings he was given only twenty minutes, during which time he was badly baited and badgered by the committee.[8]

By the end of December committee chairman Flood informed Tumulty that the sentiment in the House was so strong as to make the passage of some sort of resolution on the Irish question a certainty. Wilson was not pleased by the prospect of the House expressing an opinion on Ireland, and he told Tumulty that such a measure would be an embarrassment to him.[9] Through the influence of Tumulty at the White House and Polk at the Department of State Gallagher was prevailed upon to change the wording from a claim for 'freedom' and 'independence' to merely 'self-determination'. The resolution came before the House during the late evening of 3–4 March, as the session of Congress was drawing to a close. Through the shrewd parliamentary efforts of Congressmen Gallivan, Mann, McLaughlin and Flood the resolution was placed in a favourable position on the calendar, well ahead of other more important business. It was supported in debate by many of the same arguments expressed at the committee hearings: America's debt to Ireland, the war aims, and Irish nationality and historical claims. Its opponents said that passage of the resolution would disrupt the unity of the Allies, embarrass Wilson and meddle in the affairs of Great Britain. Ireland, it was pointed out, was part of an Allied power, not defeated Germany or outcast Russia to whom orders could be given. The resolution was passed by a vote of 216 to 45 in the small hours of the morning as the session closed. But it was passed too late to receive the required action from the Senate. Alan J. Ward has suggested that Congress regarded the mildly phrased resolution as merely a gesture of sympathy and nothing more.[10]

Irish-American nationalists continued to deluge their congressmen with petitions, memorials and resolutions demanding that Ireland be given self-determination and that the American government intercede in Paris to see that this was done. Dutiful senators and representatives had these items read into the *Congressional Record*, thus to be distributed across the country. Irish-Americans were also able to extract resolutions from various state legislatures requesting President Wilson to use his good offices at the Peace Conference to see that self-determination was applied to Ireland. Massachusetts, Wisconsin, Rhode Island, New Hampshire and Nevada all sent their official appeals to the President.[11]

Irish-American nationalists were by no means idle in the weeks after the armistice. Their immediate task was to rebuild their demoralised organisations to their pre-war strength in order to make the Irish-American ethnic group an effective political pressure bloc. This they did through a series of spectacular public meetings throughout the country. The first effort to bring the Irish question back into the public mind and to start the local Irish nationalist organisations again working openly and without apology was made by the national council of the FOIF which planned 'Self-Determination for Ireland Week' to be held throughout the country from 8 to 15 December 1918. During the week meetings were held in various cities demanding that the United States support Irish national aspirations. The largest and most important of these meetings was held in Madison Square Garden in New York on 10 December and featured as the principal speaker Cardinal O'Connell of Boston. To an audience of over 25,000 people the cardinal said that the Allied leaders had told the people that the war had been fought for justice, the rights of small nations and the right of self-determination. 'The war can be justified only by the universal application of those principles,' he said. 'Let that application begin with Ireland.'[12] In saying that Ireland was the test of the sincerity of the Allies, the cardinal unquestionably spoke for the majority of interested Irish-Americans. What was of importance was that a member of the hierarchy had made such a speech in public; it marked a significant public shift from the Church's wartime policy of forbidding Irish agitation. The meeting, as did others, passed resolutions which were cabled to President Wilson, then on his way to Paris, asking him to obtain self-determination for Ireland.[13]

News in late December of the significant election victory in Ireland of the Sinn Féin candidates worked as a rationale for further mass meetings in the United States to promote the Irish question. Although there was some division among the nationalist leaders as to how the victory should be interpreted, Irish-American nationalists met under the auspices of the Clan na Gael in New York on 5 January 1919 and there provided a platform for Dr McCartan to announce that the Irish Republic had separated itself from Great Britain. McCartan also pointed out that the Polish-Americans had sent $8,000,000 to Poland, and he asked the Irish-Americans to do the same or better for Ireland. Judge Cohalan avoided mention of an 'Irish Republic' and confined his remarks at the meeting to Irish self-determination, as did Liam Mellows. The following evening, 6 January, the IPL held another public meeting in New York where the idea of an 'Irish Republic' was more enthusiastically received. This meeting significantly drew to the platform several native American liberals, the Rev. Norman Thomas and Dr Lovejoy Elliott among them, who had not previously been associated with the Irish movement.[14]

In late 1918 the Irish-American leaders called the third Irish Race Convention in Philadelphia for 22 and 23 February 1919 for the purposes of unifying the Irish community in the United States and demonstrating to American politicians the political significance in America of the Irish question, although they disagreed among themselves as to what kind of a nationalist programme to promote in Ireland. To make the greatest possible impact on the American public a broad spectrum of opinions was represented among the speakers. In addition to those Irish-American nationalist leaders whose presence might be expected, Michael J. Ryan of the defunct Redmondite UIL was invited to give a major address, and several native American politicians, including Senator William E. Borah, Governor Sproul of Pennsylvania and Mayor Smith of Philadelphia, spoke or made introductions. This bringing together of the left and right wings of American political life was, perhaps, due less to the universal appeal of the Irish cause than to the convenience of the Irish cause as a means of striking at the compromise peace that the Versailles Treaty represented—a compromise that satisfied neither the radicals who had wanted the treaty to be agent of social change nor the conservatives who had wanted the treaty to re-establish the old order. To balance the large number of Catholic clergymen participating, the socialist-Presbyterian Rev. Norman Thomas, the Episcopalian Rev. James Grattan Mythen and the

Jewish Rabbi Joseph Krauskopf lent an ecumenical tone to the programme. The most important guest at the convention was Cardinal Gibbons of Baltimore, perhaps the most influential member of the Catholic hierarchy, who introduced resolutions calling on President Wilson to use his influence to see that Ireland got self-determination and that Ireland's representatives were given a hearing at the Peace Conference. The convention also created the Irish Victory Fund which was designed to raise over $1,000,000 for the purpose of financing political agitation in the United States and Ireland (the exact purpose of the fund became a source of bitter disagreement when de Valera wanted to use it to finance the Dáil government).[15]

The Irish Race Convention also appointed a delegation to meet President Wilson to enlist his direct support in obtaining Irish self-determination. Wilson was back in the United States in part of February and March to deal with legislation as the 65th Congress came to a close, and he was unwilling to see the delegation because of the shortness of time, in spite of appeals from Senator Walsh and Congresswoman Rankin. Tumulty finally obtained permission to arrange a meeting in New York on 4 March, after a speech at the Metropolitan Opera House on the eve of the President's return to France, but only after reasserting the President's earlier assurances to Senator Walsh and Bishop Shahan and emphasising the extent to which a refusal to see the delegation would play into the hands of Wilson's opponents.[16] However, at the meeting Wilson was upset by the presence of Judge Cohalan, who because of pre-1917 Irish–German activities was still tinged with disloyalty, and refused to see the delegation until the judge withdrew. He was further disconcerted to find that the delegation wanted not merely to present him with the resolutions of the convention but to obtain from him some assurance that he would advocate the Irish cause in Paris. Wilson did say that he was sympathetic to their feelings about Ireland, but that he was unable to exercise much influence over the domestic policy of other governments, and that he could not be held responsible for any course of action in this regard. The results of the meeting were unfortunate: Wilson had been badly provoked by the Irish-Americans, and they, in turn, were disappointed with Wilson's apparent lack of good faith about self-determination.[17]

It should be emphasised at this point that not all American opinion on Ireland after the armistice was represented by the struggles of the Irish-American nationalist leaders to win Wilson's advocacy. Fairly divergent views existed in various quarters about what position America should take towards Ireland. One abortive

effort to mould American opinion in favour of a moderate solution
to the Irish question, along the lines proposed by Sir Horace
Plunkett, was led by such people as Dr H. N. MacCracken,
president of Vassar College, J. O'Hara Cosgrave, an editor of the
New York *World*, Lieutenant-Colonel G. P. Ahern, secretary of
the Army War College, Charles McCarthy and John Quinn.[18]
Although many of the group were of Irish descent, they were outside the conventional nationalist movements and in fact represented
a financially and socially successful element in the Irish-American
community which despised the Irish 'political bosses' as typified by
Judge Cohalan. The group originally assembled before the end of
the war to endorse a programme supporting Home Rule; but within
three months they had established working committees and raised
some money with which to start a publicity campaign, in part co-
ordinated with Plunkett's trip to America in early 1919. Indeed,
McCarthy had on his own initiative written to House and Lansing
in September and, more forcefully, to Dr Sidney E. Mezes, director
of Wilson's research staff at the Peace Conference, in December.[19]

By the end of 1918 the moderate group found itself eclipsed by
the resurgence of Irish-American nationalism, and in the long run
the appeal of self-determination and the moderate tone of the Irish
Race Convention weakened their momentum. In January 1919
there were growing divisions as to whether they should continue to
talk in terms of imperial Home Rule, which some felt was a discredited concept, or whether they should shift to self-determination
which coincided with Wilson's wartime language. By the end of the
month they decided to halt their activities. Cosgrave related to
McCarthy that the feeling was that 'At this juncture moderation
seems out of the game,' and that their efforts to promote Home
Rule were out of step with the current popular appeal of self-
determination and the more radical trend of events in Ireland, so
that their movement would thus appear 'moderate and plutocratic'.[20]
Although they continued to feel that an Irish republic was out of
the question, and indeed that self-determination had its pitfalls for
a united Ireland, they supported Plunkett and trusted to President
Wilson to save the situation.

Other native Americans came to the conclusion that the Irish
question had to be resolved for reasons of expediency. Although in
January Acting Secretary of State Frank L. Polk had told Senator
Duncan U. Fletcher that Ulster would present an obstacle to any
settlement, by mid-March he and Assistant Secretary of State
William Phillips confessed to Plunkett that an 'immediate settlement' of the Irish situation was necessary to stop the hostility in
some sections of the United States that was growing towards the

League of Nations. A group of senators (Peter C. Gerry, David I. Walsh, Key Pittman, John B. Kendrick and Thomas J. Walsh) wrote to Wilson saying that both the League of Nations and the Democratic Party would be badly hurt if the Peace Conference closed without any progress made on the Irish question. W. W. Durbin, a Democratic state executive chairman, warned Tumulty that the Irish-Americans were threatening the league and defecting from the Democratic Party with the possible view to starting an Irish-American party. President Wilson was advised by Thomas L. Chadbourne that, although he had no more interest in Ireland than he did in Poland or Yugoslavia, it was vital for the future of the Democratic Party that the Peace Conference take some steps to deal equitably with Ireland. But probably few native Americans took the position of Congressman William E. Mason of Illinois, who told John Devoy that Irish self-determination was 'not an Irish question, it is not an English question, it is purely a question of American honour'. Mason reasoned that because both the Germans and the Allies had accepted Wilson's fourteen-point programme, the United States was under a moral obligation to see that the principle was applied equitably all round.[21]

Meanwhile anti-Irish feeling developed in the United States also. On 6, 7 and 9 December 1918, just a few days before the House of Representatives held hearings on the Gallagher resolution, the Senate was holding hearings on German propaganda before and during the war. A. Bruce Bielaski, a witness from the Attorney-General's office, testified in some detail about such Irish-American nationalists as James K. McGuire, Jeremiah A. O'Leary and Shaemus O'Sheel; he asserted that they all worked closely with the Germans, had probably operated on German money, and had hoped, as everyone knew, for Great Britain's defeat in the war.[22] Also during the midst of 'Self-Determination for Ireland Week' the *Christian Science Monitor* featured a series of articles interviewing distinguished native Americans such as John Bates Clark, a Columbia University economist, Dean James B. Lough of New York University, and Allen B. Pond, secretary of the war committee of the Union League Club, who all agreed on the inadvisability of the American delegation raising the Irish question at the Peace Conference.[23] The Irish-American argument that the United States had gone to war to fight for self-determination was brushed aside by F. L. Warren of Stockbridge, Massachusetts, who told Senator John Sharp Williams that America had entered the war only because it had been threatened by Germany. Arguing against the League of Nations, he said that Irish-American agitation was an example of what could happen when a foreign question became involved in domestic politics. And Irving Winslow, national secretary of the Anti-Imperialist League, complained angrily to Senator Williams of the Irish-American pressure on Wilson. 'The last blow seems final!' he said of Wilson's meeting with the Irish delegation on 4 March 1919. 'How *can* the President insult our ally—an independent nation—by a demand for dismemberment?' The dangers to Protestants in Ireland that a Catholic Home Rule government would present were outlined to Wilson in several letters urging him to ignore the demands of the 'Sinn Féiners'.[24]

II. Irish-American Diplomacy: the American Commission on Irish Independence

The representatives of the main body of the Irish-American nationalist movement were undeterred by their fruitless meeting with President Wilson on 4 March. After reconvening, the delegation appointed a subcommittee of three to go to Paris under the title of the American Commission on Irish Independence. Three distinguished Irish-Americans, Frank P. Walsh, a Kansas City lawyer, former joint president of Wilson's War Labour Conference Board and member of the Industrial Relations Commission, Edward F. Dunne, a liberal Democrat, former mayor of Chicago and former governor of Illinois, and Michael J. Ryan, a former Philadelphia City solicitor and former president of the UIL of America, were instructed to obtain safe conducts for Éamon de Valera, Arthur Griffith and George Noble, Count Plunkett, who had been selected by the Dáil to represent Ireland at Paris. If they were unable to secure the safe conducts, they were to plead the Irish case before the Peace Conference themselves and to advance all other efforts for the recognition of the Irish Republic.[25]

Arriving in France on 11 April the Irish-American delegation was immediately contacted by Seán T. O'Kelly and George Gavan Duffy, Dáil envoys to France, and Lincoln Steffens, an American journalist. Through Steffens Walsh met Ray Stannard Baker, then the director of the press bureau for the American Commission to Negotiate Peace and the person who received all official correspondence for President Wilson. Baker was cordial and offered to place their correspondence before the President and assist them in arranging an interview with Wilson at such time as they might desire. Walsh also met William C. Bullitt, from the Current Intelligence Department of the commission, who was fully informed about the Irish Race Convention and the unsatisfactory interview between Wilson and the Irish-Americans in New York. Bullitt offered to contact Lloyd George's confidential secretary, Philip

Kerr, and to talk with him about Walsh and his mission; indeed, the following day he reported to Walsh that Kerr had told him that Lloyd George would probably give the Irish delegation passports to come to France, although he would never agree to allow them to appear before the Peace Conference. On the same afternoon Walsh met E. M. House, one of the five members of the American peace commission, who said he was familiar with the Irish situation through his friend Sir Horace Plunkett and who made arrangements to meet again in a few days. On the strength of these successes, and the encouragement of Baker and Bullitt, the Irish-American delegation sent a letter to President Wilson explaining who they represented and the purpose of their mission. 'If these gentlemen', they wrote about de Valera, Griffith and Count Plunkett, 'were furnished safe conduct to Paris so that they might present their case, we feel that our mission would be . . . accomplished.' They appealed to Wilson to prevail upon Lloyd George, and they assured him that in so doing he would win the approval of millions of Americans.[26]

Perhaps as the result of the reports on the situation in Ireland he had received earlier in the month from George Creel and Sir Horace Plunkett urging the importance of an immediate settlement, Wilson agreed to meet the Irish-American delegation. In fact by the time he had returned from the United States Wilson had decided to speak with Lloyd George about the Irish problem. However, in his conversation with the Irish-Americans on 17 April he said that officially the only topic which could be discussed at the time was the treaty with Germany, but that once the terms had been reached he proposed to say to Lloyd George that the Irish in America were all united and 'intense' over the Irish question and that unless it was settled it would seriously affect British relations with America and the dominions.[27] No doubt Walsh, Dunne and Ryan would have liked Wilson to have given a more specific commitment, but at least he had assured them that he would raise the Irish question in the near future. Certainly this appeared to be progress after the disagreeable incident at the Metropolitan Opera House meeting a month earlier.

Meanwhile House had talked with Lloyd George and was shortly able to reinforce Bullitt's opinion that the delegates from Ireland would probably be allowed to come to Paris, although they could not appear before the conference. When House had seen Lloyd George he had attempted to demonstrate American interest in the Irish question by showing some resolutions which were typical of those being sent to the peace commissioners by groups in the United States.[28] Through House and Wiseman arrangements were made for the Irish-Americans to meet Lloyd George, possibly for the purpose of planning an agenda for the Irish delegation. However, the business of the Peace Conference itself caused Lloyd George to postpone twice his meeting with Walsh and the Irish-Americans. In view of these delays it was suggested—by whom is a matter of some disagreement—that the Irish-Americans should make a quick trip to Ireland to examine the situation there for themselves. They were pleased at the opportunity to go to Ireland and in fact had earlier been advised to do so by Judge Cohalan so that on their return they could 'enlighten American opinion'.[29] Actually the State Department had anticipated some dangers in precisely this situation and had therefore restricted the passports for travel exclusively in France. However, when the British government issued diplomatic visas to the Irish-American delegation the State Department felt that the matter was out of their hands.[30]

Walsh, Dunne and Ryan toured Ireland in a triumphal procession, but in doing so they wrecked the prospects of an Irish delegation going to Paris. They arrived on 3 May, and after spending several days meeting Northern nationalist leaders and visiting jails and police barracks, they returned to Dublin on 6 May, where they were greeted by a large crowd of people and a parade which took them through the city. The Irish-Americans spent ten days in Ireland, during which time they met many Sinn Féin leaders, including de Valera, Griffith and Plunkett. They were given the freedom of the city of Limerick, attended several civic functions in Dublin, addressed the Dáil and visited Mountjoy Prison. They made several speeches in which they made clear their views on Irish self-government, described their mission at the Peace Conference, and reported the unanimous support in America for the Irish cause.[31] These activities caused an explosive reaction in England. The newspapers commented at great length; Bonar Law had to answer questions in parliament for Lloyd George (and in fact said that Lloyd George would not now meet the Irish-Americans); even the king asked that Lloyd George obtain from President Wilson some 'disavowal of the action of these American Citizens'.[32] While the Irish-Americans were only half-way through their trip Lloyd George wrote to House complaining that he had permitted them to go to Ireland on the understanding that they were responsible men who genuinely wanted to investigate the conditions there; but he expressed his subsequent dismay, listing the indiscretions of the Irish-Americans in Ireland, and said that the British government could not permit such activities. House refused to take any responsibility for the delegation and said that they had not asked to go to Ireland but had simply wanted Lloyd George to receive de

Valera, Griffith and Plunkett in Paris. The Prime Minister replied that he had been given an altogether different understanding from both Sir William Wiseman and House and that he proposed to cancel the scheduled interview with the Irish-Americans.[33]

The result of the trip to Ireland of the Irish-American delegates on the efforts being made at the Peace Conference to assist in a settlement was disastrous. Through the efforts of House and Bullitt, working with the knowledge and approval of Wilson, Lloyd George had seemed willing to allow the Dáil delegation to come to Paris. However, after the reports of the activities of the Irish-American delegation reached the newspapers, parliament and the cabinet, Lloyd George had no alternative but to cease all efforts in that direction. Wilson explained the situation to an anxious Tumulty:

> By our unofficial activity in the matter we had practically cleared the way for the coming of the Irish representatives to Paris when the [Irish-]American commission went to Ireland and behaved in a way which so inflamed British opinion that the situation has got quite out of hand, and we are utterly at a loss how to act in the matter without involving the government of the United States with the government of Great Britain in a way which might create an actual breach between the two. I made an effort the day before yesterday in this matter which shows, I am afraid, the utter futility of further efforts.[34]

Wilson, who has often been regarded as indifferent if not hostile to the Irish cause, clearly felt that he and the American peace commission had through efforts in an unofficial capacity gone far to making a settlement possible, when the indiscretions of the Irish-American delegation destroyed these efforts and even the possibility for further attempts. When the Irish-Americans returned to Paris they directed new appeals to Secretary of State Lansing, emphasising their desire to have the Irish delegation obtain safe conducts, and wrote to Wilson outlining the objectives of their mission and asserting that they understood from House that Lloyd George would grant his permission. After discussing the matter with Wilson, Lansing replied to Walsh that the unofficial British and American co-operation which had allowed them to travel to Ireland and which had given hopes for securing permission for the Irish delegation to come to Paris was no longer possible. 'Certain utterances' had been made by the delegates which had caused 'the deepest offence to those persons with whom you were seeking to deal', Lansing wrote, and in view of these facts new attempts to talk with the British authorities about the delegation from Ireland 'would be futile and therefore unwise'.[35]

This rather explicit letter from the Secretary of State should normally have ended the Irish-American mission, and in fact Ryan did leave for the United States on 24 May. Walsh and Dunne were undeterred and attempted to save the situation by arguing with the American peace commissioners. They talked to House, who explained the damage that had been caused by what had reached the press, but who said he would do what he could for Ireland and that he intended to visit Ireland later in the summer. The delegation also sent several letters to Lansing arguing very legalistically that Lansing's note did not apply to them. They demanded to know exactly what 'utterances' had caused offence, and to what 'persons', and they protested vigorously that they were not attempting to 'deal' with anyone, but rather that they merely wanted the three Irish delegates to be assured safe conduct from Ireland to Paris in order to address the Peace Conference; failing that they hoped to appeal to the conference themselves. As for their views on Ireland, these had been known by everyone before their trip, and if they gave offence to anyone, it was not to the people of Ireland. But these letters to Lansing, Wilson and even Clemenceau were last-resort gestures. As Henry White, one of the five United States peace commissioners, reported to Senator Henry Cabot Lodge, the Irish-Americans had obviously not sought to make their appeal an official concern of the peace commission until after their private efforts through House had failed.[36]

Walsh and Dunne had one more meeting with both Lansing and Wilson. They told Lansing on 6 June that the American peace commissioners were obliged as public representatives to give them an interview because they were in a position to provide information about Ireland which was vital before a satisfactory peace could be concluded with Germany and Austria. They also gave Lansing a copy of the report of their trip to Ireland, which in inflammatory nationalist rhetoric described what they had seen. President Wilson, though seriously annoyed with them by late May, met Walsh and Dunne on 11 June and gave them a very frank interview.[37] He told them that there was little he could do, despite the obvious American sympathy for Ireland, and that no small nation had yet appeared before the Peace Conference other than those which had been directly involved in the war. When Walsh attempted to suggest that Wilson would do something for Ireland if he fully appreciated the revolutionary situation which existed there, the President replied:

Now, Walsh, if it is your intention to go back to America and try to put me in bad, I am going to say when I go back that we were well on the way of getting Mr DeValera and his associates over here; we were well on the way, when you made it so difficult by your speeches in Ireland that we could not do it; that it was you gentlemen who kicked over the apple cart.

When Walsh and Dunne asked Wilson about the application of his war aims of self-determination to Ireland and other small nationalities, the President said: 'You have touched on the great metaphysical tragedy of to-day,' and he as much as confessed, what Lansing had earlier feared, that he had had during the war no real knowledge of the effects of his words on people throughout the world.[38] All the problems that Walsh had mentioned could not be solved in the short time of the Peace Conference, Wilson said; he had not done as much as he had hoped, but he had made a beginning.

The interviews with Wilson and Lansing virtually ended the purposeful activities of Walsh and Dunne in Paris, although they continued to write letters, referring threateningly to the support for the Irish cause among powerful groups in the United States.[39] John A. Murphy and L. S. Trigg were sent to Paris on 28 June by the Irish Race Convention committee to continue the attempt to force the Peace Conference to deal with Ireland. Walsh and Dunne, however, returned to the United States. Measured by their original objectives, they had failed completely—de Valera and his colleagues were not permitted to go to Paris, nor were the Irish-Americans themselves allowed to appeal to the Peace Conference, and their agitation for an Irish republic was hardly effective in realising that goal among the great powers; indeed, they may have obstructed the efforts of the diplomats. Nonetheless, they were regarded as a great success by Judge Cohalan, who cabled his congratulations, and by several of the Irish envoys abroad, and in fact the goal of getting the delegation from Ireland to Paris seemed less important than the publicity campaign which the Irish-Americans carried on with great efficiency.[40] Henry White later wrote to Lansing that he had been informed that Seán T. O'Kelly felt that the Irish were satisfied not only with the Irish-American delegation but also with the actions of the members of the American peace commission and that they realised that the Irish question could not come before the conference itself. White also told Senator Lodge that what the Irish-American delegation 'wanted was publicity for the Irish cause'.[41]

Meanwhile in the United States substantial efforts were also made to induce President Wilson to bring the Irish question before the Peace Conference. The most effective instrument by which to do this was the United States Congress, which traditionally had been more sympathetic to Ireland and more amenable to the pressures of the Irish-American nationalists than either the presidency or the State Department. Direct assistance came from Senator William E. Borah, a powerful member of the Foreign Relations Committee, who throughout 1919 became, in the words of his biographer, the 'linch pin' between the Irish-American nationalists and the irreconcilable Republican senators who opposed the Versailles Treaty. After consultations with Judge Cohalan, Senator Borah introduced a resolution on 29 May which asked:

That the Senate of the United States earnestly requests the American peace commission at Versailles to endeavor to secure for Edward DeValera [sic], Arthur Griffiths [sic], and Count George Noble Plunkett [sic] a hearing before said peace conference in order that they may present the case of Ireland.[42]

The resolution was reported back to the Senate on 5 June, amended in such a way as to avoid mentioning a republican government in Ireland. When the resolution came up for a vote on the following day Senator Henry Cabot Lodge, who as a result of the Republican majority elected in November 1918 had recently become the new chairman of the Foreign Relations Committee, moved and carried an amendment to the resolution which expressed 'sympathy with the aspirations of the Irish people for a government of its own choice'. In his speech Lodge deplored that the Peace Conference had become involved in matters beyond drafting a treaty of peace with Germany which had been its original purpose. From current reports, Lodge told the Senate, the British were attempting to interpret America's Monroe Doctrine in the context of the League of Nations, which Lodge felt they had no right to do; but if they chose to do so, the Senate was perfectly free to draft statements about Britain's vital interests. The resolution was passed by a vote of 60 to 1 (Senator Williams opposing and 35 not voting).[43]

The Senate's genuine interest in Irish representation at the Peace Conference was the subject of discussion several days later during debate on the Knox resolution, designed to limit the activities of the conference to simply the treaty with Germany. Senator Thomas pointed out the incongruity of this same group supporting the Knox resolution after almost unanimously passing the Borah resolution the previous week. If the Senate were serious about the representation of small nationalities at the conference, why was there not a resolution in favour of Korean independence before the Senate as well as one favouring Ireland. As for Ireland and American war aims, Senator Thomas thundered, 'We certainly did not enter this war with the object of securing the independence of the Irish Sinn

Féin,' whom he accused of not representing Ireland and of being in collusion with the Germans. Several days later both Senators Borah and Phelan attempted to make rebuttals, but Phelan at least was hampered by the fact that he was a member of the same political party as the President.[44]

The Borah resolution forced the question of the Irish delegates fully into the open. Despite all Tumulty's warnings, there was little the President could do to prevent its passage or to anticipate effectively its objective. As he told Tumulty, 'I have tried to help in the Irish matter but the extraordinary indiscretion of the [Irish-] American delegation over here has almost completely blocked everything.'[45] When the Senate resolution arrived in Paris, Wilson, acting on the advice of the four other American peace commissioners, forwarded it to Clemenceau, president of the Peace Conference, with a minimum of comment. Clemenceau took no action on the resolution.[46] It did, of course, provide further arguments for Walsh and Dunne in their attempts to force the American peace commissioners to have de Valera brought to Paris. However, if it had ever been possible for the United States to take the initiative in such a way, through the official machinery of the Senate and the peace commission, it was no longer so after the Irish-American delegation had gone to Ireland. In terms of practical possibilities in Paris the resolution was an empty gesture, but, as Henry White wrote to Lodge, it relieved the peace commission 'of any responsibility in the matter'.[47] However, the resolution was not without some positive effects. 'We have all got new hope and courage as a result of it,' Seán T. O'Kelly wrote to Devoy on 13 June. 'Even if we are turned down by Wilson—as is not unlikely from most recent happenings—the effect of the Senate resolution will be such, in my opinion, as will secure for our cause an earlier success than most of us could dream of.' The resolution encouraged the Irish political leaders to believe that they had substantial support from America in much the same way as had the visit to Ireland of the Irish-American delegation. The Dáil sent its unanimous thanks to the Senate.[48]

Across the United States there were very mixed feelings about both the Irish-American delegation and the Borah resolution in the Senate. The *Literary Digest* commented on the delegation's trip to Ireland with some amazement, but registered no opinions from American newspapers. Charles McCarthy, an interested observer, warned Sir Horace Plunkett that Frank P. Walsh was 'a pretty dangerous individual'. Senator Borah was reminded by a Chicago businessman that the Republican Party was made up of Irishmen of the 'McKinley breed', not the 'Dunnes and Cohalans and Ryans', and further that Americans supported 'the Irish who were loyal and not with the skulking, traitorous, draft-resisting Sinn Féin'.[49] The secretary-general of the Freemasons in the southern United States told Senator Williams that America had gone too far in interfering in the Irish question, and he argued that an Irish Catholic government would persecute the Protestants in Ireland just as the Catholics in Poland were currently persecuting the Jews. Another correspondent from Chicago also warned Williams of the 'Catholic intrigue' and said the Irish-American delegation went abroad 'as Roman Catholics camophlaging as Americans'. German–Irish collusion during the war was also a source of great hostility among many Americans whose passions had not sufficiently cooled to allow them to regard with equanimity the apparent Senate support for Sinn Féin Ireland. Former Attorney-General George W. Wickersham, who had spoken out several times on the necessity of a settlement of the Irish question, thought that the Senate resolution was subversive and disgusting.[50] But the criticisms of some native Americans aside, the delegation and the resolution had substantial support.

III. The League of Nations Fight and the Irish Question

When it became clear that the Peace Conference was not going to take up the Irish question the leaders of the Irish-American nationalist organisations turned the energies and resources of their movement, with some personal malice resulting from their sufferings during the war, against President Wilson and his foreign policy. This was a step taken not without some cost, especially to those Irish-Americans who had loyalties either to Wilson or to the Democratic Party, but it also held the elements of a possible alliance with the Republicans in the 1920 elections. Indeed, the Irish-American nationalists had taken a public position on the League of Nations as early as the Irish Race Convention in February 1919, when they said that they would oppose any treaty which did not safeguard what they felt to be America's interests. As early as March and April 1919 the energies of the nationalist organisations were directed towards an attack on the league as a threat to American freedom, as an Anglo-American alliance, and as a device for strangling the Irish revolutionary movement by excluding the possibility of outside assistance. Large meetings were sponsored throughout the country by the FOIF, the IPL, Irish Self-Determination clubs and countless local Irish-American organisations for the purpose of demonstrating the dangers that the league posed to both the United States and Ireland. In early April Edward F. McSweeney a successful Boston lawyer and former chairman of the Boston Board of Port Directors, counselled Judge Cohalan about the tactics for a nation-wide campaign, advising the necessity of enlisting the support of successful and respectable Irish-Americans, of circulating anti-British propaganda in non-Irish newspapers, and of establishing a mailing list of at least 20,000 Irish sympathisers to whom appeals and information could be sent. By mid-summer the FOIF was fully embarked on just such a programme, financed by the Irish Victory Fund, and the IPL was engaged in similar activities on a somewhat smaller scale.[51]

The possible success of the drive to link the Irish question with the League of Nations issue depended upon the extent to which the Irish-American nationalists were able to join forces with other elements in American society which also opposed the league. In this they were particularly fortunate, for although the league had many supporters in the United States, it had many powerful opponents as well, especially among the Republican majority in the Senate. The most outstanding of these Senate opponents was Senator Borah, who had indicated his interest in Ireland as early as November 1918 but who also found in the Irish-American objections to the league a useful argument in his own fight against the treaty. During the spring and summer Borah consulted with Judge Cohalan in co-ordinating Irish-American and anti-league activities, and Cohalan provided the senator with access to the Irish-American leaders. Borah spoke frequently before large Irish-American audiences and told them how the League of Nations would permanently establish British rule in Ireland.[52] Borah's views on the league and Irish nationalism were probably most completely summarised in his telegram to a large Irish-American meeting in Portland, Oregon, on 1 June 1919:

The right of self determination which we were assured was involved in this war is wholly excluded from the League Covenant. . . . There is no method, no means by which a subject people struggling for their liberties can ever be heard. The denial of a hearing to the representatives of Ireland discloses in an unmistakable way that the principle of self determination had been rejected by the framers of the League. The League created an autocracy based upon the combined military power of five great nations. Under Article ten this military force is to be used to hold intact the territorial boundaries of the members of the autocracy. This not only means the subjection of all small nations to the dictation of the autocracy but it means the use of the man power of the United States to settle the territorial disputes and dynastic quarrels of Europe. The scheme is un-American, unjust to small nations and instead of being a league for peace is a league to promote war. As we love American independence, as we believe in the freedom of the Irish people, as we believe in liberty everywhere let us fight it.[53]

Here Borah outlined all of the growing fears of the Irish-Americans about the dangerous effects of the league on both Ireland and the United States. Senator Lodge of Massachusetts was also willing to use the Irish question to fight the league and the treaty, as indeed his amendment to the Borah resolution in June indicated. He observed to Henry White that the Irish-Americans were 'bitterly opposed to the League', and he felt that their antagonism towards Wilson was not altogether unjustified. By late July Lodge observed to the chairman of the Massachusetts Republican finance committee that the Irish-Americans were irrevocably 'against Wilson and the League', and he recommended that the Republicans exploit this sentiment among the traditionally Democratic Irish-Americans in Massachusetts. And Lodge himself assured a Massachusetts state senator that 'under Article 10 Americans would be prevented from giving the same kind of aid to Ireland as that which France gave to America in the Revolution' unless the United States were willing to go to war with all the members of the league.[54] Both Borah and Lodge differed in their basic objections to the league—Borah because it constituted a fundamental break with traditional American foreign policy of non-entanglement with other powers, Lodge because it subverted the constitution and by-passed the Senate—but they were conveniently given common ground on which to fight the treaty through the Irish question and other similar ethnic issues.

The combined efforts of the Irish-American leaders and the Republican senators against the League of Nations reached a high point when, through the work of Cohalan and Borah, Lodge's Senate Foreign Relations Committee allowed Irish-Americans to testify at the hearings on the peace treaty. In early July Judge Cohalan wrote to Senator Borah that there were a large number of Americans who would like to testify before the committee in regard to several causes, the Irish among them. Borah advised Cohalan to encourage these people to demand from their senators that public hearings be held, and as a result the committee listened patiently to many nationalist, ethnic and lobby groups who had grievances related to the treaty.[55] On 30 August 115 Irish-Americans appeared before the committee with Judge Cohalan as their spokesman. The judge said that he and his colleagues spoke for the 20,000,000 Americans of Irish descent who desired to see Ireland free. He told the committee that he opposed the treaty and the league because it was not in America's best interests to guarantee the status quo in Ireland and the rest of the world. Cohalan said further that an Ireland independent from Great Britain and friendly to the United States was the key to the North Atlantic and was vital to maintain the freedom of the seas and the all-important commercial freedom which would allow the United States to continue to grow in the face of British trade rivalry. Frank P. Walsh, Edward F. Dunne and Michael J. Ryan told of their frustrations in attempting to deal with the American and British peace commissions to bring the Irish delegation to Paris and gave an account of the deplorable conditions they found in Ireland. Indeed, Walsh said he had gone to Paris fully supporting Wilson and the league but that he had become convinced that the Allied statesmen had no intention of fulfilling their war promises. John A. Murphy gave a brief account of his experiences with the peace commissioners in Paris; W. W. McDowell, the Lieutenant-Governor of Montana, and Daniel C. O'Flaherty, a Protestant Irish-American from Virginia, both spoke of America's great sympathy and interest in Irish freedom; and Congressman W. Bourke Cockran gave a history of Ireland and expounded on the obligations of the United States to Ireland.[56]

The senators told the Irish-American witnesses, Frank P. Walsh later recalled, that they were sympathetic to the Irish cause and that the Irish-American nationalists were of such great assistance that but for them the league would have been quickly accepted. The committee published, along with the actual hearings, all the written materials submitted, including petitions, resolutions and statements prepared by several of the witnesses. The most important of these items was the correspondence between Walsh, Dunne and Ryan and the American, British and French peace commissions. These letters revealed Walsh's pleading inquiries and the commissioners' cold businesslike replies, but they rather unfairly omitted any mention of the very important efforts that had been made by Wilson, House and Lansing on behalf of the Irish delegation. In fact to give these letters faster and wider publicity and circulation, Senator Brandegee also had them printed in the *Congressional Record*.[57] Through Daniel T. O'Connell, director of the Irish National Bureau in Washington, at least 75,000 copies of the committee hearings were mailed out, and by 11 November O'Connell asked Borah for 5,000 copies with his frank which would allow the bureau to address them to receptive readers at public expense. The testimony of the Irish-Americans and the subsequent publication of their correspondence had its effect on public opinion and influenced the growing hostility towards the league. As Lodge wrote to Henry White, who tended to dismiss Walsh's complaints against the commission, 'I assure you that these are not men whose testimony can be whistled down by the wind whatever you may feel about the Irish.'[58]

The Irish-American nationalist organisations attacked the League of Nations by showing how it threatened Ireland's national aspirations. The FOIF, the largest of these organisations, published a series of broadsheets and pamphlets from its national office. *The League of Nations and the rights of small nations*, which came out in April 1919, was among the first FOIF attacks, and after the Peace Conference was over, Edward F. Dunne's *What Dunne saw in Ireland* gave in pamphlet form much of his testimony before the Senate committee, as did the *Statement of Hon. Daniel F. Cohalan.* The FOIF also published *Official documents from Ireland, including 'Ireland's case for independence' adopted by Dáil Éireann for presentation to the Peace Conference*, which presented all the unsuccessful Irish correspondence to the American, British and French peace commissions. Edward F. McSweeney's *Ireland is an American question* argued that the league was an instrument of British oppression and that it was designed to ensure British domination of the sea.[59] The FOIF also financed the Irish National Bureau in Washington, DC, which published a weekly *News letter*, which contained short articles suitable for reprinting, and a one- or two-page press release, the *Weekly News Bulletin*, which was circulated to newspaper reporters; both items were sent to politicians in Washington. The American Commission on Irish Independence, which did not disband after returning to the United States, printed such occasional leaflets as *America's appeal to Ireland*, which referred to an address by the first Continental Congress to the Irish parliament in 1775. The IPL, which, in addition to its regular bulletin, published anonymously a series of pamphlets which attacked the league, described in vivid statistics the territorial expansion of the British Empire as a result of the war and bemoaned the loss to the United States and gain to the Allies that the war had been. The IPL also attracted to the Irish fight against the league a number of native American liberals.[60]

Individual Irish-Americans and others also made private efforts to promote the Irish cause, often at the expense of the League of Nations. Judge Edward J. Gavegan wrote an important article for the New York *American*, 'Every race saved from bondage except the Irish', which said that America and Britain must work closely together for world peace but that Irish freedom had to come first. A book describing the efforts to bring the Irish delegation before the Peace Conference, *The invincible Irish*, was written by J. C.

Walsh, then with the Jesuit weekly *America,* who had travelled to
Ireland and France in 1919. A Hearst newspaper writer, Philip
Francis, published *The poison in America's cup,* which was wild
anglophobe propaganda directed specifically at the Irish-American
public. Perhaps one of the most effective of all publications during
the league debate was *The re-conquest of America,* written by Dr
W. J. M. A. Maloney but published anonymously and over the
imprint of a fictitious press. Supposedly a letter from Sir William
Wiseman to Lloyd George, the pamphlet described the progress
that had been made and the work yet to be done in bringing the
United States back into the Empire. It cleverly portrayed Wilson
as the weak-willed tool of British influences and the Irish and
Germans as those most resistant to British designs. The pamphlet
was reprinted several times and was also reproduced in several
newspapers and liberal journals. One of the more unlikely Irish
apologists was George Creel, who in February had served as
Wilson's special agent in Ireland. By the summer of 1919 he had
written a series of nationalist articles on Ireland which were later
published as a book; and in fact Creel found himself asked to speak
at IPL functions.[61]

Irish-American obstruction of Wilson and the league placed
great stresses on many old Democratic Party loyalties, and substantial efforts were made by Democrats either to disentangle the
Irish question from the league and the treaty or to demonstrate how
the league could most effectively provide Ireland with certain kinds
of outside assistance. As early as April 1919 one senator told
Tumulty: 'The League of Nations is the only way by which Ireland
should be able to expect a very prompt settlement of her desire for
self-government.' Wilson himself replied to one of Tumulty's many
requests on behalf of Ireland by saying: 'I firmly believe when the
League of Nations is once organized it will afford a forum not now
available for bringing the opinion of the world and of the United
States in particular to bear on just such problems.'[62] For diplomatic
reasons, Wilson was unwilling to voice this opinion in public; however, by late August even the Secretary of State was asking Wilson
for some statement of opinion which could be used to answer the
volumes of letters on the Irish question directed to the department.
During his ill-fated speaking tour across the United States in
September, when the President attempted to bring the league and
treaty issues directly to the people, he was ready to use these arguments to forestall his critics. On 17 September Wilson answered
questions put to him by the San Francisco Labour Council, which
asked why Ireland had not been heard at the Peace Conference and
where the President stood on self-determination for Ireland. Wilson's

replies were that the conference 'had no jurisdiction over any question of that sort which did not affect territories which belonged to the defeated empires'. And he went on to answer the second question:

> My position on the subject of Self-Determination for Ireland is expressed in Article XI of the Covenant, in which I may say I was particularly interested because it seemed to me necessary for the peace and freedom of the world that a forum be created to which all peoples could bring any matter which was likely to affect the peace and freedom of the world.[63]

But a week later in Colorado Wilson suffered a physical collapse, followed by a stroke, which effectively removed him from the league fight. The immediate result was that the President was never able to develop convincingly the arguments which might have countered the anti-league propaganda of his Irish-American enemies.

Loyal Democrats were willing to point out the ways in which the league could be used to assist Ireland and to accuse their Republican adversaries of duplicity in their newly found pro-Irish sympathies. Shortly after the Borah resolution had been passed Senator Phelan interrupted an important debate to point out that Article X of the league covenant posed no threat to Irish aspirations. Irish independence might be achieved by three ways: mutual agreement with Britain, successful revolution, or intervention by an outside power. Article X blocked only the third means, he said, which had failed to be a practical policy with Spain, France, or most recently Germany as the intervening power. Phelan also reminded the Senate that in 1916, when they could have done something for Ireland, only eight Republicans had supported the resolution asking for clemency for Irish prisoners. When Borah later attempted to rebut Phelan's three arguments as to how Ireland could obtain her independence Senator Thomas J. Walsh interrupted to ask if 'the Senator from Idaho is contemplating aid by this Government to the Irish people'. Borah, caught in the logical conclusion of his own argument, had to reply that if Walsh meant military aid he did not, but he felt that America should give Ireland all the moral support possible and that no American troops should be used to suppress an Irish insurrection.[64] Senator Walsh was then approached by Michael Francis Doyle, who thought that Wilson had alienated the Irish-American public and not provided much encouragement to his Irish-American friends. Doyle urged Walsh to meet Senator Phelan and Doyle to plan some strategy to counter the opposition. Actually Walsh had already conferred with Wilson some time earlier, and his plan was to introduce a resolution in the

Senate committing the United States to immediate action on the Irish question as soon as the country entered the League of Nations. Walsh introduced this resolution on 17 October, but it was called an unconvincing trick to win back Irish-American support by Senator Poindexter, and Lodge not only had the resolution tabled but two days later also read to the Senate a letter from the director of the Irish National Bureau which stated that the FOIF and all 20,000,000 Irish-Americans opposed the resolution. Walsh himself confessed to friends that the measure did not have much support, and in fact it never came up for a vote.[65]

The intrusion of the Irish question in the national debate on the league and the treaty was a source of some considerable anguish to a number of native Americans. In the Senate a protest was registered by John Sharp Williams, who on 16 October assailed the Irish-Americans, saying that those in the Senate who tied 'Americanism' to the league issue were really talking about 'pro-Germanism, Irish-Americanism, Magyar-Americanism, and Austrian-Americanism'. Williams raised the prospect of all the Americans of English, Welsh and Scottish descent banding together to promote a policy solely for the benefit of Great Britain, and indeed he went on to argue that the basic concepts of freedom and liberty, as known in America, had their origins in England. Williams was warmly supported by many upper middle-class native Americans, who applauded his comments as they had approved of his single vote against the Borah resolution. The president of Randolph–Macon College in Virginia, a state senator from Iowa, an assistant treasurer of the St Louis United States Sub-Treasury, the president of the Philadelphia Protestant Federation, and many others sent Williams their approval, along with the suggestion that Anglo-Saxon and Protestant England and America must stand together. Williams privately apologised to Phelan for anything that he said about the Irish to which the Senator might have taken offence, but two days later, when Senator Hitchcock had AOH resolutions placed in the *Congressional Record*, Williams demanded the printing of some resolutions from the Near East Relief Society asking that the American government attempt to do something about the fate of nearly 100,000 Christian and Jewish women still kept in harems in areas which were formerly parts of the Ottoman Empire. Williams's attempts to contrast injustices in the Near East with injustice in Ireland fell upon predictably deaf ears among the Irish-Americans and their friends in the Senate, who regarded Williams as a crank and a propagandist for Britain and who by this time were insisting that the Irish question was the key issue for Anglo-American post-war co-operation.[66]

The treaty of peace with Germany, which incorporated the League of Nations, came before the Senate for a vote on 19 November 1919. After three votes, two with the Lodge reservations and one with no reservations, the treaty was defeated. Cohalan quickly cabled Senator Borah: 'Heartiest congratulations. Greatest victory for country and liberty since Revolution largely due to you.' The senator returned his thanks to Cohalan and said: 'You have rendered in this fight a service which no other man has rendered or could have rendered,' which, given the size and strength of the FOIF which Cohalan dominated, was certainly true. The *Gaelic American* registered its approval with the large headline: 'SENATE'S ACTION A SPLENDID VINDICATION OF AMERICANISM' and reproduced broadsheets published by the Irish Victory Fund under the auspices of the FOIF.[67]

Because of the sentiment in the country the Senate voted on the treaty in March 1920 for a fourth time. On 17 March, the day before the treaty would come up for a vote, Senator Gerry of Rhode Island introduced a reservation to the treaty which contained something of the spirit of Senator Walsh's earlier resolution. It stated that in accepting the treaty the United States would reaffirm its commitments to the principles of self-determination, particularly as applied to Ireland, and it further suggested that as soon as Ireland obtained its independence it should be quickly admitted into the league.

> In consenting to the ratification of the treaty with Germany the United States adheres to the principle of self-determination and to the resolution of sympathy with the aspirations of the Irish people for a government of their own choice adopted by the Senate June 6, 1919, and declares that when such government is attained by Ireland, a consummation it is hoped is at hand, it should promptly be admitted as a member of the League of Nations.

When the Gerry reservation was debated the following day Senators Thomas, Williams and Kellogg attempted to include also Korean and African independence, which they said was valid if the Senate were really interested in matters of principle rather than Irish votes. Thomas insisted that Hitchcock, one of the Gerry reservation supporters, was unlikely to vote for the treaty under any conditions and that this was an attempt to obscure the real issues. The reservation was carried by a vote of 38 to 36, with Fletcher, Kellogg, Lodge, Harding and Williams among those opposing it.

The treaty was defeated the next day by a vote of 49 to 35. As Senator Borah had acknowledged, the Irish-Americans had been conspicuous in assisting to defeat the league and the treaty, although it is to be remembered that they shared the responsibility with many other groups in the United States as well.[68] If it was a 'victory' as Judge Cohalan had said, it was a negative one. Irish independence was still a long way off.

In retrospect, the anti-league agitation of the Irish-Americans seems particularly irresponsible, especially inasmuch as American abstention did not crush the league or strengthen the Irish nationalist movement or even prevent Ireland from later taking a conspicuously active part in the league's work. Nonetheless, the Irish had genuine fears about the league and Article X. As early as April 1919 the Dáil had expressed the view that the league must conform to the notions of self-determination and the rights of small nations, and very shortly after his arrival in the United States de Valera openly opposed the league and Article X. Later in Ireland the United States Senate's defeat of the treaty, and especially the passage of the Gerry reservation, were seen as an indication of Irish-American influence in American politics. Griffith told the Dáil on 29 June 1920: 'Were it not for Mr de Valera's work in the United States of America there was little doubt that with some amendments, the Peace Treaty, including article 10, would have been carried,' and he affirmed a view expressed by Harry Boland that 'The [Gerry] reservation written into the Peace Treaty made it quite clear that the League of Nations could only be adopted with Ireland as a consenting party, and the writing in of that reservation had made the Irish question an International question which could not be settled without the assent of America.'[69] Griffith's assertions illustrated the extent to which Irish nationalists misunderstood the political situation in the United States and the extent to which America would allow its foreign policy to be shaped to serve Ireland's interests.

CHAPTER 6
AMERICA DURING THE ANGLO-IRISH
STRUGGLE
1919–1921

THE Irish nationalist movement in the United States reached its high point in the years from 1919 to 1921. Shortly after the spectacular success of the Borah resolution Éamon de Valera, the President of Dáil Éireann and the only surviving commandant of the 1916 Rising, undertook a mission to America which was bound to contribute to the new aggressiveness of Irish-American nationalism after the First World War.[1] However, de Valera's nineteen-month mission to raise money and obtain recognition had its own set of problems, for while the Irish President was an important agent for publicising the Irish cause and for drawing new support from among the Irish-American population, his presence complicated the already fragile relationships within the leadership circles. Eventually, even the single objective of Irish independence could not hold the Irish-American nationalist movement together, and during the summer and autumn of 1920, when agitation might have been expected to be at its peak, the nationalist organisations were divided and quarrelling. Nevertheless, by extraordinarily imaginative devices the Irish cause was kept before the American public despite these divisions. But, to be sure, these achievements were not made without some cost, for by at least 1920 a substantial body of organised anti-Irish opinion had developed as a reaction against the nationalist clamour. Indeed, it was a commentary on the exceptional vigour of the Irish-American community that the nationalist movement succeeded as it did under these conditions.

I. De Valera's Tour of the United States

Éamon de Valera made his first public appearance in the United States on 23 June 1919 when he held a reception at the Waldorf-Astoria Hotel in New York.[2] Then, and more explicitly at a press

F

conference on the following day, de Valera told newspaper reporters that the objectives of his mission to America were to obtain a loan of about $5,000,000 and to secure the recognition of the Irish Republic. A week later de Valera began the first of several speaking tours across the United States, wherein he was honoured and fêted by both public officials and private citizens. De Valera spoke before state legislatures, conferred with governors, was given the freedom of several cities, and received two honorary doctorates. As always, he addressed large public audiences, describing the iniquities of British rule in Ireland, the inherent right of Ireland to be free, and from at least mid-July criticising the League of Nations, should it make no provision for Ireland. It was a spectacular performance which marked the beginning of a crucial episode in the Irish nationalist movement in the United States, and perhaps de Valera's travels throughout America, more than any event since the 1916 Rising, dramatised for the American people the dimensions of the Irish struggle. In fact de Valera was such an effective publicist and agitator that the British government decided that he must be prevented from returning to Ireland.[3]

These tours were extremely important in publicising the Irish cause and in the minds of many were reminiscent of the American sojourns in 1917–18 of Ignance Jan Paderewski and Thomas Garrigue Masaryk labouring to obtain American assistance for the aspirant Polish and Czechoslovak states. Insofar as his mission in the United States captured the idealistic imagination of the American people, de Valera's nineteen months in the country were overwhelmingly successful. For example, James E. Murray reported to Senator Thomas J. Walsh: 'The enthusiasm manifested by the people of Butte on that occasion [de Valera's address to 10,000 people in Butte, Montana, on 25 July 1919] was the most marvelous I have ever witnessed.'[4] Frank P. Walsh sent an enthusiastic report to Seán T. O'Kelly that de Valera had spoken before the governors and legislatures of Maryland and Delaware, and he said he had 'no idea that the cause could make the headway which it has in this country'. Even de Valera's critics were forced to concede the popular acclaim that was given him. George W. Wickersham, a strong Home Ruler, complained that it was 'heartsickening' that the Irish leader 'had receptions in the principal cities of the country, such were given to Joffre and Viviani and Balfour, when they were here in the spring of 1917'; and the Boston lawyer Moorfield Storey thought it 'very disquieting' that in Cleveland 'The Irish [de Valera] were received with great enthusiasm, while the King and Queen [of Belgium] received little notice.'[5] The few occasions on which public officials refused to extend full acknowledgment to Ireland or de

Valera—the mayor of Baltimore introducing him as a 'stranger', the governor of Virginia introducing him as a 'visitor' rather than as the President of the Irish Republic, and the mayor of Philadelphia refusing to discuss the Irish question with him—merely served to underscore the frequency with which the mission was cordially received. The Irish-American newspapers were, of course, wildly enthusiastic in their support of the Irish mission, although within eight months the *Gaelic American* was openly criticising de Valera and several other Irish nationalists in the United States. The editorial opinion of native American newspapers varied from the hostility of the *Christian Science Monitor* to the warmth of the Chicago *Tribune*.[6]

De Valera began work immediately to float a loan to provide revenue for financing the Dáil government. The idea of an American loan had first been seriously proposed by Frank P. Walsh, Edward F. Dunne and Michael J. Ryan in their discussions with Irish leaders during their trip to Ireland in May 1919. However, when shortly after his arrival de Valera specifically suggested to a group of Irish-American leaders that the loan be made through the sale of 'bonds' in the name of the Republic of Ireland he was told that such a transaction by an unrecognised government would be illegal in the United States.[7] But to maintain the apparatus of a *de facto* government it was important to raise the money in the accepted language of international finance. A satisfactory compromise was achieved with 'bond-certificates' which were within the law because they were not actually 'bonds' but which were close enough in terminology to be thought of as such. De Valera and others stated that the bond-certificates were not to be considered financial investments, and Walsh gave specific instructions to the state chairmen that the term 'bond' should never be used to mean 'bond-certificate', but the difference was not discernible to a public who had only a year before seen the United States government raising money by the sale of 'Liberty Bonds'.[8]

To sell the bond-certificates a national campaign was planned, under the responsibility of the American Commission for Irish Independence (Frank P. Walsh, Edward F. Dunne and Michael J. Ryan) and directed by James O'Mara, a Limerick businessman who was, along with de Valera and Bishop Fogarty, a trustee of the Dáil Éireann funds. The campaign was very loosely organised: state and city chairmen were appointed from the headquarters in New York, but they then had complete control of the sales in their districts. Frank P. Walsh advised the chairmen to work with the existing Irish-American societies in their areas—the AOH, the FOIF, the Knights of Columbus, or even the clergy—in order to save time and avoid duplication. Although the actual selling did not begin until 17 January 1920, the publicity campaign was started in August with de Valera's tours. Accompanied by McCartan, Boland, Seán Nunan, O'Mara, and others, de Valera devoted much of his energy to seeing that all the communities which he visited had some plans for selling the bond-certificates before the entourage moved on, and in the process he obtained, as far as he could, the endorsement of local civic officials and the clergy. In New York de Valera sold the first bond-certificate to Mayor John F. Hylan and was given the freedom of the city in return, while 40,000 canvassers began their assignments. De Valera was also invited to Albany as the guest of Governor Alfred E. Smith when the state assembly adopted a resolution endorsing the bond-certificate drive. Altogether $5,123,640 were raised by the sale of bond-certificates, and more than half of that amount was brought to Ireland for the use of the Dáil government.[9]

Despite its obvious success, the bond-certificate campaign was not without its corresponding difficulties also. Many of these problems were within the nationalist movement in America. John J. Splain, chairman of the campaign in Connecticut, complained to W. Bourke Cockran that it was 'hard to get our people enthused in this matter' and that he got 'poor co-operation' from both the Irishmen and the Irish-Americans directing the campaign. The same complaint was made by Dr W. Patrick Slattery, the Iowa state chairman, who was 'disappointed and disgusted' with the lack of interest shown by Irish-Americans in the bond-certificate campaign. The national president of the AOH and the chairman of the campaign in Indiana, James E. Deery, wrote to Peter Golden that the Indianapolis chairman had resigned less than two weeks after the drive began and he had not been able to find a replacement; of those whom Deery asked, 'they all appear to be interested, [but] they refuse to take any active part because so and so is taking an active part'. Golden himself was having trouble organising support in Cincinnati.[10]

The near illegality of the whole bond-certificate sale carried with it some danger of government restriction. A Boston publisher and bookseller wrote to President Wilson to ask if the government had given tacit approval to the Irish bond-certificates by allowing them to be exchanged at par value for Liberty Bonds. Frank P. Walsh was eventually sent a stern note from the Secretary of the Treasury warning that such practices must stop. The feeling in the State Department was that the administration was allowing an outrageous situation to develop. 'To close our eyes and do nothing to prevent our territory being used to further rebellion against a friendly nation is not very creditable to our Government and makes us morally responsible for the situation in Ireland today,' wrote one Foreign Service officer. Senator John Sharp Williams felt that the sale of the bond-certificates was clearly illegal and that de Valera, Walsh, Dunne and Ryan were 'indictable under the United States statute for "setting on foot missions of military enterprise against the do-minions of a foreign state at peace with the United States" ', but he lamented that it would be impossible to get a conviction because of the Irish sympathy in the country. The *Wall Street Journal*, the leading financial newspaper in the United States, agreed with Senator Williams that the sale of the bond-certificates was contrary to international law and that Britain's failure to protest did not make it less so. The paper pointed out that purchasers could not be given a valid pledge of a return, although it concluded disparag-ingly that they were mainly bought by 'Irish domestic servants, and others of like or lower standards of intelligence'.[11]

The campaign by de Valera and the Irish-American nationalists to obtain American diplomatic recognition for the Irish Republic was far less successful than the bond-certificate drive. Rather un-systematic agitation for some kind of acknowledgment of an Irish Republic had been under way since at least the general election of 1918. However, with de Valera's arrival in the United States in June 1919 recognition became a declared objective of the Irish-American nationalist movement, and de Valera and his entourage, as well as the American Commission for Irish Independence and the Irish bond-certificate sales staff, promoted the idea of the existing and functioning Irish Republic and the importance of American diplo-matic recognition. Because efforts to extract open support from Wilson at the Peace Conference had failed, and because throughout part of 1919 and 1920 Wilson was incapacitated by his stroke, the Irish nationalists turned their attention towards Congress in their efforts to obtain recognition for Ireland. In late May 1919 Congress-man William E. Mason introduced a bill to appropriate funds for the 'salaries of a minister and consuls to the republic of Ireland'.[12] If the House of Representatives acted favourably on such a resol-ution, it would amount to congressional recognition of Ireland, although only the President could actually appoint the minister and consuls whose salaries had been provided. The House Foreign Affairs Committee held public hearings on the bill on 12 and 13 December. A delegation led by Mason, Judge Cohalan and Frank P. Walsh attended the hearings and argued that there were pre-cedents for congressional recognition, that a *de facto* government had been functioning in Ireland since 1918, and that America was obliged to see that Ireland got independence because of Wilson's pledges during the war. The hearings were followed by extensive efforts by Irish-American nationalists to obtain support for the resolution in the House of Representatives, the Senate and the administration. But despite the agitation in its favour, the bill was not reported by the committee. In May, towards the close of the session, Congressman Mason discussed the situation with de Valera, Cohalan and several other Irish-American and political leaders, and a new resolution was drafted expressing sympathy for 'the aspirations of the Irish people for a government of their own choice'. This resolution found no favour with the committee either, and Mason's attempt to rally support in the House by introducing a flurry of Irish resolutions failed to produce any results. The congressional session ended without the House voting on any of the resolutions. Nevertheless, Congress did take some unofficial action in the form of a letter drafted by Peter F. Tague of Massachusetts and signed by nearly a hundred fellow Congressmen protesting to Lloyd George against the imprisonment of Irishmen without trial.[13]

The question of American recognition was also raised through protests about the British representation in Washington. When Sir Auckland Geddes arrived to assume his responsibilities as British Ambassador an attempt was made to insist that he did not represent the Irish Republic. On 29 April 1920 de Valera cabled President Wilson from Augusta, Georgia, to assert that Geddes had not been sent by the Irish government and did not speak for the Irish people. Through the organisation of Dr Maloney a group of women picketed the British Embassy, carrying signs insisting that the United States could no longer maintain diplomatic relations with Great Britain while outrages, specifically the shooting of Lord Mayor MacCurtain, were being perpetrated in the Irish Republic. The pickets were involved in a scuffle with pro-British Washington ladies and were arrested by the police. Upon their release on bail the pro-Irish women proceeded to picket the White House and the State Department offices, carrying signs featuring (among other slogans) quotations from speeches by Bainbridge Colby, the new Secretary of State, which he had made after the 1916 Rising. These activities, while affording the Irish movement some publicity and asserting the claims of the Republic, attempted to force recognition in areas which were well defined by custom and law. Wilson could hardly have been expected to refuse Geddes's credentials, and picketing the British Embassy violated the standard obligation of a host country protecting diplomatic envoys from insults or threats.[14] Of course, a large number of books and pamphlets were published advocating the recognition policy. The FOIF published such pamphlets as *Ireland and secession, an answer to Lloyd George* by

Thomas H. Mahony and *English atrocities in Ireland* by Katherine Hughes. John X. Regan's *What made Ireland Sinn Féin* and Mahony's *Similarities between the American and Irish revolutions* were private attempts to assist Irish recognition.[15]

By the early summer of 1920, and certainly after the end of the congressional session, the most promising means of obtaining American recognition of Ireland was by persuading the American political parties to adopt an Irish plank in their platforms for the 1920 presidential election. Actually in years past both parties had passed resolutions on the Irish question (the Democrats in 1888 and both parties in 1892), although they had been merely expressions of sympathy rather than promises of future policy. Agitation began well before the conventions to encourage individual politicians to support an Irish plank, although by the time of the Republican convention there were such divisions within the nationalist movement that both de Valera and Judge Cohalan led delegations to Chicago to work for the acceptance of their own planks. Presumably Cohalan felt that because the Mason resolution had not been acted upon by the Republican-dominated House of Representatives those same people gathered at Chicago would not endorse a resolution calling for recognition of the Irish Republic, so he favoured a statement in support of simple self-determination for Ireland. De Valera got his supporters to propose a resolution calling for the recognition of 'the elected government of the Republic of Ireland'.[16] The Republican resolutions committee voted to accept Cohalan's proposal, but de Valera's public repudiation of it for its failure to demand the diplomatic recognition that the Dáil government needed caused them to drop an Irish plank altogether. De Valera next went to the Democratic convention in San Francisco in late June, where he was unable to get the Democratic platform committee to accept either a recognition, or later a compromise, plank.

Thus neither major party adopted the Irish nationalist cause as part of its official programme, although despite the failure to secure any endorsement such perennial optimists as Frank P. Walsh observed that great progress towards recognition was being made and that 'The public demonstration there [in Chicago] was worth, to my mind, even more than the strongest plank that could have been drawn and put in the Republican platform.' On the contrary, the American Consul in Dublin reported to the State Department that news of the failure of the Republican Party to endorse a plank supporting the Irish cause 'came as a shock to Sinn Féiners in Ireland', even though efforts were now being made to show that it was the best policy not to identify too closely with either party.[17]

II.   The Split in the Irish-American Nationalist Movement

By the summer of 1920 the Irish nationalist movement in America suffered from serious internal tensions which could no longer be concealed. The split in the movement caused the breakdown of the uneasy coalition of active Irish-Americans, which effectively crippled agitation for months. This split has often been analysed simply in terms of the incompatible or perverse personalities of Devoy, Cohalan and de Valera. No doubt these leaders were difficult men who were jealous of their prerogatives, over-sensitive to criticism, and accustomed to being obeyed. The antecedents of the split, however, could be traced back as early as 1914, and the pattern was clear in 1918 when the IPL and Mrs Sheehy-Skeffington challenged the Clan na Gael and the FOIF through their continued activity during the war. By 1919 a large number of Clan and FOIF leaders had become convinced that the straightest path to Irish independence lay through American politics and diplomacy; de Valera and others favoured a more direct policy of simply subsidising the Irish revolution, with the Irish-Americans serving as overseas auxiliaries directed from Ireland.[18] Thus a conflict of principle developed when attempts were made to divert the resources controlled by the Irish-American leaders away from their propaganda efforts in the United States and towards the financing of the revolution in Ireland. In these circumstances the overbearing and dogmatic qualities of the leaders themselves aggravated and burdened the broadly based movement which was already strained by diversity.

The first major source of irritation had been the bond-certificate drive, although the leaders of the FOIF had voluntarily agreed to curtail the Irish Freedom Fund drive and had made available considerable sums of money in order to give the bond-certificate drive and de Valera sufficient cash with which to carry out a national campaign. However, there were difficulties that most of the leaders seemed to recognise. John J. Splain wrote to Frank P. Walsh that de Valera's demands obstructed the bond-certificate work, and the action of de Valera and his entourage in Portland, Oregon, led to the resignation of Thomas A. Mannix, who had figured prominently in the anti-League of Nations fight.[19] Walsh himself admitted the tensions in the movement, and indeed used the conflicts as an argument for personal sacrifice for the Irish cause. He explained to Seán T. O'Kelly: 'The position which I am taking is, that we are trying to aid Ireland, not tell her what to do, and that her chosen leader is De Valera, and that he, finally, must decide every question.'[20] This proved difficult advice to follow, however, when de

Valera acted without consulting the Irish-American leaders and when he made decisions about matters which were as much American as they were Irish.

A crisis was reached in early February 1920 when de Valera gave an interview to the *Westminster Gazette* and the New York *Globe*, in which he said that Britain could give Ireland independence and still protect its security by implementing a policy similar to America's Monroe Doctrine. The United States, de Valera argued, had permitted Cuba to be independent, although through the Platt amendment it had taken care to guarantee that Cuba could never become a base of attack against the United States nor be dominated by another power. To be sure, Cuba was technically sovereign and independent, but it had become politically unstable and dominated by the United States, and as such it provided an unsuitable model for future Anglo-Irish relations. The analogy was suggested by de Valera in the hope of stimulating a dialogue between the British government and the Irish leaders, but its effect was to create the impression in the United States and Ireland that de Valera was willing to accept as a solution to the Irish question something far less than an independent republic.

To a great many Irish-Americans, already piqued at de Valera's attempts to dominate their organisations, the interview caused a bitter outcry, and even de Valera's strongest supporters thought that the interview had dangerous implications. For over a month the editorials of the *Gaelic American* denounced de Valera for attempting to subvert Ireland's independence and sovereignty and argued that an arrangement between Ireland and Britain similar to the Platt amendment would be disastrous.[21] Some thought that the split would take place then as a result of Devoy's editorials. Dr Maloney was 'alarmed lest the gang [Cohalan and Devoy] knife de Valera', and Mrs Golden lamented: 'Of course we've known the split would come but too bad it had to come during the bonds.' On 20 February 1920 de Valera appealed to Judge Cohalan to stop the attacks against him in the *Gaelic American*, but the judge replied in a devastating attack that he did not control the policy of that newspaper, although he agreed with its assertions that the Cuban analogy which de Valera had used had seemed contrary to the expressed desires of the Irish people. Cohalan then called a meeting of nearly one hundred leading Irish-Americans in New York on 19 March, to which de Valera was not invited, ostensibly for the purpose of preventing a split in the nationalist movement. Apparently it was hoped that these leaders would agree to ask de Valera to return to Ireland and leave the handling of the agitation in America to the Irish-Americans. However, through the efforts of

Joseph McGarrity, de Valera was brought to the meeting, where he defended himself against the charges of Cohalan by asserting that the judge and Devoy had hoped to destroy him. After ten emotional hours the meeting closed with a not very successful attempt to reconcile differences.[22]

The tension within the Irish-American nationalist movement was not allowed to diminish. Within a month's time James O'Mara, acting as one of the trustees of the Dáil loan, demanded that the money raised through the Irish Victory Fund be turned over to the Dáil government. The national council of the FOIF refused to do this, saying that the money would be used for its intended purpose— that being, roughly, to educate public opinion and to maintain agitation in America and Ireland, but not to provide revenue for an Irish government. If this direct challenge to the leadership of the FOIF had not been enough, the misadventures of the Irish delegations at the American political conventions in June 1920 forced the divisions into public view again. As a result de Valera decided that the FOIF required 'immediate and thorough' reorganisation; he told the Illinois state council of the FOIF that they should make their organisation 'as widely democratic as possible', with all officers and committees elected rather than appointed. The summary expulsion in July of the IPL, which included many of de Valera's strongest supporters, from associate membership of the FOIF augmented the growing hostility within the movement and laid the FOIF leaders open to the charge of autocratic practices.[23] De Valera appealed in a public letter to the recently elected president of the FOIF, Bishop Gallagher of Detroit, to call an Irish Race Convention in the autumn in order to restore confidence in the organisation and provide the machinery through which differences could be worked out 'by the will of the majority of the members' rather than by 'arbitrary suspensions and expulsions by the Executive'. The bishop turned de Valera down. Failing to obtain a race convention, where broad popular support could have been developed for whatever changes de Valera requested, he submitted to Bishop Gallagher a series of amendments to the constitution of the FOIF for consideration at the national council meeting due to be held in New York on 17 September. However, once again his attempts to force changes upon the FOIF that would weaken the control of its present leaders were unsuccessful. In an emotional meeting, in some ways not unlike the so-called 'trial' of de Valera in March, the new proposals were defeated, and de Valera left the meeting in the company of his supporters.[24]

In addition to efforts made by the Irish leaders in America to obtain the unqualified support of the Irish-American leaders,

attempts were also made from Ireland to end the difficulties. Seán
T. O'Kelly cabled John Devoy after the Republican Party convention to 'end effectively [the] infamous allegations against president
[de Valera]' because they were weakening the movement at home
and abroad. The situation was also discussed with some alarm in
the Dáil, which of course defined the problem in de Valera's terms.[25]
During the late summer of 1920 Harry Boland, then Irish envoy to
the United States, was able to work out a pledge of co-operation
from the Clan na Gael, but when the editorial policy of the *Gaelic
American* seemed impervious to change, Boland, acting on the
authority of the Supreme Council of the IRB, severed the connection between the Clan and the Brotherhood on 22 October.
Several weeks later at a meeting of the Clan executive Devoy, John
A. McGarry, John A. Murphy, Joseph Liddy and Michael McGrail
defended the Clan's policy and denounced Boland's action against
the objections of Joseph McGarrity and Hugh Montague. As a
result of the meeting McGarrity and Montague declared their
antagonists on the executive expelled from the Clan, and Luke
Dillon, whom they appointed treasurer of the 'reorganised' Clan na
Gael, sent out letters to all known Clan members asking them to
give their allegiance to the new leaders. Although the reorganised
Clan made some progress in Philadelphia, San Francisco and
Chicago, Devoy tended to hold the loyalties of a majority of the
Clan members, especially in New York, the Clan's main source
of strength.[26]

De Valera next took the remarkable step of circumventing
Cohalan and Devoy by creating his own Irish-American organisation. On 9 November he sent telegrams to over one hundred
Irish-Americans asking them if they could come to Washington for
a conference to plan a national campaign to 'secure official recognition for [the] Irish Republic'. De Valera told the people who
assembled at the meeting on 16 November that he had hesitated to
form a new organisation, hoping that the existing ones would give
him their assistance, but his hopes had been 'shattered' on the eve
of the national elections and he now called on them to form a new,
open and democratic partnership to support the Irish cause. The
American Association for the Recognition of the Irish Republic was
created at the conference, and Edward L. Doheny, the California
oil millionaire who had sponsored de Valera's minority report at
the Democratic national convention in June, was made national
president.[27] Doheny had not been active in Irish-American nationalist affairs, although he seemed particularly suitable because he
was both rich and the nephew of Michael Doheny, the Young
Irelander. He was also to be something of a refreshing new face and

a public show-piece. (In the long run, however, Doheny's connection with the AARIR backfired when, albeit after he had left the organisation, he became implicated in the great Teapot Dome oil reserve scandals in 1923. Doheny seemed then to be merely another of the corrupt old Irish-American leaders who continued to reflect badly on the national cause.)

The energies of the two Irish-American nationalist organisations were, for the next several months, devoted to internal problems—the FOIF and the Clan to maintain what strength and enrolment they could, and the AARIR to create a system of state and local branches throughout the country. Diarmuid Lynch, national secretary of the FOIF, wrote to all the regular and associate branches accusing de Valera of using a 'flying squadron' to destroy the smooth-running organisation which five months earlier had the enemies of America and Ireland 'on the run'. Lynch also outlined the extent to which the FOIF and the Irish Victory Fund had not only financed the whole movement in the United States but had also subsidised de Valera's mission and the bond-certificate drive. The *Gaelic American* lashed out at de Valera, saying that his amendments to the FOIF constitution would have ruined it and that expulsion of the Clan was outrageous: 'No better work for Ireland was ever done in living memory and yet those who did it are treated as enemies of Ireland.' The AARIR, using some of the bond-certificate money and campaign workers, and the members of the IPL, began consolidating their new organisation: they established a national headquarters in Washington, created the Benjamin Franklin Bureau in Chicago, elected Peter Golden national secretary and undertook a pamphlet campaign. A large convention was called on 18–20 April 1921 in Chicago where the national character of the organisation was fully established; such Irish-American leaders as Rossa F. Downing, Judge John Goff and Father Peter C. Yorke figured prominently. The convention was a success, although requests made by de Valera for new fund-raising projects without prior consultation with either O'Mara or Boland created some bad feeling. De Valera, however, had in December 1920 slipped secretly back to Ireland.[28]

De Valera's objective in founding an organisation under the control of the Irish leaders was understandable enough, although why he chose to direct the AARIR irrevocably towards recognition of an Irish Republic is less clear. As McCartan and several others have observed, by November of 1920 it was no longer possible to hope for official acknowledgment or recognition of the Irish Republic. Nevertheless, the AARIR expended great energy in promoting the idea of American recognition. Dr Maloney published an intriguing pamphlet in which he argued that the Senate had already extended recognition to Ireland in its resolution in June 1919 asking that the Peace Conference give a hearing to the Irish delegation. The anonymous pamphlet *We must recognize the Irish Republic* said that the United States owed support and recognition to Ireland and that the Irish cause and the American cause were identical. Other pamphlets emphasised the republican character of the new Ireland. The testimony of Mary MacSwiney before the American Commission on Conditions in Ireland was reprinted, and explained the creation of the present republic. Mrs Alice Stopford Green's *The Irish Republican Army* asserted that the function of the IRA, one of the finest fighting bodies in the world, was to protect the Republic and allow its institutions to continue functioning throughout Ireland.[29] None of this moved the United States towards recognition, however, and indeed, as de Valera himself confessed to the Dáil when he returned to Ireland, 'If I were President of the United States myself . . . I could not, and would not, recognize Ireland as a Republic.' By the spring of 1921 Major Kinkead admitted that 'we will have great difficulty' securing the passage by Congress of any measure which would extend recognition to Ireland, although Frank P. Walsh suggested to James O'Mara that the AARIR was then strong enough to 'bring organized pressure to bear on the newspapers throughout the country' in order to broaden the campaign for the Irish cause.[30]

Meanwhile, of course, valuable time had been lost during the bickering between the rival factions in America. Efforts were made to deal with the very important events which were taking place in Ireland and the United States, but they met with little success. The hunger-strike of Lord Mayor Terence MacSwiney drew appeals to the American government from diverse sources. Secretary of State Colby was willing to consider making an unofficial appeal to the British Embassy and to listen patiently to Frank P. Walsh, James K. McGuire and Daniel C. O'Flaherty (the Under-Secretary of State had already told Cardinal O'Connell that the government had no legal grounds for intervention in MacSwiney's case), but the tired and sick Wilson lashed out at a rather tactless telegram to him by telling Tumulty: 'This is more than futile; it is grossly impertinent.'[31]

The 1920 presidential election was another source of frustration. The Irish-Americans, having laboured diligently for months to destroy Wilson and the Democratic Party, found that Senator Warren G. Harding, the Republican candidate for President, regarded Ireland as a British domestic problem. Appeals to Wilson from James M. Cox, the Democratic candidate, to give some assistance by making a public statement about the ways the League of Nations could serve Ireland fell upon deaf ears. Franklin D. Roosevelt, the Democratic vice-presidential candidate, wrote in all truthfulness to his British friend Colonel Arthur Murray, MP: 'I wish to goodness you could find some way of taking it [the Irish question] out of our campaign over here!'[32] But the Republican majority was so large that it was unlikely that the Irish-American vote had much influence one way or another.

Several other independent projects by Irish-American groups proved to be fiascos—boycotting British manufactured goods, causing labour strikes among workers servicing British steamships, and the efforts of the Irish 'Consul' in New York 'prohibiting' American commerce with Ireland through British ports—and they led to lawsuits, angry letters and the possibility of government action. Nor did the nationalist movement thrive on the constitutional front. To be sure, with the opening of the new Congress in April 1921 numerous resolutions were introduced in both houses asking for recognition of the Irish Republic or expressing concern over conditions in Ireland. However, in spite of several impassioned speeches by Senators LaFollette, Borah and Norris, no hearings were held on any of them and none were reported from the committees.[33]

III.   The American Commission on Conditions in Ireland and the American Committee for Relief in Ireland

While the Irish and Irish-American leaders were struggling for control of the nationalist movement in the United States, new avenues were explored to maintain agitation and, in so far as possible, to enlist the support and participation of native Americans. Several projects were undertaken, the most notable being the American Commission on Conditions in Ireland and the American Commission for Relief in Ireland, both the inventions of the fertile mind of Dr W. J. M. A. Maloney. The first project was carried out through the co-operation of Oswald Garrison Villard, the editor of the liberal New York *Nation* and a relation by marriage to Maloney. Villard agreed to send out invitations to every senator and state governor and a large list of distinguished Americans to form a 'Committee of One Hundred' which would assume the power to appoint a small commission to investigate the violent political situation in Ireland. De Valera himself was sceptical, but when assured by Maloney that 'the Commission is merely a mask to place the Irish case before the tribunal of the civilized world', although hostile witnesses would be included to maintain a degree of objectivity, he agreed. By early October some 130 people had responded and were able to meet and select the eight-member commission: chairman L. Hollingsworth Wood, a New York lawyer active in liberal causes and a member of the Society of Friends; vice-chairman Dr Frederick C. Howe, a New York lawyer and former international affairs expert for the American Commission to Negotiate Peace; Jane Addams, the Chicago social worker; the Rev. Norman Thomas, the socialist Presbyterian minister and editor of *World Tomorrow*; James Maurer, Pennsylvania labour leader; Major Oliver Newman, soldier and journalist; Senator David I. Walsh of Massachusetts; and Senator George W. Norris of Nebraska. The commission was a very distinguished one, although its decidedly liberal membership made it suspect in some quarters.[34]

The commission disengaged itself from the *Nation* as soon as money, raised by subscription through the magazine, permitted them to do so, and they opened offices in Washington, DC, at the Hotel LaFayette. Its objectives, as the vice-chairman, Frederick C. Howe, said later at the first public session, were

> to learn as nearly as possible just what the conditions in Ireland are and what has brought them about. It plans to conduct a series of public hearings in Washington. It will hear witnesses who present themselves representing English and Irish opinion.

Invitations were to be extended to people in Ireland who had figured in the reprisals by the British forces, and British government authorities were asked to send representatives; from the testimony of these witnesses the commission would attempt to determine what was happening in Ireland and who was responsible. The British government, of course, was not pleased with the prospect of Americans passing judgment on their attempts to suppress rebellion in Ireland. Geddes informed the Foreign Office that the project was 'obviously designed to embarrass us as naturally no evidence can be forthcoming from this side', and he thought anyone attempting to present the British argument should be discouraged because it could not be done effectively in the circumstances. Nonetheless, he felt it would be a mistake to prevent people such as Mrs MacSwiney from leaving Ireland because that would be more damaging than her testimony. Dr William MacDonald, secretary of the commission, was informed that the British government would not actively assist the commission but that it would not withhold passports from those attempting to give testimony.[35]

The hearings themselves were extremely effective in providing a means of informing the American public of British outrages in

Ireland, although the thirty-eight witnesses, as had been anticipated, were in large part either participants in the Irish nationalist movement or openly sympathetic to it. The first session of hearings took place on 18 and 19 November 1920 in Washington. Denis Morgan, chairman of Thurles Urban District Council, and John Derham, town councillor of Balbriggan, both addressed the commission and told of atrocities committed in their communities by the crown forces. Morgan related how the Black and Tans had subjected himself and his family to great personal danger and how his home and public house had been burned because of his alleged Sinn Féin sympathies. Derham described the British reprisals in Balbriggan which resulted in the destruction of a section of that village. Francis Hackett, a writer for the *New Republic* and the author of *Ireland: a study in nationalism*, and his wife, Signe Toksvig, gave grim reports about the conditions in Ireland they had observed; and three other Americans gave reports of unpleasant encounters with British authorities in Ireland while visiting relatives. The second set of hearings, on 8, 9 and 10 December, was even more spectacular, featuring the widow and the sister of Terence MacSwiney, who told of the long vigil maintained by the late Lord Mayor. Four former members of the Royal Irish Constabulary gave lurid tales of how the constabulary had become increasingly alienated by the practices of the uncontrollable Black and Tans and Auxiliaries. These particular hearings were dramatically underscored by the burning of sections of Cork city centre two nights later. Subsequent hearings held in late December 1920 and January 1921 included among the witnesses Lawrence Ginnell, a former Redmondite MP and now a Sinn Féin member of the Dáil; the sisters of the late Lord Mayor MacCurtain of Cork; two representatives of the British branch of the Women's International League; Louie Bennett, secretary of the Irish branch of the Women's International League; J. L. Fawsitt, Consul-General of the Irish Republic in New York; and Donal O'Callaghan, the Lord Mayor of Cork. All this testimony, fully covered by newspaper reporters, was important in keeping the nationalist point of view before the American public during a time when factionalism within the Irish-American nationalist movement had destroyed the normal machinery for propaganda and agitation.[36]

In other ways the commission was less successful. Criticism was levelled at it by native Americans because the witnesses were overwhelmingly nationalist in their sympathies, and, for this reason, several members of the Committee of One Hundred later resigned. The *Gaelic American* also opposed the commission as a device to divert Irish-American attention away from the split in the movement, although it later supported the report. But there were other problems as well. The commission moved slowly, holding hearings over three months. Its *Interim report,* which described what the commission was attempting to do and talked generally about the British terror campaign, was not published until March 1921, and the final volume, *Evidence on conditions in Ireland* did not appear until July 1921, almost too late to be of propaganda value.[37] Even Villard confessed: 'Our report had a much better reception in England than it did here.' Furthermore, the fact that the Benjamin Franklin Bureau distributed free copies of both volumes created financial problems for the commission. By May the chairman of the commission told Frank P. Walsh: 'Altogether the three main movers in this enterprise are feeling pretty unhappy.'[38]

Relief operations were another avenue of agitation which could be maintained despite the divisions in the nationalist movement. Of course, relief efforts had been made in 1916, although they had been an almost exclusively Irish-American enterprise. In 1920, in part because of the publicity work of the American Commission on Conditions in Ireland, but to no small degree because of the dimensions of the reprisals themselves, much larger and more ambitious projects were proposed. Attempts were first made during the autumn of 1920 to secure the assistance of the American Red Cross in sending aid to Ireland; however, with the burning of parts of Cork on the night of 11–12 December an appeal was received directly from Lord Mayor O'Callaghan. Dr Livingstone Farrand, national director, sensitive to the political implication of relief in Ireland, consulted the Department of State, the British Embassy and the British Red Cross. On the strength of the report from the British director that no one was homeless as a result of the destruction, although eventually jobs would be affected, the American Red Cross informed people such as Mrs Peter Golden that they felt that no action could be taken. Appeals directly to the Secretary of State for advice about the distribution of clothing and assistance were turned aside with the suggestion that the Irish Red Cross might be willing to help. Although these attempts to secure the intervention of the Red Cross failed, private efforts such as that of Mrs Séamus O'Doherty, then in the United States, were successful. Through the Irish-American Club of Philadelphia Mrs O'Doherty was able to send the s.s. *Honolulu* to Cork in late December loaded with 1,700 tons of food and clothing.[39]

A more spectacular private effort undertaken by Dr Maloney was also successful, although initially his attempts among friends in New York to create interest in sending a relief ship to Ireland had not been very promising. Through the influence of Judge Richard

Campbell and Senator David I. Walsh, Maloney enlisted the aid and financial resources of Edward L. Doheny, the California oil millionaire who had recently been appointed national president of the AARIR. Doheny wrote a cheque for $10,000 and agreed to underwrite the whole $247,000 if necessary. Maloney attempted again to win support for his project by holding a luncheon meeting in New York, but five days before the meeting sections of Cork were burned by the British forces. Armed with this news and a cable appealing for aid from James G. Douglas, a leading Dublin member of the Society of Friends, Maloney changed his plans and advocated the creation of a national organisation to co-ordinate and direct relief to Ireland. This new proposal was enthusiastically accepted by the guests at the luncheon, who formed themselves into the executive committee of the American Committee for Relief in Ireland. This committee, which included twenty-three distinguished Irish-Americans, began work to make a national appeal for funds and create a broadly based organisation to collect them. Doheny advanced the committee $250,000, which enabled them to begin work then and to cable $25,000 to Douglas immediately.[40]

Maloney also suggested that a delegation be sent by the American Committee for Relief in Ireland to investigate the conditions in Ireland and to confer with people there as to how relief operations could be most effectively handled. A group of eight men, several of them members of the Society of Friends with previous experience in European relief operations, was appointed and left in late January for England and Ireland, where they immediately began talks with Friends' relief committees in both countries. After securing permission to travel throughout Ireland from General Macready, on the condition that their relief work would be 'non-political' and carried out in an 'impartial spirit', the delegation proceeded to make an inspection tour of the country lasting nearly two months, during which they visited ninety-five towns, villages and creameries which had been destroyed or damaged by the British forces. From their own observations and from conversations with people in the distressed areas, as well as from the advice of relief organisations in Ireland, the delegation compiled a report for the American Committee for Relief in Ireland from which estimates of the type and amount of relief necessary were calculated. A close relationship was quickly established between the delegation and James G. Douglas of the Irish White Cross Society, and indeed the decision was made to carry out the relief through that society rather than attempt to administrate it themselves.[41]

Meanwhile in the United States the committee began work to

raise the money to finance the relief projects. On the advice of Herbert Hoover, Captain John F. Lucey, who had worked with Hoover in Belgian relief, was placed in charge of the fund drive and James A. Healy was made assistant secretary of the executive committee. A large national council was created with 134 members, many of them native Americans, and a list of dignitaries as honorary vice-chairmen, including eighteen state governors, three former cabinet members, as well as labour leaders, social workers, philanthropists and editors. Although the membership of the national council was heavily Irish-American, the number of native Americans was significant. Furthermore, letters of endorsement were solicited from such public figures as Vice-President Calvin Coolidge, Secretary of Commerce Herbert Hoover, Secretary of War J. Wingate Weeks, former Secretary of the Treasury William G. McAdoo, former head of the war industries board Bernard Baruch, former Ambassador to Germany James W. Gerard, and many others. By far the most significant letter came from President Warren G. Harding, who wished the committee 'the fullest measure of success'. He told Judge Morgan J. O'Brien:

The people of America never will be deaf to the call for relief in behalf of suffering humanity, and the knowledge of distress in Ireland makes quick and deep appeal to the more fortunate of our own land where so many of our citizens trace kinship to the Emerald Isle.[42]

Armed with this official endorsement, the committee began its national appeal on St Patrick's Day, 1921, issuing an open letter entitled 'A summons to service' to all Americans and asserting that the people of Ireland were then suffering more than had the people of Belgium. 'We are not concerned', it said further, 'with the causes of this suffering, our appeal is solely humanitarian, absolutely nonsectarian, and strictly non-political.' They estimated that $10,000,000 was needed quickly and that only the American people could provide the money. The public appeal enlisted the support of such celebrities as John McCormack, who gave three benefit concerts to raise money, in addition to the assistance of the Catholic Church and various Irish-American organisations. Geddes sent home anxious reports that the committee had raised $2,000,000 and had pledges for a further $3,000,000. Actually the committee raised the impressive sum of $5,223,497, most of which was sent to Ireland through James G. Douglas and the Irish White Cross Society.[43]

The very success of the American Committee for Relief in Ireland

created diplomatic problems for the British and American governments. Indeed, a very complicated situation had developed. The
endorsement of the relief movement by President Harding and
others had appeared to lend the approval of the government, and
in fact, along with widespread reports of destitution in Ireland, it
had stimulated contributions. When Samuel Duff McCoy, secretary
to the delegation sent to Ireland, returned to the United States in
late April he conferred with G. Howland Shaw, the State Department's director of Western European affairs, explaining that the
British military authorities in Ireland had first said they would
permit non-partisan relief to be distributed, but that when the
delegation decided to work through the Irish White Cross Society
which was in operation before they arrived, the British broke their
agreement. As an alternative, McCoy suggested that the administration of the relief funds be assumed by the Department of State
as had been done in Belgium during the war, since he thought the
department was certain to become involved anyway. Sir Auckland
Geddes learned of these proposals informally and sent a worried
dispatch to the Foreign Office analysing the situation as one fraught
with danger. An open rejection, Geddes thought, would cause
Congress to pass a resolution in favour of recognition of an Irish
Republic which might result in the resignation of Secretary of State
Charles Evans Hughes and his replacement by former Senator
Albert B. Fall, then Secretary of the Interior, a leader of the anti-
British western oil interests. The Foreign Office was genuinely
alarmed, and Lord Curzon, with the approval of the cabinet, drafted
a cable to Geddes that the British government could in no way
accept the suggestion that the Department of State assume the
administration of, or the responsibility for, relief in Ireland.[44]
Geddes informed Secretary Hughes that the suggestions of the
American committee were 'entirely unacceptable', although Hughes
hoped that the British government would be able to accommodate
some kind of relief operation in Ireland in order to forestall the
indignant public outburst which was certain to follow a flat rejection
of any kind of Irish relief. Indeed, Geddes recommended some sort
of compromise, perhaps with the British Red Cross doing the relief
work, and he was supported in this by Sir William Tyrrell, now
Assistant Under-Secretary at the Foreign Office, but the government
was adamant in its refusal.[45]

The discomfiture of the State Department and the American government, in addition to that caused by the endorsement of Harding
and members of his cabinet, was made all the greater by the reports
which the department began to receive from the United States
Consul in Dublin, Frederick T. F. Dumont. Just a few days before

Harding wrote his letter, Dumont sent the State Department a report in which he questioned the objectivity of the Irish White Cross personnel with whom the American delegation had conferred. He asserted that there was no widespread distress in Ireland, and that in fact the cargo of the relief ship, s.s. *Honolulu,* which had arrived in mid-January, had been stored in Cork and not distributed. These observations were shown to Hughes and President Harding, and a request for more information was sent to the Dublin, Cork and Belfast consulates. Dumont's subsequent reports were equally disquieting to the department, and they provided substantial evidence that, as the British authorities had insisted, there was little economic distress in Ireland as a result of the civil disorders and that indeed Ireland was probably more prosperous than ever before. Furthermore, Dumont said of the American relief funds: 'It can be stated with confidence that they are to be used to relieve the Treasury of Sinn Féin, and permitting it to devote its funds entirely to the forwarding of the revolutionary movement in Ireland.'[46] This bold assertion, that the American relief money was to be used to subsidise the families of those fighting the British, thus relieving the Dáil of that responsibility, was received with grave concern by the department, and Secretary Hughes himself asked Dumont to 'send all specific information which you may be able to obtain as to the introduction of American funds into Ireland, particularly when, in your opinion, these funds are to be used for the purposes of the Republican Army'.[47]

Nevertheless, despite the considerable degree of tension which had developed between the two governments over the Irish question, Hughes was willing to use the Irish situation in order to extract concessions from Great Britain on the issues of the Anglo-Japanese alliance and Anglo-American naval rivalry—the two questions that were of greatest concern to the administration. The State Department had been probing the British government about termination of this treaty for almost a year, but on 23 June 1921 Hughes told the British Ambassador rather pointedly that renewal of the alliance would probably provoke the rallying of all anti-British elements in the United States and would very likely lead to a congressional debate on a resolution calling for the recognition of the Irish Republic.[48] The degree to which Hughes's remarks to Geddes constituted a threat that the United States government would support insurrection in Ireland unless Britain broke off the Anglo-Japanese alliance, to state the matter baldly, is difficult to measure. However, it is significant that the Secretary of State took pains to link the two issues in his talk with the British Ambassador and that the arrangements both for the truce between the British and the Dáil and for the Washington Conference on naval disarmament and Asian affairs coincided on 11 July 1921.

Closely allied to the State Department's worries about the use of relief funds for revolutionary purposes was the fear that weapons might be sent from the United States to supply the Irish Republican Army. There had been rumours of arms shipments from America as early as January and May 1920, although by the end of the year British intelligence sources failed to trace any substantial number of weapons to the United States. However, by early June of 1921 the report of the Irish Chief Secretary to Lord Curzon that information had been acquired suggesting that the Irish Republican Army was in possession of a number of machine-guns caused some genuine anxiety in the State Department. The fortuitous discovery, several days later, of 495 machine-guns and ammunition on board the coal ship s.s. *East Side*, destined to sail to Ireland, seemed to offer conclusive proof that arms traffic between the United States and Ireland existed. The Under-Secretary of State asked the Secretary of the Treasury to be kept informed of the details of this and any similar arms seizures, and Hughes had an uncomfortable interview with Geddes wherein the ambassador noted the dangers of the situation and Hughes was able to defend himself only by asking for specific details about the arms shipments to which Geddes had alluded.[49] With the acquisition of Dumont's observations on the use of the relief fund simultaneously with the discovery of the machine-guns on the s.s. *East Side* and the possibility of a congressional resolution recognising the Irish Republic, the State Department found itself, and the state of Anglo-American relations on the eve of the truce, in an extremely difficult situation.

IV.   Native American Reaction

Perhaps inevitably, the extensive and prolonged Irish agitation in the United States from 1919 to 1921 provoked a hostile reaction from many native Americans. Antagonism towards immigrant groups and Catholics was always close to the surface in American life, as has been shown in earlier chapters, but by the 1920s the nativist and xenophobic tendencies which had been stimulated by the First World War, the Russian Revolution, the peace treaty, and probably the activities of de Valera and the Irish-Americans, gave rise to a degree of anti-Irish sentiment in the United States which went well beyond the occasional speech by Senator Williams or pamphlet by George L. Fox. Organised resistance to the de Valera mission, the bond-certificate drive and the FOIF first centred round a delegation of Ulster Protestants led by William J. Coote,

MP for South Tyrone, who arrived in the United States in November 1919 to make a tour of the country presenting the Unionist arguments. Speaking from the pulpits of large Protestant churches throughout the country, Coote and the six clergymen who accompanied him outlined the dangers presented by Irish nationalism to the Protestant minority and the degree to which the Catholic hierarchy dominated the people. They published, and distributed where they visited, a small pamphlet, *Facts about Ireland for the consideration of American citizens,* which attempted to refute the nationalist propaganda by asserting that Ireland had never been a nation in the modern sense, that it was not oppressed or overtaxed, and that the Sinn Féin movement was responsible for whatever lawlessness or disorder that existed. An independent Ireland, it said, would only unleash religious strife. Irish nationalists often played into Coote's hands, such as when they disrupted him at Grace Methodist Episcopal Church in New York by shouting 'Up the Irish Republic!' and 'Long live de Valera!' Coote could effectively make the point that the Unionists were attempting to save Ireland from people like that.[50]

Encouraged by Coote's mission, a number of Boston anglophiles founded the Loyal Coalition for the purpose of preserving the close and friendly Anglo-American relations that had existed during the war and that were presently being threatened by the Irish ferment in the United States. Led by Demarest Lloyd, the son of the Wisconsin Progressive Henry Demarest Lloyd, and Randolph Wellford Smith, the Loyal Coalition traded heavily on native American racial and religious biases and on the recent fear of Irish collusion with German and Soviet agents. Their first project was a series of public lectures on Anglo-American topics by such distinguished speakers as former president Eliot of Harvard, Moorfield Storey, William Roscoe Thayer, George Haven Putnam, Rear-Admiral William Sowdon Sims, and Captain Arthur E. Runnells of the Canadian Intelligence Service. In addition to a newspaper campaign in New England, the Loyal Coalition attempted to warn the government directly of the Irish menace. Lloyd advised Secretary Colby that the State Department should ignore the 'Irish American influences [attempting] to precipitate a diplomatic controversy with Great Britain over the treatment by the British Government of disturbers of the peace in the south and west of Ireland'.[51] They also sent complaints to Washington protesting about both the various Irish resolutions before Congress in 1920 and 1921, suggesting that the House of Representatives 'confine their attention to American problems', and about the legality of the Irish bond-certificates. Members of the Loyal Coalition travelled to Chicago and San

Francisco to fight the inclusion of an Irish plank in the party platforms, and they struggled throughout the election campaign to keep
the candidates from making statements on the Irish question. They
also denounced the American Commission on Conditions in
Ireland as 'Mr Villard's meddling', but they promised Senator
Williams that they intended 'to see that the truth is known'. These
protests were not made without some personal cost, however, and
the Loyal Coalition was attacked collectively and individually. In
the House of Representatives Congressman Gallivan said they were
'distinctly a treasonable, secret, anti-American body of American
and provincial Tories, Britishers of a sort, and other alienminded
conspirators, officered by some cranks and a few criminals, and
financed by anti-American sources'.[52]

Native Americans were often disturbed by the violence of the
Irish-American demonstrations. Irish political rhetoric and action
had always been fairly extreme, but when directed at American
Presidents or war heroes it produced a vehement reaction. Hearing
Irish-Americans 'applauding de Valera and hissing our President
made millions of us rage', wrote one disgruntled New Yorker, and
he spoke for many others. A striking instance of the tendency for
Irish-Americans to create bad feeling for Ireland by their obnoxious
behaviour was the habit of destroying the Union Jack when found
in the displays of the flags of the Allies which decorated many
buildings for several years after the war. Irish-Americans not only
threatened the close relations between Great Britain and the United
States; many Irish sympathisers made no attempt to disguise the
fact that they wanted war with England. Congressman Gallivan had
told the House of Representatives that Britain had 'no right to
object' to American assistance to Ireland, and Judge Cohalan
answered 'yes' to the question of Congressman Connolly as to
whether he would support war with Britain to secure Irish freedom.
Senator Williams, who insisted that he had always supported Irish
Home Rule, deeply resented the recent efforts of the Irish-
Americans to use the United States as 'a cat's paw to pull Irish
chestnuts out of the fire'. Amory Blaine, the hero of F. Scott
Fitzgerald's popular novel *This side of paradise,* agreed with a
friend about the lack of dignity of the Irish Republic because the
Irish-Americans in the reception committee rode through the town
with 'their arms around the President'; and Sinclair Lewis's fictitious
creation George Babbitt approved of a newspaper account of a
meeting which 'demanded that this Mick agitator, this fellow
DeValera, be deported', claiming that all of the trouble-makers in
America were being paid with German gold and that the United
States had no business meddling in Irish affairs.[53]

Ireland and Irish agitation also became the subject of a series of books and pamphlets which challenged the idea of Irish nationalism and often attacked the role of Irish-Americans in American politics. One of the most thoughtful volumes was *Ireland and England*, a study of Anglo-Irish relations by Edward Raymond Turner, a history professor at the University of Michigan. Turner argued that Irish independence would not be wise for either Ireland or Britain, although the English desire to do justice to Ireland could be most successfully accomplished through some scheme of Home Rule. A more popular book, also destined to be more controversial, was *A straight deal or the ancient grudge* by the celebrated author of *The Virginian* and friend of Theodore Roosevelt, Owen Wister. Wister talked about the importance of maintaining close Anglo-American solidarity, and he struck out at the historical arguments of the Irish in claiming American support in their rebellion. If America owed support to any Irishman, Wister said, it was to the 'Orange' Irish who aided in the founding of the republic and not to the 'Green' Irish who had given America the Civil War draft riots, Tammany Hall politics and the Molly Maguires, and who had assaulted United States sailors in Queenstown in 1918. The scholar and literary critic Henry Seidel Canby, who had been lecturing at Oxford during the war, discouraged an Irish settlement until sectarian passions diminished in Ireland. An exchange of letters between Moorfield Storey and Michael J. Jordan in the Boston *Herald* discussing the attempts of the Irish-Americans to force the Irish question into American foreign relations was reprinted as a small pamphlet, as were several short articles by George L. Fox. Through his writings and testimony at congressional hearings Fox had become known as an anti-Irish spokesman, but the publication of *Light on the Irish question, More light on the Irish question, Lest we forget how disloyal the Irish Sinn Féin Roman Catholics were and are* and *Poisoning the wells* established his reputation. Two books which made some impression in the United States, but which were written abroad, were R. C. Escouflaire's *Ireland an enemy of the Allies?*, which described Ireland's treacherous relations with the Germans during the war, and Richard Dawson's *Red terror and green*, which told of Ireland's post-war relations with the unspeakable Bolsheviks.[54] All of these books questioned the merits of Irish nationalism, often because of Anglo-American sympathy, anti-Catholic feeling, or simply a distrust of the Irish, whether in American politics or in the world war.

These anti-Irish feelings among native Americans eventually focused on the controversy surrounding a speech in London on 7

June 1921 by Rear-Admiral William Sowdon Sims. Actually Sims had earlier incurred the wrath of the Irish-American nationalists when he published his war memoirs, *The victory at sea*, where he devoted several pages to the Irish, discussing the collaboration between the Sinn Féin and the Germans and the attacks of Sinn Féin Irishmen on American sailors in Queenstown. But Sims also added:

> During the nearly two years which the American naval force spent in Europe only one element in the population showed them any hostility or even unfriendliness. At the moment when these lines are being written a delegation claiming to represent the 'Irish Republic' is touring the United States, asking Americans to extend their sympathy and contribute money toward the realization of their project. . . . But it seems that now when this same brotherhood is attempting to stir up hatred in this country against our Allies in the war, there is a certain pertinence in informing Americans just what kind of treatment their brave sailors met with at the hands of the Sinn Féin in Ireland.[55]

These allegations that the nationalists in Ireland had collaborated with the Germans, had beaten up American sailors and were now attempting to destroy the wartime alliance ran directly counter to the arguments of the Irish-American nationalists that the United States owed a long and great debt to Ireland which could only be paid by full support in Ireland's struggle for independence. In fact the Irish-Americans struck back at Sims, denying that there was extensive Irish–German collusion or that Irishmen treated American seamen with anything but open cordiality, and they labelled Admiral Sims as an un-American slave-minded tool of the British.[56]

Thus when Sims told the English-Speaking Union in London in 1921 that the Sinn Féin movement had 'the blood of British and American boys on their hands' and that the Irish-American nationalists were 'none of them Americans at all' but like zebras, 'either black horses with white stripes or white horses with black stripes'—although actually they were 'jackasses' with votes—it was followed by an explosion of Irish-American anger in the United States.[57] The *Gaelic American* assailed Sims, calling him 'a bumptious, swaggering fellow, without intellect or ordinary common sense, who owed his promotion to favouritism and newspaper puffery', and the *Sinn Féiner* called him 'Jackass' Sims. The AARIR and the FOIF sent letters to the Navy Department, Congress and the President protesting against Sims's comments on the Irish. Senator Medill McCormick protested to Secretary of the Navy

Edwin Denby, and Senators Reed and Norris deplored Sims's statements; Senator Pat Harrison of Mississippi introduced a resolution to have Sims's remarks investigated by the Naval Affairs Committee; Congressmen Kindred and Gallivan introduced similar resolutions in the House; and Congressman Manly said confidently that President Harding would have to repudiate the admiral. Sims cut short his visit to England and returned to the United States, to be greeted in New York by rival groups of supporters and opponents, and he was given a mild rebuke by Denby and a pleasant chat with the President.[58]

The matter should have been allowed to drop, but on 20 July Senator Thomas J. Walsh told the Senate that he could not understand why the sympathy for the Irish question 'seems to suffer from a widespread neglect, if not a positively hostile sentiment'. The public was 'deaf', he said, to Ireland's appeals and to the Black and Tan reprisals, and he concluded the reason was due 'in no small part to the charge repeatedly made by Admiral Sims that the Irish were disloyal during the war'; Sims had given the impression that through their collusion with the Germans the Irish had prolonged the war and caused American deaths. Walsh said that these charges were without basis but that their propagation had unfairly crippled American support for the Irish cause. Although Walsh was warmly supported by many Irish-Americans in these statements, the *Christian Science Monitor* seized on the speech as a confession by an Irish-American leader that the Irish cause did not in fact have the national support that had often been claimed for it.[59]

It was certainly incorrect to say, as Senator Thomas J. Walsh had, that America had been altogether 'deaf' to the Irish cause or that Ireland had never gained any widespread support throughout the country. The cordial reception de Valera received from the American public, despite his controversy with the Irish-American nationalist leaders, and the freedom he and his staff enjoyed to carry out their mission across the United States testifies to that, as does the interest and sympathy shown in the efforts of the American Committee for Relief in Ireland to win public support in the United States. But interest and sympathy could not be sustained indefinitely. By 1921 it was becoming noticeable that a point of diminishing returns had been reached and that increasingly Americans were being alienated by this activity as well as won over in support. Moorfield Storey had seen the situation of many native Americans as early as April when he wrote to Lord Bryce suggesting that the British policy of repressing Irish nationalists was misguided: 'Here the experiment of giving the Sinn Féiners ample rope is having the usual salutary result. They have stimulated an intense feeling against themselves, and at least two vigorous societies have been formed in Boston to counteract their propaganda.'[60] When the truce came in July 1921 it found the Irish cause in America for the first time meeting organised opposition as well as support.

CHAPTER 7
AMERICA AND THE FOUNDING OF THE IRISH FREE STATE
1921–1923

WITH the Anglo-Irish truce in 1921 American opinion reflected the shift from military to political attempts to resolve the Irish question. British attempts between 1919 and 1921 to legislate a modest form of Irish self-government in the North and the South, and which brought Northern Ireland into existence, had been generally scorned by nationalist sympathisers whose demands had exceeded these proposals.[1] However, both Irish-Americans and native Americans regarded the truce and peace negotiations as evidence of Britain's willingness to grant to Ireland the degree of sovereignty which the nationalists had claimed. News of the Treaty and the creation of the Irish Free State hastened this belief that the struggle was over and that Ireland was free. The civil war won little support in the United States, despite the efforts of republican propagandists. In fact the civil war was almost as great a source of disillusionment to many Irish-Americans who had dreamed of a happy and prosperous Ireland freed from Britain's grip as it was a source of satisfaction to some native Americans who regarded it as proof of the deficiencies of the Irish character.

I. Irish-Americans: the Anglo-Irish Treaty and the Civil War

Irish-American nationalist agitation fell off sharply as the result of the truce between British and Irish forces on 11 July 1921. The truce was regarded as an admission of defeat by the British after the success of the Sinn Féin candidates in the general election of 1921 and the burning of the Custom House in Dublin, in much the same way that most Americans regarded the armistice as the surrender of the Germans in 1918. Even during the preliminary talks the *Sinn Féiner* featured headlines:

IRISH REPUBLIC TRIUMPHS
BRITAIN MOVES FOR PEACE

For most Irish-American leaders, who may have had a clearer understanding of the delicacy of the situation, the truce imposed a degree of restraint that they had previously never found necessary or desirable, with the result that during the summer of 1921 there was a marked lull in nationalist activities. The *Gaelic American* continued to warn its readers that de Valera was about to betray the Irish Republic for some kind of Home Rule or dominion status, but neither the Clan na Gael, which held a highly secret convention in Boston on 4 and 5 July, nor the FOIF, which directed its energies towards creating an anti-British foreign policy, initiated any major programmes during the remainder of 1921.[2] The AARIR was not much more active in stimulating agitation, although it too called for congressional action to force Britain to pay her debts to the United States and warned of British development of air and naval stations in Ireland which it was felt could only be used against the United States. In the circumstances surrounding the talks between de Valera and Lloyd George even the most innocent gestures of goodwill could be misinterpreted. W. Bourke Cockran introduced a resolution in Congress which expressed a desire that the negotiations lead to a 'complete reconciliation' between the 'English Government and the Irish people'. He was given a stern scolding by Miss Mary MacSwiney, still in the United States, for weakening the Irish negotiating position by not referring to the Irish government. Perhaps to avoid exactly these problems none of the resolutions introduced during the spring, and which had given the State Department such concern, were pressed, and no new resolutions were introduced until late autumn when it was felt that they might strengthen the hand of the Irish negotiators in London.[3]

There was a mixture of optimism and caution among the Irish-American leaders. Even before the truce was declared Basil M. Manly commented to Frank P. Walsh that de Valera was negotiating with the British government 'in magnificent style' and that Ireland was in a favourable position. Walsh himself observed that he found 'the Irish spirit very enthusiastic in America'. Senator Thomas J. Walsh was confident that 'Through the statesmanlike efforts of President DeValera and his able associates a solution of their troubles . . . is at hand.'[4] Despite their factional differences, both FOIF and Clan leaders sent their congratulations to de Valera for his firmness in dealing with the British and his conduct of the negotiations. Nevertheless, the Irish White Cross Society and Clemens J. France (the agent of the American Committee for

Relief in Ireland) felt that there was a possibility of a resumption of hostilities in Ireland, which would result in a blockade of money and supplies into the country; they thus requested that relief funds be sent once again. The committee in the United States complied at once, and the sum of $472,062 was sent off on 2 September, to be followed by weekly remittances similar to those forwarded before the truce.[5]

In October the agitation was vigorously resumed through a second bond-certificate drive in the hope of raising money against a possible breakdown of the Anglo-Irish negotiations, which had just opened, and of strengthening the bargaining position of the Irish delegation in London. Stephen O'Mara had been sent to the United States to replace his brother James in order to direct the second external loan for the Dáil which had been authorised for the amount of $20,000,000. Despite the fact that this amount was twice that of the first loan, the campaign, which opened on 15 October, was limited to Washington, DC, and Illinois.[6] Departing from the policy of ambiguous references to the uses for the money, O'Mara stated that the money would be used to resist aggression and to support the Dáil government. In late October he explained to his Washington chairman, A. J. Barrett, how vital it was that the campaign be successful there, in part because of the British presence at the Washington naval disarmament talks. 'Failure here will be quickly registered at Downing Street where the Irish Peace Conference sits,' O'Mara wrote. 'News of success will as quickly be borne there.' O'Mara instructed Barrett to seek the support of the wealthy Irish-Americans throughout the country and make it clear to them 'that one dollar now is of more importance and will be far more highly appreciated than ten times that amount when Ireland is free'.[7] Having restricted themselves to merely Washington and Illinois, and operating without the support of the Clan or the FOIF, the chances of the second bond-certificate drive were not very promising. Nonetheless, Frank P. Walsh felt that the possibilities were unlimited and wrote that the Irish in America could 'raise fifty million dollars almost as easily as they raised the eleven million [during the first loan and relief campaign]', and Michael Collins later told the Dáil that the peace negotiators in London had been assured that Irish-Americans could supply 'a million dollars a month' in the event of war being resumed. With the report of the signing of the Treaty in London, the bond-certificate campaign was called off with over $600,000 collected.[8]

The signing of the Anglo-Irish Treaty in London on 6 December 1921 was as momentous an event for the Irish-Americans as it was for the Irish at home. Similarly it was regarded as an acceptable settlement, although it offered something less than a republic and it reaffirmed provisions for the exclusion of a large part of Ulster. An important meeting of wealthy Irish-Americans, AARIR leaders and sympathetic politicians was held in Washington on 8 December, originally for the purpose for exploring methods of continuing support for Ireland should negotiations fail. The meeting was significant because a number of prominent leaders, such as Bishop Shahan and W. Bourke Cockran, spoke out in favour of the Treaty. Senator Thomas J. Walsh observed that 'It was the unanimous opinion that the agreement brought substantial freedom to Ireland and ought to be accepted,' and he told several people that Irish-Americans should not encourage the rejection of the Treaty while they remained safe in the United States. Boland and O'Mara also spoke, and although they were critical, it was understood by several observers that they did not oppose the Treaty; indeed, they used the occasion to call off the second bond-certificate campaign.[9]

Many of the national leaders of the AARIR also quickly endorsed the Treaty. Edward L. Doheny, the national president, said that the way was now cleared for harmonious Anglo-American relations, and one of the vice-presidents said he was 'delighted with the result of the Irish peace negotiations'.[10] Even the knowledge of de Valera's disapproval of the Treaty did not deter the leaders of the AARIR. The state directorate met in Washington on 14 December and declared its 'neutrality' in regard to the evident disagreement within the Dáil and the government, but several days later the national executive met and sent a cable to 'congratulate the government and the people of the Republic of Ireland on the magnificent struggle they have made for liberty and on the great progress they have already made towards its achievement'. It was clearly a hint to accept what was already at hand. Frank P. Walsh probably spoke for many when he confessed that although he had reservations about the Treaty, he thought it was a 'big step forward' and that 'it puts mighty weapons in our hands for the final consummation of Ireland's complete independence'.[11]

However, despite this initial endorsement of the Treaty by many of its leaders, the AARIR soon found itself badly divided. Even before the meeting of the national executive a memorandum was drawn up outlining the reasons for keeping the organisation functioning. On 4 February 1922 members of the national executive met again, but with fewer than twenty members present, and in New York rather than at the national headquarters in Washington. At this meeting they reversed their earlier position and extended their support to de Valera and the maintenance of the Irish Republic. An Irish Republic Defence Fund was created and, according to

Rossa F. Downing, all members of the AARIR were expected to contribute or were expelled. Many opposed this policy, which ran directly counter to the decision of the Dáil to accept the Treaty, with the inevitable result that the leadership slipped into the hands of the more dogmatic republicans and the membership quickly shrank. In fact within several days of this major policy-making meeting Doheny announced that he had not been informed of it and that because of the Dáil's acceptance of the Treaty and the creation of the Irish Free State he found himself the president of an organisation whose goals had been accomplished. An angry national secretary protested to Doheny immediately, disputing the appropriateness of his continuing in office, considering his views.[12] Many of the members of the AARIR opposed the change in policy of the national executive and the tactics used to accomplish it. By mid-March Frank P. Walsh informed Stephen M. O'Mara that the organisation was 'absolutely shot to pieces', and Downing later substantiated this by commenting that the membership had declined to a mere 75,000. The *Irish World*, which since the split in the Irish movement in 1920 had been the organ of the AARIR, rejected the Treaty from the first. It denounced it in bitter terms, calling it 'the Treaty of surrender' and, after news of its acceptance by the Dáil, announcing that the 'Irish Republic still lives'.[13] The *Irish World* became an uncompromising spokesman for the republican position in the United States and started a slanderous campaign against the supporters of the Treaty and the Irish Free State.

The reactions of the FOIF and the Clan na Gael to the Treaty followed a different pattern. Diarmuid Lynch of the FOIF, Laurence J. Rice of the Clan, and Judge Cohalan all issued immediate protests about its provisions, especially those dealing with the crown and British defence precautions. The *Gaelic American* announced that the Irish delegation had brought back mere 'Home Rule within the Empire'. Holding its national convention on 10 and 11 December, the FOIF issued a statement which said clearly that the organisation did not endorse the Treaty or the Irish Free State, that their opinion had not been asked, and that they regarded any Irish acceptance of the Treaty as a choice made under duress. They proclaimed that 'A free and independent Republic, separated from the Empire . . . is the only solution of the Irish national problem.'[14] However, John J. Splain recorded that most of the members of the convention felt that the dominion status offered in the Treaty was all that could then be extracted from Britain because de Valera's actions in the United States during 1920 had compromised the position of the Republic. While condemning the Treaty, the *Gaelic American* attacked de Valera for objecting to it because his compromises and

G

blunderings had made it inevitable. By January 1922 the paper was beginning to support the Irish Free State and those in the Dáil who voted with the majority. By mid-February Devoy wrote to Michael Collins: 'Our best men here, under the existing conditions, favour giving the "Free State" a chance to do what it can for Ireland,' and he went on to condemn de Valera's presumed loyalty to a republic which he himself had destroyed. Increasingly the *Gaelic American* asserted that de Valera's republican followers had been duped and deluded and that de Valera was encouraging civil war. Judge Cohalan advised his friends to say that the Free State should be supported as a means to an end and that de Valera should be repudiated in favour of Collins. On 28 March 1922 the national council of the FOIF published a statement on the conditions in Ireland, blaming de Valera for the disunity there and giving support to the Irish Free State, through which 'very material advantages can be gained for Ireland'.[15]

During this crisis in Ireland and the United States over the acceptance of the Treaty, the American Committee for Relief in Ireland, which had no ideological commitments to a republic at all, quickly exercised its influence in defence of the Treaty and social stability in Ireland. As soon as the terms of the Treaty were published in the United States the executive committee cabled its congratulations to de Valera and the Dáil, adding that the American people 'earnestly hope for the ratification of the treaty by Dáil Éireann'. Within two weeks Clemens J. France reported the nature of the growing divisions within the Irish government and the important position that the United States could play in the situation. The position of the Irish Free State could be vastly strengthened by the immediate establishment of a Consul-General in Dublin with 'broad powers' and a sympathy for 'Irish National aspirations' and by the development of strong commercial ties with the United States.[16] Nearly a month later France and James G. Douglas outlined another plan by which the committee could support the Irish Free State, which they suggested had the approval of the 'great majority of the Irish people'. They proposed that the money which was currently being given to individuals suffering distress should be diverted into creating jobs in order to insure social and economic stability. 'If the people of Ireland find themselves getting back to work, the Irish Government will hold the great majority which now is in its favor. It might lose that majority if the present stagnation in agriculture and industrial pursuits continues.'[17] By this means the committee was able to help stabilise the situation in Ireland. Sir Horace Plunkett, who through Lawrence Godkin met the members of the executive committee, observed that their attitude was 'sympathy with the Collins Griffith party as they presumably had the majority of people at their backs [and] a readiness to help Ireland financially'. Indeed, in the mind of Captain Monteith, the Irish Republic was betrayed by American moneyed and capitalist interests who wanted to stop the revolution in order to permit American investment in and exploitation of the new Irish state.[18]

Meanwhile the growing disunity among the nationalist leaders in Ireland was dramatically revealed to the Irish in America in the form of two rival delegations sent to tour the United States on behalf of their respective factions. James O'Mara, Piaras Béaslaí, and Seán Mac Caoilte (and later Denis McCullough) were sent by the Provisional Government with instructions 'to get in touch with political and other circles likely to be useful in this country'—in short to win support among the Irish-Americans for the Treaty and the Irish Free State and to raise money with which to fight the coming election. Arriving on the same ship were Austin Stack and J. J. O'Kelly (followed shortly by Countess Markievicz and the sister of Kevin Barry), representing the anti-Treaty faction, whose purpose it was to raise money for the election in order to fight the Treaty supporters and to marshal republican sympathy among the Irish-Americans. A committee of the AARIR protested to Collins and de Valera that such a display of disunity would 'prove disastrous here', and they offered to divide equally all money which Irish-Americans themselves raised for the Irish election.[19] However, neither side could afford to call back their delegations. Harry Boland had written to Frank P. Walsh in late February: 'We will require the support of all friends of the Republic in America now more than ever . . . and we will need a great deal of money to enable us to successfully place our case before [the Irish people]' in the coming election. The pro-Treaty forces needed no money, but they wanted American support nonetheless.

Thus both groups began tours across the country, denouncing their opponents in Ireland with all the malice and vituperation that had previously been reserved for the British government. Stack and O'Kelly opened republican offices in New York and announced the creation of an election campaign fund, while O'Mara worked to cement an alliance with the FOIF and the disaffected members of the AARIR in favour of the Treaty as an immediate, albeit temporary, solution to the Irish problem. The result of this spectacle, made all the more serious by the allegations of the *Gaelic American* that de Valera—that 'half-breed Spanish-American Jew'—was encouraging civil war in Ireland and by the counter-allegations of the *Irish World* that Griffith and Collins—the leaders of the 'Freak State'—were traitors, was extremely demoralising to the Irish-

American community.[20] But de Valera got the money for his election campaign, and Collins and Griffith got the support of Devoy and Judge Cohalan.

Very shortly events in Ireland were to surpass even this. The results of the June election provided a clear majority for the Irish Free State, which (superficially at least) weakened the ideological position of the republicans in the eyes of Americans. The *Gaelic American*, which had been predicting de Valera's collapse, jubilantly published the headlines 'DEVALERA DECISIVELY BEATEN' and claimed that 'Routed in elections he seeks by Mexican methods to overcome the decision of the people by force.' The shelling of the Four Courts and the subsequent outbreak of civil war in Ireland were calamitous to Irish-American morale. Shocked observers who had followed Irish affairs for years were bewildered as the Irish leaders, many of whom had travelled in America and were known to Irish-Americans, were removed from the scene in a grim succession of deaths: Griffith and later Ginnell from overwork; Collins, Boland and Brugha in action; Mellows, Childers and O'Connor by reprisals. John Quinn wrote to Douglas Hyde in disgust: 'I would not shed the blood of a single Irish wolf-hound for the difference between a republic and a free state.'[21] Archbishop Curley of Baltimore returned from a trip to Ireland to announce that 'de Valera is the [Pancho] Villa of Ireland', a contemptuous reference to banditry in Mexico, and Bishop Turner of Buffalo stated that ninety per cent of the Irish people supported the Irish Free State.[22] Dr W. J. M. A. Maloney and the Very Rev. Peter E. Magennis, in Ireland during August of 1922, met representatives of the Free State government and the republican forces and attempted without success to arrange a truce between the warring factions. On 29 September the national council of the FOIF met to denounce the civil war with 'horror and dismay', asserting that it was 'a crime against Ireland and an outrage on the spirit of true democracy'. While some Irish-American supporters of the Free State balked at the government's final policy of executing republican prisoners, the *Gaelic American* never flinched.[23]

The republicans in Ireland realised that despite their control of the AARIR, their claim to the sympathies of the Irish-American community was no longer strong. In fact once again the leader of the AARIR clashed with his executive and had to be replaced. James E. ('Red') Murray, a distinguished labour lawyer and later a liberal senator from Butte, Montana, elected in May 1922 to replace Edward L. Doheny after the latter had given public support to the Treaty, was forced out of office in August because in the civil war crisis he had attempted to use the AARIR to demand a reconciliation of the two factions rather than simply throw the support of the organisation behind the republicans. Nevertheless, the republicans were stoutly defended by the *Irish World*, which denied the significance of the general election of June 1922, arguing that the so-called Independent candidates were merely anti-republicans in disguise and not genuinely independent. When fighting broke out it described the Irish government as an 'illegal junta' created by the British, and it referred to the Free State army as 'hirelings' and later as 'Green and Tans'. Furthermore, a series of republican delegations were sent to the United States to raise money to finance resistance in Ireland and to rally support. Mrs Muriel MacSwiney and later Mrs Hannah Sheehy-Skeffington, despite their differences, toured the country in an attempt to create an Irish Republican Soldiers' and Prisoners' Dependants' Fund, and with Judge John W. Goff as chairman and Frank P. Walsh as vice-chairman, they travelled throughout the country and raised a substantial amount of money. J. J. O'Kelly and Joseph O'Doherty were sent to the United States in the autumn to continue the work of the Stack–O'Kelly–Markievicz mission of the previous spring, although even de Valera seemed to have little confidence in their chances of winning assistance from Irish-Americans on a national level.[24]

The republicans had further difficulties in the United States, beginning in September of 1922, when the Free State government began legal proceedings to obtain possession of the $2,500,000 worth of Irish bond-certificates still in New York banks. The injunctions issued by the courts froze the moneys in the banks and deprived the republicans of access to them during the most critical period of the civil war and in the dark days immediately thereafter. (Although the matter was not fully resolved until 1931, the New York State Supreme Court decided in 1927 that neither the Irish Free State government nor the republican forces had a legitimate claim to the bond-certificates, which had been raised in the name of an Irish republican government, declared by the judge to be non-existent. The bond-certificates were thus placed in the hands of receivers and returned to the purchasers. The struggle for possession of these bond-certificates, fought in the newspapers as well as in the courts, was a spectacular contest which provided an opportunity for both the Free State government and the republicans to assert their claims to legitimacy before world opinion.)[25]

The reprisals carried out by the Free State forces in late 1922 created a moderate response in favour of the republicans which Lawrence Ginnell, the new republican envoy to America, and John F. Finerty, the tough new president of the AARIR, were able to exploit. Finerty, the son of a prominent Irish-American nationalist leader, newspaper editor and politician and who was himself a lawyer for the United States Railroad Administration, an agency of the federal government of which he was deputy director, gave British authorities considerable cause for alarm. Even so, Irish-American attempts to get Congress to pass resolutions deploring the reprisals or extending recognition to the republican government stood no possible chance of success, and in fact Basil M. Manly advised Frank P. Walsh against any organised agitation in Congress because it would reveal clearly how weak the republican cause was in the United States. However, republican propaganda was distributed through the newly founded *Irish Legation Circular* which Ginnell directed, and Finerty used his able administrative talents to rejuvenate the ailing AARIR.[26] Optimistic reports were sent back to Ireland about the possibility of raising money for the republican cause among the Irish-Americans, but it soon became clear to Ginnell that even the present leadership of the AARIR was very badly divided, and a conference of the national leaders in early March failed to obtain encouragement for a new bond-certificate campaign. Financial problems plagued the organisation; in November 1922 the national office appealed to the republicans in Ireland for a loan of between $1,000 and $2,000 to keep its doors open, and by the spring of 1923 the leadership of the AARIR was irrevocably divided over the question of whether or not to expel the New York chapter because of its failure to contribute money to keep the national organisation running. Ginnell's death in April 1923, internal dissension and the declining fortunes of the republicans in Ireland prevented the effective rebuilding of a national organisation.[27]

The civil war in Ireland came slowly and inconclusively to a close in the spring of 1923, as more and more republican army leaders were killed or captured and, finally, as de Valera and Frank Aiken issued orders to cease operations and to hide weapons. The *Irish World*, which in March had assured its readers that the Free State was on the brink of collapse, refused to admit that the republicans had been defeated and emphasised that de Valera had merely ordered a ceasefire, not a surrender. The *Gaelic American* was contemptuous of de Valera's efforts to negotiate, and it fully supported the Cosgrave government in its refusal to compromise or deal leniently with the republicans. The arrest of de Valera, who came out of hiding to campaign in the election of August 1923, aroused appeals from diverse sources across the United States for American intervention to ask that his life be spared.[28] Senator Thomas J. Walsh spoke to both Secretary of State Hughes and President Coolidge about an American protest against his possible execution, and large public meetings were held in New York. These appeals were broadened early in 1924 to ask that clemency be obtained for all Irish political prisoners, and in fact one resolution to that effect was even introduced in Congress. John F. Finerty attempted, as had Irish-American leaders in years past, to involve the American Red Cross, this time by requesting that the Red Cross investigate conditions in Irish Free State prisons.[29] But these efforts compared badly with the spectacular national agitation which had been aroused over the 1916 prisoners or the hunger-strike of Terence MacSwiney in 1920. In 1924 prominent Americans such as Mayor John F. Hylan of New York, Governor Channing H. Cox of Massachusetts and Archbishop Curley of Baltimore extended congratulations and hopes for success to the Irish Free State.

Indeed, almost as an anticlimax in October 1924, without any national agitation or petitions, without congressional resolutions or public hearings, the United States government extended diplomatic recognition to the Irish Free State. Scrupulously observing diplomatic protocol, the British Ambassador expressed the wish of his government to have the relations between the United States and the Irish Free State carried out directly through an Irish minister. Accordingly on 7 October 1924 Dr Timothy A. Smiddy presented his credentials to President Coolidge. The United States eventually responded in 1927 with the appointment of Frederick A. Sterling, a career diplomat, as Envoy Extraordinary and Minister Plenipotentiary. Sterling was succeeded in 1934 by the first of a series of Irish-Americans, W. W. McDowell, the former Lieutenant-Governor of Montana and close friend of Senator Thomas J. Walsh. Recognition did not end the Irish question in America, but it did symbolise the closing of the last great phase of American opinion on Ireland.[30]

Irish-American ethnic identity has flourished in the United States over the years, and even some forms of Irish-American nationalism continued for several more decades—indeed achieving some prominence in recent years—but the Irish question never again became the burning issue in American social and political life that it had been between 1919 and 1923. By 1927 the bitter animosities within the Irish-American community which grew out of the split in 1920 and the divisions over the civil war began to die down sufficiently to permit a reconciliation between Major Kinkead, a former vice-president of the AARIR, and Devoy and Judge Cohalan. By 1934 Cohalan had sufficiently put the turmoil of the Wilson era behind him to be on socially cordial terms with Wilson's old foreign affairs adviser, E. M. House. For all except the very few, Ireland was left to go its own way.[31]

II.   Native Americans and the New Ireland

The reaction of native Americans to the truce and the Treaty was not unlike that of the great majority of Irish-Americans, except perhaps that the indifference came more rapidly. Increasingly insensitive to the Irish question during 1921, as Senator Walsh had complained in the Senate, many native Americans also equated the truce with an Irish triumph, or at least an end to the Irish question. A. Lawrence Lowell, who had followed events in Ireland closely, felt that the negotiations would produce a settlement because 'It is inconceivable that either the British Government or Sinn Féin should not accept almost anything rather than return to the previous condition of violence.' When the Treaty was signed the British government was congratulated by such diverse sources as former Ambassador John W. Davis and the Rotary Club of Orange, New Jersey. Even Harry Boland, who voted against the Treaty himself, admitted to the Dáil that 'The great public opinion of America is on the side of this Treaty.'[32] Americans failed to appreciate the arguments over the oath and the relationship of Ireland to the Empire, and they were distressed by the growing disharmony among the Irish leaders. 'Yes, we are pleased with the promise of an Irish settlement which the conference at London offered,' wrote the former president of Harvard, Charles W. Eliot, 'but we have been disappointed at the long delay in acepting it on the part of the Sinn Féiners.' One native American from Trenton, New Jersey, wrote to Senator Williams: 'I most sincerely and profoundly rejoice that there is now a project (if hate does not get the better of reason) that Ireland may win practical independence and a chance to work out her own salvation in her own way.' This may have been a superficial comment on the complexities of the Irish situation, but it reflected the sentiments of many Americans. Furthermore, by the spring of 1922 Americans who were interested in such foreign problems as the Irish question found their attention being drawn to newer issues like the Greco-Turkish War and Japanese expansion. Native American newspapers overwhelmingly supported the Treaty as a fair settlement of the Irish question.[33]

The outbreak of civil war in Southern Ireland and sectarian strife in the North did not encourage confidence among native Americans about the capacity of the Irish for self-government. In response to inquiries from Senator Truman H. Newberry about the fate of Catholics in Belfast, Secretary of State Hughes commented: 'Conditions are of course deplorable both in Dublin and in Belfast, but as you know, both the north and the south of Ireland have at the present time their own Governments,' although he confessed that neither government was 'able as yet to assure safety to the people'. But even while the civil war and the reprisals were at their worst, not all native Americans were discouraged. President Harding told Plunkett on 15 January 1923 : 'If only peace came, I tell you Sir Horace Ireland would be the richest country in the world with her glorious climate and soil.'[34] Nonetheless, there was a growing impatience with the continuation of fighting in Ireland and Irish-American clamour in the United States. The State Department not only refused to intervene on behalf of de Valera and the republican prisoners in 1923 and 1924, but in response to Senator Walsh's direct comparison of United States treatment of the Confederate President Jefferson Davis after the American Civil War with de Valera's arrest and possible execution in late 1923, Secretary Hughes replied coldly that Davis 'had not for a year or two carried on guerilla warfare and tried to murder officers of the American Government'.[35] In short, Americans had little interest in the intricacies of Irishmen fighting among themselves.

To be sure, the Treaty gave the anti-Irish elements in the United States no pleasure, unless perhaps to the extent that it resulted in civil war in Ireland and confirmed their beliefs about the Irish character. Predictably, George L. Fox warned of the great danger of the possibility of Ulster falling under the jurisdiction of a Catholic government and asserted that a Free State, a dominion or a republic 'all mean the same thing'. As early as 10 December 1921 the disagreement over the terms of the Treaty provided the opportunity to refer to 'Ire-Land' and to joke about Irish 'factions' and the probability that once the Anglo-Irish conflict settled down the Irish would 'begin fighting again over their "peace" '.[36] Such books as Andrew Gerrie's *Ireland's woes and Britain's wiles*, published in July 1922, placed the responsibility for Ireland's difficulties squarely on the Irish, pointing out their predisposition to factionalism and their destructive refusal to compromise as the source of Ireland's difficulty. In July 1922, with the shelling of the Four Courts barely over, this was a difficult argument to refute. Indeed, the observation made in 1916 by Madison Grant in his book *The passing of the great race*, the fourth edition of which went through six printings between 1920 and 1924, that 'An independent Ireland worked out on a Tammany model is not a pleasing prospect' seemed to have been borne out in the cruelties of the civil war.[37]

III. Conclusions

The Irish question was an important issue in American public life for nearly two decades during the early twentieth century. Predictably, Americans of Irish descent were the most concerned, informed and opinionated on the Irish situation in the United States. But there were also important divisions within the Irish-American community over the forms of Irish nationalism and the kind of political system they hoped to see established. As the prospects for Home Rule brightened under Redmond and the Asquith government from 1910 onwards, the great majority of Irish-Americans gave their support to the Irish Parliamentary Party and the concept of a Dublin government subordinate to Westminster. Home Rule, however, while badly weakened by Unionist intransigence in 1914 and by the Easter Rising in 1916, was perhaps more than anything else a casualty of the First World War. The decline of Irish-American support for Redmond and the UIL can be linked specifically to British postponements of the implementation of self-government in Ireland in 1914, 1916, and again in 1918; perhaps nothing illustrates this better than the unsuccessful attempts of Irish-American moderates in 1919.

Certainly revolutionary Irish-American nationalism represented a small body of opinion until the European war created new circumstances which they were able to exploit, although by 1917 American war priorities imposed obvious restrictions on their freedom to create an anti-British policy of revolutionary Irish nationalism. Clearly by 1919, as the result of the British failure to implement Home Rule, the 1916 Rising and—of perhaps incalculable importance—the Wilsonian rhetoric of self-determination during the war, Irish-Americans seemed unanimous in their support of some form of separation from Great Britain. They were further inspired by the creation of modern Poland, Czechoslovakia and Yugoslavia, as well as by the ideals of the revolutionary Irish-American nationalists. The visit to the United States by de Valera in 1919 and 1920 rallied Irish-American opinion behind the concept of Irish independence and started in motion various projects to raise money and carry out agitation on several fronts. Irish-American unanimity on the principle of separation survived even the disastrous split in the movement in 1920, as both factions claimed unqualified devotion to the principle of independence. For most Irish-Americans the Treaty and the Irish Free State provided a satisfactory degree of independence, if not actually a republic, and only the most dedicated and doctrinaire republican ideologues refused to accept this.

Native American opinion on the Irish question, unlike Irish-American opinion, started from no common agreement on the virtue of Irish self-government. Nevertheless, substantial numbers of native Americans warmly supported Irish nationalist claims. Indeed, every President from Taft to Coolidge could be found to have made statements, both public and private, in favour of Irish self-government, and they were joined in this, particularly at moments of great importance in the Irish nationalist movement, by many Americans whose sentiments could not have been designed to win votes. Native Americans supported Ireland for ideological reasons: because they were democrats or federalists and felt that every people had a right to the government of their own choice, or because they included Ireland's claims for nationhood among the obligations of the war aims, or because of anglophobic and anti-imperialist convictions. Others favoured Irish self-government for more practical reasons in the hope that its realisation would relieve American domestic politics of the *raison d'être* of militant Irish-American nationalism or that it would allow the United States to develop cordial diplomatic relations with Great Britain. These views were not institutionalised in organisations, as was Irish-American opinion, with the result that they appeared fragmentary and disorganised and tied to specific incidents affecting the nationalist cause. But the opinion of these native Americans was no less important for that, since they represented a degree of power, influence, wealth and respectability that was often lacking in the Irish-Americans. Of course, a great many native Americans opposed Irish nationalism, often for reasons of religious, racial or anti-immigrant feelings, and during and after the war for reasons of pro-British sympathy. To a large extent also, anti-Irish feeling in the United States was a direct reaction to Irish-American agitation and corresponded in intensity to the periods of most blatant Irish-American nationalism.

The cumulative effect of this body of opinion on the Irish question was not without some importance to the eventual resolution of Ireland's national aspirations. Although the United States government was obviously susceptible to the political pressure which the Irish-Americans were able to exert in their hope of making American foreign policy an instrument of Irish nationalist ambitions, no administration was willing to allow the country's vital interests to be influenced by Irish-American demands. Thus the government entered the First World War on the side of the Allied powers, refused to demand that Britain grant independence to Ireland as the *sine qua non* of participation in the war and the peace, and refused to extend premature diplomatic recognition to the Dáil government. Within the confines of a broader policy of friendly relations with Britain, however, the United States government was willing to use its influence on behalf of prisoners in 1916, to encourage a settlement in 1917, to promote Anglo-Irish talks in 1919, and to assist in relief operations in Ireland in 1916 and 1921. The Irish-Americans had only moderate success in extracting assistance from Congress, which, although willing to provide a national platform for Irish agitation, was not prepared to take decisive action except when its objectives coincided with those of the Irish-Americans, as in the defeat of the arbitration treaties and the Versailles Treaty. In fact the nationalist leaders themselves were partially responsible for the failure of the Irish to utilise the Peace Conference for anything but propaganda purposes and for the failure of either political party to endorse the Irish cause in the presidential election campaign of 1920.

To an extent American opinion on the Irish question was more important to the British government than to the American. Because of the insecurity of Britain's position during the war and in the 1920s, American opinion on the Irish and other questions became a factor to be carefully considered by the British government. In September 1914, in May 1917, and again in late 1919 and 1920 the cabinet justified its attempts to deal with Ireland in the hope of placating American and dominion opinion. By the spring of 1921 the British government was presented with problems of enormous pro-Irish agitation (to a degree involving the American government), of growing Anglo-American naval rivalry, and of certain financial dependence on the United States. The anxious reports of British diplomats in Washington showed that there was the possibility of congressional recognition of the Dáil government and of private assistance to Ireland in the form of weapons and more money. These were all elements encouraging the British to make some accommodation with the Dáil government, although they were not forced to capitulate (for example, despite renewed agitation and fund-raising in November 1921 by the Irish-Americans, the British government remained firm in the limits of what it would concede to the Irish delegation in London).

Possibly American agitation was most important in influencing the nationalist movement in Ireland itself. Money raised in the United States kept both the constitutional and the revolutionary movements alive in Ireland even when their policies seemed quite impractical; and, of course, after the war the Irish Victory Fund, the bond-certificate drives and the relief efforts alone raised over $12,000,000 (and there were many private funds and remittances as well). Particularly important, however, as a consideration by the Irish leaders in increasing their demands from local autonomy to republican independence was the prospect of large-scale assistance or intervention from the United States. Nationalist leaders in Ireland were probably mistaken in their estimations of the importance of the visit of the Irish-American delegation to the Peace Conference in 1919, of the Borah resolution, of the defeat of the Versailles

Treaty, and of the enthusiastic reception given de Valera in the United States; but that mistake seems to have given them sufficient confidence to make a bolder struggle against Great Britain. Certainly American opinion made feasible a far stronger kind of nationalism in Ireland than would otherwise have been possible.

APPENDIX

GLOSSARY OF NAMES

ASQUITH, Herbert Henry (1881–1947) Liberal Prime Minister from 1908 to 1916. Although nominally committed to Home Rule for Ireland, Asquith was reluctant to act on the matter in the face of Unionist objections or the crisis of the First World War.

BAKER, Ray Stannard (1870–1946) One of the most successful journalists of the Progressive era and the author of an important book, *Following the color line* (1908), Baker enjoyed the confidence of President Wilson. While on a mission in Europe in 1918 Baker went to Ireland at Wilson's request on the eve of the conscription crisis, and on the basis of travels and talks submitted a report to the government on conditions in Ireland. In 1919 Baker served as director of the press bureau for the American Commission to Negotiate Peace, where he was in a position to place Irish matters before the President.

BALFOUR, Arthur James (1848–1930) Although he had been Irish Chief Secretary in the government of his uncle, Lord Salisbury, and Prime Minister of a Conservative government from 1902 until 1906, Balfour is primarily important in this study as Foreign Secretary from 1916 to 1919. One of the objectives of Balfour's mission to the United States in 1917 was to return to the British government a clear view of where the Wilson administration and the American people stood on the issue of an Irish settlement. It is not certain that he was altogether candid in that task.

BOLAND, Harry (1887–1922) A member of the Dáil, Boland accompanied de Valera in the United States, forming in effect part of his staff. Boland succeeded Dr McCartan as Dáil envoy to the United States in 1919.

BONAR LAW, Andrew (1858–1923) Born in Canada and raised in Scotland, Bonar Law became a successful merchant and then a powerful force in the Conservative Party. He was one of the principle leaders of the Unionist resistance to Home Rule between 1912 and 1914. He became a member of the coalition government in 1915 and remained in the cabinet until early 1921. He was out of office while the Anglo-Irish Treaty was concluded, but succeeded as Prime Minister in 1922 upon Lloyd George's resignation.

BORAH, William E. (1865–1940)   Republican senator from Idaho from 1903 to 1940. Generally described as an 'isolationist', Borah opposed the war and opposed the peace. Indeed, after the death of Henry Cabot Lodge in 1924 he became chairman of the Senate Foreign Relations Committee and opposed most of the foreign policy initiatives of subsequent administrations. Of all the senators hostile to the Versailles Treaty, Borah was the most successful in working with the dissident Irish-Americans and merging his own objectives with theirs.

BRYAN, William Jennings (1860–1925)   United States Secretary of State from 1913 to 1915. He was nominally sympathetic to Home Rule.

CARSON, Sir Edward Henry (1854–1935)   A very successful Irish lawyer, Carson emerged as the leader of the Unionist defiance of the Asquith government's Home Rule legislation. His joining the coalition government in 1915 was viewed with alarm by supporters of Home Rule.

CASEMENT, Sir Roger (1864–1916)   Made famous, indeed knighted, for his humanitarian efforts in Africa and South America, Casement is of note in this study because of the role he played in the United States in the summer of 1914 and because of the degree of support that rallied around efforts to prevent his execution in 1916. In both instances Casement was an unusual but powerful figure in the minds of Americans.

COCKRAN, W. Bourke (1854–1923)   A congressman from New York with a great reputation for oratory. For years Cockran was a spokesman for the constitutional Irish-American nationalists, but he grew disillusioned with the policies of Redmond by 1914.

COHALAN, Daniel F. (1865–1946)   A successful lawyer, a judge in the Supreme Court of the State of New York, and a powerful force in the politics of that state. A member of the Clan na Gael since his early manhood, Cohalan was one of the founders of the FOIF and indeed became a national figure in Irish-American circles through his services to that organisation and to the Irish Victory Fund. By 1919 Cohalan was perhaps the dominant figure in Irish-American nationalist affairs. His greatest success was linking the Irish nationalist movement with the anti-League of Nations movement, but his subsequent efforts to influence American politics as an Irish-American leader contributed to the fissures which already existed within the nationalist movement and helped make the ultimate split appear to be simply a personality clash between himself and de Valera.

COLBY, Bainbridge (1869–1950)   United States Secretary of State from 1920 to 1921 at the very end of President Wilson's administration. Colby was a man of liberal political views and had spoken out on the Irish question following the 1916 Rising. His words to some extent came back to haunt him as he attempted to serve as Secretary.

COLUM, Pádraic (1892–1972)   Poet and playwright, and one of the youngest members of the Irish literary revival. He was living in New York in 1916, and after the Rising took a leading role in nationalist activities. Colum became a national officer in the Irish Progressive League.

COLLINS, Michael (1890–1922)   Famous for his military leadership during the Anglo-Irish War, Collins is important in this work as the Dáil Minister for Finance responsible for the two Irish bond-certificate drives and also as one of the individuals who rallied support for the Anglo-Irish Treaty and the Irish Free State.

COOTE, William J. (1863–1924)   A Unionist MP from South Tyrone who led a delegation of Ulster Unionists to the United States in 1919–20 to speak to Protestant audiences in the hope of counteracting the many nationalist and republican speakers. Coote and his delegation became a lightning-rod attracting widespread attention from both pro- and anti-nationalist elements in the United States.

CREEL, George (1876–1953)   A prominent journalist who was trusted by President Wilson. He was given the important assignment of directing the War Information Bureau during the war, and in 1919 he was sent by Wilson on a special mission to Ireland to investigate the political situation after the first meeting of Dáil Éireann. Although Creel remained a devoted supporter of Wilson, he turned his writing talents towards Ireland and later in 1919 published a very powerful and effective book entitled *Ireland's fight for freedom.*

CURZON OF KEDLESTON, George Nathaniel Curzon, 1st Marquis (1859–1925)   British Foreign Secretary from 1919 until 1924 under Lloyd George, Bonar Law and Baldwin.

DE VALERA, Éamon (1882–1975)   Born in New York of an Irish mother and a Cuban father and raised in Ireland by his mother's family, de Valera's career as a mathematics professor was cut short by the 1916 Rising, which left him the only surviving commandant. De Valera was chosen President by Dáil

Éireann, and after it became clear that he would not be invited to the Paris Peace Conference, he went to the United States to win support and raise money for Ireland. Always controversial, de Valera became involved in the policy disputes that flourished among the leaders of the Irish-American nationalist movement. His strong will and prestige contributed to the public aspects of the split and perhaps made compromise more difficult. Once the split came, de Valera was subjected to a bitter attack, which increased during and after the civil war.

DEVOY, John (1842–1928) Described by Patrick Pearse as 'the greatest of the Fenians', Devoy lived most of his adult life in New York as a bachelor, solely devoted to the cause of revolutionary nationalism. By the period of this study he was old, deaf and increasingly irascible; his newspaper, the *Gaelic American*, was hard-hitting and uncompromising. All this made him a towering figure among Irish-American nationalists. Because of his prestige and his newspaper, the clash between himself and de Valera was particularly bitter and destructive. After the Anglo-Irish Treaty he supported the Irish Free State.

DOHENY Edward L. (1856–1935) The nephew of Michael Doheny, the Young Irelander, Edward L. Doheny became a millionaire in the oil business in California and Mexico. Brought into Irish-American activities through his underwriting of the American Committee for Relief in Ireland, Doheny was selected by de Valera to lead the new AARIR because of his family connections, the prestige his wealth conferred, and because he constituted a break from the existing Irish-American leadership. Doheny left the AARIR when de Valera wanted to use the organisation to fight the Treaty. Doheny's subsequent notoriety over his involvement in the 'Teapot Dome' oil reserves scandal must have been an embarrassment to many Irish-Americans.

DOUGLAS, James G. (1887–1954) A leading Dublin member of the Society of Friends. Because of his reputation for honesty and integrity, Douglas performed many services as mediator and broker during the Anglo-Irish and civil wars. Because of these qualities he was trusted also with the funds of the American Committee for Relief in Ireland. He later became an Irish Free State senator.

DOYLE, Michael Francis (1876–1960) A Philadelphia lawyer who did some occasional work for the State Department and who was active in Democratic Party politics, Doyle represented Casement both in a libel suit in the United States and as part of his trial defence in London. Doyle also urged Wilson to see that Ireland got some political concessions after the war.

DUNNE, Edward F. (1853–1937)   A successful lawyer, judge, mayor of Chicago, and reform governor of Illinois. He was selected by the Irish Race Convention in 1919 to serve on the American Commission on Irish Independence.

EGAN, Maurice Francis (1852–1924)   An author, lecturer, and diplomat, Egan served as United States Ambassador to Denmark from 1907 to 1918. His efforts on behalf of Ireland were usually made through the Church.

EGAN, Patrick (1841–1919)   Prominent in the Irish Land League and the *Times* forgery case of 1888, Egan later made a career for himself in America, including an appointment as United States Minister to Chile. During the period of this study Egan remained a devoted follower of Redmond.

FINERTY, John F. (1885–1969)   The son of Colonel J. F. Finerty, a Chicago journalist and congressman, John F. Finerty was himself a lawyer and deputy director of the United States Railroad Administration. He more or less took over the AARIR after the outbreak of the civil war in Ireland and he looked after the legal interests of the republicans for many years afterwards.

FOX, George L. (1852–1931)   A schoolmaster in New Haven, Connecticut, who fought for years to counteract and refute Irish propaganda and agitation in the United States. He testified before congressional committees and wrote numerous pamphlets, but without very great success.

FRANCE, Clemens J. (1877–1959)   He had been executive secretary of the Port of Seattle and had done relief work in Belgium during the war. France was appointed by the American Committee for Relief in Ireland to lead a delegation to Ireland to inspect the damage caused by the Anglo-Irish War and to make recommendations for specific financial aid. France also advised in the drafting of the constitution of the Irish Free State. He had one brother, Senator Joseph I. France of Maryland, who as a Progressive Republican generally supported Irish measures in Congress, and another brother, Royal W. France, who served as treasurer for both the American Commission on Conditions in Ireland and the Committee of One Hundred.

GAFFNEY, T. St John (1864–1944)   Born and educated in Ireland, Gaffney was appointed to the United States consular service in 1905 as a reward for his services to the Republican Party. His outspoken anti-British, pro-Irish and pro-German statements made him a good host for Casement in Munich, but not a satisfactory diplomat. He resigned from the service under a cloud, and always believed that the United States wrongly entered the First World War because of Wilson and his pro-British administration.

GALLAGHER, Michael J. (1866–1937)   Bishop of Detroit, Gallagher served as national president of the FOIF in 1920. He effectively held that organisation behind Judge Cohalan during the split in the Irish-American nationalist movement. Bishop Gallagher later supported and encouraged the controversial rightwing priest, Father Charles E. Coughlin.

GEDDES, Sir Auckland Campbell (1879–1954)   A successful surgeon who entered government service during the war and was by 1919 a member of the cabinet. He figures in this study as British Ambassador to the United States from 1920 to 1924.

GOLDEN, Peter (d. 1926)   An Irish-American poet and Gaelic singer who toured the United States on a lecture circuit. He became involved in Irish affairs at a national level by raising money for relief for Ireland in 1916. Golden was elected general secretary of the newly formed, aggressive, left-wing IPL in 1917. One of the earliest opponents of Devoy and Cohalan, Golden supported de Valera in the split and was elected national secretary of the AARIR in 1920.

GREY OF FALLODEN, (Sir) Edward Grey, 1st Viscount (1862–1933)   British Foreign Secretary under Campbell-Bannerman and Asquith from 1905 to 1916, during which time his good personal relations with Page, House, Spring Rice and, even at a distance, President Wilson, worked to ease British–American relations through a dangerous period. It is uncertain how important he regarded the Irish question in this connection. Nevertheless, one of the main objectives of his abortive mission to the United States in 1919 was to come to an understanding with Wilson on the Irish question.

GRIFFITH, Arthur (1872–1922)   Established as a prominent figure in Irish political affairs in 1904 with the publication of *The resurrection of Hungary, a parallel for Ireland* and with the founding of the Sinn Féin party the following year Griffith's importance in this work stems from his role in leading the Dáil while de Valera was in the United States.

HARDING, Warren G. (1865–1923)   President of the United States from 1921 to 1923, Harding took no action on behalf of Ireland, but he did make some public statements and received some Irish spokesmen.

HOBSON, Bulmer (1883–1969)   A youthful member of the IRB who was engaged in a number of nationalist activities in Ireland and who also served as a communications link between the IRB and the Clan na Gael from 1907 until the outbreak of the First World War.

HOUSE, Edward M. (1858–1938)   President Wilson's private adviser on foreign affairs from 1913 to 1918, at which time he was made a member of the American Commission to Negotiate Peace. House was the channel through which Wilson's views on Ireland were occasionally expressed to the British government, and he was also accessible to Irish-Americans and Irishmen, such as Sir Horace Plunkett, for placing opinions before Wilson.

HUGHES, Charles Evans (1862–1948)   United States Secretary of State from 1921 to 1925. He was not disposed to take a sympathetic attitude towards Ireland, but he was willing to use the Irish situation to attempt to extract concessions from Britain on matters that did concern him, such as the Anglo-Japanese treaty.

JORDAN, Michael J. (b. 1865)   National secretary of the UIL, Jordan remained loyal to Redmond during the war, and joined Stephen McFarland and Dr John G. Coyle in fighting to keep open the national headquarters of the UIL.

KEATING, John T. (d. 1915)   A leading Chicago member of the Clan na Gael, Keating rose to prominence during the reunification of the Clan in 1903, and along with Devoy and Joseph McGarrity became one of the Revolutionary Directory.

LANSING, Robert (1864–1928)   United States Secretary of State from 1915 to 1920, Lansing was not particularly sympathetic to Irish nationalist aspirations, but he did see clearly how President Wilson's language gave the Irish and others reason to hope for American assistance and that therefore something would have to be done for them. At the Peace Conference he attempted to be helpful, but only unofficially. On the other hand, despite his sympathy for the British, especially during the war, Lansing refused to aid them in Irish matters in the United States.

LESLIE, (Sir) Shane (John) Randolph (1882–1971)   Leslie came from a prominent Anglo-Irish family, and through his mother's sisters he was a nephew of Moreton Frewen and a cousin of Winston Churchill; by marriage he was a brother-in-law of W. Bourke Cockran. At university he converted to Catholicism and later he also converted to Home Rule. All these connections gave him an excellent entrée into a variety of circles in England, Ireland and the United States. Throughout most of the war he worked for Redmond and the Home Rule movement in the United States by attempting to promote a favourable image of the Irish and by editing the short-lived magazine *Ireland*. His friendship with Joseph Tumulty, Cardinal Gibbons, Lord Reading and others of similar station gave him unique opportunities to press the Home Rule case.

LLOYD, Demarest (1883–1937)   Lloyd was the son of the distinguished author and Progressive spokesman Henry Demarest

Lloyd. He helped to found the Loyal Coalition in 1920, which attempted by meetings, speeches and correspondence with public men to fight the influence of the Irish nationalists in the United States and to align American foreign policy with that of Britain —in short, to re-create the wartime coalition.

LLOYD GEORGE, David (1863–1945) Welsh Liberal politician and Prime Minister in the coalition and Liberal governments between 1916 and 1922, Lloyd George's position on the Irish question is difficult to ascertain. Nominally in favour of Home Rule, he failed to get any measure implemented in 1916, and from 1919 to 1921 prosecuted a vigorous war in Ireland against republican forces. Nevertheless, he negotiated the Anglo-Irish Treaty which granted dominion status to twenty-six counties in Ireland— a measure that was not popular among his supporters and which took some political courage.

LODGE, Henry Cabot (1850–1924) Republican senator from Massachusetts. Although a quintessential representative of the native American establishment, Lodge never forgot that he also represented a large Irish-American constituency. As chairman of the Senate Foreign Relations Committee Lodge attempted to balance the values of native Americans, the nationalist aspirations of his Irish-American constituents, the needs of his party and his own views of America's best interests.

LOWELL, A. Lawrence (1856–1943) President of Harvard University and the author of numerous books on contemporary affairs, Lowell, who had many friends in England and Ireland, was an interesting sounding-board of enlightened native American views on the Irish question.

LYNCH, Diarmuid (1878–1950) Although Lynch lived for several years in the United States, supporting himself by teaching Irish dancing, he went back to his native Ireland and participated in the 1916 Rising. He returned to the United States and in 1918 was elected national secretary of the FOIF, a post he held for many years.

McCARTAN, Patrick (1878–1963) Assisted through medical school by Joseph McGarrity, McCartan had a long career in Irish revolutionary affairs, beginning with membership in the IRB. Dr McCartan was sent to the United States in the summer of 1917 on the first leg of an abortive mission to Russia, but became 'Envoy of the Provisional Government of Ireland' to the United States, a position subsequently confirmed by the Dáil in 1919. In that position he was a key figure in Irish nationalist agitation during both the war and de Valera's mission. In late 1920 he was instructed to resume his mission to Russia. After the

Irish struggle McCartan continued to move back and forth between Ireland and the United States, and although nominally out of Irish politics, he stood as a presidential candidate in 1945.

McCARTHY, Charles (1873–1921)   One of the minor celebrities of the Progressive movement. The author of a widely read book, *The Wisconsin idea* (1912), and the principle creator of the legislative reference library, he gave his efforts and prestige to the moderate Irish-American nationalists in 1918 and 1919.

McGARRITY, Joseph (1874–1940)   A prosperous Philadelphia businessman, and also something of a poet, McGarrity emerged in the top levels of the Clan na Gael in 1903. He was very active in supporting Irish nationalists in the United States—particularly Dr McCartan—and he was instrumental in founding the *Irish Press* in Philadelphia. McGarrity broke with Devoy and Cohalan during the split and backed de Valera, both then and during the civil war.

McLAUGHLIN, Joseph (1869–1926)   Elected to Congress in 1916, failed to be renominated in 1918 (possibly for his Irish activities), but was elected again in 1920. He was also the national president of the AOH in the United States and the editor of the *National Hibernian.*

MALONEY, W. J. M. A. (1882–1952)   A physician who had been wounded serving with the British army at Gallipoli. He went to New York and became one of the most effective of all the Irish nationalist propagandists. Through his marital connection with O. G. Villard, Maloney was largely responsible for the American Commission on Conditions in Ireland, and he was also instrumental in launching the American Committee for Relief in Ireland. He became a bitter foe of Judge Cohalan.

MASON, William E. (1850–1921)   Twice elected to the United States Senate, Mason was serving in the House of Representatives during the period examined by this study. While a congressman, Mason was the author of several pro-Irish resolutions.

MURPHY, John A. (d. 1922)   A prominent Clan member from Buffalo, Murphy was sent to Ireland with John Gill in 1916 to distribute relief money after the Rising. In 1919 he and L. S. Trigg were sent to Paris to continue the work of the American Commission on Irish Independence when Walsh, Dunne and Ryan returned to the United States.

O'LEARY Jeremiah A. (b. 1881)   An active revolutionary nationalist, O'Leary became involved, along with James T. McGuire and John T. Ryan, in efforts to forge an Irish–German alliance in the United States. One of the foremost anglophobes in the country, O'Leary was president of the American Truth

Society and editor of the anti-British periodical *Bull.* O'Leary was the object of a public attack by Wilson for a rude letter he had written to the President during the 1916 election campaign. O'Leary continued his anti-British activities after the United States entered the war and was as a result imprisoned, an event which he described in his sensational book, *My political trial and experiences* (1919).

O'MARA, James (1873–1948)   The eldest son of a prosperous Limerick family, O'Mara served briefly as an Irish Parliamentary Party MP, but resigned in 1907. He was elected as a Sinn Féin candidate in December 1918. In the autumn of 1919 both de Valera and Griffith asked him to go to the United States to direct the bond-certificate drive and he was made one of the trustees of the Dáil Éireann funds. He resigned this position, along with membership in the Dáil, in May 1921 over policy disagreements with de Valera.

O'MARA, Stephen M. (1885–1926)   The younger brother of James O'Mara, Stephen served as Lord Mayor of Limerick after the assassination of George Clancy in March 1921. After his brother's withdrawal from the financial affairs of the Dáil in May 1921, Stephen was placed in charge of the fund-raising activities in the United States and appointed a trustee of Dáil funds.

PAGE, Walter Hines (1855–1918)   United States Ambassador to Britain from 1913 to 1918, Page was not sympathetic to the Irish cause, particularly when Irish affairs complicated British-American relations. Page was certainly one person who was influenced by the circulation of passages from the alleged Casement diaries.

PHELAN, James D. (1861–1930)   A Democratic senator from California. He was a strong supporter of Irish resolutions in the Senate, but he maintained his loyalty to Wilson and the party also.

PLUNKETT, George Noble, Count (1851–1948)   A papal count, a scholar, and the father of the executed 1916 rebel leader Joseph Mary Plunkett, Count Plunkett was put forward for parliament by Sinn Féin at the 1917 North Roscommon by-election, defeating the Irish Parliamentary Party candidate. He emerged as a venerable figure in the Dáil in 1919 and was included with Griffith and de Valera among the three Irish representatives seeking an audience at the Paris Peace Conference.

PLUNKETT, Sir Horace Curzon (1854–1932)   Styled by his biographer an 'Anglo-American Irishman', Plunkett was a remarkable figure who bridged all three worlds. A younger son of Lord Dunsany, Plunkett was born into a family with very good Irish and English connections, and, as a result of his ranching in Wyoming for ten years, he had considerable experience in the United States also. Plunkett rose to prominence in both Ireland and America as an advocate of improved agriculture through co-operative societies. From 1916 to 1918 Plunkett was a major channel of information on the Irish question between both the British and the American governments. The fact that Plunkett chaired the Irish Convention made many Americans confident of its success.

POLK, Frank L. (1871–1943)   Counselor of the Department of State from 1915 to 1919, and then Under-Secretary of State until 1920. It was often left to Polk to handle Irish questions within the department.

QUINN, John (1870–1924)   A man of great versatility, Quinn was a highly successful New York lawyer, a brilliant art collector, the patron of Yeats, Joyce and Pound, and a dabbler in politics. Although his interest in Irish nationalism dates from at least the turn of the century, he emerges in this study as Casement's host and benefactor in 1914 and one of his most effective defenders in 1916. Quinn played a very important role, at the highest levels, among the moderate nationalists between 1916 and 1919.

READING, Rufus Daniel Isaacs, 1st Marquis of (1860–1935)   A successful barrister who served in the Asquith government as Attorney-General and was made Lord Chief Justice in 1913. In 1915 and 1917 Reading served on missions to the United States connected with the financing of the war effort. In January 1918 he succeeded Spring Rice as British Ambassador. He shared Spring Rice's opinions about the importance of the Irish question as a factor in Anglo-American relations.

REDMOND, John Edward (1856–1918)   A Parnellite who became the leader of the reunited Irish Parliamentary Party in 1900. With Home Rule a real prospect after 1910, Redmond's prestige and following grew greatly in the United States. Support for Redmond began to erode first as Home Rule legislation seemed to be successfully obstructed by the Unionists and then by his efforts to enlist Irish support for the war in 1914. He was further crippled both at home and in the United States by British policy after the 1916 insurrection and by the collapse of the Irish Convention and the onset of the conscription crisis. During this time the massive UIL of America, which he had dominated, withered away to nothing.

ROOSEVELT, Theodore (1858–1919)   Although out of office during the period of this study, former President Roosevelt was always sympathetic to a moderate solution of the Irish question, and he never hesitated to express his views or to hear Irishmen in the United States.

RYAN, Michael J. (1862–1943) A successful lawyer and city solicitor for Philadelphia, Ryan was for years national president of the UIL of America. His pro-German opinions during the war took him out of the moderate wing and led to his ultimate estrangement with Redmond and the UIL. Along with T. B. Fitzpatrick, national treasurer, he advised closing the offices of the UIL until after the war. In 1919 he became a member of the American Commission on Irish Independence.

SIMS, William Sowdon (1858–1938) Rear-Admiral Sims commanded United States naval squadrons sailing out of Cobh (Queenstown) from 1917 to 1919, during which time he grew to dislike Irish nationalists. In his war memoirs, *The victory at sea* (1919), and later in speeches he did not hesitate to criticise what he called the 'Sinn Féin Irishmen'. This made him a controversial figure, attacked by Irish-Americans and defended by native Americans.

SHEEHY-SKEFFINGTON, Mrs Hannah (d. 1946) A member of a prominent Irish family, Mrs Sheehy-Skeffington married one of Dublin's more notable eccentrics, Francis Sheehy-Skeffington, who was wrongfully shot by a British officer in 1916. Mrs Sheehy-Skeffington, herself a suffragette and a liberal thinker, made an extremely effective propagandist writing, travelling and speaking tour in the United States from 1916 to 1922. Unlike all other Irish nationalists in the United States, she actually had an opportunity to express her views to President Wilson as well as to Theodore Roosevelt.

SPRING RICE, Sir Cecil Arthur (1859–1918) British Ambassador to the United States from 1913 to 1918, Spring Rice should have been a perfect diplomat for the circumstances. A member of an Anglo-Irish family (his sister was part of the crew of the *Asgard* at the Howth gun-running) and a personal friend of Theodore Roosevelt (he was best man at Roosevelt's wedding), he was posted to Washington at a time when these qualifications were not necessarily an advantage. Although always painfully aware of the Irish question in American affairs, Spring Rice's nervousness made him less than effective in communicating to both the United States government and his own on Irish matters.

TAFT, William Howard (1857–1930) Republican President of the United States from 1908 to 1912. Although not holding public office during most of the period of this book, Taft could generally be counted on for a statement favourable to a constitutional settlement of the Irish question.

TUMULTY, Joseph P. (1879–1954)   President Wilson's private secretary, having served him since he was governor of New Jersey. An Irish-American himself, Tumulty served as a useful link between Wilson and a broad range of Irish-American groups.

VILLARD, Oswald Garrison (1872–1949)   An heir to the Northern Pacific Railroad fortune of the Villards and the newspaper tradition of the Garrisons. He ran the New York *Evening Post* and the *Nation* and, through his connection with Dr Maloney and his liberal sympathies, took up the Irish cause. It was in large measure through his efforts and the machinery of the *Nation* that the American Commission on Conditions in Ireland was started in 1920.

WALSH, David I. (1872–1947)   Several times Democratic senator from Massachusetts. Although Walsh supported Irish measures in the Senate, he was not generally active in Irish-American nationalist affairs.

WALSH, Frank P. (1864–1939)   A distinguished Kansas City labour lawyer who rose to national prominence with his appointment as joint president (with William Howard Taft) of Wilson's War Labour Conference Board and a member of the National War Labour Board. A delegate to the 1919 Irish Race Convention, Walsh was made chairman of the American Commission on Irish Independence which went to Paris and Ireland. After its return to the United States the commission testified before the Senate Foreign Relations Committee at the treaty hearings, and it also served as a kind of executive staff for the de Valera mission. Walsh was often accused of using his position to advance a political career of his own, but he gave very good service to the nationalist movement.

WALSH, Thomas J. (1859–1933)   A Democratic senator from Montana, Walsh was probably the most outstanding Irish-American politician in the government. Sympathetic to the Irish cause but not an active nationalist, ironically it was Walsh's investigation that exposed the scandal surrounding Edward L. Doheny's involvement in the 'Teapot Dome' oil fraud.

WHITE, Henry (1850–1927)   The lone Republican member of the American Commission to Negotiate Peace in 1919, White had relatively little to do with the Irish, but he kept his friend Henry Cabot Lodge informed about their affairs at the Peace Conference.

WILLIAMS, John Sharp (1854–1932)   A Democratic senator from Mississippi and a strong supporter of Wilson and of an Anglo-American understanding. His unrestrained attacks on the Irish-Americans for disrupting Anglo-American affairs made him the darling of the pro-British spokesmen in the United States and drove most Irish-American nationalists apoplectic with rage.

WILSON, Woodrow (1856–1924) Democratic President of the United States from 1912 to 1920. Although he led the normally pro-Irish Democratic Party, and although he was of distant Irish extraction himself, Wilson tended to see himself as a statesman in the British Liberal tradition of Gladstone. Moderately sympathetic to a parliamentary solution to the Irish question, Wilson's actions were often limited by his dislike of Irish-American politicians and also by what he regarded as the larger issues of the war and the peace, a solution for which depended upon some form of British co-operation.

WISEMAN, Sir William (1885–1962) After being wounded in the war, Wiseman was placed in charge of British intelligence in New York. He soon gained the confidence of E. M. House. Through House and Wiseman an effective communications system was established which enabled both the British and the American governments to communicate unofficially without having to use diplomatic channels. Opinions on the Irish situation were several times sounded out through this House–Wiseman network.

NOTES

Chapter 1
INTRODUCTION: THE IRISH IN AMERICA,
1840–1910
(pp 1–13)

1. Sir Esmé Howard to Sec. of State, 24 June 1924, and Sec. of State to British Ambassador, 28 June 1924, 701.4111/487, and C. P. Slemp (secretary to the President) to Sec. of State, 7 Oct. 1924, 701.41d11/18, *Papers relating to the foreign relations of the United States, 1924*, ii, pp 246–8 (series hereafter referred to as *Foreign relations*); and *N.Y.T.*, 8 Oct. 1924.

2. *N.Y.T., Ibid.*; Howard to Austen Chamberlain, 8 June 1925, Annual Report, 1924 (P.R.O., F.O. 371/10651); and D. W. Harkness, *The restless dominion: the Irish Free State and the British Commonwealth of Nations, 1921–31* (New York, 1970), pp 63–7.

3. The term 'Irish-American' is generally accepted as referring to the Catholic Irish who immigrated to the United States in large numbers during the nineteenth century; they formed an ethnic group which only in the twentieth century began to emerge prominently in social and economic areas of American life. By the late nineteenth century Protestant Irishmen from Ulster were known in the United States by all but the most pedantic as 'Scotch-Irish', and they were more closely identified with the native Americans than with the Irish-Americans, although exceptions could always be found.

4. The Irish-Americans were the first wave of the great European migration to the United States in the nineteenth century; in 1850, while numbering only 961,719, the Irish immigrants accounted for 42·8 per cent of the foreign-born in the country. Irish immigration was eventually exceeded by the larger number of arrivals from Germany and other countries, but as late as 1920 there were 4,136,395 Americans born in Ireland or with Irish parents. Department of Commerce, Bureau of the Census, *Thirteenth census of the United States taken in the year 1910* (Washington, 1911), i, p. 24, and *Fourteenth census of the United States taken in the year 1920* (Washington, 1922), ii, pp 29, 695 and 897. See also A. Schrier, *Ireland and the American migration 1850–1900* (Min-

neapolis, 1958), passim. It is impossible to determine the exact number of Irish-Americans (including the third and fourth generations), but the nationalist leaders in the United States seemed to agree that the figure was 20,000,000. See Peter Golden to Congressmen, 18 April 1918 (N.L.I., Golden Papers, MS. 13141, folder ii); Frank P. Walsh and E. F. Dunne to Joseph E. Grew, 2 June 1919 (New York Public Library, Walsh Papers, box 124); and Judge Daniel F. Cohalan speaking to the Senate Foreign Relations Committee, 30 Aug. 1919, U.S. Congress, Senate, Committee on Foreign Relations, *Treaty of peace with Germany* (Senate doc. no. 106, 66th Congress, 1st Session) 1919, pp 787–944.

5. See F. S. L. Lyons, 'The two faces of Home Rule' in K. B. Nowlan (ed.), *The making of 1916: studies in the history of the Rising* (Dublin, 1969), pp 99–123.

6. T. N. Brown, *Irish-American nationalism 1870–1890* (Philadelphia, 1966), pp 19–24 and passim. Several other scholarly works that are useful are F. E. Gibson, *The attitudes of the New York Irish towards state and national affairs 1848–1892* (New York, 1951), O. Handlin, *Boston's immigrants* (1941; repr. Cambridge, 1959), and C. Wittke, *The Irish in America* (Baton Rouge, 1956).

7. Handlin, pp 152–3; J. M. Donohoe, *The Irish Catholic Benevolent Union* (Washington, 1953), p. 83; and J. Devoy, *Recollections of an Irish rebel* (New York, 1929), pp 18, 20 and 47. See also Gibson, p. 68; W. D'Arcy, *The Fenian movement in the United States 1858–1886* (Washington, 1947), passim; Wittke, pp 150–60; and E. R. R. Green, 'The Fenians abroad' in T. D. Williams (ed.), *Secret societies in Ireland* (Dublin, 1973), pp 79–89.

8. Thomas N. Brown argues that Fenianism 'was a product' of the American Civil War. Brown, p. 43.

9. Devoy, p. 47; and Gibson, pp 177–8; see also *Ibid.*, pp174–7. There is some speculation about the seriousness of the United States government in encouraging the Fenian plans during and after the war. Certainly the government wanted to press upon the British the full implications of their encouragement of the Confederacy by allowing the c.s.s. *Alabama* and the Laird rams to be built in British shipyards. American support for the Fenians demonstrated that supplying aid to rebels was a two-way business, and even after the war the spectre of governmental support for the Fenians worked to keep diplomatic pressure on the British to pay the damage claims for United States shipping lost because of the *Alabama.* B. Jenkins, *Fenians and Anglo-American relations during Reconstruction* (Ithaca, 1969), passim.

10. Devoy, pp 251–60 and 284–5; M. Davitt, *The fall of feudalism in Ireland* (New York, 1904), p. 125; Brown, pp 66–7, 88–9 and 91–3; T. W. Moody, 'The New Departure in Irish politics, 1878–9' in H. A. Cronne, T. W. Moody and D. B. Quinn (ed.), *Essays . . . in honour of James Eadie Todd* (London, 1949), pp 310–13 and 320–5; and *Devoy's post-bag*, ed. W. O'Brien and D. Ryan (Dublin,

1948–53), i, pp 267 and 280. See also J. T. McEnnis, *The Clan-na-Gael and the murder of Dr Cronin* (Chicago, 1889), pp 53–7, for growth of the Clan.

11. Prior to the American Civil War the Democratic Party had split into several factions over the questions of slavery and sectionalism. The war ended with the Republican Party as the dominant political force in the country, but the election of 1876 demonstrated that the Democrats had so rebuilt their organisation that the Republicans remained in office only by highly questionable methods. For a full exposition of this situation see Brown, pp 135–6 and 159.

12. See *Ibid.*, p. xvi; and McEnnis, pp 140–6. Major H. Le Caron, pseud. [T. M. Beach], *Twenty-five years in the secret service,* (London, 1892), pp 178–92, 219–26 and 290–8; C. C. Tansill, *America and the fight for Irish freedom* (New York, 1957), pp 77–8; Devoy, p. 346; D. Ryan, *The phoenix flame* (London, 1937), pp 209–10; McEnnis, pp 123–284; H. M. Hunt, *The crime of the century* (1889), p. 576; and Brown, pp xvi, 151–7 and 174–7. T. F. McGrath, *History of the Ancient Order of Hibernians* (Cleveland, 1898), pp 54–8 and 79–81; and J. J. Bergin, *History of the Ancient Order of Hibernians* (Dublin, n.d.), pp 36–44.

13. Dr Emmet had spoken out violently against Parnell shortly after the split, and as president of the federation he circulated letters condemning Parnell as having betrayed the Irish people and stolen their money. The federation's operating funds rose sharply with the prospect of Home Rule and then fell off dramatically:

1891	$20,628.49
1892	39,727.80
1893	33,227.75
1894	5,500.00
1895	2,000.00

Dr Emmet felt that if the Irish Party had been able to unite, the federation could have supplied them with at least $50,000 a year. T. A. Emmet, *Incidents of my life* (New York, 1911), pp 290–4, 303–14 and 428–9. See also F. S. L. Lyons, *The Irish Parliamentary Party* (London, 1951), pp 202, 213 and 216.

14. See Davitt, pp 696–7; and F. S. L. Lyons, *John Dillon: a biography* (London, 1968), p. 320.

15. Ryan, p. 278; M. G. MacBride, *A servant of the queen* (Dublin, 1950), pp 180–7; *Devoy's post-bag,* ii, pp 340–4; F. O'Donoghue, 'Ceannt, Devoy, O'Rahilly and the military plan' in F. X. Martin (ed.), *Leaders and men of the Easter Rising: Dublin 1916* (London, 1967), p. 195; and Tansill, pp 120–2.

16. Efforts to defeat the ratification of the first treaty resulted in the founding of the *Gaelic American* as an organ under the control of the Clan; efforts to defeat the second treaty successfully brought Irish-American and German-American groups into co-operative action for the first time and turned the thinking of some nationalist leaders towards Germany as a new factor in the Irish situation.

Ryan, pp 279–80; *Devoy's post-bag,* ii, p. 330; and *G.A.*, 16 Feb. 1907. The three organisations were the Cumann na nGaedheal, the Dungannon Clubs and the National Council; the first two of these were amalgamated in 1907 to form the Sinn Féin League, which was in 1908 joined by the National Council to form the body known simply as Sinn Féin. B. Hobson, *Ireland yesterday and tomorrow* (Tralee, 1968), pp 10–12. Maud Gonne MacBride collected £1,000 in 1896 and again in 1901 for Griffith's newspaper, largely from Clan sources. MacBride, pp 192–3; and Tansill, pp 122–4.

17. D. Lynch, *The I.R.B. and the 1916 insurrection* (Cork, 1957), pp 10–20; P. G. Cambray, *Irish affairs and the Home Rule question* (London, 1911), p. 127; J. McGurrin, *Bourke Cockran: a freelance in American politics* (New York, 1948), pp 228–32; B. L. Reid, *The man from New York: John Quinn and his friends* (New York, 1968), pp 40–3, 49–51 and 114–19; Hobson, *Ireland,* pp 37–8; L. N. Le Roux, *Tom Clarke and the Irish freedom movement* (Dublin, 1936), pp 82–5 and 96–105; and 'Extracts from the papers of the late Dr Patrick McCartan', pt 1, *Clogher Rec.,* v, no. 1 (1963), pp 38–45.

18. J. Higham, *Strangers in the land,* (1955, repr. New York, 1963), pp xii–xiii. 5–9, 28–31 and 78–87; A. B. Paine, *Thomas Nast, his period and his pictures* (New York, 1904), pp 151, 163 and 191; J. C. Vinson, *Thomas Nast, political cartoonist* (Athens, 1967), passim; W. V. Shannon, *The American Irish* (New York, 1936), pp 27–46; and Wittke, pp 119–20.

19. G. E. Woodberry, *Torch* (1905; repr. New York, 1920), pp 7 and 9; E. A. Ross, *Social control* (New York, 1922), p. 439; J. W. Burgess, *Political science and comparative constitutional law* (Boston, 1890), i, pp 4, 19 and 33; and H. F. Osborn, Preface to M. Grant, *The passing of the great race* (New York, 1916). See also C. G. Bowers, *Beveridge and the Progressive era* (Boston, 1932), p. 121; J. R. Dos Passos, *The Anglo-Saxon century and the unification of the English-speaking peoples* (New York, 1903), pp xi and 190; G. L. Beer, *The English-speaking peoples* (New York, 1917), p. 191; and S. K. Humphrey, *The racial prospect* (New York, 1920), passim. For a general discussion see Higham, passim; and R. Hofstader, *Social Darwinism in America* (1944; repr. Boston, 1955), passim. See also H. Lea, *The day of the Saxon* (1912; repr. New York, 1942), p. 240; F. J. Stimson, *Popular law-making* (New York, 1912), p. 3; J. Fiske, *American political ideas* (New York, 1885); and J. K. Hosmer, *A short history of Anglo-Saxon freedom* (New York, 1890).

20. G. L. Fox, *Poisoning the wells* (privately printed, New Haven, [*c.* 1921]; Wittke, p. 103; and Grant, p. 55.

21. *Ibid.,* pp 53 and 75; Brown, pp 24 and 31–41; and O. Wister, *A straight deal or the ancient grudge* (New York, 1920), pp 251–66.

Chapter 2
THE CLIMAX OF HOME RULE AND THE REBIRTH
OF REVOLUTION, 1910–1916
(pp 14–54)

1. Ryan to Redmond, 27 Feb. 1910, Egan to Redmond, 18 Feb. 1910, and Sullivan to Redmond, 8 Feb. 1910 (N.L.I., Redmond Papers).
2. *N.Y.T.*, 23 Jan., 2 March and 16 May 1910.
3. *Lit. Dig.*, xl, no. 3 (15 Jan. 1910), pp 91–2, and xl, no. 8 (19 Feb. 1910), pp 337–8; and New York *American,* 17 March 1910.
4. Ryan to Redmond, 27 Feb. 1910, and T. B. Fitzpatrick to Ryan, 28 March 1910 (N.L.I., Redmond Papers). Ten months later Judge Martin J. Keogh expressed a similar concern about factions. Keogh to Redmond, 29 Nov. 1910 (*Ibid.*). *N.Y.T.*, 9 Feb. 1910; *Lit. Dig.*, xli, no. 19 (5 Nov. 1910), p. 785; and Reid to Philander C. Knox, 21 Dec. 1910 (L.C., Knox Papers, AcDR H–7, Information series B).
5. The money raised in 1909 and 1910 opened the party once again, as indeed it had during the Parnell era, to the criticism that the fabric of the United Kingdom was being destroyed by foreign money, and Redmond became known as the 'dollar dictator'. D. Gwynn, *The life of John Redmond* (London, 1932), p. 184; H. Fyfe, *T. P. O'Connor* (London, 1934), pp 221–2; Cambray, pp 115–16; W. B. Wells, *The life of John Redmond* (New York, 1919), p. 62; and Keogh to Redmond, 29 Nov. 1910 (N.L.I., Redmond Papers).
6. Reid to Knox, 9 and 21 Dec. 1910 (L.C., Knox Papers, AcDR H–7, Information series B). *N.Y.T.*, 14 Dec. 1910.
7. Sullivan to Redmond, 8 Feb. 1910, and Egan to Redmond, 18 Feb. and 1 March 1910 (N.L.I., Redmond Papers). Roosevelt to Robert John Wynne, 11 April 1910, *The letters of Theodore Roosevelt*, ed. E. Morison et. al. (Cambridge, 1954), vii, pp 68–9.
8. Keating to Devoy, 18 Dec. 1911 (N.L.I., Devoy Papers, box J–L). For details of Taft's instructions to pursue this matter through the British Foreign Office, the Canadian representatives at the coronation of George V, and the Canadian government directly, see N.A., 342.112D58/19, –/20, –/21, –/22, and –/32, box 4106; A. J. Ward, 'America and the Irish problem, 1899–1921', *I.H.S.*, xvi, no. 61 (March 1968), p. 72; and A. J. Ward, *Ireland and Anglo-American relations, 1899–1921* (London, 1969), pp 63 and 67–8.
9. Spring Rice to Grey, 30 March 1914 (P.R.O., F.O. 800/84); M. F. Egan, *Memoirs of a happy life* (London, 1924), passim; and T. St J. Gaffney, *Breaking the silence* (New York, 1930), passim. Wilson was severely criticised by many Protestants for making the Jesuit-trained Tumulty his secretary; it was alleged that Tumulty held back correspondence dealing with Protestant affairs and promoted Catholic interests. Wilson publicly defended Tumulty, but he re-

ceived a large amount of anti-Irish and anti-Catholic mail on the issue, which may have given him second thoughts about publicly endorsing Irish matters in subsequent years. (L.C., Wilson Papers, file VI, box 61, Roman Catholic Affairs)

10. Carefully accessible to moderate nationalists, Wilson was clearly unsympathetic, in spite of his Presbyterian and Scotch-Irish background, towards the defiant Ulster Unionists, with whom he avoided contact altogether. J. Tumulty, *Woodrow Wilson as I know him* (Garden City, 1921), pp 392–7.

11. L.S.W.T. to Hannay, Jan. 1911 (T.C.D., Hannay Papers). See also Hosmer, pp 322–3; Dos Passos, p. 190; and Beer, p. 191.

12. See A. J. Ward, 'Frewen's Anglo-American campaign for federalism, 1910–21', *I.H.S.*, xv, no. 59 (March 1967), pp 256–75; and *N.Y.T.*, 31 July 1910. Cockran and Frewen were related to each other through marriage.

13. Roosevelt to Gill, 17 Jan. 1911, *Roosevelt letters,* vii, p. 209; and Tumulty, p. 395.

14. *N.Y.T.*, 31 July 1910; Roosevelt to Gill, 17 Jan. 1911, *Roosevelt letters,* vii, p. 209; and L.S.W.T. to Hannay, Jan. 1911 (T.C.D., Hannay Papers).

15. *N.Y.T.*, 22 Jan. and 7 and 8 Feb. 1912; and *Lit. Dig.*, xliv, no. 8 (24 Feb. 1912), pp 365–6, and xliv, no. 9 (2 March 1912), p. 416. Cable to Redmond, 12 April 1912 (N.Y.P.L., Cockran Papers, box 18). The cable, which was also published in the press, was signed by 15 prominent Irish-Americans, including James A. O'Gorman, Martin J. Keogh, John D. Crimmins, John Quinn, William J. Gaynor, Morgan J. O'Brien, W. Bourke Cockran and William McAdoo.

16. Cockran to Redmond, 13 April 1912 (N.Y.P.L., Cockran Papers, box 18). 'The bill does not seem to be particularly satisfying to either Nationalist or Unionist', *Lit. Dig.*, xliv, no. 17 (27 April 1912), p. 877, and xliv, no. 18 (4 May 1912), p. 927. See also Lyons, *Dillon,* p. 328; Gwynn, *Redmond,* p. 202; and Keogh to Redmond 27 May 1912 (N.L.I., Redmond Papers).

17. *N.T.Y.*, 22 July 1912. In September the New York *Times* asserted further that if the Irish nationalists had the right to leave the British system, the Unionist minority in the North had the right to remain with Great Britain; nonetheless, the paper condemned the tactics of the Unionists by saying that it was 'good politics' but 'poor patriotism' to disrupt the country by 'arousing religious and sectarian passions that have always been the plague of Ireland'. *Ibid.*, 14 and 29 Sept. 1912. *Lit. Dig.*, xlv, no. 14 (5 Oct. 1912), pp 553–4.

18. See Keogh to Redmond, 5 Feb. 1913 (N.L.I., Redmond Papers); 17 Jan. 1913, *Congressional Record*, 62nd Congress, 3rd Session, vol. 49, p. 1695; and Ford to Roosevelt, 23 Jan. 1913 (L.C., Roosevelt Papers, series I/box 239).

19. Bryan to Ford, 7 Feb. 1913 (N.L.I., Redmond Papers); *N.Y.T.*,

H

18 Jan. 1913; and *Lit. Dig.*, xlvi, no. 8 (22 Feb. 1913), pp 389–90. Roosevelt to Redmond, n.d., *Roosevelt letters*, vii, p. 740; and *Hansard 5* (Commons), liii, 11487. The letter was read in parliament on 10 June 1913.

20. Cockran to Frewen, 14 Feb. 1913 (N.Y.P.L., Cockran Papers, box 16); *N.Y.T.*, 11 May 1912; *Living Age*, cclxxix, no. 3620 (22 Nov. 1913), p. 502; and *Lit. Dig.*, xlviii, no. 25 (20 June 1914), p. 1477. See also Catholic University of America Archives, Fenian Materials, box 3.

21. *N.Y.T.*, 10 June and 28 Sept. 1913; see also *Ibid.*, 17 July and 21 Sept. 1913 and 12 Feb. 1914; *Living Age*, cclxxx, no. 3634 (28 Feb. 1914), pp 566–7; and *Lit. Dig.*, xlvi, no. 26 (28 June 1913), pp 1419–20, xlvii, no. 14 (4 Oct. 1913), pp 567–8, and xlvii, no. 17 (25 Oct. 1913), pp 745–6.

22. Jordan to John Purroy Mitchel (mayor of New York), 5 March 1914 (L.C., Mitchel Papers, box 6); *N.Y.T.*, 11 March 1914; McCarthy to Plunkett, *c.* March 1914 (Wisconsin State Historical Society, McCarthy Papers, MSS KU, box 14); and Lodge to Frewen, 25 March 1914 (L.C., Frewen Papers, box 42).

23. Cockran revealed his essential moderation by telling Frewen that although he knew of no instance where a people of different religions and ethnic origins had been separated and then reunited into one nation, 'if the only alternative to partition of the Island be subjugation of one section to the other, I should hesitate long before approving either course'. Cockran to Frewen, 25 March and 19 May 1914 (N.Y.P.L., Cockran Papers, box 16).

24. Reid, p. 185; and Cockran to Frewen, 25 March 1914 (N.Y.P.L., Cockran Papers, box 16).

25. *Lit. Dig.*, xlviii, no. 14 (4 April 1914), pp 747–8, and no. 15 (11 April 1914), pp 813–14; *N.Y.T.*, 24, 25 and 29 March 1914; and Lowell to Bryce, 22 May 1914, and Bryce to Lowell, 17 June 1914 (Bodl., Bryce Papers, vol. 8, fol. 49, and vol. 22, fols 255–6).

26. Page to Wilson, 1 May 1914 (Harvard University Library, Page Papers, bms Am 1090.1/35); J. W. Gerard, *My four years in Germany* (New York, 1917), p. 100; and Tumulty, p. 397.

27. *N.Y.T.*, 26 and 27 May and 11, 27 and 29 July 1914.

28. Ryan to Devoy, 14 Jan. 1910 (N.L.I., Devoy Papers, box RU–S).

29. Keating to Devoy, 22 Jan. 1910 (N.L.I., Devoy Papers, box J–L). See also Keating to Devoy, 11 Nov. 1911, for suggestions as to how to maintain control of the Clan and keep up interest (*Ibid.*); and Devoy, p. 373.

30. Carroll to Devoy, 7 Feb. 1913, *Devoy's post-bag*, ii, pp 403–4; and Clan na Gael circular, March 1913 (N.L.I., Devoy Papers, box U.B.). One of the major arguments of the circular was that Redmond had no right to say that Home Rule would be the final settlement of the Irish question; another was that Redmond was wrong in claiming that Home Rule would permit an Anglo-American rapprochment.

31. Keating to Devoy, 11 Aug. and 23 May 1911, and 'Petition of the United German-American and United Irish-American Societies of New York to the United States Senate', 20 May 1911 (N.L.I., Devoy Papers, box J–L and box James Larkin); Congressman J. A. Hamill to Devoy, 19 July 1911, and A. P. Hayes to Devoy, 9 May 1911 (N.L.I., Devoy Papers, box E–J and box RU–S); Ryan, p. 285; and also C. Spring Rice, memorandum on 'Arbitration treaty between the United States and Great Britain' (P.R.O., F.O. 800/83). For a full analysis of Taft's struggles with the Bryce arbitration treaty see Ward in *I.H.S.*, xvi, no. 61 (March 1968), pp 71–2; Ward, *Ireland* pp 64–9; and D. F. Fleming, *The treaty veto of the American Senate* (New York, 1930), pp 90–109.

32. *G.A.*, 18 April 1914; Consul-General (Boston) to F.O., 9 March 1914 (P.R.O., F.O. 371/2154); *The life and letters of Walter H. Page*, ed. B. J. Hendrick (London, 1922–26), i, pp 242–3, 256–9 and 267; Spring Rice to Tyrrell, 17 Feb. 1914 (P.R.O., F.O. 800/84); Spring Rice to Tyrrell, 27 Jan. 1914, *The letters and friendships of Sir Cecil Spring Rice*, ed. S. Gwynn (London, 1929), ii, p. 201; and Spring Rice to Tyrrell, 30 March 1914 (P.R.O., F.O. 800/84).

33. For example, 'We Irish in America would be glad to hear that England had suffered defeat and disaster at the hands of Germany.' Chicago *Citizen*, 7 Jan. 1911, cited in Cambray, p. 134; J. T. Keating to Devoy, 4 Feb. 1914 (N.L.I., Devoy Papers, box J–L); *G.A.*, 31 Jan. 1914; D. Gwynn, *The life and death of Roger Casement* (London, 1930), pp 213–17; and R. MacColl, *Roger Casement* (London, 1956), pp 123–6.

34. Devoy to Cohalan, 29 Nov. 1911, cited in Tansill, pp 125–6; *G.A.*, 28 Feb., 7 and 14 March, 18 April and 2 May 1914; Lynch, pp 19–24; Hobson, pp 48 and 74; L. N. Le Roux, *Patrick H. Pearse* (Dublin, 1932), p. 25; Hobson to Devoy, 11 Oct. 1913, *Devoy's post-bag*, ii, pp 412–13 and 415; Tansill, pp 122–35; John B. Yeats to Lily Yeats, 29 July 1914, J. B. Yeats, *Letters to his son, W. B. Yeats, and others*, ed. J. Hone (London, 1944), p. 186; and Reid, pp 114–18.

35. *G.A.*, 3 and 31 Jan. and 7 Feb. 1914; O'Rahilly to Devoy, 6 April 1914, O' Mara to Devoy, 1 May 1914, Ryan to Devoy, 6 May 1914, and Burke to Devoy, 6 May 1914, *Devoy's post-bag*, ii, pp 426 and 433–5; and Tansill, p. 158.

36. F. Tobin to Reidy, 19 May 1914 (N.L.I., Devoy Papers, box T–Z). Circular letter to Clan from J. McGarrity, D. A. Spellissy and P. J. Griffin, 2 June 1914 (N.Y.P.L., Maloney Collection, McGarrity Papers, box 12); and *G.A.*, 6 June 1914. It should be noted, however, that by June more than six months had passed since the founding of the Irish Volunteers in Dublin. Alan J. Ward suggests that the emergence of militant Ulster resistance in 1911 saved revolutionary nationalism, but in the United States the prospects and the activities of the Irish-American revolutionaries did not

begin to improve significantly until well after the Irish Volunteers had been started in 1913–14. See Ward, *Ireland*, p. 70.

37. Ryan to Devoy, 30 June 1914, *Devoy's post-bag*, ii, p. 453. See also Devoy to McGarrity, 14 June 1914 (N.Y.P.L., Maloney Collection, McGarrity Papers, box 16); minutes of a meeting of the American Volunteer Fund Committee, 5 July 1914 (N.L.I., Devoy Papers, box Misc.); American Volunteer Fund Committee to Redmond (cable), 6 July 1914 (N.L.I., Redmond Papers); B. Hobson, *A short history of the Irish Volunteers* (Dublin, 1918), pp 130–1. This degree of moderation, while perhaps surprising, is not inconsistent with the sentiments of the Clan circular of March 1913 discussed earlier in this chapter.

38. Devoy to Hobson, 3 July 1914, *Devoy's post-bag*, ii, p. 458; Devoy to McGarrity, 18, 22 and 27 June and 2 July 1914 (N.Y.P.L., Maloney Collection, McGarrity Papers, box 16). Devoy, McGarrity, Tom Clarke and others referred to the reorganisation of the Volunteers first as a 'surrender' and finally as a 'betrayal'.

39. Casement to Mrs Green, 26 July 1914 (N.L.I., A. S. Green Papers, MS. 10464/10); *Devoy's post-bag*, ii, p. 463; and Hobson, *Ireland*, p. 53. *G.A.*, 11 July 1914; 'Extracts from the papers of the late Dr Patrick McCartan', pt 2, *Clogher Rec.*, v, no. 2 (1964), p. 189; and Casement to Cockran, 27 July 1914 (N.Y.P.L., Cockran Papers, box 17).

40. *Irish World*, 25 July 1914; Irish Volunteer Fund circular, *c.* 23 July 1914 (N.L.I., Devoy Papers, box Misc.); Robert E. Ford, circular letter, 28 July 1914 (*Ibid.*, box E–J); Devoy, p. 393; and Casement to Cockran, 27 July 1914 (N.Y.P.L., Cockran Papers, box 17).

41. The participation of the AOH was not then altogether surprising, as it had become increasingly politically orientated (and would become more so under the leadership of Joseph A. McLaughlin). While its present president, James J. Regan, pledged the support of the organisation to Redmond, Sir Roger Casement, who attended the national convention in Norfolk in late July, observed: '*All* here without exception almost are against Redmond's surrender to Ulster and a very little thing now would rent the Party irrecoverably with the Irish in America.' Devoy, he said, 'speaks for the prob [*sic*] majority I think—and it is absurd for Redmond to claim that he has the Irish here behind him'. Casement to Mrs Green, 26 July 1914 (N.L.I., A. S. Green Papers, MS. 10464/10). See also *N.Y.T.*, 11 July 1914; and *Lit. Dig.*, xlix, no. 2 (11 July 1914), pp 53–4, and no. 3 (18 July 1914), p. 98.

42. As early as 30 December 1913 Spring Rice had pointed out to Grey that if there were civil conflict in Ireland, the Irish-Americans would be quick to respond to it. At the height of the Curragh incident he again warned that 'Should there be fighting in Ireland men and guns will most certainly be sent from America.' Grey seemed muddled by this information and could not figure out 'to

whom the men and guns will be sent'. No instructions were sent to Spring Rice, but he was told that if fighting did indeed break out in Ireland, his request for instructions 'will be born in mind'. Spring Rice to Grey, 30 Dec. 1913 (P.R.O., F.O. 800/83); Spring Rice to F.O., 26 March 1914 (see also minute of the same date), and Tyrrell to Spring Rice, 28 March 1914 (P.R.O., F.O. 800/84). See the growing British concern as registered in the following dispatches: Colville Barclay to F.O., 5 and 20 July 1914 (P.R.O., F.O. 371/2187), and R. L. Nosworthy to Grey, 13 July 1914 (P.R.O., F.O. 371/2185); and minute by Percy, 15 July 1914, on Barclay to F.O., 5 July 1914 (P.R.O., F.O. 371/2187).

43. Casement to Devoy, 21 July 1914, *Devoy's post-bag*, ii, p. 463; and Casement to Cockran, 27 July 1914 (N.Y.P.L., Cockran Papers, box 17). Mac Néill to McGarrity (cable), 10 Aug. 1914 (N.Y.P.L., Maloney Collection, McGarrity Papers, box 13); and Casement to Mrs Green, 29 July 1914 (N.L.I., A. S. Green Papers, MS. 10464/10).

44. Howth also coincided with the maturation of the various fund-raising activities in the United States so that $5,000 was cabled to Mac Néill the following day. Hobson has said that the Volunteers never lacked money after Howth. Hobson, *A short history*, p. 65. Casement won Quinn's support for the Volunteers, and Quinn in turn wrote to Mayor John Purroy Mitchel, the grandson of the Young Irelander John Mitchel: 'In view of the open arming and treason of Ulster . . . The only hope [for Home Rule] is the arming of the National Volunteers.' Quinn to Mitchel, 31 July 1914 (L.C., Mitchel Papers, box 7); M. J. Barry to McGarrity (cable), 23 July 1914 (N.Y.P.L., Maloney Collection, McGarrity Papers, box 12); Casement to Mrs Green, 26 July 1914 (N.L.I., A. S. Green Papers, MS. 10464/10); and Reid, pp 187–9.

45. Devoy, pp 416–17; *G.A.*, 1 Aug. 1914; *Irish World*, 1 Aug. 1914; and *N.Y.T.*, 29 July 1914.

46. Asquith reported to the king that in the cabinet meeting to decide to pass the Home Rule Bill 'Sir E. Grey laid especial stress, in view of the situation in the United States, upon the necessity at the earliest foreseeable date of putting the Irish Bill on the Statute Book, though not into immediate operation.' Minutes of cabinet meeting, 'Thursday and yesterday', 12 Sept. 1914 (P.R.O., CAB. 41/35/43).

47. *N.Y.T.*, 12 Aug. 1914; *The war from this side* (Philadelphia, 1915), i, p. 163; *N.Y. Herald*, 18 Sept. 1914; Roosevelt to Lee, 22 Aug. 1914, *Roosevelt letters*, vii, p. 812; and *Lit. Dig.*, xlix, no. 15 (10 Oct. 1914), p. 678.

48. *Irish World*, 15 and 22 Aug., 26 Sept., 3, 10, 17 and 31 Oct. and 7 Nov. 1914.

49. Redmond to Ryan, 17 Sept. 1914, and Ryan to Redmond, 2 Oct. 1914, cited in Gwyn, *Redmond* pp 416–18.

50. F. X. Martin (ed.), *The Irish Volunteers, 1913–15* (Dublin, 1963),

pp 9–10. See Gwynn, *Redmond*, p. 420; and Egan to Redmond, 12 and 20 Oct. 1914 (N.L.I., Redmond Papers). Dillon to Cockran, 22 Oct. and 10 Nov. 1914 (N.Y.P.L., Cockran Papers, box 18). Arguing with Cockran some weeks later, Dillon made the telling point, 'If the promise to be loyal to the Empire does not imply the promise to help the Empire in such a war as this, it means practically nothing.' Dillon to Cockran, 23 Nov. 1914 (*Ibid.*). Dillon to Captain J. O'D. Storen, 8 Nov. 1914 (N.Y.P.L., Cockran Papers, box 18). John T. Keating, the Chicago Clan leader, was confident that Dillon's cable would, 'split the old party irreparably'. Keating to Devoy, 7 Nov. 1914, *Devoy's post-bag*, ii, p. 469.

51. Gwynn, *Redmond*, pp 417–19; S. Leslie, *The Irish issue in its American aspect* (London, 1918), p. 183; and Fitzpatrick to Redmond, 5 March 1915 (N.L.I., Redmond Papers).

52. Coyle to Redmond, 11 and 18 Dec. 1914, Barry to Redmond, 31 Oct. 1914, Fitzpatrick to Redmond, 15 Dec. 1914, and Jordan to Redmond, 31 Dec. 1914 (N.L.I., Redmond Papers). See also Patrick Egan's statement that the loss of the *Irish World* was not as bad as it seemed because 'A large number of the old timers of the League have ceased to read the *Irish World*.' Egan to Redmond, 24 Nov. 1914 (*Ibid.*).

53. Plunkett diary, 19 Dec. 1914 (Plunkett Foundation, Plunkett Papers); Pillsbury to Bryce, 25 March 1915, and Bryce to Pillsbury, 13 April 1915 (Bodl., Bryce Papers, vol. 23, fol. 25); Sanderson to Bryce, 3 March 1916 (*Ibid.*, vol. 18, fols 99–100); Egan to T. J. Hanna, 2 March 1915 (N.L.I., Redmond Papers); and Manning to Devoy, *c.* 23 Aug. 1915 (N.L.I., Devoy Papers, box M).

54. *Lit. Dig.*, xlix, no. 25 (19 Dec. 1914), p. 1216, and li, no. 5 (31 July 1915), p. 201; and Philadelphia *North American*, 2 July 1915, cited in *The war from this side*, i, pp 97–101.

55. Jordan to Redmond, 31 Dec. 1914 and 25 Feb. 1915, Egan to Jordan, 27 Feb. 1915, Fitzpatrick to Redmond, 5 March 1915, and Jordan to Egan, 5 March 1915 (N.L.I., Redmond Papers).

56. National Executive Committee to Ryan, 6 March 1915, Ryan to Stephen McFarland, 9 March 1915, McFarland and R. J. Waddell to Jordan, 12 March 1915, and Jordan to Redmond, 9 April 1915 (*Ibid.*).

57. The first attempt to curtail expenses had come some time earlier with the suspension of the UIL *Bulletin*. Ryan to McFarland, 9 March 1915, Coyle to Redmond, 5 April 1915, and Egan to T. J. Hanna, 9 March 1915 (*Ibid.*). For a detailed description of the fight in New York see the report of R. J. Waddell (secretary of the Municipal Council) to J. P. Gaynor, 16 March 1915 (*Ibid.*).

58. Boyle to Redmond, 3, 6 and 14 May 1915 (*Ibid.*); and Leslie, *Irish issue*, p. 183.

59. See Gwynn, *Redmond*, pp 432–3; Theodore Roosevelt to Redmond, 1 June 1915 (N.L.I., Redmond Papers); and Percy to Balfour, 6 June 1915 (B.M., Balfour Papers, Add. MS. 49748, vol. lxvi).

60. Fyfe, pp 235–8. With $10,000 cash and $5,000 later Egan felt he could start a newspaper in the United States which would give both the league and the party full support. Egan to Redmond, 20 Oct. 1914, and Egan to T. J. Hanna 12 Dec. 1914, Gallagher to Redmond, 2 Dec. 1914, Jordan to Redmond, 31 Dec. 1914, and Egan to T. J. Hanna, 7 May 1915 (N.L.I., Redmond Papers); and Dillon to Cockran, 4 Jan. 1915 (N.Y.P.L., Cockran Papers, box 18).

61. Redmond to Boyle, 13 Oct. 1915 (N.Y.P.L., Cockran Papers, box 18); Leslie, *Irish issue*, pp 181–2; Leslie to Redmond, 2 and 6 March 1916 (N.L.I., Redmond Papers). Although there was some feeling among the embassy staff in Washington that *Ireland* was 'too neutral to be of any great value, either to the Allied or even to the Nationalist cause', both Spring Rice and the Foreign Office were delighted by the progress that it seemed to make. Their feelings were that more might be done immediately. Memorandum from the British Embassy, Washington, to F.O., 10 and 27 March 1916, and minutes (P.R.O., F.O. 371/2793).

62. *G.A.*, 15 and 22 Aug. 1914; and O'Sheel to McGarrity, 18 Aug. 1914 (N.Y.P.L., Maloney Collection, McGarrity Papers, box 14). *G.A.*, 29 Aug., 12 Sept. and 3 and 17 Oct. 1914.

63. These meetings took place every week in some part of the country and were sponsored either by the large national organisations or by local groups; in either case they were fully reported in the Irish-American press. For specific instances see *G.A.*, 7 Nov. and 12 Dec. 1914; see also *Ibid.*, 30 Jan., 13 March, 12 June, 31 July, 28 Aug. and 2 Oct. 1915.

64. *Ibid.*, 3 and 31 Oct. and 7 Nov. 1914. Donnelly to Cockran, 25 Sept. 1914 (N.Y.P.L., Cockran Papers, box 18); and Casement to Mrs Green, 14 Sept. and 11 Oct. 1914 (N.L.I., A. S. Green Papers, MS. 10464/10).

65. Keating to Devoy, 7 Aug. and 7 Nov. 1914, *Devoy's post-bag*, ii, pp 465 and 469; and Casement to Mrs Green, 14 Sept. and 11 Oct. 1914 (N.L.I., A. S. Green Papers, MS. 10464/10).

66. Devoy, pp 403–6; *Documents relative to the Sinn Féin movement*, p. 3, H.C. 1921 [Cmd 1108], xxlx, 429; Reid, pp 188–9; Gwynn, pp 251–2; Casement to Mrs Green, 11 Oct. 1914 (N.L.I., A. S. Green Papers, MS. 10464/10); and Ward, *Ireland*, pp 75–6.

67. E. Larkin, *James Larkin, Irish labour leader, 1876–1947* (London, 1965), pp 187–94; and F. von Rintelen, *The dark invader* (London, 1933), pp 166–7 and 180.

68. 'Extracts from the papers of the late Dr Patrick McCartan', pt 2, *Clogher Rec.*, v, no. 2 (1964), pp 190–1; Lynch, p. 24; Devoy, pp 404 and 459; Le Roux, p. 154; and P. Béaslaí, *Michael Collins and the making of a new Ireland* (London, 1926), i, pp 57–8.

69. P. H. Pearse, *From a hermitage*, Bodenstown series, no. 2 (Dublin, 1915); P. H. Pearse, *Ghosts*, Tracts for the times, no. 10 (Dublin, 1916); The O'Rahilly, *The secret history of the Irish Volunteers*,

Tracts for the times, no. 3 (Dublin, 1915); Sir R. Casement, *The crime against Europe: a possible outcome of the war of 1914* (Philadelphia, 1915); 'An Irish-American' [Shaemus O'Sheel], *The catechism of Balaam, Jr.*, (New York, 1915); and 'By the author of *The catechism of Balaam, Jr.*' [Shaemus O'Sheel], *A trip through headline land* (New York, 1915). *The catechism of Balaam, Jr.* was estimated to have had a circulation of 300,000 copies and to have been translated into several languages. U.S. Congress, Senate, Subcommittee of the Judiciary Committee, *Hearings on brewing and liquor interests and German propaganda*, 65th Congress, 3rd Session (Washington, 1919), p. 1426. See also D. A. Wallace, *The revelations of an American citizen in the British army* (New York, 1916); American Truth Society, *The conquest of the United States* (New York, 1915); and J. A. O'Leary, *The fable of John Bull* (New York, 1916).

70. F. Koester, *The lies of the Allies* (New York, 1916); E. A. Steiner, *The confession of a hyphenated American* (New York, 1916); S. I. Szinnyey, pseud. [S. I. Stephen], *Neutrality* (Chicago, 1916); *British versus German imperialism* (New York, 1915); J. K. McGuire, *The King, the Kaiser and Irish freedom* (New York, 1915); J. K. McGuire, *What could Germany do for Ireland?* (New York, 1916); and Gaffney, p. 144.

71. McGinn to Devoy, 12 Oct. 1915, *Devoy's post-bag*, ii, pp 480–1; Devoy to McGarrity, 14 Oct. 1915, and Devoy to Clan brothers (printed circular), 29 Dec. 1915 (N.Y.P.L., Maloney Collection, McGarrity Papers, box 16); *Documents relative to the Sinn Féin movement*, p. 9; Tansill, p. 188; *G.A.*, 11 March 1916; J. J. Splain in W. G. Fitz-Gerald (ed.), *The voice of Ireland* (Dublin, 1924), p. 228; McLaughlin to Devoy, 21 Feb. 1916 (N.L.I., Devoy Papers, box M); and 'Appeal re Irish Race Convention, 1916' (*Ibid.*, box Misc.). Indeed, the Irish-American community was divided as to the merits of a convention. Congressman Michael Donohoe complained to McLaughlin that such activity undermined Redmond and played into the hands of Carson. Donohoe to McLaughlin, 19 Feb. 1916 (N.Y.P.L., Maloney Collection, McGarrity Papers, box 12).

72. Cited in Tansill, p. 189; and *Documents relative to the Sinn Féin movement*, p. 9. All the national officers and 15 of the 17 members of the executive committee were members of the Clan. *G.A.*, 11 March and 1 April 1916; and Devoy, pp 451–7.

73. *Lit. Dig.*, lii, no. 12 (18 March 1916), p. 703. See also Leslie to Redmond, 6 March 1916 (N.L.I., Redmond Papers); and New York *Herald*, 5 March 1916.

74. Brooklyn *Citizen*, 6 March 1916; *Lit. Dig.*, lii, no. 12 (18 March 1916), pp 702–3; and memorandum from the British Embassy, Washington to F.O., 10 March 1916, and minutes (P.R.O., F.O. 371/2793).

Chapter 3
1916 AND ITS AFTERMATH, 1916–1917
(pp 55–88)

1. See *N.Y.T.*, New York *World* and Washington *Post*, 25 April 1916 (the New York *World* had only a small article on p. 2); Chicago *Tribune*, 25 April 1916 (the *Tribune* published leaders reading 'FOIL GERMAN–IRISH PLOT' and suggested that Ireland might have been invaded and in a state of rebellion); and *C.S.M.*, 26 April 1916. American newspapers were further hampered in obtaining news about the rising in Dublin because they had no correspondents there and had to send their London reporters to Ireland on special assignment; the first travelled with the Irish Chief Secretary, Augustine Birrell, on a British destroyer and arrived in Dublin on Saturday 29 April, cabling articles which appeared in the American press on Monday 1 May. See *C.S.M.*, 1 May 1916, and Washington *Post*, 26 April 1916.

2. *C.S.M.*, 26 April 1916; New York *World*, 26 April 1916; Washington *Post*, 28 and 30 April 1916; New York *World*, 26 April 1916; Chicago *Tribune*, 26 April 1916; and Boston *Transcript*, cited in *Lit. Dig.*, lii, no. 19 (6 May 1916), pp 1263–4. D. M. Tucker, 'Some American responses to the Easter rebellion, 1916', *The Historian*, xxix (Aug. 1967), pp 605–18; and O. D. Edwards, 'American aspects of the Rising' and 'Appendix II: press reaction to the Rising in general' in O. D. Edwards and F. Pyle (ed.), *1916: the Easter Rising* (London, 1968).

3. New York *World*, 26, 27 and 30 April 1916; *N.Y.T.*, 26 April and 2 and 3 May 1916; *C.S.M.*, 2 May 1916; Washington *Post*, 26 April 1916; and Chicago *Tribune*, 2 May 1916.

4. *N.Y.T.*, 29 April and 2 May 1916; in this view they were joined in part by the *C.S.M.*, 29 April 1916. See also New York *Evening Mail*, 28 April 1916; Chicago *Tribune*, 28 April 1916; Washington *Post*, 2 May 1916; and *Lit. Dig.*, lii, no. 19 (6 May 1916), pp 1263–5. Tucker discusses briefly the split in the staff of the *New Republic* between Francis Hackett, an Irish-American with strong nationalist sympathies, and Walter Lippmann and Herbert Croly, who felt that Britain should not be weakened during the war. Tucker in *The Historian*, xxix (Aug. 1967), pp 612–13.

5. New York *World*, 6, 9, 10 and 13 May 1916. The *World* later published a damning editorial of the government's handling of the Bowen-Colthurst case. New York *World*, 8 June 1916.

6. Washington *Post*, 7 May 1916; Chicago *Tribune*, 5 May 1916; *N.Y.T.*, 4 May 1916; Des Moines *Capital*, cited in the Chicago *Tribune*, 11 May 1916; and *C.S.M.*, 6, 13 and 26 May 1916. The *Christian Science Monitor* seemed irresistibly drawn to discussing the rebellion, and in fact on 16 May 1916 published a fairly comprehensive summary of the Rising, complete with facsimile reproductions of the Proclamation and the proposed postage stamps for the Republic. *C.S.M.*, 16 May 1916. The *Literary Digest* noted the

unanimity of American editors in disapproving of the executions as well as the Rising. *Lit. Dig.*, lii, no. 20 (13 May 1916), p. 1355. Later in the summer, after first impressions had already been made, the July issue of the radical journal *The Masses* featured articles by Louise Bryant, James Larkin and the editor Arturo Giovannitti praising and explaining the Rising. By November the liberal pacifist Roland Hugins, in a book discussing the termination of the war, wrote that British greed and hypocrisy had driven Ireland into revolt and that England had robbed Ireland of her 'economic and political liberty'. R. Hugins, *The possible peace* (New York, 1916), p. 156.

7. Kellogg to Plunkett, 27 April and 21 May 1916, and Lowell to Plunkett, 13 May and 5 July 1916 (Plunkett Foundation, Plunkett Papers); and McCarthy to Plunkett, 10 May 1916 (Wisconsin State Historical Society, McCarthy Papers, MSS KU, box 27).

8. Butler to Bryce, 13 May 1916 (Bodl., Bryce Papers, vol. 3, fol. 262); Low to Bryce, 20 May 1916 (*Ibid.*, vol. 7, fol. 331); Straight to Bryce, 21 June 1916 (*Ibid.*, vol. 19, fol. 155); and Dr W. T. Sullivan to Bryce, 7 July 1916 (*Ibid.*, fol. 194).

9. R. M. Stuart Wortley to Frewen, 2 May 1916 (L.C., Frewen Papers, box 46); New York *Nation*, 18 May 1916; and J. Kilmer, *Poems, essays and letters,* ed. R. C. Holliday (New York, 1918), i, p. 77.

10. New York *World*, 26 April 1916. See Colby to Judge Cohalan, 20 May 1916 (L.C., Colby Papers, box 2).

11. Bullard to House, 1 May 1916 (Bodl., Nathan Papers, vol. 477). Bullard, notwithstanding his desire to break down the Irish–German alliance in the United States, had been shocked by the British handling of the Irish rebellion. He told E. M. House: 'Everything for which British Liberalism has stood, as contrasted to Prussian Junkerism, has been brushed away.' Bullard to House, 23 May 1916, cited in A. S. Link, *Wilson: campaigns for Progressivism and peace, 1916–1917* (Princeton, 1965), p. 13. Thompson to Plunkett, 1 May 1916 (Plunkett Foundation, Plunkett Papers); Bullard to House, 1 May 1916 (Bodl., Nathan Papers, vol. 477); and Bullard to Plunkett, 1 May 1916, and Plunkett diary, 4, 7 and 13 May 1916 (Plunkett Foundation, Plunkett Papers). Shane Leslie suggested much the same kind of plan to Redmond, hoping that proof of a German betrayal would work to discredit the revolutionaries in the United States and move sympathy to the constitutionalists. Leslie to Redmond, 16 May 1916 (N.L.I., Redmond Papers).

12. House to Plunkett, 25 April and 16 June 1916 (Plunkett Foundation, Plunkett Papers). See also Plunkett to House, 25 and 29 May 1916 (*Ibid.*).

13. Roosevelt to Lee, 7 June 1916, *Roosevelt letters*, viii, pp 1054–5; and Roosevelt to Plunkett, 9 July 1916 (Plunkett Foundation, Plunkett Papers). See also Plunkett to Roosevelt, 27 June 1916 (L.C., Roosevelt Papers, series 1/box 304).

14. In the *G.A.*, 29 April 1916, Devoy said that there had been no Irish informers or British spies to give away the information about the German arms ship, 'but that deficiency was supplied by the Washington Government'. See also *G.A.*, 27 May 1916. This assertion was repeated in his memoirs, Devoy, pp 465–71, and again in Tansill, pp 193–4. However, in private Devoy seemed more assured; he sent McGarrity the following thinly disguised letter: 'I know you will be anxious after hearing of the fire in our home to learn if we all came off safe. I am glad to be able to inform you that all the papers relating to the property were saved except one little scrap, and that will not be much of a loss. The sale will come off on time and everything looks all right. We were very anxious for the whole day, but when the firemen got through with their work of salvage we found we had no cause for worry.' 'David Jones' [Devoy] to 'Dear Friend' [McGarrity], 19 April 1916 (N.Y.P.L., Maloney Collection, McGarrity Papers, box 16). Thomas W. Gregory (Attorney-General) to Sec. of State, 21 April 1916 (N.A., WOLF VON IGEL CASE, 701.6211/307½). In fact Spring Rice complained to Grey on 28 April that the 'United States authorities have not issued any account of the nature of the documents seized in von Igel's apartment'. Spring Rice to Grey, 28 April 1916 (P.R.O., F.O. 371/2851).

15. American Embassy, London, to Sec. of State, 25 April 1916 (N.A., WOLF VON IGEL CASE, 701.6211/367); and Lansing to American Embassy, London, 1 May 1916 (*Ibid.*). Tumulty telephoned Lansing on Thursday 27 April, saying that the government had been accused of informing the British of the plans of the Irish revolutionaries. See Lansing desk diary, 27 April 1916 (L.C., Lansing Papers).

16. See Spring Rice to Grey, 28 April 1916 (P.R.O., F.O. 371/2851); Spring Rice to Grey (cable), 19 May 1916 (P.R.O., F.O. 800/86); Spring Rice to Grey, 19 May 1916 (P.R.O., F.O. 371/2795); and Frost to Sec. of State, Oct. 1916 (N.A., 841.00/32, roll 6).

17. H. Res. 235, 12 May 1916, *Congressional Record*, 64th Congress, 1st Session, vol. 53, p. 7899. Two more resolutions appealing to the British government to exercise restraint with the Irish prisoners were introduced in the House by Thomas Gallivan of Chicago (H. Res. 244) and Murray Hulbert of New York (H. Res. 245). All three resolutions were sent to the Foreign Affairs Committee, which did not report any of them; nonetheless, their introduction was an indication of the sentiments of the Congress and the popular pressures put upon it. *Ibid.*, pp 8358 and 8427. 16 May 1916, *Congressional Record, Appendix*, 64th Congress, 1st Session, vol. 54, p. 959; 17 May 1916, *Congressional Record*, 64th Congress, 1st Session, vol. 53, pp 8125–6; and S. Res. 196, *Ibid.*, pp 8140–41. Two days after the Kern resolution had been introduced Senator James E. Martine of New Jersey told the Senate that he opposed the methods England had used to suppress the Rising and said

that the ruthless execution of prisoners made British claims in the war seem hypocritical.

18. Polk to Stone, 27 May 1916 (Yale University Library, Polk Papers, drawer 77, file 133). 1, 2 and 13 June 1916, *Congressional Record*, 64th Congress, 1st Session, vol. 53, pp 9026–7, 9150 and 9482. See also 1 June 1916, *Hansard* 5 (Commons), lxxxii, col. 2932.

19. See Polk to William Rasquin, Jr, 10 May 1916 (Yale University Library, Polk Papers, drawer 77, file 133); and Washington *Post*, 19 and 20 May 1916. See Edwards in Edwards and Pyle, pp 160–3; for a conflicting interpretation see Ward, *Ireland*, pp 117–18.

20. Lord Eustace Percy, who was in the United States during the Rising, later wrote that the rebellion was no more welcome to moderate Irish-American nationalists than to the British government. Lord E. Percy, *Some memories* (London, 1958), p. 50. Chicago *Tribune*, 26 April 1916. These interviews were later syndicated and published in several other newspapers. See the Boston *Transcript*, cited in *Lit. Dig.*, lii, no. 19 (6 May 1916), pp 1263–74; and New York *World*, 29 April 1916.

21. Among those participating were Michael J. Jordan and T. B. Fitzpatrick. *C.S.M.*, 2 and 3 May 1916. Spring Rice to Grey, 4 May 1916 (P.R.O., F.O. 800/86); and Reid, pp 232–3.

22. McFarland to Redmond, 4 May 1916, Ryan to Redmond, 15 May 1916, and Leslie to Redmond, 16 May 1916 (N.L.I., Redmond Papers); and *Ireland*, cited in *Lit. Dig.*, lii, no. 20 (13 May 1916), p. 1355.

23. Leslie to Redmond, 16 and 20 May 1916, and Barry to Redmond, 25 May 1916 (N.L.I., Redmond Papers); and Godkin to Plunkett, 5 July 1916 (Plunkett Foundation, Plunkett Papers). See also 'Easter Week' and 'Apology' in Kilmer, i, pp 131–2 and 163–4.

24. *Irish World*, 29 April 1916; *G.A.*, 26 and 29 April and 6 May 1916; and *C.S.M.*, 1 May 1916. See also a handbill dated 30 April 1916 announcing the mass meeting (P.R.O., F.O. 371/2793); Edwards in Edwards and Pyle, p. 159; and New York *World*, 2 May 1916.

25. *G.A.*, 6 May 1916.

26. *G.A.*, 6 and 13 May 1916. The *Gaelic American* also claimed that John Redmond had applauded the executions in parliament. See A. C. Ross (British Consul in San Francisco) to Foreign Secretary, 11 May 1916 (P.R.O., F.O. 371/2793). Resolutions were also introduced in the Massachusetts House of Representatives demanding that there be no more executions of Irish prisoners. Frederick P. Leay (British Consul in Boston) to Spring Rice, 10 May 1916 (*Ibid.*). 'Men of 1916' in J. McGarrity, *Celtic moods and memories* (Dublin, 1938), p. 96.

72. Colby to Cohalan, 20 May 1916 (L.C., Colby Papers, box 2). *C.S.M.*, 15 May 1916; *G.A.*, 20 May 1916; and Edwards in Edwards and Pyle, p. 159. Subsequent meetings were held in Lowell, Westfield, New Haven, Providence, Rochester, Hoboken,

Chicago, and again in New York, although they were increasingly concerned with raising relief funds. Leslie, *Irish issue*, pp 188 and 190–1.

28. New York *World*, 26 May and 14 and 25 June 1916; and *C.S.M.*, 26 May 1916.
29. *N.Y.T.*, 7 and 11 July 1916. House told Wilson that conservative forces in the cabinet had prevented the acceptance of Lloyd George's Home Rule proposals. House to Wilson, 30 July 1916, cited in Link, *Wilson*, p. 38. *N.Y.T.*, 25, 26 and 31 July 1916. Roland G. Usher, the author of several popular books on international relations, wrote a feature article for the magazine section of the New York *Times*, 6 Aug. 1916. Usher argued that Redmond's refusal to accept diminished Irish representation in Westminster was unreasonable because it was not fair for the Irish to have their own local government and still dominate the House of Commons. R. G. Usher, 'The plight of Home Rule', magazine section, *N.Y.T.*, 6 Aug. 1916. New York *World*, 26 July 1916; *Lit. Dig.*, liii, no. 8 (19 Aug. 1916), p. 399; and *G.A.*, 17 and 24 June and 15 and 29 July 1916.
30. *C.S.M.*, 26 May 1916; *N.Y.T.*, 30 June 1916; New York *Evening Mail*, 30 June 1916; and New York *World*, 30 June 1916.
31. Lowell to Plunkett, 5 July 1916 (Plunkett Foundation, Plunkett Papers); Straight to Bryce, 21 June 1916 (Bodl., Bryce Papers, vol. 19, fol. 155); Roosevelt to Arthur Hamilton Lee, 7 June 1916, *Roosevelt letters*, viii, pp 1054–5; and G. L. Fox, *Roger Casement and John Redmond* (n.p., 1916).
32. Robert P. Troy, Richard O'Connor and John Mulhern to Wilson, 19 May 1916, and Phelan to Wilson, 22 May 1916 (L.C., Wilson Papers, file VI, no. 3152, box 520). 22 May 1916, *Congressional Record*, 64th Congress, 1st Session, vol. 53, p. 8454. Tumulty to Polk, 2 and 9 June 1916 (Yale University Library, Polk Papers, drawer 77, files 134 and 136); and Polk to Tumulty, 3 June 1916 (L.C., Wilson Papers, file VI, no. 3152, box 520).
33. Wilson to Troy, 7 July 1916, Troy to Phelan, 23 June 1916, and Phelan to Tumulty, 28 June 1916 (L.C., Wilson Papers, file VI, no. 3152, box 520). See p. 18 above; and Tumulty, p. 396. Tumulty to Meyer London, *c.* 30 June 1916, and memorandum by Tumulty, *c.* summer 1916 (L.C., Wilson Papers, file VI, no. 3085, box 520).
34. Doyle to Tumulty, 28 and 29 April 1916 (L.C., Wilson Papers, file VI, no. 3085, box 520). It should be mentioned that Doyle's assurances to Tumulty that he represented no Irish-American organisation were not strictly correct; although he charged no fee himself, his expenses (at least $5,000) were paid by the Clan na Gael and perhaps by the Germans. See Devoy, pp 477–8. Memorandum by Joseph McGarrity, 3 June 1916 (N.Y.P.L., Maloney Collection, McGarrity Papers, box 12). G. de C. Parmiter, *Roger Casement* (London, 1936), p. 283; and *Documents relative to the Sinn Féin movement*, p. 15. Tumulty to Lansing, 29 April

1916, and Woolsey to Tumulty, *c.* 30 April 1916 (L.C., Wilson Papers, file VI, no. 3085, box 520). Woolsey said that Doyle probably wanted the government to act on behalf of Casement as it had on behalf of Nurse Edith Cavell, although he regarded the situations as entirely different. Mrs Newman to Wilson, 30 April 1916, Tumulty to Wilson, 1 May 1916, and Wilson to Tumulty, 2 May 1916 (*Ibid.*); Polk to Doyle, 31 May 1916 (Yale University Library, Polk Papers, drawer 77, file 134); and Doyle to Tumulty, 30 May 1916, Doyle to Polk, 30 May 1916, and Polk to Tumulty, 2 June 1916 (L.C., Wilson Papers, file VI, no. 3085, box 520).

35. 'Memorandum account of interview with Doyle', enclosed in Spring Rice to Grey, 17 June 1916, and Grey to Samuel, 16 June 1916 (P.R.O., F.O. 800/86 and 112). MacColl, p. 251; A. Noyes, *The accusing ghost of Roger Casement* (London, 1957), pp 164–9 and 187; Doyle to Tumulty, 6 July 1916 (L.C., Wilson Papers, file VI, no. 3085, box 520); and Doyle to Grey, 19 July 1916, and minutes (P.R.O., F.O. 800/112).

36. Quincy to Tumulty, 30 June 1916, and F. H. Krebs, memorandum of a meeting with President Wilson, 7 July 1916 (L.C., Wilson Papers, file VI, no. 3085, box 520); Lansing to Page, 1 July 1916 (N.A., 841.00/17a, roll 6); and Page to Sec. of State, 3 July 1916 (Yale University Library, Polk Papers, drawer 77, file 135). The letter was seen by at least Wilson, Lansing, Polk and Tumulty. Alan J. Ward has quite rightly concluded that the so-called 'black diaries' had little effect in the United States, except perhaps to further discredit the British government. Ward, *Ireland*, p. 123.

37. Doyle to Tumulty, 6 and 19 July 1916, Tumulty to Wilson, 20 July 1916, and Wilson to Tumulty, 20 July 1916 (L.C., Wilson Papers, file VI, no. 3085, box 520). Alan J. Ward has shown that Wilson similarly refused to intervene in the executions of nationalist leaders in Central Europe. Ward, *Ireland*, p. 116; and Ward in *I.H.S.*, xvi, no. 61 (March 1968), p. 79.

38. Senator Martine also referred to the court procedure as a 'so-called trial'. S. Res. 223, *Congressional Record*, 64th Congress, 1st Session, vol. 53, pp 10251–2 and 11146–7.

39. 19 and 22 July, *Ibid.*, pp 11305 and 11429. S. Res. 236 and 237, *Ibid.*, pp 11430–4. See also *C.S.M.*, 24 July 1916. *Congressional Record*, 64th Congress, 1st Session, vol. 53, pp 11519–26 and 11678–88.

40. The minority of the committee consisted of Pittman, O'Gorman and Stone (chairman). Stone told the Senate: 'From practically every point of view, and especially from the point of view of Sir Roger Casement, the whole proceeding has been a mistake.' The report became S. Res. 241. 29 July 1916, *Ibid.*, pp 11770–3 and 11782. Of the several senators who spoke against the resolutions all, even Williams, expressed the confidence or the hope that the British government would not execute Casement. It would be wrong to say that Casement did not stir the sympathies of the

Senate, but it would be fair to note that many voting for the resolution, particularly the Democrats, also had an eye on the November elections.

41. See Polk to Page, nos 3606 and 3608, 2 Aug. 1916, 841.00/20 and –/20a, *Foreign relations, 1916, supplement,* pp 870–1. See also Polk to Tumulty, 2 Aug. 1916 (L.C., Wilson Papers, file VI, no. 3085, box 520). The cable arrived in London at about midnight, after the embassy had closed. After decoding the following day, it was ready for delivery to the Foreign Office by 10 a.m. London time. F. L. Polk, 'Memorandum on Casement resolution', 17 Aug. 1916 (N.A., 841.00/23½, roll 6). For a full account see *Page letters,* ii, pp 167–8; and also Laughlin to Lansing, 3 Aug. 1916, 841.00/21, *Foreign relations, 1916, supplement,* p. 871.

42. Grey seemed reluctant to understand either the significance or the content of the Senate resolution. In a memorandum on the resolution he noted that Wilson had sent it without instructions and that the text referred only to 'political prisoners' which Casement was not. See memorandum by Grey, Aug. 1916 (P.R.O., F.O. 371/2798); cabinet papers, 5 and 24 Aug. 1916 (P.R.O. CAB. 37/153 and 154); and Grey to House, 28 Aug. 1916, *The intimate papers of Colonel House,* ed. C. Seymour (Boston, 1926), ii, pp 317–18. Laughlin reported back to the State Department that the resolution had been delivered. Grey, he said, 'did not promise an answer but said he would communicate the Senate's resolution to the Prime Minister and probably lay it before the Cabinet'. Laughlin to Lansing, 3 Aug. 1916, 841.00/21, *Foreign relations, 1916, supplement,* p. 871.

43. Spring Rice to Grey, 2 and 4 May and 4, 26 and 29 July 1916 (P.R.O., F.O. 800/86); Reid, p. 235; Quinn to Spring Rice, 27 July 1916, and Spring Rice to Grey, 28 July 1916 (P.R.O., F.O. 371/2798); and Quinn et al. to Grey, 28 July 1916 (P.R.O., CAB. 37/152/32). See I. B. W. Bennett (president of Negro Fellowship League, Chicago) to George V, 14 July 1916 (P.R.O., F.O. 371/2798). Lodge to Grey in cable from Spring Rice to Grey, 29 July 1916, and Grey to Spring Rice, 2 Aug. 1916 (P.R.O., F.O. 800/86). Grey instructed Spring Rice to tell Senator Lodge that his 'friendly message about Casement' was appreciated and considered by the government but that no reprieve could be granted because of the seriousness of Casement's acts. See also minutes of cabinet meeting, 2 Aug. 1916 (P.R.O., CAB. 41/37/29); and Spring Rice to Grey, 2 Aug. 1916 (P.R.O., F.O. 371/2798). Spring Rice cabled again the next day to say that he had been informed by Frank L. Polk that Wilson had not desired that any appeals be made in his name. The Foreign Office was not pleased at such a suggestion from Spring Rice. Spring Rice to Grey, 3 Aug. 1916 (P.R.O., F.O. 800/86). Minutes of cabinet meeting, 2 Aug. 1916, sent to king (P.R.O., CAB. 41/37/29). See also 'Memorandum of conversation between Page and Asquith', 1 Aug. 1916, 763.72/

13495, *Foreign relations, 1916, supplement*, p. 45; *Page letters*, ii, p. 168; R. Jenkins, *Asquith* (London, 1964), pp 452–4; and Polk to Lansing, 3 Aug. 1916 (L.C., Lansing Papers, vol. 20).

44. Washington *Post*, 3 Aug. 1916; New York *World*, 3 and 4 Aug. 1916; Chicago *Tribune*, 4 Aug. 1916; and *G.A.*, 12 Aug. 1916.

45. J. Quinn, 'Roger Casement, martyr: some notes for a chapter of history by a friend whose guest he was when the war broke out', magazine section, *N.Y.T.*, 13 Aug. 1916, pp 1–4. Quinn's temper was calmed somewhat by his friend Spring Rice and by Captain Guy Gaunt, but he remained indignant at the British use of materials which compromised Casement's reputation. Reid, pp 236–9.

46. In May Joseph McGarrity considered sending a 'Green Cross Ship' with relief supplies to Ireland, as he did again in 1921, but he did not do so. 'Secret report, internal conditions, neutral countries', Philadelphia, 22 May 1916 (P.R.O., F.O. 371/2793). McCormack to Mitchel, 12 May 1916 (L.C., Mitchel Papers, box 10); *N.Y.T.*, 24 May 1916; and *G.A.*, 27 May and 3, 10 and 17 June 1916.

47. John D. Moore to Golden, 28 June 1916 (N.L.I., Golden Papers, MS. 13141); *G.A.*, 24 June and 29 July 1916; Waddell to Redmond, 18 July 1916 (N.L.I., Redmond Papers); and K. O'Doherty, *Assignment America: de Valera's mission to the United States* (New York, 1957), pp 22–3.

48. Spring Rice to Grey, 9 June and 21 July 1916 (P.R.O., F.O. 800/86); Polk to American Embassy, London, 26 July 1916 (Yale University Library, Polk Papers, drawer 77, file 133); and Page to Sec. of State, 28 July 1916 (N.A., 341.112k29/66, box 3972). In late September B. II. Thompson of Scotland Yard commented that Gill was 'merely a Sinn Féin in disguise'; he thought that in the future no similar relief funds should be allowed in Ireland. Thompson to Campbell, 28 Sept. 1916 (P.R.O., F.O. 371/2795). See also Tumulty to Moore, Mayor James M. Curley, J. J. McNellis and M. J. Murphy, 27 July 1916, and Farley to Wilson, 3 Aug. 1916 (L.C., Wilson Papers, file VI, no. 3152, box 521); and Moore to Wilson, 1 Aug. 1916 (N.A., 341.112k29/73, box 3972).

49. *G.A.*, 5 Aug. 1916; and 'Report of John Archdeacon Murphy as delegate in Ireland to the Irish Relief Fund of America', n.d., (N.L.I., Devoy Papers, box Misc.). Cardinal Farley had in a circular referred to the 'unspeakable want and distress' in Ireland as the result of the suppression of the Rising, and the Foreign Office was at a loss as to how to refute such statements effectively. Minutes on Irish Relief Fund in Chicago, 1 Jan. 1917 (P.R.O., F.O. 371/3063).

50. Rev. Edward Flannery to Tumulty, 10 Aug. and 24 Aug. 1916 (L.C., Wilson Papers, file IV, no. 61, box 81). William M. Leary, Jr, also points out that neither the *Gaelic American* nor the *Irish World*, although they detested Wilson, were very enthusiastic

about Hughes. W. M. Leary, 'Woodrow Wilson, Irish Americans, and the election of 1916', *Jn. Amer. Hist.,* liv (June 1967), pp 57–72. See also L. L. Gerson, *The hyphenate in recent American politics and diplomacy* (Lawrence, 1964), pp 65–6; and Link, *Wilson,* chapters 1–4.

51. See Washington *Times,* 4 Aug. 1916; New York *Evening Mail,* 7 Aug. 1916; and Phelan to Tumulty, 4 Aug. 1916 (L.C., Wilson Papers, file VI, no. 3085, box 520). This resolution was never reported by the Committee on Rules, but it did indicate the sentiment in the House. 9 Aug. 1916, *Congressional Record,* 64th Congress, 1st Session, vol. 53, p. 12405; and McGuire to Wilson (telegram), 5 Aug. 1916 (L.C., Wilson Papers, file VI, no. 3085, box 520). Tumulty to Polk, 7 Aug. 1916 (Yale University Library, Polk Papers, drawer 77, file 136); and Polk to Tumulty, 7 Aug. 1916 (L.C., Wilson Papers, file VI, no. 3085, box 520). In his analysis of the situation William M. Leary, Jr, suggests that the delay was probably caused by 'administrative incompetence' rather than through any deliberate calculation. Leary in *Jn. Amer. Hist.,* liv (June 1967), p. 62.

52. Ashurst to Lansing, 25 Aug. 1916 (N.A., 841.00/26, roll 6); memorandum on letter from Doyle to Tumulty, 28 Aug. 1916, Lansing to Tumulty, 2 Sept. 1916, and Tumulty to Lansing, 7 Sept. 1916 (L.C., Wilson Papers, file VI, no. 3085, box 520); and Lansing to Tumulty, 16 Sept. 1916 (L.C., Lansing Papers, vol. 21). Memorandum on letter from Doyle to Tumulty, 29 Sept. 1916 (L.C., Wilson Papers, file VI, no. 3085, box 520). See also Lansing to Tumulty, 16 Sept. and 2 Oct. 1916 (L.C., Lansing Papers, vol. 21). Tumulty was indignant at the thought that he had asked Lansing to make an 'incorrect statement', but he did want some official announcement which would relieve the pressure on the White House. Tumulty to Lansing, 3 Oct. 1916 (*Ibid.*). See Polk to Tumulty, 5, 6 and 12 Oct. 1916, and Tumulty to Polk, 11 Oct. 1916 (L.C., Wilson Papers, file VI, no. 3085, box 520); press release by Polk, 9 Oct. 1916 (Yale University Library, Polk Papers, drawer 77, file 137); and Tumulty to Doyle, 14 Oct. 1916, and Doyle to Tumulty, 18 Oct. 1916 (L.C., Wilson Papers, file VI, no. 3085, box 520).

53. *N.Y.T.,* 30 Sept. 1916; and J. A. O'Leary, *My political trial and experiences* (New York, 1919), p. 46.

54. Tumulty says in his memoirs that the campaign improved considerably from that point on, and A. S. Link records that E. M. House told the French Ambassador that O'Leary's telegram had been one of the decisive elements in the election. Tumulty, p. 214; and Link, *Wilson,* p. 105. See the New York *World,* New York *Evening Post,* Brooklyn *Citizen,* Brooklyn *Standard Union,* Philadelphia *Record,* Chicago *Journal,* Chicago *Herald,* and Springfield *Republican,* cited in *Lit. Dig.,* liii, no. 16 (14 Oct. 1916), p. 935; *Nation,* 5 Oct. 1916, p. 312; and *New Republic,* 7 Oct. 1916, p.

233. Edward A. Steiner's book published in December 1916 condemned both the Irish-Americans and German-Americans for attempting to make their ethnic problems issues in domestic American politics. E. A. Steiner, *Nationalizing America* (New York, 1916), pp 224–5.

55. In California the Irish-American Democratic vote probably went for Wilson. See, for example, Rev. Peter C. Yorke to Devoy, 23 Nov. 1916 (N.L.I., Devoy Papers, box T–Z); *G.A.*, 18 Nov. 1916; J. B. Duff, 'The Versailles Treaty and the Irish-Americans', *Jn. Amer. Hist.* lv (Dec. 1968), p. 585; and Leary in *Jn. Amer. Hist.*, liv (June 1967), pp 65–72. F. P. Leay (British Consul in Boston) reported that both the AOH and the Knights of Columbus had supported Wilson in the 1916 election. Leay to J. Joyce Broderick, (British Embassy), 11 Dec. 1916 (P.R.O., F.O. 371/3071).

56. See Colonel Ricard O'Sullivan Burke to Devoy, 6 Dec. 1916, *Devoy's post-bag*, ii, p. 571; and *G.A.*, 23 July, 5 Aug. and 14 Oct. 1916. See also D. Macardle, *The Irish Republic: a documented chronicle of the Anglo-Irish conflict* (1937; repr. New York, 1965), p. 191; Tumulty to Lansing, 21 Sept. 1916, Lansing to AMEMBASSY, 30 Sept. 1916, Lansing to Tumulty, 28 Sept. 1916, and Victor Wellesley (for the Foreign Office) to Page, 1 Nov. 1916 (N.A., 341d11/1 and –/2, box 4094); and Spring Rice to Grey, 14 Sept. 1916, U.S. Chargé d'Affaires to F.O., 3 Oct. 1916, and F.O. to Spring Rice, 9 Oct. 1916 (P.R.O., F.O. 371/2795).

57. See Plunkett to James Byrne, 14 June 1916 (Plunkett Foundation, Plunkett Papers); R. Monteith, *Casement's last adventure* (Dublin, 1953), pp 230–8; Luke Dillon to Devoy, 21 Feb. 1917 (N.L.I., Devoy Papers, box CF–D); M. Skinnider, *Doing my bit for Ireland* (New York, 1917), passim; N. Connolly, *The unbroken tradition* (New York, 1918), pasim; F. O'Donoghue in Lynch, pp 187–8; P. McCartan, *With de Valera in America* (Dublin, 1932) pp 5–14; M. Joy et. al., *The Irish rebellion of 1916 and its martyrs* (New York, 1916), passim; and John D. Moore to Golden, 28 June 1916 (N.L.I., Golden Papers, MS. 13141). Larkin, pp 219–29. Purely American efforts included F. P. Jones, *History of the Sinn Féin movement and the Irish rebellion of 1916*, with an introduction by Judge J. W. Goff (New York, 1917).

58. *N.Y.T.*, 20 Dec. 1916 and 7 Jan. 1917. Shane Leslie felt that she was the most damaging of the Irish refugees because of the strength of her complaints against the British government. Leslie, *Irish issue*, p. 184. Sperling observed: 'We could hardly have done worse than decide to keep her in Ireland and then let her escape.' Minutes on Mrs H. Sheehy-Skeffington, 17 Feb. 1917 (P.R.O., F.O. 371/3071). For her own account see H. Sheehy-Skeffington, *Impressions of Sinn Féin in America* (Dublin, 1919); and see also Sir F. Vane, *Agin the governments* (London, 1929), p. 273. See also Roosevelt to Mrs Sheehy-Skeffington, 18 Jan. 1917, and Roosevelt to Sir Francis Fletcher Vane, 18 Jan. 1917 (L.C.,

Roosevelt Papers, series 3A/vol. 101). Because of the nature of the letter, Roosevelt took the precaution of sending it to Vane in care of the American Ambassador in London. With a smallness that characterised some of the least admirable features of the Wilson administration, Page turned the letter over to Balfour, who, before delivering it to Vane, had it copied and was able to take steps to see that it could not be answered. Roosevelt eventually got a reply from Vane which said that Mrs Sheehy-Skeffington's statements were largely true. Roosevelt to Page, 18 Jan. 1917, Page to Roosevelt 15 March 1917, and Vane to Roosevelt, 29 May 1917 (*Ibid.* and series I/box 337); Roosevelt to Vane, 18 Jan. 1917, and Vane to Roosevelt (letter stopped by the Foreign Office), 20 March 1917 (P.R.O., F.O. 800/211).

59. See Leslie to Redmond, 10 Nov. 1916, Jordan to Redmond, 29 Nov. 1916, and R. McGhee to Redmond, 10 Jan. 1917 (N.L.I., Redmond Papers). J. Joyce Broderick in the British Embassy was less optimistic in his report to the Foreign Office. He stated that the UIL had 'practically passed out of existence' and that Redmond himself could not make a successful tour of the United States under the existing conditions. J. J. Broderick, 'Memorandum on Irish-Americans', 19 Jan. 1917 (P.R.O., F.O. 371/3071). *N.Y.T.*, 9 March 1917; and *C.S.M.*, 9 and 15 March 1917. Springfield *Republican*, St Louis *Republic*, *Irish World, Gaelic American, Ireland*, cited in *Lit. Dig.*, liv, no. 12 (24 March 1917) pp 805–6.

60. Leslie to Redmond, 9 and 15 March 1917, and Archbishop Glennon to Redmond, 30 March 1917 (N.L.I., Redmond Papers).

Chapter 4
IRELAND AND THE AMERICAN WAR CRISIS,
1917–1918
(pp 89–120)

1. The United States government was informed of the German decision on 31 January, and diplomatic relations were broken off on 3 February.

2. A. Murray, *At close quarters* (London, 1946), pp 1–14; W. B. Fowler, *British–American relations, 1917–1918* (Princeton, 1969), pp 158–9; and 'Relations between the United States and Great Britain', 8 March 1917 (Yale University Library, House Papers, Wiseman, Sir Wm).

3. Wilson to Lansing, 10 April 1917, 841d.00/103½, *Foreign relations, the Lansing papers, 1914–1920*, ii, pp 4–5; and *Page letters*, ii, pp 255–6. The recent Russian revolution had eliminated the other embarrassment of a non-democratic government.

4. Page to Sec. of State, 18 April 1917 (N.A. 841d.00/106, roll 214).

5. Page to Wilson, 4 May 1917, *Page letters*, ii, pp 259–60; and Page to Wilson, 4 May 1916 (Harvard University Library, Page Papers, bms Am 1090.1/35). *Lit. Dig.*, liv, no. 19 (12 May 1917), p. 1400.

6. Sydney Brooks, the English journalist, paid his respects to Wilson

before returning home and also suggested that the President discuss the Irish question with Balfour, impressing upon him the bad
feeling which Ireland caused and the obstruction that Ireland
presented to Anglo-American co-operation. Brooks to Wilson, n.d.,
and Tumulty to Wilson, 20 April 1917 (L.C., Tumulty Papers,
box 2); and Tumulty, pp 398–9. Wilson replied to Tumulty: 'Confidentially (for I beg that you will be careful not to speak of or
intimate this), I have been doing a number of things about this
which I hope may bear fruit.' *Ibid.*, p. 399.

7. Cabinet minutes, dated 10 April 1917, suggest the instructions
with which Balfour left London: 'Mr Balfour undertook to make
special enquiry, and to telegraph the War Cabinet, as to the
importance of the Irish Question in connection with our relations
with the United States of America.' War Cabinet 116 (min. 23),
10 April 1917 (P.R.O., CAB. 23/2); and F.O. memorandum,
London, 10 and 13 April 1917 (P.R.O., F.O. 800/208). See also
Spring Rice to F.O., 13 April 1917 (P.R.O., F.O. 800/242).

8. R. Lansing, *War memoirs of Robert Lansing* (New York, 1935),
p. 277; Tumulty to Lansing, 19 April 1917 (L.C., Lansing Papers,
vol. 26); Tumulty to Lansing, 26 April 1917, and Lansing to
Tumulty, 28 April 1917 (*Ibid.*, vol. 27); and Tumulty to Lansing,
30 April 1917, and Lansing to Tumulty, 5 May 1917 (N.A.,
841.00/41, roll 6).

9. Nevertheless, he devoted disproportionate space in his report to
American opinion on the Irish question and noted that both the
embassy and the State Department limited his freedom to travel
in the United States for fear of Irish-inspired incidents. Balfour to
Lloyd George, 23 June 1917 (P.R.O., CAB. 1/25/5). On 30 April
Lord Robert Cecil asked if Wilson had broached the Irish problem
and Balfour replied that no one in the government had mentioned
Ireland by that time. Kenneth Young, Balfour's recent biographer,
suggests that Wilson did raise the Irish question in conversation
but agreed that the implementation of self-government should be
left until after the war. Cecil to Spring Rice, 30 April 1917, and
Balfour to Cecil, 2 May 1917 (P.R.O., F.O. 371/3070); and K.
Young, *Arthur James Balfour* (London, 1963), p. 384.

10. H. Res. 49, 13 April 1917, *Congressional Record,* 65th Congress,
1st Session, vol. 55, p. 663; and H.J. Res. 71, 28 April 1917, *Ibid.*,
p. 1558. H.J. Res. 88, 14 May 1917, *Ibid.*, p. 2305. See also 4
May 1917, *Congressional Record, Appendix,* 65th Congress, 1st
Session, vol. 55, pp 151–2. H.J. Res. 127 and H. Con. Res. 17, 25
July 1917, and H.J. Res. 129, 26 July 1917, *Congressional Record,*
65th Congress, 1st Session, vol. 55, pp 5474 and 5532–3. None of
these resolutions ever emerged from the Foreign Affairs Committee to reach a vote in the House, but their introduction was
still of some importance.

11. 30 April 1917, *Congressional Record, Appendix,* 65th Congress,
1st Session, vol. 55, p. 161. Both Congressmen Mason and

McLaughlin signed the cable, although seven days later one asked for independence and the other for a republic in the course of their speeches; very probably they would have gladly accepted anything concrete as an adequate settlement. 4 May 1917, *Ibid.*, pp 151–2 and 158–9. For Gallivan's resolution (H. Res. 479) see 30 Jan. 1917, *Congressional Record*, 64th Congress, 2nd Session, vol. 54, p. 2296.

12. Leslie to Redmond, 15 March 1917 (N.L.I., Redmond Papers). See 'When the Sixty-Ninth comes back', Kilmer, i, p. 110; and Reid, p. 400. In fact Lowell, president of Harvard, observed that the effect of the Irish question on Irish-American participation in the war was 'slightly exaggerated'. See Plunkett diary, 27 April 1917 (Plunkett Foundation, Plunkett Papers).

13. See Northcliffe to Bullock, 22 April 1917, cited in J. Quinn 'Memorandum on Irish Home Rule', 24 April 1917 (L.C., Roosevelt Papers, series I/box 330). The series of letters was later reprinted as a pamphlet, *American opinion on the Irish question* (New York, 1917). The New York *Times* commissioned a series of articles about the war which mentioned the resolution of the Irish question which was later published in book form. 'Cosmos', *The basis of durable peace* (New York, 1917), p. 11.

14. See *The Times,* 26 April 1917. Quinn arranged for Roosevelt to write and supplied him with detailed information on Ireland and the recent activities of Home Rule sympathisers. Quinn, 'Memorandum on Irish Home Rule', 24 April 1917 (L.C., Roosevelt Papers, series I/box 330). In late 1917 Roosevelt not only stated again that he thought the Irish should be given Home Rule within the Empire, but he also attacked those Irish-Americans 'whose blind hatred of England makes them disloyal to America'. T. Roosevelt, *The foes of our own household* (New York, 1917), pp 29 and 61. Through his father-in-law Leslie obtained the comment of Taft. S. Leslie, *Long shadows* (London, 1966), pp. 192–7. Other contributors were Dr Charles W. Eliot, Dr Nicholas Murray Butler, Alton B. Parker, Ambassador James W. Gerard and Colonel George Harvey. A federal solution to the Irish question was proposed in a privately printed pamphlet, F. S. Oliver, *The Irish question, federation or secession* (New York, 1917). *The Times*, 26 April 1917. While these letters received the enthusiastic support of Lord Bryce and the American correspondent of *The Times*, they were not universally welcomed. Professor W. Alison Phillips of Trinity College, Dublin, a strong Unionist and later the author of a book on the Anglo-Irish war which was very hostile to nationalist aspirations, thought the letters showed how poorly Americans understood the Irish situation: the Irish were full partners in the United Kingdom; on the other hand Americans had been most unwilling to allow the southern states to secede in 1860. *Ibid.*, 30 April 1917. The editors tended to agree with Phillips. *Ibid.*, 25, 26 and 27 April and 2 May 1917.

15. Joseph Brennon, et al. to Redmond, 22 April 1917, cited in Quinn, 'Memorandum on Irish Home Rule', 24 April 1917 (L.C., Roosevelt Papers, series I/box 330). The signators included John D. Crimmins, W. Bourke Cockran, Colonel Emmet, Lawrence Godkin, John Quinn and Judges Keogh and Dowling.

16. [J. Quinn], 'Notes of recent American opinion and action on the Irish Home Rule question', 2 June 1917 (N.L.I., Quinn Papers, MS. 1751, also to be found in the Plunkett Papers).

17. *C.S.M.*, 4 May 1917; and M. J. Ryan to Redmond, 28 April 1917, and Jordan to Redmond, 7 May 1917 (N.L.I., Redmond Papers). Redmond's response was to cable for financial support. See Redmond, circular letter, 11 May 1917, and O'Brien et al. to Redmond, 11 May 1917 (*Ibid.*).

18. Plunkett went to Washington to see Balfour, and there he worked with Leslie to draft an article for the New York *World* which promoted the idea of Irish-American leaders meeting with Balfour to work out some kind of solution to the Irish question. Plunkett was also in close communication with House and Spring Rice, and Leslie was with Tumulty and Spring Rice; thus they were able to operate in such a way as to keep British and American officials informed of their activities. Plunkett diary, 19 April 1917 (Plunkett Foundation, Plunkett Papers); and Leslie, *Long shadows,* pp 190–1.

19. Plunkett diary, 25 April 1917 (Plunkett Foundation, Plunkett Papers); and Quinn to Roosevelt, 1 May 1917 (L.C., Roosevelt Papers, series I/box 331). Fathers Sigourney Fay and John J. Wynne were originally to be included but were replaced by Fitzgerald. Quinn to Otto Carmichael, 30 April 1917 (L.C., Wilson Papers, file VI, no. 3926, box 558).

20. The final details of the meeting were worked out between Quinn and Balfour's secretary, Sir Eric Drummond. Quinn to Drummond, 1 and 2 May 1917 (P.R.O., F.O. 800/208); and [Quinn], 'Notes of recent American opinion and action on the Irish Home Rule question', 2 June 1917 (N.L.I., Quinn Papers, MS. 1751, and Plunkett Papers). See also Leslie, *Irish issue,* pp 200–1; and transcript of the Irish deputation's interview with Balfour, 4 May 1917 (P.R.O., F.O. 800/208).

21. Balfour to P.M., 5 May 1917 (P.R.O., F.O. 371/3070). At a later date Balfour talked with a second delegation of Irish-Americans, who told him much the same thing. Balfour to Lloyd George, 23 June 1919 (P.R.O., CAB. 1/25/5).

22. Godkin to Plunkett, n.d., and Quinn to Plunkett, 19 June 1917 (Plunkett Foundation, Plunkett Papers). Godkin had been pleased that Balfour promised to report the views expressed in the meeting to his government. Reid, p. 329; Plunkett to Betty Balfour, n.d., cited in Countess of Fingall, *Seventy years young* (London, 1938), p. 377; and Leslie to Mrs A. S. Green, 22 May 1917 (N.L.I., Duffy Papers, MS. 5581).

23. Circular letter to Clan officers and members, 28 April 1918 (N.L.I., Devoy Papers, box U.B.); and *G.A.*, Feb. to April 1917. The *Gaelic American* opposed the break in diplomatic relations with Germany and the attempts of the government to prepare the country for war, and the FOIF held large meetings throughout the country in support of those congressmen who opposed Wilson's Armed Merchantmen Act and the Overman Espionage Bill. In fact the paper was severely criticised for publishing protests against the war after Congress had passed Wilson's declaration, a point which Devoy justified because the weekly newspaper had been printed several days before it was sold. *Ibid.*, 7 and 14 April 1917. As Pat Mullen, the author of *The man of Aran*, later wrote, no Irishmen in America wanted to fight Germany; they wanted to fight England if anyone. P. Mullen, *Come another day* (London, 1940), p. 225. *G.A.*, 14 April 1917. A telegram prepared by Judges Edward J. Gavegan, John W. Goff and John Jerome Rooney was sent to Wilson, Vice-President Marshall and Speaker of the House Champ Clark, pledging support for the war, praising the Irish rebels of 1916, and asking Wilson to speak out for justice and independence for Ireland. *Ibid.*; and 10 April 1917, *Congressional Record*, 65th Congress, 1st Session, vol. 55, p. 508. See also *G.A.*, April and May 1917, especially 21 and 28 April 1917.

24. *Congressional Record*, 65th Congress, 1st Session, vol. 55, p. 703; J. F. Waters to Wilson, 4 May 1917 (L.C., Wilson Papers, file VI, no. 3926, box 558); *Congressional Record, Appendix*, 65th Congress, 1st Session, vol. 55, pp 158–9; and *Congressional Record*, 65th Congress, 1st Session, vol. 55, p. 3312.

25. S. MacManus, *Ireland's case* (New York, 1917). The book went through at least seventeen editions, sold over 70,000 copies, and indeed was still in print several years later. See also Tumulty to Crimmins, 5 May 1917 (L.C., Tumulty Papers, box 2); and John D. Moore to Wilson, 12 May 1917 (L.C., Wilson Papers, file VI, no. 3926, box 558). Wilson was advised to look at the results of the North Roscommon and South Longford by-elections and not listen to men with Irish-sounding names who said Ireland would settle for something less than independence.

26. *G.A.*, 28 April and 12 May 1917; and *Irish World*, cited in *Lit. Dig.*, liv, no. 19 (12 May 1917), p. 1400. The Loyal Orange Institution of Muscatine, Iowa, also made a protest about who spoke for the sentiments of America. See Charles F. Fulham to Spring Rice, 15 May 1917 (P.R.O., F.O. 371/3070). When Balfour addressed Congress each senator and representative was sent a letter suggesting that they 'Ask Mr Balfour—Why are you called by the Irish Bloody Balfour?' G. Viereck, *Spreading germs of hate* (New York, 1930), p. 220; and A. Willert, *The road to safety* (London, 1925), p. 76.

27. War Cabinet 101, 22 March 1917 (P.R.O., CAB. 23/2). Plunkett later confessed in a short essay that Lloyd George, 'having to

consider the unsettled Irish Question as a factor in America's attitude to the British . . . turned his mind again in search for a settlement'. Sir H. Plunkett, 'Ireland's problems' in *These eventful years, the twentieth century in the making* (London, 1924), i, p. 519. R. B. McDowell, *The Irish Convention, 1917–18* (London, 1970), pp. 185–6. Certainly Americans could find the analogy between the Irish Convention and their own Constitutional Convention of 1787 if they chose to do so. For a press résumé see the *Lit. Dig.*, liv, no. 22 (2 June 1917), p. 1688, lv, no. 6 (11 Aug. 1917), p. 17, lv, no. 8 (25 Aug. 1917), pp 17–18, and lv, no. 13 (29 Sept. 1917), p. 20. Page had reported that the chances for a settlement were slim because 'the Catholic bishops and priests really do not want home rule', and that the Irish politicians were not anxious to see the Irish question resolved either. Page to Sec. of State, 19 May 1917 (N.A., 841.00/42, roll 6); and Page to Wilson, 22 June 1917 (Harvard University Library, Page Papers, bms Am 1090.1/35). The final report of the Convention was given to Wilson by Lord Reading on 8 May 1918. Reading to Tumulty, 8 May 1918 (L.C., Wilson Papers, file VI, no. 3926, box 558); S. Leslie, *American wonderland* (London, 1936), p. 64; Willert, p. 91; and Fowler, pp 159–60.

28. Compare the chapters 'Sinn Féin and the Dublin insurrection' and 'The American point of view' with Roosevelt's letter to Russell, 6 Aug. 1917, *Roosevelt letters,* viii, pp 1217–21; G. Russell, H. Plunkett, and J. Quinn, *The Irish Home-Rule Convention* (New York, 1917); G. Russell, *Thoughts for a convention* (Dublin, 1917); and also [Quinn], 'Notes of recent American opinion and action on the Irish Home Rule question', 2 June 1917 (N.L.I., Quinn Papers, MS. 1751); and Reid, pp 330–1. See also Plunkett to Redmond, 19 June 1917, and Plunkett to Karl Walter, 10 Sept. 1917 (Plunkett Foundation, Plunkett Papers); and Plunkett to George Gavan Duffy, 23 July 1917 (N.L.I., Duffy Papers, MS. 5581).

29. Leslie, *Irish question,* pt 2. In 1918 Francis Hackett, a writer for the liberal *New Republic* magazine, published a book arguing for dominion Home Rule (although in later editions he bent the argument to support independence). F. Hackett, *Ireland: a study in nationalism* (New York, 1918). Arthur Gleason, who visited Ireland during the war, wrote a description of Irish political life in terms of a division between the old parliamentarians and the newer more aggressive economic and social thinkers. He looked for some kind of moderate solution and condemned the Irish-Americans for their irresponsible extremism. A. Gleason, *Inside the British Isles* (New York, 1917), pp 174–91.

30. Walter to Plunkett, 19 Jan. 1918, and Plunkett diary, 18 Jan. 1918 (Plunkett Foundation, Plunkett Papers); F. E. Smith to P.M., 8 Jan. 1918 (P.R.O., F.O. 371/3429); Colville Barclay to F.O., 18 and 19 Jan. 1918, and minutes (P.R.O., F.O. 371/3428); R.

Sperling, minutes on America and the Irish question, 2 Feb. 1918 (P.R.O., F.O. 371/3428); and Barclay to Balfour, 4 April 1918 (P.R.O., F.O. 371/3430).

31. See Redmond, circular letter, 2 May 1917, and Leslie to Redmond, 18 May 1917 (N.L.I., Redmond Papers). Leslie suggested that in view of the war situation the delegation might include some soldiers, such as Redmond's brother or Captain Stephen Gwynn. Leslie to Redmond, 21 May 1917 (*Ibid.*). Leslie observed that there was some dialogue between previously antagonistic factions; Judge Cohalan had had a meeting with Michael J. Ryan, he said, and in Chicago there was greater unity among the Irish than any time since the Cronin murder in 1889. Leslie to Redmond. c. May 1917 (*Ibid.*). But this view was over-optimistic, as Leslie himself later revealed to Mrs Alice Stopford Green. He said about Redmond and the Irish Parliamentary Party: 'I think everything has been done that was possible from this side to put the Irish Party in a position to retrieve themselves. The British Government have been held up from Washington and told to rehabilitate Redmond.' Leslie to Mrs A. S. Green, 22 May 1917 (N.L.I., Duffy Papers, MS. 5581).

32. Before O'Connor sailed John Dillon suggested that he minimise the war but speak to Wilson's pronouncements about small nations, that he keep away from the British Embassy, and not take England's part in the war. This advice proved difficult to follow. Lyons, *Dillon*, pp 418–19. Washington *Evening Star*, 6 July 1917. See also Page to Wilson, 22 June 1917 (Harvard University Library, Page Papers, bms Am 1090.1/35); and Tumulty to Wilson, 25 June 1917, and Wilson to Tumulty, n.d. (L.C., Tumulty Papers, box 2).

33. Leslie to Redmond, 30 June 1917 (N.L.I., Redmond Papers). In fact there had been incidents at the memorial services in New York for Redmond's brother. Leslie to Dillon, 26 Aug. 1917, cited in Lyons, *Dillon*, p. 424. Reid, p. 328; and Quinn to Lawrence Godkin, 24 July 1917 (Plunkett Foundation, Plunkett Papers).

34. As O'Connor told a friend, in addition to the names he was called by the Irish-American press, he was accused of being a millionaire through the sale of Ireland to England. Attacks were directed against him personally through the press and by means of handbills. Fyfe, pp 266–70; and Hazleton to Leslie, 26 Sept. 1917 (N.Y.P.L., Cockran Papers, box 18). For an example of O'Connor's speeches see the pamphlet, *Mr T. P. O'Connor, M.P., in Chicago,* (n.p., n.d.); and Hazleton to Redmond, 5 Dec. 1917 (N.L.I., Redmond Papers). O'Connor wrote to Dillon that in spite of the war there had been no movement back to the Parliamentary Party, although he was confident that Sinn Féin was defunct in the United States. Fyfe, pp 268 and 271.

35. *Ibid.,* pp 268–70; and Hazleton to Redmond, 5 Dec. 1917 (N.L.I., Redmond Papers). Even the former ally of Sir Edward Carson,

F. E. Smith, found O'Connor to be a sad and much abused figure in the United States. Sir F. E. Smith, *My American visit* (London, 1918), pp 70–1. See also Reading to Lloyd George, 5 May 1918 (Beaverbrook Library, Lloyd George Papers, F 60/2/69); Hazleton to Leslie, 26 Sept. 1917 (N.Y.P.L., Cockran Papers, box 18); and Fyfe, p. 271. O'Connor remained in the United States until the summer of 1918; upon his return to England he gave a pessimistic report to the House of Commons. In closing O'Connor warned the House: 'After the War Americans of Irish blood will still be of Irish blood, and will still open their hearts to the call of the motherland of their race, and I tell you in language that is unmistakable that, unless you reconcile Ireland you will never reconcile the American race of Irish blood, and if you do not reconcile them, you will never have the whole heart and soul of America with you in upholding the peace of the world.' 7 Aug. 1918, *Hansard* 5 (Commons), cix, cols 1439–55.

36. The result of this retrenchment policy was a diminution of public activity which was perceptible by most close observers of the Irish-American community. See Spring Rice to F.O., 14 June 1917 (P.R.O., F.O. 800/242); and Hazleton to Leslie, 26 Sept. 1917 (N.Y.P.L., Cockran Papers, box 18). As a matter of public policy the *Gaelic American* attacked the Irish Convention in violent editorials as a trick designed by Lloyd George to discredit the Irish cause, and it also kept up a constant series of denunciations of T. P. O'Connor and Richard Hazleton with such effect that their efforts to raise money and rebuild the fortunes of their party were unsuccessful. Rev. Peter C. Yorke to Congressman Julius Kahn (California), 2 July 1917; FOIF to Kahn, 7 July 1917 (L.C., Wilson Papers, file VI, no. 4095, J. W. Preston); and *C.S.M.,* 30 Aug. 1917. See K. Walter to Plunkett, 31 Aug. 1917, for a description of the meeting as an anti-English 'demonstration' (Plunkett Foundation, Plunkett Papers); and McCartan, pp 17–18.

37. Tansill, pp 234–40; and Sheehy-Skeffington, *Impressions of Sinn Féin in America,* passim; *N.Y.T.,* 23 Sept. 1917; McCartan, pp 18–28; Reid pp 323–5; 'Questions for John A. Connolly', c. Nov. 1917 (N.L.I., Devoy Papers, box James Larkin); and F. Strother, *Fighting Germany's spies* (Garden City, 1918), for facsimiles of some of the von Igel papers. See also O'Leary, pp 159–468; and a 'wanted' notice for John T. Ryan (N.L.I., Devoy Papers, box Misc.). Ryan was born in the United States and was a Spanish-American War veteran as well as a lawyer. He was wanted for 'aiding and assisting German spies in New York'. *G.A.,* 26 Jan. 1918; and T. G. Patten to Devoy, 19 Jan. 1918, and T. F. Murphy to Devoy, 24 Jan. 1918 (N.L.I., Devoy Papers, box T–Z).

38. See Reid, pp 322–3; King to Williams, 13 Feb. 1918 (L.C., Williams Papers, box 34); and *C.S.M.,* 27 Feb. 1918.

39. U.S. Congress, Senate, Subcommittee of the Senate Judiciary Committee, *Hearings on the National German–American Alliance,*

65th Congress, 2nd Session, 1918, pp 63, 126–7 and 268–70. The Princeton University professor Christian Gauss also condemned Irish–German collusion in the United States in his book. C. Gauss, *Why we went to war* (New York, 1918), pp 231–2; W. Barry, *The world's debate* (New York, 1917), pp 291–2; and E. T. Clark, *Social studies of the war* (New York, 1919), pp 47 and 66–86.

40. See McCartan, pp 11–14. Having accepted the two documents from McCartan, Tumulty was advised by Frank L. Polk at the State Department to simply 'file' them and not reply. See Polk to Tumulty, 8 Aug. 1917 (L.C., Wilson Papers, file VI, no. 3926, box 558). However, when the documents were printed in the *Congressional Record* at the request of Senator Lewis the more uncompromising view of Senator Smoot prevailed and they were removed. 30 July 1917, *Congressional Record*, 65th Congress, 1st Session, vol. 55, p. 5542. Only one month earlier Wilson had refused to see an Irish-American delegation led by a Father O'Callaghan. See Tumulty to Wilson, 10 Dec. 1917, and Wilson to Tumulty, 11 Dec. 1917 (L.C., Wilson Papers, file VI, no. 3926, box 558).

41. Mrs Sheehy-Skeffington to Devoy, n.d., *Devoy's post-bag*, ii, p. 519; and Mrs Sheehy-Skeffington to Golden, n.d. (N.L.I., Golden Papers, MS. 13141, folder xi).

42. Leslie, *American wonderland*, p. 62; James D. Phelan to James K. McGuire, 14 Feb. 1918 (American Irish Historical Society, Cohalan Papers, drawer 4); and Mrs Sheehy-Skeffington to Devoy, n.d., *Devoy's post-bag*, ii, p. 520.

43. H.J. Res. 204, 4 Jan. 1918, *Congressional Record*, 65th Congress, 2nd Session, vol. 56, p. 617; and S. Con. Res. 18, 16 March 1918, *Ibid.*, p. 3595. See also the resolutions introduced in the summer of 1917, which were more in line with the revolutionary rather than the constitutional nationalists, pp 92–3 above. McCartan, p. 14. Mrs Sheehy-Skeffington met Speaker of the House Champ Clark, Senator LaFollette, Congresswoman Rankin and several Irish-American politicians. See Mrs Sheehy-Skeffington to Golden, 10 Jan. 1918 (N.L.I., Golden Papers, MS. 13141, folder xi); Sheehy-Skeffington, *Impressions of Sinn Féin in America*; and report by Shaemus O'Sheel of his assistance to Mrs Sheehy-Skeffington, Jan. 1918 (N.L.I., Devoy Papers, box Misc.).

44. *G.A.*, 1 Sept. 1917; and McCartan, p. 39. See bulletin for a mass meeting at Terrace Garden in New York, 25 Oct. 1917 (N.L.I., Golden Papers, MS. 13141). The Irish labour leader James Larkin was in New York when the league was being formed, but he had a low opinion of it and its leaders. Larkin, pp 220–2.

45. Minutes of the first meeting of the Irish Progressive League (N.L.I., Golden Papers, MS. 13141, folder ii). Mrs Sheehy-Skeffington and Dr Gertrude B. Kelly also attended the first meeting, and while the former was not an officer or a member of the executive

committee, she, along with Golden, Mrs Hickey and Dr Kelly, tended to dominate the league's activities. The IPL later included in its programme the establishment of the 'Irish Embassy' in Washington with Dr McCartan as 'Envoy of the Provisional Government of Ireland'. The financial responsibility for these projects was assumed by the FOIF after the war. See league circular, n.d., appealing for money to establish Miss Katherine Hughes and Pádraic Colum in the bureau, and *Bulletin of the Irish Progressive League*, no. 2 (25 March 1918) (N.L.I., Golden Papers, MS. 13141). By early February de Valera asked Dr McCartan to extend the thanks of the Irish people to the league for their efforts to see that the principle of self-determination be applied to Ireland. De Valera to McCartan, 7 Feb. 1918 (N.L.I., Devoy Papers, box CF–D).

46. Mrs Sheehy-Skeffington to Golden, 20 March 1918 and n.d. (N.L.I., Golden Papers, MS. 13141). She said she had to laugh at the ' "ultra" patriots', who after her meeting with Wilson could 'now safely "stand behind the President" '. Mrs Hickey's deputation was at the White House on 8 April 1918. Mrs Hickey to Tumulty, 9 April 1918 (L.C., Wilson Papers, file VI, no. 3926, box 558).

47. Golden to Devoy, 1 March 1918 (N.L.I., Devoy Papers, box E–J); and John Kennedy (business manager of the *Gaelic American*) to Mrs Sheehy-Skeffington, 15 Jan. 1918 (N.L.I., Golden Papers, MS. 13141, folder xi); report by Shaemus O'Sheel of his assistance to Mrs Sheehy-Skeffington, Jan. 1918 (N.L.I., Devoy Papers, box Misc.); Monteith, pp 230–1; and McCartan, pp 36–9.

48. Golden to Devoy, 2 March 1918 (N.L.I., Devoy Papers, box E–J).

49. Balfour to House, no. 72, 2 April 1918 (Yale University Library, House Papers, Balfour, Arthur James). For cabinet discussions of the importance of American opinion on conscription in Ireland, and for the decision to ask House's advice, see War Cabinet 376A (min. 1), 28 March 1918, and War Cabinet 379A (min. 2), 1 April 1918 (P.R.O., CAB. 23/14).

50. Wilson to House, 3 April 1918 (Yale University Library, House Papers, Balfour, Arthur James); and Fowler, pp 160–3.

51. See Ward in *I.H.S.*, xvi, no. 61 (March 1968), p. 82. Lloyd George's memoirs suggest that the government was cognizant of the dangers that conscription presented both in Ireland and the United States, but that there was simply no alternative if the age limit were to be raised in England. D. Lloyd George, *War memoirs of David Lloyd George* (London, 1933), v, p. 2668. The cabinet minutes suggest that Lloyd George did not think that the Irish in the United States would object to the Irish in Ireland being subject to conscription as they were themselves. War Cabinet 385, 6 April 1918 (P.R.O., CAB. 23/6).

52. Egan to Wilson, 10 April 1918, and Wilson to Egan, 12 April 1918 (L.C., Wilson Papers, file VI, no. 3926, box 588).

53. Wiseman to House, 25 April 1918 (Yale University Library,

House Papers, Wiseman, Sir Wm, 47). See also War Cabinet 389 (min. 9), 11 April 1918 (P.R.O., CAB. 23/6).

54. Wiseman confessed to House that he did not know how Wilson could avoid the appeals from various quarters, and he complained that Page was advising the British government 'to take strong measures'. Letter contained in House to Wilson, 26 April 1918 (L.C., Wilson Papers, file II, box 166).

55. Leslie to Tumulty, 23 April 1918 (*Ibid.*, file VI, no. 3926, box 558). See also H. M. Hyde, *Lord Reading* (London, 1967), p. 281.

56. Leslie to Reading, 25 April 1918 (L.C., Wilson Papers, file VI, no. 3926, box 558); and Wiseman to House, 25 April 1918 (Yale University Library, House Papers, Wiseman, Sir Wm, 47). Plunkett's first thought was that Wilson might indeed have a role to play in salvaging a situation through the Lord Mayor's trip. Plunkett diary, 21 April 1918 (Plunkett Foundation, Plunkett Papers). Page to Lansing, 24 April 1918, and Lansing to Wilson, 25 April 1918 (L.C., Wilson Papers, file II, box 166); and William Phillips to Wilson, 3 May 1918 (N.A., 841.00/71, roll 6).

57. Wilson to William Phillips, 4 May 1918 (*Ibid.*, –/76, roll 6). Plunkett understood that the Lord Mayor realised how coldly he would be received in the United States and was in fact 'praying that the passport would be refused'. Plunkett to K. Walter, 24 May 1918 (Plunkett Foundation, Plunkett Papers). Lansing to AMEMBASSY, London, 6 May 1918 (N.A., 841.00/71, roll 6).

58. Instead the long vellum documents were mailed to Wilson, outlining Ireland's grievances and the illegality of extending conscription to Ireland contrary to the wishes of Irish political and religious leaders. Laurence O'Neill (Lord Mayor of Dublin) to Wilson, 11 June 1918 (Wilson Papers, file II, box 168). Within several weeks a letter from Sir Edward Carson and a group of Ulster Unionists was also sent to Wilson arguing that the Southern Irish had no right to resist conscription. Carson et al. to Wilson, 1 Aug. 1918 (*Ibid.*, box 172).

59. R. S. Baker, *American chronicle* (New York, 1945), pp 335–7; see also Plunkett diary, 26 June 1918 (Plunkett Foundation, Plunkett Papers). 'Leaders agree seriousness of situation can scarcely be exaggerated.' Baker to Polk, contained in a cable from Page to Sec. of State, 16 May 1918 (N.A., 841.00/80, roll 6).

60. Walter Long to Reading, 16 May 1918 (B.M., Balfour Papers, Add. MS. 49741, vol. lix). The following day Reading was also informed that the Irish were appealing to Wilson and that he should tell the President that 'any views he may express must necessarily greatly influence the situation'. Long to Reading, 17 May 1918 (*Ibid.*). Actually the cabinet had made a decision to arrest de Valera and several others seven months before, although the decision was not implemented until after the conscription crisis broke and when Long had been delegated by the war cabinet to deal with Ireland. See War Cabinet 255A, 23 Oct.

1917 (P.R.O., CAB. 23/13), and War Cabinet 408 (min. 11), 10 May 1918 (P.R.O., CAB. 23/6).

61. Lansing's comment on the Irish nationalists was: 'Without denying that the fundamental idea of the Sinn Féiners has merit, their present willingness to cooperate with the Germans shows a blindness to the great issues to [*sic*] the war and a willingness to sacrifice democracy to their own selfish ends which seems utterly unpardonable.' In fact he felt that if the Sinn Féiners assisted Germany, the government should help suppress them, but that these documents did not show that. Lansing to President, 19 May 1918, and Lansing to AMEMBASSY, 20 May 1918 (N.A., 841.00/87a, roll 7).

62. Reading to Long, 20 May 1918, and Reading to ——, 22 May 1918 (B.M., Balfour Papers, Add. MS. 49741, vol. lix). Eventually the British government took the responsibility for the publication of the documents.

63. Wiseman to Drummond, 3 June 1918 (P.R.O., F.O. 800/223). It might be added that at the request of Congressman Tinkham of Boston the State Department inquired after the condition of Éamon de Valera after his arrest on 17 May 1918. See Rev. Thomas J. Wheelwright (half-brother of de Valera) to Tinkham, 23 May 1918, William Phillips to Irwin B. Laughlin, 19 June 1918, and Page to Sec. of State, 20 July 1918 (N.A., 341d.1121 VALERA, EAMON DE/41 and –/42 and 341.112D491/29, box 4095, jacket no. 2).

64. See *C.S.M.*, 18 April 1918. The *Monitor* also published the views of several leaders of the Loyal Orange Institution who thought that if Home Rule were given it should be preceded by conscription. *Ibid.* Leaders of the Loyal Orange Institution were also writing to President Wilson insisting that the Irish question should not be allowed to intrude on the war effort. They asked Wilson to continue to reject 'the O'Learys' of the Irish community, and they assured him that soon those who still 'play his game will be as despised as he'. George E. Bemister, Grand Master, and James Jaynes, Grand Secretary, of the Grand Lodge of Massachusetts, to Wilson, 21 May 1918, Ford to Tumulty, 26 May 1918, Lynch to Tumulty, 22 May 1918, and Kinkead to Wilson, 27 May 1918 (L.C., Wilson Papers, file VI, no. 3926, box 558).

65. *C.S.M.*, 20 April 1918. Senator Phelan of California read a message from McEnerney containing similar sentiments to the Senate on 18 April 1918. *Congressional Record*, 65th Congress, 2nd Session, vol. 56, pp 5237–9. For a vigorous rebuttal see Rev. Peter C. Yorke, *America and Ireland, an open letter to Mr Garrett W. McEnerty* [sic] (San Francisco, 1918) published by the FOIF. See O'Connor to Phelan, 13 April 1918, and O'Connor to Tumulty, 26 April 1918 (L.C., Wilson Papers, file VI, no. 3926, box 558); and Lansing to Wilson, 29 May 1918 (N.A., 841d.00/9A, roll 213). In late June Phelan wrote to tell Wilson that any comment he made

on the Irish situation would have a good effect. Wilson replied: 'I realize, of course, the critical importance of the whole Irish Question, but I do not think it would be wise for me in any public utterance to attempt to outline a policy for the British Government with regard to Ireland.' In this he was holding to his earlier policy. Phelan to Wilson, 29 June 1918, and Wilson to Phelan, 1 July 1918 (L.C., Wilson Papers, file VI, no. 3926, box 558); and Gerald F. M. O'Grady to Walsh, 19 July 1918, and Walsh to O'Grady, 30 July 1918 (L.C., Walsh Papers, file B, box 190).

66. See *G.A.*, 13, 20 and 27 April 1918; *Lit. Dig.*, lvii, no. 4 (27 April 1918), p. 14; and McCartan, pp 42–3.

67. *N.Y.T.*, 5 May 1918 (L.C., Wilson Papers, file VI, no. 3926, box 558); and *G.A.*, 4 May 1918. Mrs Sheehy-Skeffington was also prevented by police from addressing a meeting at Providence, Rhode Island. *C.S.M.*, 10 May 1918. See McCartan, pp 45–6. McCartan said this memorandum had been drafted by Maloney. The IPL printed and circulated a broadsheet entitled *Ireland's attitude on conscription* which argued that conscription was contrary to both the will of the people and the expressions of Ireland's leaders, and Peter Golden had written to a number of American political figures to elicit some word of official approval or sympathy for the resistance movement, although the responses tended to show growing American hostility rather than support. *Ireland's attitude on conscription* (n.p., n.d.); Golden to Congressmen, 18 April 1918, and replies (N.L.I., Golden Papers, MS. 13141, folder ii); and Jeremiah Carroll to Senator William E. Borah, 4 May 1918 (L.C., Borah Papers, box 188).

68. FOIF committee on conventions, *To the men and women of the Irish race in America* (New York, 1918). Goff's petition in fact caused some disturbance. Father Hurton had asked to see Wilson; he was refused, but on 21 June he gave the petition to Tumulty, despite Tumulty's comment that 'speeches of the most seditious character' had been made at the meeting. Thus the presentation of the petition to Tumulty represented an attempt to accommodate the Irish-American nationalists. The public announcement of this presentation brought an immediate protest from the Intelligence Branch of the War Department, which claimed that unless the petition were repudiated it would seriously 'embarrass the cause of the Allies'. It was, however, allowed to stand. See Tumulty to Wilson, 24 May 1918, Wilson to Tumulty, 25 May 1918, Tumulty to Wilson, n.d., re Miss Marguerite Maginnis to Wilson, 21 May 1918, and War Department correspondence re news articles in the Washington *Post*, 22 June 1918 (L.C., Wilson Papers, file VI, no. 3926, box 558).

69. Full descriptions may be found in the *G.A.*, 25 May 1918; *C.S.M.*, 20 May 1918; Splain in Fitz-Gerald, pp 230–2. McCartan, pp 46–7; and Tansill, pp 270–4. As a result of his activities connected with the convention and the 4 May meeting in New York, Father

Magennis was reprimanded by Cardinal Farley who refused to tolerate such overt political action by the clergy within his arch-diocese. Indeed, contrary to the allegations of the *Christian Science Monitor* the hierarchy in the United States made several specific orders to its clergy to cease Irish revolutionary activity. See *Lit. Dig.*, lvii, no. 10 (8 July 1918), p. 30. The British Ambassador noted the cardinal's rebuke of Father Magennis with some interest, and in fact Reading reported several instances of bishops insisting that their clergy not take part in Irish agitation. Reading to F.O., 22 May 1918 (P.R.O., F.O. 371/3488), and 28 and 30 May 1918 and 5 July 1918 (P.R.O., F.O. 371/3430); and Spring Rice to Balfour, 21 Dec. 1917 (P.R.O., F.O. 371/3428).

70. For examples of the less than total commitment of many Irish-American leaders, as well as serious rivalry and division within the movement, see the disillusioned letters of Mrs Sheehy-Skeffington ('Situation here re. Irish is as everywhere else—timidity & axes to grind! Most of my best help comes from Americans with not a drop of our blood.') and Liam Mellows ('. . . back again to this maelstrom of bitterness & perversity. . . . Prejudice is rampant—fierce—unbelievable.') to Peter Golden. Mrs Sheehy-Skeffington to Golden, n.d. and 26 April 1918, and Mellows to Golden, 2 and 8 Aug. 1918 (N.L.I., Golden Papers, MS. 13141, folder xi). There are many instances of friction within the revolutionary movement in the United States, several of which have been cited here and earlier, but see also the statement of Francis A. Campbell of the Boston FOIF that Mrs Sheehy-Skeffington had 'outstayed her use-fulness in this country, and the sooner she returns to Ireland the better for the cause'. *C.S.M.*, 22 May 1918; and F. O'Donoghue in Lynch, pp 192–3.

71. See Mrs McWhorter to Tumulty, 6 June 1918, and Mrs McWhorter to Wilson, 9 July 1918 (L.C., Wilson Papers, file VI, no. 3926, box 558); and *Congressional Record*, 65th Congress, 2nd Session, vol. 56, pp 9607–9. To give the gesture maximum publicity, Congress-man Gallagher described the 'Mothers' Mission' in Congress and had the petition and letter printed in the *Congressional Record*, as did Senator Lewis in the Senate, but only over the objections of Senator King. 18 July 1918, *Ibid.*, p. 9159. See the Irish Progressive League circulars (N.L.I., Golden Papers, MS. 13141, folder ii).

72. See Splain in Fitz-Gerald, p. 232; and McCartan, pp 48–54. These articles were reprinted in 1919 in W. J. M. A. Maloney, *The Irish issue* (New York, 1919), and more remarkably as part of the hear-ings of the House Committee on Foreign Affairs on the Gallagher resolution. U.S. Congress, House of Representatives, Committee on Foreign Affairs, *The Irish question*, Hearings on H.J. Res. 357 (House doc. no. 1832, 65th Congress, 3rd Session), 1919.

73. For caustic criticism see Congressman Milton H. Welling to John D. Moore, 20 Sept. 1917 (N.L.I., Devoy Papers, box Misc.); McCartan, pp 33–5 and 252–8; 21 Feb. 1918, *Congressional Record*,

65th Congress, 2nd Session, vol. 56, pp 2482–3; and see *C.S.M.*, 15 and 16 March 1918; and Mrs Sheehy-Skeffington to Devoy, 9 March 1918, *Devoy's post-bag*, ii, pp 524–5. Actually the British government had agreed to allow the United States the option of not applying the regulations of the treaty to Irishmen in America if they chose. Thomas F. Logan to Frank L. Polk, 21 Feb. 1918, and L. H. Woolsey to Polk, 2 March 1918 (Yale University Library, Polk Papers, drawer 77, file 138). Less than a year earlier Martin Conboy had served as Liam Mellows's defence lawyer on a charge of illegal exit from the United States, after Mellows's unsuccessful attempt to go to Germany and Russia. *C.S.M.*, 25 Oct. 1918.

74. Buffalo *Express, Ohio State Journal*, Kansas City *Times* and St Louis *Post-Dispatch*, cited in *C.S.M.*, 24 April 1918; and New York *Herald* and New York *World*, cited in *Lit. Dig.*, lvii, no. 4 (27 April 1918), p. 14, and no. 9 (1 June 1918), p. 25.

75. *C.S.M.*, 11, 19 and 25 April and 11 May, 1918; New York *Times* and Detroit *Free Press*, cited in *Ibid.*, 24 and 25 April 1918. See also the Boston *Herald and Journal*, 4 and 11 Feb. 1918.

76. New York *Evening Post*, New York *Commercial*, Chicago *Daily News* and Brooklyn *Eagle*, cited in *Lit. Dig.*, lvii, no. 4 (27 April 1918), p. 13, and no. 9 (1 June 1918), p. 25.

77. Golden to Congressmen, 18 April 1918 (N.L.I., Golden Papers, MS. 13141, folder ii). The *C.S.M.* of 18 April 1918 said that the feeling in Washington among senators and representatives was that conscription should be extended to Ireland; public expression like this may have prompted the IPL to write to individual politicians. *C.S.M.*, 18 April 1918.

78. King to Golden, 26 April 1918, and Gronna to Golden, 1 May 1918 (N.L.I., Golden Papers, MS. 13141, folder ii). Congressman William S. Greene of Massachusetts replied that Americans had not been consulted about conscription either and that the United States government could hardly object to the means by which Great Britain raised troops to defend herself. Greene to Golden, 26 April 1918 (*Ibid.*). Congressman Louis C. Crampton of Michigan said that Golden's suggestion that Irishmen were justified in resisting conscription was 'traitorous to our own land'; America, Canada England and other countries had accepted conscription; 'I can see no objection to Ireland performing its part.' Crampton to Golden, 30 April 1918 (*Ibid.*). Congressman T. S. Williams of Illinois attacked hyphenate immigrant groups in the United States and said the sooner they abandoned their ethnic ties the better it would be for America; in the meantime he found 'the attitude of the Irish people' on the war crisis to be 'very disappointing'. Williams to Golden, 30 April 1918, Claypool to Golden, 27 April 1918, Church to Golden, 4 May 1918, and LaFollette to Golden, 1 May 1918 (*Ibid.*).

79. J. F. Weilbright, Elmer E. Weaver and W. S. Rychman to Wilson,

I

24 April 1918 (L.C., Wilson Papers, file II, box 166). Senator John Sharp Williams of Mississippi told a correspondent that if Ireland did not begin to help the Allies in the war, there would not be anyone willing to support her claims at the Peace Conference. Williams to T. H. Synon, 5 Sept. 1918 (L.C., Williams Papers, box 40); and also McCarthy to Plunkett, 9 Sept. 1918 (Wisconsin State Historical Society, McCarthy Papers, MSS KU, box 37).

80. See, for example, G. L. Fox, *Ireland and the Union* (New Haven, 1918); G. L. Fox, *Sound truth about the Irish question* (New Haven, 1918); and Leslie to Dillon, 9 Aug. 1918, cited in Lyons, *Dillon*, p. 442.

81. Jameson to the *aide-de-camp* of General J. J. Pershing, 11 June 1917 (L.C., Roosevelt Papers, series I/box 339); Jameson to Tumulty, 8 Feb. 1918; and Benedict Crowell (Acting Secretary of War) to Tumulty, 16 March 1918 (L.C., Wilson Papers, file VI, no. 3926, box 558). Spring Rice to Sir Eric Drummond, 12 Oct. 1917, Balfour to the Army Council, 15 Oct. 1917, and B. B. White (Secretary of the Army Council) to Drummond, 19 Oct. 1917 (P.R.O., F.O. 371/3124).

82. McCarthy to Plunkett, 17 June 1918, and McCarthy to Tumulty, 17 June 1918 (Wisconsin State Historical Society, McCarthy Papers, MSS KU, box 37); McCarthy to AE [George Russell], *c.* summer 1918 (*Ibid.*); Plunkett diary, 14 and 17 Aug. 1918 (Plunkett Foundation, Plunkett Papers); and M. Digby, *Horace Plunkett: Anglo-American Irishman* (Oxford, 1949), p. 241. See also C. McCarthy, 'Memorandum on Irish conditions', 12 Sept. 1918, and McCarthy to E. M. House, 4 Oct. 1918 (Wisconsin State Historical Society, McCarthy Papers, *Ibid.*); Lansing to Wilson, 13 Sept. 1918 (N.A., 841D.00/15A, roll 213); and Wilson to Lansing, 17 Sept. 1918 (N.A., 841d.00/16½, roll 213); Shane Leslie suggested an Irish legion to Tumulty, but later withdrew it. Leslie to Tumulty 22 April 1918 (L.C., Wilson Papers, file VI, no. 3926, box 558); and Leslie to W. J. M. A. Maloney, 25 July 1918 (N.Y.P.L., Maloney Collection, box 11); for public comment on these proposals see *Lit. Dig.*, lvii, no. 4 (27 April 1918), pp 13–14, and lviii, no. 4 (27 July 1918), p. 14.

83. Murray, pp 81–4; and also B. B. White to F.O., 15 Jan. 1918, and Colville Barclay to F.O., 25 Jan. 1918 (P.R.O., F.O. 371/3488). See also Lord Dunraven to A. Bonar Law, *c.* summer 1918 (Beaverbrook Library, Lloyd George Papers, F 30/2/16); Austin to Wilson, 18 June 1917 (L.C., Wilson Papers, file VI, no. 3926, box 558); Digby, p. 242; Plunkett diary, 15 Sept. 1918 (Plunkett Foundation, Plunkett Papers); and Plunkett to Balfour, 2 Oct. 1918, Balfour to W. G. S. Adams, 4 Oct. 1918, and Samuel M. Power to Sir Eric Drummond, 8 Oct. 1918 (P.R.O., F.O. 800/211).

Chapter 5
IRELAND AND THE PARIS PEACE CONFERENCE,
1919
(pp 121–148)

1. See, for example, Wilson's famous speech to the Washington
diplomatic corps on 4 July 1918 at Washington's tomb at Mount
Vernon, Virginia, that after the war 'The settlement of every
question, whether of territory, of sovereignty, of economic arrangement, or of political relationship, [must be] upon the basis of the
free acceptance of that settlement by the people immediately concerned.' *A day of dedication: the essential writings of Woodrow
Wilson*, ed. Albert Fried (New York, 1965), p. 329. See L. L.
Gerson, *Woodrow Wilson and the rebirth of Poland* (New Haven,
1953), passim. For an excellent series of short studies of the
attitudes of various ethnic groups towards Wilson and the Peace
Conference see J. P. O'Grady (ed.), *The immigrants' influence on
Wilson's peace policies* (Lexington, 1967).

2. See poster for Irish Progressive League meeting, 12 Nov. 1918
(N.L.I., Golden Papers, MS. 13141); Colum to Tumulty, 14 Nov.
1918 (L.C., Wilson Papers, file VI, no. 3926, box 558); and *Irish
World*, 16 Nov. 1918. The memorial was delivered by the national
secretary of the FOIF, James J. Hoey. Memorial to Wilson, 30
Nov. 1918 (A.I.H.S., Cohalan Papers, drawer 1). McLaughlin to
Wilson, 2 Dec. 1918 (L.C., Wilson Papers, file II, box 180–A). The
New Orleans AOH sent Wilson a petition signed by 720 people
asking for self-determination for Ireland. (*Ibid.*, file VI, no. 3926,
box 558). Walsh to Wilson, 2 Dec. 1918 (L.C., Walsh Papers, file
B, box 190). Walsh received a large number of letters and petitions
from the AOH, the FOIF and his constituents asking that he use
his influence to secure assistance for Ireland. Personal appeals were
also directed towards Wilson's confidants and to his rivals, but with
the same hope of influencing the President's action in favour of
Ireland. See J. B. Cahill to E. M. House, 13 Dec. 1918 (Yale
University Library, House Papers, Cahill, James B.); Congressman
G. E. Campbell to Tumulty, 24 Dec. 1918 (L.C., Wilson Papers,
file VI, no. 3926, box 558); and Mrs Mary Fogarty to Senator
W. E. Borah, 12 Nov. 1918 (L.C., Borah Papers, box 188).

3. Wilson to Walsh, 3 Dec. 1918 (L.C., Walsh Papers, file B, box
190); and Tumulty, p. 410.

4. Wilson to Bishop Shahan, 3 Dec. 1918 (L.C., Wilson Papers, file
VI, no. 3926, box 558); Tumulty, p. 404; and Ward, *Ireland*, pp
185–6. See also K. R. Maxwell, 'Irish-Americans and the fight for
treaty ratification', *Public Opinion Quarterly*, xxxi, no. 4 (winter
1967–68), pp 620–41; Duff in *Jn. Amer. Hist.*, lv (Dec. 1968), pp
582–98; Lansing diary, 20 and 30 Dec. 1918 (L.C., Lansing
Papers); and R. Lansing, *The peace negotiations* (Boston, 1921),
pp 86–7.

5. Creel to Wilson, 1 March 1919 (L.C., Wilson Papers, file VIIIA,

box 22). Wilson had read the report by at least 20 March, although his reply was so non-committal that it is impossible to say if it altered his judgment in any way. See also G. Creel, *Rebel at large* (New York, 1947), pp 216–22; and G. Creel, *The war, the world, and Wilson* (New York, 1920), p. 202. Wilson also instructed Tumulty to prepare a memorandum on Ireland and whatever commitments he had made to the Irish-Americans. See Tumulty to Wilson, 28 Feb. 1919 (L.C., Tumulty Papers, box 3). Gelfand's recent study of the American policy planning staff at the Peace Conference would seem to indicate that Ireland was not seriously considered, although it was the subject of four economic reports. L. E. Gelfand, *The inquiry: American preparations for peace, 1917–1919* (New Haven, 1963), p. 361.

6. Lundeen (H.J. Res. 354), 2 Dec. 1918, *Congressional Record*, 65th Congress, 1st Session, vol. 57, p. 19; McLaughlin (H.J. Res. 355), *Ibid.*; Gallagher (H.J. Res. 357), 3 Dec. 1918, *Ibid.*, p. 66; Kennedy (H.J. Res. 362), 9 Dec. 1918, *Ibid.*, p. 231; and Rankin (H.J. Res. 363), 10 Dec. 1918, *Ibid.*, p. 280. For Senate see Phelan (S.J. Res. 203), 26 Dec. 1918, *Ibid.*, pp 842–3.

7. These included Dr Patrick McCartan ('Envoy of the Provisional Government of Ireland'), Diarmuid Lynch (secretary of the FOIF), Pádraic Colum (for the IPL), John A. Murphy (representative of relief operations in Ireland in 1916), Richard F. Dalton (for the United Irish-American Societies), Mrs Mary McWhorter (president of the Ladies' Auxiliary of the AOH) and Miss Katherine Hughes (for the Irish Women's Council of America). R. T. Hanrahan, a Chicago contractor and Irish-American nationalist, wrote to James Reidy to say that a delegation was leaving for Washington to testify; he said they were a 'respectable crowd too'. Hanrahan to Reidy, 9 Dec. 1918 (N.L.I., Devoy Papers, box E–J). U.S. Congress, House of Representatives, Committee on Foreign Affairs, *The Irish question*, Hearing on H.J. Res. 357 (House doc. no. 1832, 65th Congress, 3rd Session), 1919. For the request of Chairman Flood to have the hearings printed in a separate volume see *Congressional Record*, 65th Congress, 3rd Session, vol. 57, p. 4351. See also McCartan, pp 59–62; O'Doherty, pp 27–8; and Tansill, pp 287–8.

8. U.S. Congress, *The Irish question*, Hearings on H.J. Res. 357 (House doc. no. 1832, 65th Congress, 3rd Session), pp 58–64. Fox expressed his disgust at the whole proceedings in a letter to J. St L. Strachey; he thought the resolution and the hearings were 'the product of the most shameless falsehood, chicanery, blackmail and bull dozing, that one can conceive of'. Fox to Strachey, 24 March 1919 (Beaverbrook Library, Strachey Papers, folder 3, 1919–21). Several months later the New York *Times* asserted that these hearings had been the public act which effectively reactivated the revolutionary Irish-Americans after the war. *N.Y.T.*, 2 March 1919.

9. See Tumulty to Wilson, 31 Dec. 1918, and Wilson to Tumulty, 7
   and 30 Jan. 1919 (L.C., Tumulty Papers, boxes 2 and 3). Wilson
   said: 'I frankly dread the effect on British public opinion with
   which I am daily dealing here of a Home Rule resolution by the
   House of Representatives and I am afraid that it would be impossible to explain such a resolution here, but I willingly trust your
   discretion in handling the matter at Washington. It is not a question of sympathy but of international tactics at a very critical
   period.' Wilson to Tumulty, 30 Jan. 1919 (*Ibid.*, box 3).
10. See Tumulty to Wilson, 5 Feb. 1919 (*Ibid.*); and Polk to Lansing,
    3 Feb. 1919 (N.A., 841d.00/11a, roll 213). Polk had earlier told
    Colonel Arthur Murray that some kind of resolution was certain
    to be passed but that he would use his influence to have it 'properly
    worded'. Murray to Reading, Drummond and Tyrrell, 10 Dec.
    1918 (Beaverbrook Library, Lloyd George Papers, F60/3/3). On
    6 February Gallagher introduced a new resolution (H. Con. Res.
    67) with the milder wording, and on 11 February Chairman Flood
    submitted his report, amended to support the milder 'self-deter-
    mination'. *Congressional Record*, 65th Congress, 3rd Session, vol.
    57, pp 2868 and 3174. See also O'Grady, pp 69–70; and 4 March
    1919, *Congressional Record,* 65th Congress, 3rd Session, vol. 57,
    pp 5026–7. For text of various extended speeches see 3 March
    1919, *Ibid., Appendix,* pp 239, 240–2, 282–3, 347–8, and 406–10.
    The success of the Gallagher resolution should not be seen as a
    clear victory for Irish nationalist sentiments. As much as anything
    else it represented the co-operation between the Republicans and
    the Irish-American congressmen. The latter were certainly anxious
    for Congress to make some kind of statement about Ireland, but
    the Republicans were concerned largely with preventing several
    items of legislative importance from being acted upon before the
    65th Congress ended. By this stratagem the Republicans forced
    Wilson to call the new 66th Congress, elected in November with
    Republican majorities in both houses, into session early to deal
    with this legislation. Normally the new Congress would not have
    sat until December 1919—well after the period during which
    Wilson might have successfully presented the peace treaty to the
    American people without the systematic criticism of the Repub-
    lican-dominated Senate. (As a consequence of this manoeuvre the
    Republican Henry Cabot Lodge, a personal antagonist of Wilson
    as well as the senator of a strongly Irish state, replaced the
    Democrat William J. Stone as chairman of the critically important
    Senate Foreign Relations Committee.) Indeed, while the Gallagher
    resolution was being debated in the House the Senate was discus-
    sing Lodge's 'round robin'; 39 senators signed the declaration that
    they did not find the League of Nations covenant acceptable (only
    33 votes were needed to defeat the treaty). The new 66th Congress
    not only defeated the treaty, but the Senate also collaborated with
    the Irish-Americans to pass their own resolution on the Irish

question. For a close analysis of these events see T. A. Bailey, *Woodrow Wilson and the lost peace* (1944; repr. Chicago, 1963). Ward, *Ireland*, pp 176–7.

11. See *Congressional Record*, 65th Congress, 3rd Session, vol. 57, pp 844–6, 1071–2, 3741, 3866, 4157–8, 4844 and 4949. Legislative appeals were dated: Massachusetts, 25 Feb. 1919; Wisconsin, 26 Feb. 1919; Rhode Island, 5 March 1919; New Hampshire, 12 March 1919; and Nevada, 26 March 1919 (N.A., 841d.00/25, –/26, –/28 and –/39, roll 213). The Massachusetts resolution was also presented to the Senate by Lodge. 20 May 1919 *Congressional Record*, 66th Congress, 1st Session, vol. 58, pp 48–9.

12. See Splain in Fitz-Gerald, p. 232. Of course, even before 'Self-Determination for Ireland Week' Irish-American nationalists were attempting to start public agitation. James J. Caniffe wrote to Devoy on behalf of Father Peter C. Yorke in San Francisco in late November to say that work had begun there to hold Wilson and the Allies to their war promises about self-determination; the FOIF and the United Irish Societies had already held a successful joint meeting. Caniffe to Devoy, 26 Nov. 1918 (N.L.I., Devoy Papers, box C–CA); *N.Y.T.*, 11 Dec. 1918. Conflicting accounts of how Cardinal O'Connell came to speak in New York can be found in McCartan, pp 57–8, and Tansill, pp 277–9. Other major meetings were held in Philadelphia, Brooklyn, San Francisco, New Orleans and Chicago.

13. Seven months earlier Father Magennis was censured by Cardinal Farley for his Irish nationalist activities in New York. Cardinal O'Connell had caused the British Embassy some considerable alarm in November 1918 when he raised the Irish question in his greetings to the English and French bishops in the United States on an official mission. See C. Barclay to F.O. (circulated to the King and the War Cabinet), 10 Nov. 1918 (P.R.O., F.O. 371/3430); and Monsignor A. J. Barnes to Sir Eric Drummond, 25 Nov. 1918 (Beaverbrook Library, Lloyd George Papers, F 60/2/75). *N.Y.T.*, 11 and 16 Dec. 1918; and *Irish World*, 14 Dec. 1918.

14. McCartan, pp 63–72; and *G.A.*, 11 Jan. 1919. McCartan's activities as 'Envoy of the Provisional Government of Ireland' were a matter of annoyance to the British Embassy, which protested to the State Department. C. Barclay to W. Phillips, 18 Dec. 1918 and 7 Jan. 1919, and Alvey A. Adee (for Acting Secretary of State) to Barclay, 17 Feb. 1919 (N.A., 841d.00/612 and –/621, boxes 7367 and 7368). For conflicting interpretations of these events compare McCartan, pp 70–8, with Tansill, pp 292–5. For an analysis of the growing liberal, progressive and radical disillusionment with Wilson and the Peace Conference see W. J. Helbich, 'American liberals in the League of Nations controversy', *Public Opinion Quarterly*, xxxi, no. 4 (winter 1967–68), pp 577–96.

15. *G.A.*, 18 Jan. 1919; and *Irish World*, 4 Jan. 1919. Actually there were growing differences among the leaders of the Clan and the

FOIF and the Irish exiles in America over the question of whether a republic existed in Ireland and, if so, how completely it should be supported from America. Indeed, it is still difficult to know just what the forces were behind the convention. See McCartan, pp 79–88; O'Doherty, pp 18–19 and 35–6; Tansill, pp 296–302; and Cohalan to Borah, 18 Feb. 1919 (L.C., Borah Papers, box 194). The convention was attended by 5,132 delegates from Irish-American organisations across the country. Splain in Fitz-Gerald, pp 232–4. Philadelphia *Record,* 24 Feb. 1919; *N.Y.T.,* 24 Feb. 1919; *G.A.,* 1 and 8 March 1919; and *Irish World,* 1 March 1919. Another important result of the convention was that the FOIF assumed the financial responsibility for the Irish National Bureau in Washington, which had been started by the IPL and run by Miss Katherine Hughes. By mid-summer the Boston lawyer and politician Daniel T. O'Connell had been appointed director. 'The achievements of the Irish Progressive League', *Bulletin of the Irish Progressive League,* no. 4 (Sept. 1919) (N.L.I., Golden Papers, MS. 13141).

16. See Tumulty to Wilson, 24 Feb. 1919, and Miss Rankin to Wilson, 28 Feb. 1919 (L.C., Wilson Papers, file VI, no. 3926, box 558). Tumulty wrote to Wilson: 'Regardless of what we may think of Cohalan and his crowd, there is a deep desire on the part of the American people to see the Irish question settled in the only way it can be settled—by the establishment of a Home Rule Parliament in Dublin.' Tumulty to Wilson, 28 Feb. and 1 March 1919 and n.d., and Wilson to Tumulty, n.d. (L.C., Tumulty Papers, box 3). Before meeting with the delegation Wilson assured Lord Reading that he would not commit himself to raise the Irish question at the Peace Conference. Reading to F.O., 4 March 1919 (P.R.O., F.O. 371/4245).

17. The delegation also included former governor Edward F. Dunne, Michael J. Ryan, Bishop Shahan, Michael Francis Doyle, Major Eugene F. Kinkead, Mayor John P. Grace, John J. Splain, Judge O'Neill Ryan, Dr William Carroll, John E. Milholland, the Rev. James Grattan Mythen and the Rev. Norman Thomas. In Cohalan's place Judge Goff, Bishop Muldoon and Frank P. Walsh spoke for the delegation. Others in the delegation to whom Wilson might have objected were Michael J. Ryan, who had made no secret of his pro-German views before 1917, Michael Francis Doyle, who had served as one of Casement's lawyers and had been a fairly vociferous anti-British spokesman, and the Rev. Norman Thomas, who had been a prominent socialist and pacifist critic of the Wilson administration during the war. Splain in Fitz-Gerald, p. 234; *G.A.,* 8 March 1919; *N.Y.T.,* 10 March 1919; and McCartan, pp 275–6. Ray Stannard Baker later wrote that Wilson told him the delegation had been 'so insistent . . . that I had hard work keeping my temper', and David Hunter Miller recorded that Wilson said on his return to Paris that the delegation had made

him very 'angry' and that his impulse had been to tell them 'to go
to hell'. See Baker, pp 385–6; D. H. Miller, *The drafting of the
covenant* (New York, 1928), i, p. 294; and S. Bonsal, *Unfinished
business* (Garden City, 1944), p. 149. Both John J. Splain and
Major Eugene F. Kinkead recorded the opinion of the delegation
that Wilson would not do anything for Ireland. Nonetheless, four
days later Major Kinkead sent Wilson a letter pleading with him
to consider the results of the recent election in Ireland and apply
to Ireland the concept of self-determination which he had enunci-
ated during the war. Kinkead to Wilson, 8 March 1919 (L.C.,
Wilson Papers, Sec. VIII, box 15). The appeal was a strong personal one inasmuch as Kinkead had been one of a delegation
which had asked Wilson to enter politics in 1909.

18. In their early resolutions they stated: 'We believe in the adoption
of a generous plan of Home Rule, with a united Ireland, incorporated in some federal plan within the United Kingdom.' See
'Memorandum of informal conference held at the Century Club',
2 Nov. 1918, and resolutions, *c.* 15 Nov. 1918 (Wisconsin State
Historical Society, McCarthy Papers, MSS KU, box 37).

19. McCarthy to House, 9 Sept. and 4 Oct. 1918 (Wisconsin State
Historical Society, McCarthy Papers, MSS KU, box 37); Lansing
to Wilson, 13 Sept. 1918, and Wilson to Lansing, 17 Sept. 1918
(N.A., 841d.00/15A and –/16½, roll 213); and McCarthy to Mezes,
16 and 28 Dec. 1918 (Yale University Library, House Papers, III
B, drawer 34, file 48). Wilson disliked and distrusted McCarthy,
and he discouraged Lansing, and presumably House as well, from
relying on his judgment. Perhaps for this reason the inquiry
devoted very little time to a consideration of the Irish question,
despite McCarthy's correspondence with Dr Mezes. McCarthy
resented both the convention led by Irish-Americans who had
recently been accused of being pro-German and the anti-Irish tone
of the *Christian Science Monitor.* McCarthy to J. S. Cullinan, 27
and 30 Dec. 1918. However, Richard Campbell, a successful New
York lawyer, gave a very enthusiastic report of the convention.
Ahern to McCarthy, 16 Jan. and 4 Feb. 1919, and Campbell to
McCarthy, 21 Jan. and 15 and 26 Feb. 1919 (Wisconsin State
Historical Society, McCarthy Papers, MSS KU, boxes 37, 38 and
39).

20. Cosgrave to McCarthy, 1 Feb. 1919, Campbell to McCarthy, 15
Feb. 1919, McCarthy to Plunkett, 17 Feb. 1919, McCarthy to
Campbell, 3 March 1919, and McCarthy to Miss N. E. Murphy,
21 March 1919 (*Ibid.*).

21. Polk to Fletcher, 7 Jan. 1919 (Yale University Library, Polk
Papers, drawer 77, file 139); Plunkett diary, 15 March 1919
(Plunkett Foundation, Plunkett Papers); Gerry et al. to Wilson,
8 March 1919 (L.C., Walsh Papers, file B, box 190); Durbin to
Tumulty, 23 April 1919 (L.C., Wilson Papers, file VI, no. 3926,
box 558); Chadbourne to Wilson, 3 March 1919 (*Ibid.*, file VIII

A, box 22); and Mason to Devoy, 27 Dec. 1918 (N.L.I., Devoy Papers, box M).

22. U.S. Congress, Senate, Subcommittee of the Senate Judiciary Committee, *Brewing and liquor interests and German propaganda*, Hearings pursuant to Senate Res. 307 (65th Congress, 2nd and 3rd Sessions), 1919, pp 1392, 1496–7, 1408–26, 1542–4 and 1577. In fact both Larkin and O'Leary came up for trial in 1919. For details see O'Leary, passim; and Larkin, pp 237–43. The IPL, which was currently being prevented from holding meetings by the New York police, attempted to raise money for O'Leary's defence. See IPL appeal, and Golden to Police Commissioner Enright, 10 Dec. 1918 (N.L.I., Golden Papers, MS. 13141, folder ii); and *G.A.*, 22 Feb. 1919.

23. *C.S.M.*, 3, 4 and 9 Dec. 1918.

24. Warren to Williams, 10 Feb. 1919, and Winslow to Williams, 19 March 1919 (L.C., Williams Papers, box 44); and four identical letters to Wilson from B. L. Jones, C. J. Fletcher, J. H. Bribben and C. B. Smith, 25 March 1919 (L.C., Wilson Papers, file VI, no. 3926, box 558).

25. *G.A.*, 5 April 1919; *Irish World*, 5 April 1919; D. F. Cohalan to Paris Peace Conference, 25 March 1919 (A.I.H.S., Cohalan Papers, drawer 1); Redmond S. Brennan to American Commission on Irish Independence, 31 March 1919, William J. Moran to Walsh, 31 March 1919, and Walsh diary, 17 April 1919 (N.Y.P.L., Walsh Papers, box 124); and 'Notes of an interview of Secretary Lansing with Frank P. Walsh', 6 June 1919 (L.C., Lansing Papers, vol. 43). It had been suggested to Diarmuid Lynch in early 1919 by Griffith, Collins and Brugha that a delegation of Irish-Americans be sent to Paris to assist Irish representatives in obtaining a hearing at the conference. Lynch, pp 197–8.

26. Walsh diary, 14 and 15 April 1919 (N.Y.P.L., Walsh Papers, box 124); E. F. Dunne in Fitz-Gerald, p. 223; and Walsh et al. to Wilson, 16 April 1919 (Yale University Library, House Papers, Walsh, Frank P.).

27. Plunkett to Wilson, 2 March 1919, and Polk to Wilson, 6 March 1919 (L.C., Wilson Papers, file VIII A, box 22, and Sec. VIII, box 15); Wilson to Plunkett, 25 March 1919 (Plunkett Foundation, Plunkett Papers); Miller, i, p. 294; Bonsal, p. 149; Walsh diary, 17 April 1919 (N.Y.P.L., Walsh Papers, box 124); and *G.A.*, 26 April 1919.

28. See Thomas Canfield to House, *c.* 17 March 1919, and House to Canfield, 21 April 1919 (Yale University Library, House Papers, Canfield, Thomas).

29. Cohalan to Walsh, 28 March 1919 (N.Y.P.L., Walsh Papers, box 124). The circumstances surrounding the two weeks between the Irish-American delegation's initial contacts with the American authorities and their trip to Ireland are still ambiguous. The papers of the three major participants—Walsh, House and Lloyd

George—are all somewhat contradictory in their accounts. After the delegates returned to Paris rather hostile notes were sent back and forth. Walsh claimed that House had told him de Valera *would* be granted safe conduct; House later said he thought de Valera *might* be granted safe conduct; Lloyd George said that he wanted to talk with Walsh merely to present the English arguments to the delegates. Walsh understood that Lloyd George wanted them to go to Ireland; Lloyd George thought that House wanted them to go; Sir William Wiseman, who arranged their going, thought that Wilson wanted them to go. See American Commission on Irish Independence to Wilson, 20 May 1919 (*Ibid.*); Lloyd George to House, 9 May 1919, and 'Notes on conversation between Colonel House and Walsh, Dunne and Ryan', 23 May 1919 (Yale University Library, House Papers, Lloyd George, David, and III B, drawer 34, file 51); and War Cabinet 567A, 14 May 1919 (P.R.O., CAB. 23/15).

30. Polk suggested that the exact situation should be described to the press so that it would be understood that 'the British have brought all this trouble on themselves by visaing their passports for England and Ireland'. See F. L. Polk, 'Memorandum respecting passports of Irish-Americans', 15 May 1919 (Yale University Library, House Papers, III B, drawer 34, file 51); and John W. Davis (American Ambassador to England) to Polk, 16 May 1919 (Yale University Library, Polk Papers, drawer 77, file 133). See also Lord Reading to F.O., 4 March 1919 (P.R.O., F.O. 371/4245).

31. 9 May 1919, *Dáil Éireann, miontuarisc an chéad Dála, 1919–1921; minutes of the proceedings of the first parliament of the Republic of Ireland, 1919–1921, official record* (Dublin, [1921]), pp 82 and 99–108. For vivid accounts of the trip see the Dublin *Freeman's Journal*, 3–13 May 1919. For reports back to the United States and details of their travel and activity see *G.A.*, 10, 17 and 24 May 1919; *Irish World*, 24 May 1919; and *N.Y.T.*, 2–15 May 1919. Daily report, 14 May 1919 (Yale University Library, House Papers, III B, drawer 34, file 51). Dunne, in fact, cabled the Chicago *Daily News* that seventy-five per cent of the Irish people favoured a republic. See Dunne in Fitz-Gerald, p. 224.

32. 14 May 1919, *Hansard* 5 (Commons), cxv, col. 1582; and Walter Long to Lloyd George, 8 May 1919, and Lord Stamfordham to Lloyd George, 9 May 1919 (Beaverbrook Library, Lloyd George Papers, F 33/2/62). At the war cabinet meeting on 14 May 1919 the Irish Chief Secretary, Ian Macpherson, said that the Irish-Americans had very much aggravated a delicate situation by their inflammatory speeches and their careless use of their passports, and he saw a direct increase in unrest in Ireland as a result of their visit; Bonar Law decided to announce in parliament that Lloyd George would not meet the Irish-Americans back in Paris. War Cabinet 567A, 14 May 1919 (P.R.O., CAB. 23/15). This view was later supported by the American Ambassador to Britain, John W.

Davis. See Davis to Sec. of State, 28 May 1919 (N.A., 841d.00/57, roll 213).

33. Lloyd George to House, 9 May 1919 (Yale University Library, House Papers, Lloyd George, David); and Bonsal, pp 174–6. He also said that in view of the present situation he would inform the Viceroy in Ireland to take whatever steps 'necessary in the interests of peace and order'; thus when Walsh applied to the military to visit Westport he found his travel had been restricted. Lloyd George to House, 10 May 1919 (Yale University Library, House Papers, Lloyd George, David). The New York *Times* reported that the British authorities were 'incensed' at the delegates and that House would no longer serve as 'intermediary' between them and the British. *N.Y.T.*, 14 and 15 May 1919.

34. Wilson to Tumulty, 9 June 1919 (L.C., Tumulty Papers, box 3). Given the delicacy of the situation, it is difficult to understand what prompted the Irish-Americans to figure so prominently in blatantly nationalistic activities; the previous missions of Ray Stannard Baker and George Creel had demonstrated that Americans could investigate conditions in Ireland, even conferring with nationalist leaders, without calling undue attention to themselves, and of course as representatives of President Wilson they were much more noteworthy. Colonel Bonsal, a military adviser for the American peace commission, related a conversation in which Dunne confessed that their passionate speeches were the result of too much Irish whiskey, although this explanation could hardly cover the entire trip even if true. See Bonsal, pp 177–8. Ward doubts that Wilson had 'cleared the way' for the Irish delegation in any case. Ward, *Ireland*, p. 183.

35. Lansing sent the letter to Wilson for his recommendations. See Walsh et al. to Lansing, 17 May 1919, and Walsh et al. to Wilson, 20 May 1919, and Lansing to Walsh, 24 May 1919 (N.Y.P.L., Walsh Papers, box 124). If Wilson, as Seth Tillman has recently suggested, refused to allow the Irish question to 'come to the surface', he had no objection to working on it at another level. S. Tillman, *Anglo-American relations at the Paris Peace Conference of 1919* (Princeton, 1961), p. 200.

36. *Irish World*, 7 June 1919. 'Notes on conversation between Colonel House and Walsh, Dunne and Ryan', 23 May 1919 (Yale University Library, House Papers, III B, drawer 34, file 51); and Walsh to Lansing, 26 and 27 May 1919 (N.Y.P.L., Walsh Papers, box 124). Walsh and Dunne sent letters to each of the five members of the American peace commission and forwarded over thirty cables from Irish-American organisations to Wilson. Failing to obtain any favourable response, they then requested an interview with the American peace commission, which was turned down along with the comment that a discussion of the Irish situation did not fall within the purview of the American peace commission. See Walsh to Wilson, 28 May 1919, Walsh and Dunne to J. C. Grew, 29 May

1919, and Walsh and Dunne to Grew, 2 June 1919 (*Ibid.*); Walsh to Wilson, 31 May 1919, and Lansing, White, House and General Tasker H. Bliss to Wilson, 31 May 1919 (Yale University Library, House Papers, Walsh, Frank P., and III B, drawer 34, file 49A). These efforts by the Irish-American delegation were fully reported in America. See *G.A.*, 7 June 1919; and White to Lodge, 29 May 1919 (Massachusetts Historical Society, Lodge Papers, Henry White box).

37. See 'Notes of an interview of Secretary Lansing with Frank P. Walsh', 6 June 1919 (L.C., Lansing Papers, vol. 43). The report, copies of which were also sent to members of the British government, the king and leading London newspapers, was obviously designed to appeal over the heads of diplomats and governments to public opinion, especially in America and Ireland; it was certainly not likely to increase the chances of de Valera, Griffith and Plunkett going to Paris. The British government was, of course, troubled by the publication of the report, and the Irish Office printed a ten-page refutation of the allegations contained in it. See War Cabinet 579 (min. 4), 13 June 1919 (P.R.O., CAB. 23/10), and G.T. no. 7485, 14 June 1919, 'Statement of Irish-American delegates' (P.R.O., CAB. 24/81); *Hansard* 5 (Commons), cxvii, cols 607–8; and American Commission on Irish Independence [F. P. Walsh and E. F. Dunne], *Report on conditions in Ireland with a demand for investigation by the Peace Conference* (Paris, 1919). When Ray Stannard Baker told Wilson on 29 May that Walsh and Dunne were in his office every day Wilson replied that he did not know how long he could keep himself from condemning their 'miserable mischief-making'. 'They see nothing', he said, 'except their own small interest.' Baker, p. 435. Henry White, while not so annoyed with the Irish-Americans, wrote to Senator Lodge that it was 'difficult to deal frankly with' them because 'they are apt to turn whatever one writes or says to them to the furtherance of their views, irrespective of the facts'. White to Lodge, 19 June 1919 (Massachusetts Historical Society, Lodge Papers, Henry White box). The final meeting between the delegates and Wilson was arranged through the efforts of Tumulty and Admiral Grayson. See Grayson to Tumulty, 13 June 1919 (L.C., Tumulty Papers, box 3).

38. Compare with Wilson to Tumulty, 9 June 1919 (L.C., Tumulty Papers, box 3), cited on p. 134 above. Interview between Wilson, Walsh and Dunne, 11 June 1919, taken from U.S. Congress, *Treaty of peace with Germany*, pp 836–8; see also Dunne in Fitz-Gerald, p. 224.

39. Frank P. Walsh, who had strong connections in the American labour movement, obtained a pro-Irish resolution from the powerful American Federation of Labour, which was presented to Lansing. See Walsh to John Fitzpatrick, 12 and 15 June 1919, and Frank Morrison to Walsh, 22 June 1919 (N.Y.P.L., Walsh Papers,

box 124); Walsh and Dunne to Lansing and the American Commission to Negotiate Peace, 20 June 1919 (L.C., Lansing Papers, vol. 43); and Tumulty to Wilson, 21 June 1919 (L.C., Tumulty Papers, box 3).

40. Back in the United States Walsh, Dunne and Ryan undertook to relate their experiences in great detail. See *G.A.*, 12, 19 and 26 July 1919; *Irish World*, 21 June 1919; and P. S. O'H[egarty] to George Gavan Duffy, 23 May 1919 (N.L.I., Duffy Papers, MS. 5582). From Rome O'Hegarty wrote that Bishop Fogarty and Father O'Flanagan regarded the trip to Ireland as a great 'success'. Seán T. O'Kelly, Dáil envoy in Paris, said that the delegation had 'done wonders' and had kept the Irish matter before the eyes of the public, the press and the Peace Conference; he wanted the thanks of Ireland extended to them for 'the untold services they have rendered in this fight'. O'Kelly to Devoy, 13 June 1919 (N.L.I., Devoy Papers, box N–OL). See also Cohalan to Walsh and Dunne, 3 June 1919 (N.Y.P.L., Walsh Papers, box 124).

41. White to Lansing, 26 Aug. 1919 (L.C., Lansing Papers, vol. 46); and White to Lodge, 4 Sept. 1919 (Massachusetts Historical Society, Lodge Papers, Henry White box). Walsh's comment to Griffith that 'Ireland was making more noise than all other small nations combined [in Paris]' would seem to raise questions as to how serious they were in hoping to deal with Lloyd George. 17 June 1919, *Dáil Éireann proc. 1919–21*, p. 117.

42. See M. C. McKenna, *Borah* (Ann Arbor, 1961), p. 158; Cohalan to Borah, 12 and 27 May 1919, and Borah to Cohalan, 14, 23 and 28 May 1919 (L.C., Borah Papers, box 551); and 29 May 1919 (S. Res. 48), *Congressional Record*, 66th Congress, 1st Session, vol. 58, p. 393. See also Cohalan's objections to the amended form, Cohalan to Borah, 5 and 10 June 1919 (A.I.H.S., Cohalan Papers, drawer 3); Cohalan to Borah, 25 June 1919 (L.C., Borah Papers, box 551); and 5 June 1919 (S. Report no. 6), *Congressional Record*, 66th Congress, 1st Session, vol. 58, pp 671–2. When Senator Borah asked for the immediate consideration of the resolution Senator Williams objected, saying that the resolution was 'ill advised and really none of our business'. *Ibid.*

43. 6 June 1919, *Ibid.*, p. 729. Lodge justified his actions and the vote of the Senate on the same terms to both Henry White and Lord Bryce. See Lodge to White, 23 June 1919, and Lodge to Bryce, 10 June 1919 (Massachusetts Historical Society, Lodge Papers, Henry White and Bryce boxes). See also Frank L. Polk to Lansing, 6 June 1919 (L.C., Lansing Papers, vol. 43); *Congressional Record*, 66th Congress, 1st Session, vol. 58, p. 729; *G.A.*, 14 June 1919; and *Irish World*, 14 June 1919.

44. *Congressional Record*, 66th Congress, 1st Session, vol. 58, pp 1374 and 1726–30.

45. See Tumulty to Wilson, 4 June 1919, Tumulty to Admiral

Grayson, 7 June 1919, and Wilson to Tumulty, 7 June 1919 (L.C., Tumulty Papers, box 3).

46. Wilson to Lansing, 10 June 1919, Lansing, White, House and Bliss to Wilson, 10 June 1919, Wilson to Lansing, 16 June 1919, and American Commission to Negotiate Peace to M. Clemenceau, 16 June 1919 (L.C., Lansing Papers, vol. 43). See also 'Minutes of the daily meetings of the Commissioners Plenipotentiary', 21 June 1919, 184.00101/93, *Foreign relations, Paris Peace Conference, 1919,* xi, p. 242; and Lansing to President, 3 Oct. 1919 (N.A., 841d.00/52, roll 213).

47. See Walsh and Dunne to American Commission, 13 17 and 20 June 1919, and J. C. Grew to Walsh, 21 June 1919 (L.C., Lansing Papers, vol. 43); Grew to Walsh, 17 June 1919 (N.Y.P.L., Walsh Papers, box 125); 'Minutes of the daily meetings of the Commissioners Plenipotentiary', 14 June 1919, 184.00101/88, *Foreign relations, Paris Peace Conference, 1919,* xi, p. 234; and White to Lodge, 6 June 1919 (Massachusetts Historical Society, Lodge Papers, Henry White box).

48. O'Kelly to Devoy, 13 June 1919 (N.L.I., Devoy Papers, box N–OL). For similar views see Art Ó Briain to Paris Office, 12 June 1919, and O'Kelly to Ó Briain, 15 June 1919 (N.L.I., Ó Briain Papers, MS. 8422); and 17 June 1919, *Dáil Éireann proc. 1919–21,* pp 113–14.

49. *Lit. Dig.,* lxi, no. 10 (7 June 1919), pp 25–6; McCarthy to Plunkett, 4 April 1919 (Plunkett Foundation, Plunkett Papers); and John E. McEldowney to Borah, 7 June 1919 (L.C., Borah Papers, box 550).

50. John H. Cowles to Williams, 6 June 1919, W. Weishaar to Williams, 7 June 1919, Milledge L. Bonham to Williams, 7 June 1919, and Richard Zerega to Williams, 11 June 1919 (L.C., Williams Papers, box 45); and Wickersham to Lord Bryce, 15 June 1919 (Bodl., Bryce Papers, vol. 21, fol. 192).

51. O'Grady, pp 76–7; *G.A.,* 3 May 1919; *Irish World,* 30 March 1919; and Splain in Fitz-Gerald, p. 233. See also McSweeney to Cohalan, 2 April 1919 (N.L.I., Devoy Papers, box M); W. V. DelaHunt to Golden, 19 May 1919 (N.L.I., Golden Papers, MS. 13141, folder ii); Gerson, *The hyphenate,* p. 102; and S. Adler, *The isolationist impulse: its twentieth-century reaction* (New York, 1957), p. 83.

52. See Borah to Mrs Fogarty, 20 Nov. 1918 (L.C., Borah Papers, box 188). The causes of the hostility of the Republican senators to Wilson and the treaty do not fall within the scope of this study, although they obviously have considerable bearing on the alliance between the Irish-Americans and the senators. For a complete analysis see T. A. Bailey, *Woodrow Wilson and the great betrayal* (1945; repr. Chicago, 1963), passim; McKenna, pp 158 and 283–4; Cohalan–Borah correspondence, May–Sept. 1919; Irish Self-Determination Club, Omaha, to Borah, 2 March 1919, Harry Cun-

ningham et al. to Borah, 2 March 1919, John V. Sullivan to Borah, 8 March 1919, and Joseph McCaffery and James J. Murphy to Borah, 26 March 1919 (L.C., Borah Papers, box 551).
53. Borah to Dr A. C. Smith, 31 May 1919 (punctuation changed from telegram form), and Borah to Thomas Mannix, 29 March 1919 (*Ibid.*).
54. Lodge also argued with White that the Irish-American delegates 'were not allowed to present their case as they should have been permitted to present it'. Lodge to White, 2 July and 2 Oct. 1919 (Massachusetts Historical Society, Lodge Papers, Henry White box;) Lodge to John W. Weeks, 31 July and 14 Aug. 1919 (*Ibid.*, Peace, League, Political box).
55. Cohalan to Borah, 11 July 1919, and Borah to Cohalan, 14 July 1919 (L.C., Borah Papers, box 551).
56. U.S. Congress, *Treaty of peace with Germany*, pp 757–903. Many of Cohalan's arguments were also developed in his pamphlet published by the FOIF. D. F. Cohalan, *Freedom of the seas* (New York, 1919). Also see J. A. McGarry to Cohalan, 7 Jan. 1920 (A.I.H.S., Cohalan Papers, drawer 3). Walsh, Dunne and Ryan submitted to the committee copies of their correspondence with the American, British and French peace commissions and gave detailed memoranda of their conversations with Wilson and others. See also F. P. Walsh, 'Impressions of Ireland', *Nation*, cviii (7 June 1919), p. 907; and *G.A.*, 6 and 13 Sept. 1919. Irish-American nationalists also assisted in the testimony of other dissatisfied minority groups. See Ward, *Ireland*, p. 198. Senator Williams told Lodge that in fairness the committee should also be willing to hear testimony from Ulster Unionists. Williams to Lodge, 2 Sept. 1919 (L.C., Williams Papers, box 47).
57. Walsh to Seán T. O'Kelly, 17 Sept. 1919 (N.Y.P.L., Walsh Papers, box 124); and 2 and 3 Sept. 1919, *Congressional Record*, 66th Congress, 1st Session, vol. 58, pp 4611–19 and 4650–718. For a bitter denunciation of this practice by Congress see resolutions from the East Lansing, Michigan, American Legion Post to Wilson, 21 Feb. 1920 (L.C., Wilson Papers, file VI, 3926, box 558).
58. O'Connell to Borah, 13 Nov. 1919, and John B. Sullivan to Borah, 30 Sept. 1919 (L.C., Borah Papers, boxes 550 and 551); and Lodge to White, 2 Oct. 1919 (Massachusetts Historical Society, Lodge Papers, Henry White box).
59. *The League of Nations and the rights of small nations* (New York, 1919); E. F. Dunne, *What Dunne saw in Ireland* (New York, 1919); D. F. Cohalan, *Statement of Hon. Daniel F. Cohalan* (n.p., 1919); *Official documents from Ireland, including 'Ireland's case for independence' adopted by Dáil Éireann for presentation to the Peace Conference* (New York, 1919); and E. F. McSweeney, *Ireland is an American question* (New York, 1919). C. C. Tansill has asserted that such pamphlets as *The Irish Republic can pay*

its way and E. F. McSweeney's *America first* (Boston, 1920) reached a circulation of 700,000 and 100,000 copies respectively. Alan J. Ward suggests that the FOIF may have spent nearly $750,000 of the Irish Victory Fund on anti-league efforts. Tansill, p. 332; and Ward in *I.H.S.*, xvi, no. 61 (March 1968), p. 87.

60. See *America's appeal to Ireland* (Chicago, n.d.); *That traitorous League of Nations* (New York, 1919); *The lion's share* (New York, 1919); *Profit and loss in peace making* (New York, 1919); *Revolution and co-operation* (New York, 1919); and *Defeat to all Democrats* (New York, 1919). Liberal supporters of the IPL included the Rev. Norman Thomas, Dr Lovejoy Elliott, Scott Nearing, Lincoln Colcord, Frank Harris, Alfred W. McCann, Harry Weinberger, Joseph D. Cannon, James Maurer, Edward F. Cassidy and Leonora O'Reilly. See 'The achievements of the Irish Progressive League', *Bulletin of the Irish Progressive League,* no. 4 (Sept. 1919), Colcord to Golden, 29 July 1919, and Golden to Colcord, 5 Aug. 1919 (N.L.I., Golden Papers, MS. 13141, folder vi); and Amos Pinchot, 'Speech on the League of Nations', n.d. (L.C., Pinchot Papers, file 102).

61. New York *American,* 16 March 1919; J. C. Walsh, *The invincible Irish* (New York, 1919); P. Francis, *The poison in America's cup* (New York, 1919); *The re-conquest of America* (New York, 1919); and McCartan, pp 121–32. Frank P. Walsh told Seán T. O'Kelly in mid-September that it was 'a splended thing'. Walsh to O'Kelly, 17 Sept. 1919 (N.Y.P.L., Walsh Papers, box 124); and G. Creel, *Ireland's fight for freedom: setting forth the high lights of Irish history* (New York, 1919). Creel's book was first serialised in the New York *Sunday American,* July–Aug. 1919. In spite of his interest in Ireland, Creel supported Wilson and the league and criticised several Irish-American leaders, which won him the enmity of the *Gaelic American. G.A.,* 16 Aug. 1919; and *Leslie's Weekly,* 2 Aug. 1919. The inability of the Clan leaders to recognise the importance of Creel's book for the Irish movement was a source of some despair to Frank P. Walsh. Walsh to Seán T. O'Kelly, 17 Sept. 1919 (N.Y.P.L., Walsh Papers, box 124). In the end Creel's book, along with several others on Ireland, was distributed to members of the House of Representatives and the Senate. D. T. O'Connell to Cohalan, 21 April 1920 (A.I.H.S., Cohalan Papers, drawer 2).

62. —— to Tumulty, 7 April 1919 (L.C., Wilson Papers, file VI, no. 3926, box 558); and Tumulty, p. 404.

63. See Office of the Secretary, Department of State, to Wilson, 22 Aug. 1919 (L.C., Lansing Papers, vol. 45). The friends of the league felt that Wilson should emphasise precisely this point—that the league could help Ireland in order to win back Irish-American support. See Dr Joseph Hugh McGready to Wilson, 5 Sept. 1919 (L.C., Wilson Papers, file VI, no. 3926, box 558); William Scallon to Walsh, 18 Sept. 1919 (L.C., Walsh Papers, file B, box 190);

Senator James Hamilton Lewis to American Commission on Irish Independence, 20 Sept. 1919, and Frank P. Walsh to Lewis, 24 Sept. 1919 (N.Y.P.L., Walsh Papers, box 124); Charles McCarthy to Joseph F. O'Connell, 26 Aug. 1919 (Wisconsin State Historical Society, McCarthy Papers, MSS KU, box 40); and *G.A.*, 27 Sept. 1919. The *Gaelic American* denied Wilson's interest and said that without British agreement the United States could never raise the Irish question in the league. Wilson's friends saw his statements as the beginning of the long-awaited rebuttal of the violent Irish-American critics. William Scallon to Senator Thomas J. Walsh, 18 Sept. 1919 (L.C., Walsh Papers, box 190). Frank P. Walsh wrote to Wilson immediately after the interview asking for a clearer statement as to whether Wilson favoured applying the principle of self-determination to Ireland; no answer was received. Walsh to Wilson, 17 and 19 Sept. 1919 (N.Y.P.L., Walsh Papers, box 124). See also Tumulty, pp 405–7; and Gerson, *The hyphenate,* p. 83. For a description of Clan activities during Wilson's tour see Viereck, p. 227.

64. Of the eight, he pointed out, six were Progressives. 26 and 30 June 1919, *Congressional Record,* 66th Congress, 1st Session, vol. 58, pp 1787–8 and 2077–80. See also Phelan to J. K. McGuire, 29 July 1919 (A.I.H.S., Cohalan Papers, drawer 4). Walsh also accused Borah and the irreconcilable Republicans of using Ireland to obscure the real issues, and that their inconsistency was revealed in their contradictory demands that the United States keep out of European quarrels while at the same time insisting that the United States would be prevented by the league from assisting Ireland's struggle for independence. 28 July 1919, *Congressional Record,* 66th Congress, 1st Session, vol. 58, pp 3323–8. Walsh was supported in this argument by the former governor of Montana. A. E. Spriggs to Walsh, 31 July 1919 (L.C., Walsh Papers, file B, box 190). These arguments were promptly repudiated by Irish-Americans. D. D. Murphy to Borah, 1 July 1919 (L.C., Borah Papers, box 551).

65. Doyle to Walsh, 4 Sept. 1919, and Walsh to Wilson, 17 July 1919 (L.C., Walsh Papers, file B, box 190); 17, 18 and 20 Oct. 1919 (S. Res. 215), *Congressional Record,* 66th Congress, 1st Session, vol. 58, pp 7048, 7105–15 and 7156–7; and Walsh to Mrs A. E. Spriggs, 25 Nov. 1919 (L.C., Walsh Papers, file B, box 190). S. Adler has suggested that by joining forces with the irreconcilable Republicans the Irish-American nationalist leaders made the chance for any compromise worked out by Republican and Democratic moderates, such as Senator Walsh, quite impossible. Adler, p. 84. J. B. Duff has concluded that after June 1919 Senators Walsh and Phelan were the only Irish-American politicians still supporting Wilson. Duff in *Jn. Amer. Hist.,* lv (Dec. 1968), p. 598.

66. 16 Oct. 1919, *Congressional Record,* 66th Congress, 1st Session, vol. 58, pp 7005–7. Senator Phelan responded to Williams that all

of the blessings of Anglo-Saxon liberty about which Williams had talked so glowingly had not yet reached across the Irish Sea. Lodge recognised in Williams's speech further ammunition which the Republicans could use in their campaign to lure the Irish vote into their own camp. See Lodge to John L. Weeks, 17 Oct. 1919 (Massachusetts Historical Society, Lodge Papers, Peace, League, Political box). For comments on the speech see L.C., Williams Papers, boxes 48 and 49. For evidence of support for the league on strictly Protestant and Anglo-Saxon lines see K. R. Lancaster, 'The Protestant churches and the fight for ratification of the Versailles Treaty', *Public Opinion Quarterly*, xxxi, no. 4 (winter 1967–68), p. 605; Williams to Phelan, 17 Oct. 1919 (L.C., Williams Papers, box 48); and 18 Oct. 1919, *Congressional Record*, 66th Congress, 1st Session, vol. 58, p. 7107. Some pamphlet-writing was done by those who rejected the Irish-American nationalists' arguments against the league. See J. A. Connolly, *The still vexed Irish question* (n.p., n.d.); and *The elements arrayed against the R.C. Irish* (n.p., n.d.). Their effect was probably negligible.

67. Cohalan to Borah, 19 Nov. 1919, and Borah to Cohalan, 22 Nov. 1919 (L.C., Borah Papers, box 551); *G.A.*, 29 Nov. 1919; *Irish World*, 6 Dec. 1919; and Bailey, pp 236–64.

68. 17 and 18 March 1920, *Congressional Record*, 66th Congress, 2nd Session, vol. 59, pp 4457, 4479–507 and 4522. There had been some discussion between Borah and the Irish-American leaders about an Irish reservation as early as July 1919. See Rossa F. Downing to Cohalan, 24 July 1919 (N.L.I., Devoy Papers, box J–L). Senator Harding later justified his vote against the reservation to Frank P. Walsh by pointing out that sixteen of those who had voted for it also voted against the treaty with the other reservations. Harding to Walsh, 24 March 1920 (N.Y.P.L., Walsh Papers, box 124). For an indignant reaction to the Gerry reservation see Moorfield Storey to Lord Bryce, 22 March 1920 (Bodl., Bryce Papers, vol. 10, fols 132–3). In answer to the question, to what extent were the Irish-Americans responsible for the defeat of the treaty, Alan J. Ward asserts that in 1919, as with the arbitration treaties, the Irish were only successful in obstructing the treaty ratification in the Senate to the degree that their interests coincided with the interests of a powerful group in the Senate. In this case a significant number of Republicans felt that American sovereignty, the prerogatives of the Senate and the future of their party were at stake. In the case of the Versailles Treaty the Irish were also joined by disgruntled ethnic groups from Eastern and Southern Europe and from Asia. See Ward in *I.H.S.*, xvi, no. 61 (March 1968), pp 95–6; and Ward, *Ireland*, pp 187, 198 and 213.

69. 12 April 1919 and 29 June 1920, *Dáil Éireann proc. 1919–21*, pp 72–6 and 120; and *N.Y.T.*, 14 July 1919. K. R. Maxwell has shown that de Valera did not oppose the league in theory, but he quickly joined in the league fight in the United States, no doubt thereby

influencing a good number of Irish-Americans. Maxwell in *Public Opinion Quarterly*, xxi, no. 4 (winter 1967–68), p. 631. De Valera reported to the Dáil shortly after his arrival in America that the league probably would not be ratified, and when he gave his report to the Dáil upon his return to Ireland he listed the defeat of the League of Nations first among the objectives of his mission. 19 Aug. 1919 and 25 Jan. 1920, *Dáil Éireann proc. 1919–21*, pp 141 and 250.

Chapter 6
AMERICA DURING THE ANGLO-IRISH STRUGGLE, 1919–1921
(pp 149–176)

1. Once in the United States, de Valera was persuaded to style himself as President of the Irish Republic, a title which he had no authority to use until 1921. McCartan, pp 138–40.

2. De Valera, like McCartan, travelled to the United States disguised as a seaman and left his ship in New York; he had been in the United States about two weeks, visiting his mother and conferring with Joseph McGarrity before making his public appearance on 23 June. His mission to the United States has been fully described in O'Doherty; McCartan; Ward, *Ireland*, pp 214–36; Tansill, pp 340–96; Earl of Longford and T. P. O'Neill, *Éamon de Valera* (1970; repr. Boston, 1971), pp 95–114; M. J. MacManus, *Éamon de Valera: a biography* (1944; repr. Dublin, 1962), pp 87–108; M. Bromage, *De Valera and the march of a nation* (London, 1956), pp 90–107; D. Gwynn, *De Valera* (London, 1933), pp 79–114; D. Ryan, *Unique dictator, a study of Éamon de Valera* (London, 1936), pp 102–32; and *N.Y.T.*, 21, 23, 24 and 25 June 1919.

3. He left New York on 29 June, addressing crowds of people from 17,000 to 40,000 in major cities along the eastern seaboard, and then made a quick trip out to the west coast, stopping in the principal Irish-American centres. Beginning in early October, in connection with the bond-certificate drive, he toured some fifty-nine cities, largely in the western and southern parts of the country, during a two-and-a-half-month period; it was a formidable undertaking. See O'Doherty, pp 10, 48–9 and 51–9; and de Valera itinerary, *c.* Sept. 1919 (N.L.I., Devoy Papers, unmarked box). War Cabinet 624 (min. 3), 25 Sept. 1919 (P.R.O., CAB. 23/12).

4. For a discussion of the strategy to present the Irish case most effectively see Willard DeLue to D. F. Cohalan, 26 Jan. 1920 (N.L.I., DeLue Papers, MS. 8534). See Murray to Walsh, 30 July 1919, and A. E. Spriggs to Walsh, 31 July 1919 (L.C., Walsh Papers, box 190).

5. Walsh to O'Kelly, 2 April 1920 (N.Y.P.L., Walsh Papers, box 125); Wickersham to Lord Bryce, 15 July 1919, and Storey to Bryce, 22 Dec. 1919 (Bodl., Bryce Papers, vol. 21, fol. 192, and

vol. 10, fols 113–14). Indeed, questions were asked in parliament as to whether the cordial receptions accorded de Valera by various state officials did not constitute 'unfriendly acts' towards Great Britain. 6 May 1920, *Hansard* 5 (Commons), cxxviii, col. 2216.

6. See *N.Y.T.*, 26 and 27 Aug. 1919. In fact both the State Department and the British Embassy were concerned about the diplomatic implications of de Valera's stay in the United States. In December 1919 the Attorney-General advised Lansing that de Valera had been carefully observed by his department but had not broken any laws; the British felt they were safer in not protesting about de Valera's activities as long as the American government made no move in any way to recognise him or the Irish Republic. A. Mitchell Palmer to Sec. of State, 4 Dec. 1919 (N.A., 841d.00/103, roll 214); Sir William Wiseman to Sir Ian Malcolm, 1 July 1919, and R. C. Lindsay to F.O., 14 July 1919 (Beaverbrook Library, Lloyd George Papers, F 46/1/9). Certainly the confidence of nationalist leaders in Ireland was very much strengthened by the reports they received about the enthusiastic welcome given to de Valera by the American people. See 19 Aug. 1919, *Dáil Éireann proc. 1919–21*, pp 139 and 141; R. Brennan, 'Propaganda report', 21 Aug. 1919; and H. Sheehy-Skeffington and T. Kelly, 'Report of annual Árd-Chomhairle of Sinn Féin', 21 Aug. 1919 (N.L.I., Barton Papers, MS. 8786). See *G.A.*, 28 June 1919; *Irish World*, 28 June 1919; *C.S.M.*, 24 and 25 June 1919; and Chicago *Tribune*, 15 July 1919.

7. The loan was thought by some to be the most important of the several nationalist ambitions. James E. Deery to Golden, 31 Jan. 1920 (N.L.I., Golden Papers, MS. 13141). A controversy arose as to whether the Irish Victory Fund should have been sent to Ireland. Apart from the fact that the fund was not a loan and that it was a fairly small amount ($1,005,080), it was clearly raised with the object in mind of carrying out agitation, perhaps in both the United States and Ireland, but not to provide the operating revenue for an Irish government. The fund was used to finance de Valera's mission in the United States, to pay the expenses of the American Commission for Irish Independence, for grants to the bond-certificate drive, and for grants to Ireland and the Irish mission in Paris. The Irish Victory Fund was closed in August 1919. See Tansill, pp 347–8; McCartan, pp 143–5; and O'Doherty, pp 63–4.

8. Harry Boland to James K. McGuire, 11 Sept. 1919 (A.I.H.S., Cohalan Papers, drawer 2), and de Valera to Trustees, FOIF, 20 Sept. 1919 (*Ibid.*, drawer 1). The prospectus, issued in early October, said that a quota of $10,000,000 of bond-certificates would be sold in several denominations and that they could be exchanged at par value for gold bonds, which would ultimately return 5 per cent interest 'one month after the Republic has received international recognition'. The purpose of the loan was

'to finance the Elected Government of the Republic in projects of National Reconstruction and for such other purposes as the Government may decide'. (N.L.I., Devoy Papers, unmarked box). The Dáil originally authorised a loan of $1,250,000; however, after de Valera appraised the situation in America this amount was increased to $25,000,000. Of the amount authorised $10,000,000 (rather than the earlier $5,000,000) was selected as a practical goal in the hope of raising at least half that amount. See O'Doherty, pp 40–1; *Dáil Éireann proc. 1919–21*, pp 132–4, 139 and 150. De Valera said that he hoped to draw money 'only from those who seek to serve a good cause, not from those who want immediate pecuniary profit', and W. Bourke Cockran said: 'I do not mean that these bonds will be bought as commercial investments.' De Valera to Walsh, Sept. 1919 (N.Y.P.L., Walsh Papers, box 124); *N.Y.T.*, 11 Jan. 1920; and Walsh to all state and city chairmen, 8 Dec. 1919 (N.Y.P.L., Cockran Papers, box 17). The failure of the public to understand the financial risks of the Irish bond-certificates is illustrated by a letter to President Wilson asking if the money raised would purchase Ireland's independence, and, if not, whether there would be any way for the purchasers to get their money back or would it be considered 'donated to Ireland and her cause'. Joseph V. O'Connor to Wilson, 24 Jan. 1920, and Alvey A. Adee (2nd Assistant Secretary of State) to O'Connor, 12 Feb. 1920 (N.A., 841d.51/5, roll 243).

9. Walsh and Dunne seemed to have some misgivings about directing the bond-certificate drive, but agreed to do so rather than weaken the nationalist movement. Walsh to Dunne, 12 Aug. 1919, de Valera to Walsh, Sept. 1919, and Walsh to de Valera, 2 Oct. 1919 (N.Y.P.L., Walsh Papers, box 124); and P. Lavelle, *James O'Mara: a staunch Sinn-Féiner 1873–1948* (Dublin, 1961), pp 138–41. Walsh also recommended that the chairmen attempt to consolidate the Irish-American organisations for the sake of the bond-certificate drive, although this was not particularly successful. See Boland to Cockran, 20 Nov. 1919, and 'Instructions on organization for Irish bond-certificate campaign', n.d., and Frank P. Walsh to all state and city chairmen, 8 Dec. 1919 (N.Y.P.L., Cockran Papers, box 17). O'Doherty, pp 66–76 and 93–120; Lavelle, pp 144–6 and 153; F. P. Walsh, circular letter, 15 Jan. 1920 (N.Y.P.L., Cockran Papers, box 17); Monteith, pp 239–40; and John J. Splain to Cockran, 17 Feb. 1920 (N.Y.P.L., Cockran Papers, box 17). The remainder of the money raised by the sale of the bond-certificates stayed in United States banks and became the subject of several long litigations which were not settled until the 1930s. Lynch, pp 216–18.

10. Splain felt that Cohalan should have been put in charge of the bond-certificate campaign; he was convinced that those directing it did not appreciate the problems involved. Splain to Cockran, 17 Feb. 1920 (N.Y.P.L., Cockran Papers, box 17); and Splain to

Walsh, 17 Sept. 1919 (N.Y.P.L., Walsh Papers, box 124). Slattery
to Walsh, 3 Jan. 1921 (*Ibid.*, box 127); Deery to Golden, 31 Jan.
1920, and Golden to Walsh, 5 Feb. 1920 (N.L.I., Golden Papers,
MS. 13141). One friend of Golden's, very distressed at the lack
of support that the Irish-American community gave the drive,
concluded that they were 'permanently lost to Ireland'. The failure
of the Irish-Americans, and especially those with means, to support the bond-certificate campaign became a common complaint.

11. See H. B. Hastings to Wilson, 19 Dec. 1919, and Carter Glass to
Hastings, 22 Dec. 1919 (N.A., 841d.51/1, roll 243); and D. F.
Houston (Secretary of the Treasury) to Walsh, 7 Feb. 1920
(N.Y.P.L., Walsh Papers, box 125). Memorandum from O.L.M. to
Albert re Joseph V. O'Connor to Wilson, 24 Jan. 1920 (N.A.,
841d.51/5, roll 243); Williams to P. B. Forsyth, 29 Jan. 1920
(L.C., Williams Papers, box 50); and *Wall Street Journal*, 4 Feb.
1920.

12. Both Dr McCartan and C. C. Tansill give their versions of the
tangled policy in regard to the 'Irish Republic' during the first
half of 1919. McCartan refused to participate in the Irish Race
Convention because no acknowledgment of the Republic was
planned; on the other hand, precisely for this reason such moderates as Cardinal Gibbons were persuaded to take part. McCartan,
pp 70–88; and Tansill, pp 288–306. *N.Y.T.*, 24 June 1919; Frank
P. Walsh to W. Bourke Cockran, 13 March 1920 (N.Y.P.L.,
Cockran Papers, box 17). On his several tours de Valera made
specific appeals for American recognition of Ireland, and on a
local level he was often successful. An interesting example was
the Montana legislature, which passed a resolution asking that
Congress demand that the President extend recognition to Ireland;
the President, however, was also informed that the Montana
legislators voted for the resolution because 'we knew it could cut
no figure anyhow'. See —— to Wilson, 11 Aug. 1919 (L.C.,
Wilson Papers, file VI, no. 3926, box 558); and resolution of the
House and Senate of Montana, 12 Aug. 1919 (N.A., 841d.00/89,
roll 214).

13. Among the other pro-Irish witnesses were Lindsay Crawford,
John E. Milholland, Mary F. McWhorter, James K. McGuire,
Major Eugene F. Kinkead, W. Bourke Cockran, Father F. X.
McCabe, Daniel T. O'Connell, Shaemus O'Sheel, Katherine
Hughes, Joseph McGarrity and John J. Splain. For these hearings
George L. Fox organised an anti-Irish delegation, largely of Prot-
estant clergymen, who argued that no Irish Republic existed and
that the Irish question was a British domestic problem. U.S.
Congress, House of Representatives, Committee on Foreign
Affairs, Hearings on H. Res. 3404, *To provide for the salaries of
a minister and consuls to the Republic of Ireland*, 66th Congress,
2nd Session, 1920, pp 4–16, 17–40 and 40–59. Mason to Stephen
G. Porter, 17 April 1920 (A.I.H.S., Cohalan Papers, drawer 3).

In fact there was a substantial amount of opposition to the Mason resolution among native Americans. For the several versions of how the original resolution was changed see McCartan, pp 184–8; Tansill, pp 353–8; and O'Doherty, pp 86–8. See also *Congressional Record*, 66th Congress, 2nd Session, vol. 59, pp 6669, 7127, 7325, 7712, 7767, 7957, 8680, 9292–5 and 9349–50; and *Irish World*, 29 May and 5 June 1920. After some discussion Lloyd George decided to make no reply to letter. See Sir Auckland Geddes to Lord Curzon, 5 May 1920, and minutes, and F.O. to Geddes, 20 May 1920 (P.R.O., F.O. 371/4550).

14. De Valera to Wilson, 29 April 1920, and Tumulty to Bainbridge Colby, 29 April 1920 (N.A., 701.4111/336, box 6296). See Office of the Solicitor, Department of State, 'Memorandum on picketing of the British Embassy by sympathizers with the so-called Irish Republic', 3 April 1920, and Chief Special Agent, Department of State, 'Memorandum on Irish pickets', 16 April 1920 (N.A., 701.411/377, box 6296); R. C. Lindsay to Curzon, 8 April 1920 (P.R.O., F.O. 371/4550); McCartan, pp 176–81; and *Irish World*, 10 and 17 April 1920. The pickets, some of whom were Irish-American and some of whom belonged to the American Women's Pickets, were brought to Washington by Maloney, but although financed through the *Irish World*, they did not work very well with the Irish nationalist movement. Mrs Gertrude Corless, the leader of the American Women's Pickets, resented the attempts of Harry Boland to give her instructions and assignments. Mrs Corless to Mrs Peter Golden, 24 Aug. 1920 (N.L.I., Golden Papers, MS. 13141, folder vi). The conservative Irish-American leadership tended to dislike women pickets because they included a large mixture of socialists and liberal thinkers.

15. T. H. Mahony, *Ireland and secession, an answer to Lloyd George* (New York, 1920); and K. Hughes, *English atrocities in Ireland* (New York, 1920).See also L. Crawford, *The Problem of Ulster* (New York, 1920); *In darkest Ulster* (New York, n.d.); E. F. McSweeney, *America first: dedicated to the teachers and students in the schools and colleges of America* (Boston, 1920); E. F. McSweeney, *De-Americanizing young America: poisoning the sources of our national history and traditions* (Boston, 1920); *Ireland and British misrule: Lloyd George's insincerity* (Washington, 1920); W. McCormick, *Irish republican arbitration courts* (Washington, 1920); W. McCormick, *Irish electors again proclaim the Republic* (Washington, 1920); *Ireland under English intrigue* (Washington, 1920); J. X. Regan, *What made Ireland Sinn Féin* (Boston, 1921); and T. H. Mahony, *Similarities between the American and Irish revolutions* (New York, 1921). For three interesting suggestions for moderate solutions see T. C. Johnson, *The Irish tangle and a way out* (New York, 1920); P. W. Wilson, *The Irish case before the court of public opinion* (New York, 1920); and F. Weigle, *Ireland as it is today* (n.p., 1920).

16. See Tumulty to Attorney-General A. Mitchell Palmer and Senators Key Pittman, Peter Gerry and Carter Glass, 15 June 1920 (L.C., Tumulty Papers, box 4). For an analysis also see T. Hachey, 'The Irish question: the British Foreign Office and the American political conventions of 1920', *Éire–Ireland*, iii, no. 3 (autumn 1968), pp 92–106. See also Irish Committee to Henry Cabot Lodge, 1 June 1920 (Massachusetts Historical Society, Lodge Papers, box H–O); Tansill, pp 373–83; and McCartan, pp 192–200.

17. T. T. Martin to Cohalan, 12 June 1920 (A.I.H.S., Cohalan Papers, drawer 1); and statement by de Valera, *c.* summer 1920 (N.L.I., Golden Papers, MS. 13141, folder ii). The Labour Party and several state conventions of the Democrats and Republicans passed resolutions, but the Irish question did not officially become part of the presidential campaign. See Walsh to Seán T. O'Kelly, 5 Aug. 1920 (N.Y.P.L., Walsh Papers, box 126). Walsh had earlier told George Gavan Duffy that the Republicans had attempted to 'pussy foot' with the Irish but that de Valera had stood firmly for a pledge of recognition or nothing. Walsh to Duffy, 15 June 1920 (N.L.I., Duffy Papers, MS. 5582). F. T. F. Dumont (American Consul in Dublin) to Sec. of State, 15 June 1920 (N.A., 841d.00/209, roll 216). Despite the diminishing likelihood of effective pressure to force the government to recognise Ireland by October 1920, Fred K. Nielsen, Solicitor of the State Department, outlined for the Secretary the conditions for recognition of rebellious nations. His conclusion was that by all standards of international law no 'state of war' existed in Ireland and the republican government could not be regarded as a belligerent power: 'Obviously Ireland has not established its independence to such an extent as to justify her recognition by this government.' Nielsen to Sec. of State, 5 Oct. 1920 (L.C., Nielsen Papers, box 4).

18. MacManus, pp 105–8; Tansill, pp 341–4; Splain in Fitz-Gerald, pp 242–54; and Rt Rev. M. J. Gallagher, *Statement dealing with matters which arose out of the visit to the United States of America of the Hon. Éamon de Valera* (Detroit, 1921). See the often cited passage from a letter from de Valera to Griffith: 'The trouble is purely one of personalities. . . . Big as the country is, it was not big enough to hold the Judge and myself.' P. Béaslaí, *Michael Collins and the making of a new Ireland,* ii, pp 4–7. For examples of the very cool relations see Cohalan to Golden, 13 and 17 March 1919, and Golden to Cohalan, 15 March 1919 (N.L.I., Golden Papers, MS. 13141); and Dr Maloney's observation about that 'ubiquitous four flusher Cohalan'. Maloney to Oswald Garrison Villard, 2 May 1919 (Harvard University Library, Villard Papers, bms Am 1323, vol. 1878).

19. Splain complained of de Valera that 'He doesn't know America, and apparently some of those who are directing him don't know

America,' and he stated that the campaign would be going better if Judge Cohalan's suggestions had been followed. Splain to Walsh, 17 Sept. 1919 (N.Y.P.L., Walsh Papers, box 124). Walsh confessed to a friend of Mannix that a terrible mistake had been made in Portland. Mannix to Walsh, 6 Nov. 1919, and Walsh to James Robertson, 5 Dec. 1919 (*Ibid.*).

20. Walsh to Edward F. Dunne, 12 Aug. 1919, and Walsh to O'Kelly, 17 Sept. 1919 (*Ibid.*).

21. Certainly this was the editorial view of the *Globe*. See *Irish World*, 14 Feb. 1920; and McCartan, p. 151. Later in the debates on the Treaty James Burke told the Dáil: 'We started down the slippery slopes when the President agreed to accept a relation between Ireland and England similar to that between Cuba and the United States.' 4 Jan. 1922, *Iris Dháil Éireann, tuairisg oifigiúil, diosbóireacht ar an gConnradh idir Éire agus Sasana do signigheadh i Lundain ar an 6adh lá de mhí na Nodlag 1921; official report, debate on the Treaty between Great Britain and Ireland signed in London on the 6th December 1921* (Dublin, [1922]), p. 257. Dr Maloney thought de Valera's statements a serious compromise, and Mrs Golden wrote her husband: 'Indeed it seems to me nothing short of a calamity that de V. should have said it just at this time.' McGarrity disagreed with the interview but thought that it might teach de Valera to be more careful. Mrs Golden to Golden, 16 Feb. 1920 (N.L.I., Golden Papers, MS. 13141, folder vi); and McCartan, pp 150–2. On the other hand, James K. McGuire thought that it would do no harm and be 'forgotten in a week'. McGuire to Cohalan, 10 Feb. 1920 (A.I.H.S., Cohalan Papers, drawer 3). Devoy stated that his comments were 'mild, fair and friendly criticism', although in fact the general tone of the *Gaelic American* was so extreme as to make any comment seem like an attack. *G.A.*, 21 Feb. and 12 March 1920.

22. Mrs Golden to Golden, 16 Feb. 1920 (N.L.I., Golden Papers, MS. 13141, folder iv); de Valera to Cohalan, 20 Feb. 1920, and Cohalan to de Valera, 22 Feb. 1920, cited in Tansill, appendix, pp 446–9. Harry Boland to Golden, 4 March 1920, and Mrs Golden to Golden, 2 March 1920 (N.L.I., Golden Papers, *Ibid.*). Both Tansill and McCartan have vivid descriptions of this so-called 'trial' of de Valera. Tansill, pp 65–8; and McCartan, pp 160–9.

23. An illuminating illustration of the depth of the divisions within the nationalist movement is Diarmuid Lynch's resignation from the Dáil as a result of his disagreement with de Valera's concept of what should be done in the United States. See Lynch's letters to the Dáil and to his constituents dated 19 July 1920. *Dáil Éireann proc. 1919–21*, pp 188–90. Statement by de Valera *c.* summer 1920, and de Valera to Illinois state council, FOIF, 16 June 1920 (N.L.I., Golden Papers, MS. 13141, folder iii). For expulsion of IPL see Lynch to Golden, 24 July 1920, Mrs Golden to Lynch,

6 Aug. 1920, and a circular letter from Mrs Golden to newspapers and FOIF branches throughout the country, 10 Aug. 1920 (N.L.I., Golden Papers, *Ibid*).

24. De Valera to Bishop Gallagher, 6 Aug. 1920 (N.Y.P.L., Walsh Papers, box 126). Tansill, pp 386–8 and 691–2; and 'Notes for proposed call to Chicago convention' (N.L.I., Golden Papers, MS. 13141, folder ii). For the bishop's version of these events see Gallagher, *Statement dealing with matters which arose out of the visit to the United States of America of the Hon. Éamon de Valera.* See also de Valera to Diarmuid Lynch, 6 Aug. 1920 (A.I.H.S., Cohalan Papers, drawer 1). For an interesting account of the meeting and a shrewd analysis of the situation see Thomas F. Cooney to Cohalan, 24 Sept. 1920 (*Ibid.*). As R. H. Hadow, clerk in the American department of the Foreign Office, observed, 'Altogether the U.S. Irish have got two wars on hand—against England and among themselves.' Minutes, 19 Oct. 1920 (P.R.O., F.O. 371/4552).

25. O'Kelly to Devoy, 24 June 1920 (N.L.I., Devoy Papers, box N–OL). Count Plunkett told the Dáil on 6 August 1920 that there was a 'dispute between certain people in America and the President. These people thought that they in America had a right to dictate the policy of the Republic. The President naturally held a different view. . . . The trouble was now practically over. The President was sure of his ground, and the greater volume of Irish opinion in the United States had rallied to his support.' *Dáil Éireann proc. 1919–21*, p. 195. See also *Irish World*, 10 July and 28 Aug. 1920.

26. McCartan, pp 209–10; Lynch, p. 214; *Irish World*, 27 Nov. 1920; and S. Cronin, 'The Fenian tradition', *Irish Times*, 22 April 1969.

27. Lavelle, p. 182. At least some welcomed the open break with the leaders of the FOIF. Mrs Peter Golden wrote in August: 'I am convinced that whatever the cost the most important thing at this time is to give Dan [Cohalan] the knock-out blow. He must GO and what ever the I.P.L. can do to hasten his going I feel it is our duty to do.' Mrs Golden to M. E. Hickey, 11 Aug. 1920 (N.L.I., Golden Papers, MS. 13141, folder ii). *Irish World*, 27 Nov. 1920; and Lavelle, pp 184–5. See R. F. Downing, *A report* (n.p., 1920), which described the obstructionist tactics of the FOIF leaders and the need for a new organisation; and 'Report of first annual state convention, Montana AARIR', 12 Feb. 1921 (L.C., Walsh Papers, file B, box 190).

28. Lynch to FOIF, 7 Oct. and 19 Nov. 1919 (Catholic University of America Archives, Shahan Papers); and *G.A.*, 16 and 30 Oct. 1919. FOIF numbers shrank from 100,749 regular members and 174,281 associates down to a mere 20,000. O'Donoghue in Lynch, p. 241. De Valera on one occasion told the Dáil that the AARIR numbered over half a million and on another 800,000, although these

estimates seem over-optimistic. 10 May 1921, *Dáil Éireann proc.
1919–21*, p. 288; and 2 March 1922, *Dáil Éireann, tuairisg oifigiúil
(official report)* [*1921–22*] (Dublin, [1922]), p. 216. The British
Embassy in Washington understood that enrolment in the AARIR
grew through a system whereby a member was paid between 25
and 50 cents for every new person he brought into the organisation. J. Joyce Broderick to Comptroller General, Department of
Overseas Trade, 2 Feb. 1921 (P.R.O., F.O. 371/5632). Despite
the collapse of the FOIF, it held the loyalties of many of the old
Irish-American leaders. 'As for the choice between Mr Harry
Boland and Judge Cohalan, give me Cohalan,' said Dr W. P.
Slattery. 'The so-called Irish leaders that I have personally met
and who were shooting off the hot air during this entire campaign
to my mind could not successfully run a ward caucus.' Slattery
to Frank P. Walsh, 3 Jan. 1921 (N.Y.P.L., Walsh Papers, box 127).
See Golden to Mrs Golden, 20 April 1921 (N.L.I., Golden Papers,
MS. 13141, folder i); and *Irish World*, 11 and 18 Dec. 1920. For a
full report of the convention by Jeremiah A. O'Leary see *Sinn
Féiner*, 30 April 1921; and by Harry Boland see 17 Aug. 1921,
Dáil Éireann rep. 1921–22, pp 17–18.
29. McCartan, pp 216–18. On 20 October 1920 de Valera himself sent
an unsuccessful formal appeal to the American government for
recognition of the Irish Republic. See also W. J. M. A. Maloney,
The recognised Irish Republic (New York, 1920); *We must
recognize the Irish Republic* (Los Angeles, n.d.); M. MacSwiney,
The background of the Irish Republic (Chicago, 1921); and A. S.
Green, *The Irish Republican Army* (Washington, n.d.).
30. Béaslaí, ii, p. 18. Other pamphlets published by the AARIR in-
cluded A. McCormick, *The Black and Tans* (Chicago, n.d.),
Torture and terror (Chicago, n.d.), K. O'Callaghan, *The Limerick
curfew murders of March 7th, 1921* (Chicago, n.d.), J. P.
McGarigle, *The master mind* (Niagara Falls, n.d.), *America wake
up* (Chicago, n.d.), *The United States has paid its debt to France*
(Chicago, n.d.), and L. Ginnell, *Ireland's case for freedom*
(Chicago, 1921). Walsh to O'Mara, 4 May 1921, Kinkead to
Walsh, 2 May 1921, and Basil M. Manly to Walsh, 7 July 1921
(N.Y.P.L., Walsh Papers, box 110).
31. George E. Brennan to Wilson, 2 Sept. 1920, Tumulty to Wilson,
2 Sept. 1920, Wilson to Tumulty, n.d., Senator Henry F. Ashurst
to Wilson, 7 Sept. 1920, Frank P. Walsh to Wilson, 1 Sept. 1920,
Edwin A. Grozier (editor of the Boston *Post*) to Wilson, 16 Sept.
1920, and White House memorandum, 4 Sept. 1920 (L.C., Wilson
Papers, file VI, no. 5315, box 624); and Colby to Wilson, 2
Sept. 1920, Edward F. Dunne to Colby, 20 Oct. 1920, and
Frank P. Walsh to Colby, 25 Oct. 1920 (L.C., Colby Papers,
box 3–B).
32. Peter Golden to Harding, *c.* summer 1920 (N.L.I., Golden Papers,
MS. 13141, folder i–c); *Sinn Féiner*, 30 Oct. 1920; Cox to Tumulty,

10 Oct. 1920 (L.C., Tumulty Papers, box 4); and Roosevelt to Murray, 9 Oct. 1920, cited in Murray, p. 90.

33. For a good analysis of the importance of the Irish question in the 1920 presidential election see Ward, *Ireland,* pp 220–4; and also Gerson, pp 105–6. Miss Leonora O'Reilly to Frank P. Walsh, 28 May 1921, Timothy Healy (American Federation of Labour) to Walsh, 17 June 1921, and Thomas P. O'Flaherty to Walsh, 24 June 1921 (N.Y.P.L., Walsh Papers, box 110); H. S. Chapee to Department of State, 6 July 1921 (N.A., 841d.00/385, roll 218); and s.s. *Baltic* strike hand-bill (N.L.I., Golden Papers, MS. 13141, folder vi). For a list of the activities of merely the Washington, DC, Irish-Americans see R. F. Downing in Fitz-Gerald, pp 216–17. The following resolutions were introduced in Congress: Mason (H.R. 117, H. Con. Res. 4 and 5, H. Res. 26), Burke (H.J. Res. 1), and Kindred (H. Res. 21), 11 April 1921, *Congressional Record,* 65th Congress, 1st Session, vol. 61, pp 89, 99–101; Ryan (H.J. Res. 89), 27 April 1921, *Ibid.,* p. 742; O'Brien (H.J. Res. 96), *Ibid.,* p. 896. For Senate activity see LaFollette (S.J. Res. 1), 12 April 1921, and speeches, 24 and 25 April 1921, *Ibid.,* pp 152, 637–51; Norris (S.J. Res. 27), 16 April 1921, and speeches, 20 and 21 June 1921, *Ibid.,* pp 2759, 2803 and 2809–10. See also *Ibid.,* pp 899, 1144, 1403, 1721, 2123, 2256 and 2366.

34. 'Maloney's memorandum on Washington Commission on British Atrocities', McCartan, appendix vi, p. 259; also pp 210–16, 222 and 235–7. The Committee of One Hundred was extremely impressive also: eleven United States senators, six state governors, several mayors and congressmen, ten professors or university administrators, and a substantial list of editors, labour leaders, social workers, liberal journalists, and clergymen of all faiths. Among the most notable were Morris Hillquit, W. Randolph Hearst, Owen R. Lovejoy, Amos Pinchot, William Allen White, Dr W. E. B. Du Bois and Miss Abby Scott Baker. Committee of One Hundred, list of members, 23 Sept. 1920, and second list of members, 5 Oct. 1920 (Harvard University Library, Villard Papers, bms Am 1323, vol. 1878). Senator John Sharp Williams indignantly refused the invitation to serve on the Committee of One Hundred. G. C. Osborn, *John Sharp Williams* (Baton Rouge, 1943), p. 352. A staff was also appointed for the commission: Dr William MacDonald, former professor at Brown University and editor of the *Nation,* was made secretary; Royal W. France served as treasurer for both the committee and the commission; Albert Coyle transcribed the hearings; and Harold Kellock dealt with publicity.

35. Actually Howe wanted the commission to send a delegation to Ireland to investigate conditions in person; however, such plans did not materialise because of internal disagreements and the objections of the British government. Howe to Villard, Nov. 1920 (Harvard University Library, Villard Papers, bms Am 1323, vol.

1878). Sir Hamar Greenwood, Irish Chief Secretary, dismissed the idea outright, noting that the government had prevented Archbishop Mannix from entering Ireland, although he was a British subject. See minutes on cable from Geddes to F.O., 26 Nov. 1920 (P.R.O., F.O. 371/4554); and *American Commission on Conditions in Ireland: interim report* (Chicago, 1921), pp 120–5. This refusal to permit Americans to travel in Ireland provoked a protest from Senators Norris, France, LaFollette, Ransdell, Gronna, Chamberlain, Fletcher, Shields, Thomas J. Walsh and David I. Walsh, although the Department of State was compelled to admit that the British had the right to control the movement of foreigners in and out of their territories. See Senators George W. Norris et al. to Bainbridge Colby, 15 Dec. 1920, and Senator Thomas J. Walsh to Norman H. Davis, 14 Jan. 1921 (N.A., 841.00/265 and –/285, rolls 217 and 218); and Davis to each of these senators, 11 Jan. 1921 (L.C., Walsh Papers, file B, box 190). *Evidence on conditions in Ireland*, ed. A. Coyle (Washington, 1921), p. 5; and Geddes to F.O., 16 and 29 Sept. 1920, and F.O. to Geddes, 7 Oct. 1920 (P.R.O., F.O. 371/4552).

36. See *Evidence on conditions in Ireland*, ed. A. Coyle. On attempting to enter the United States, O'Callaghan was stopped because he had no passport. His subsequent statements denied his entry into the United States as a political refugee, but he was finally accepted as a 'seaman'; however, such a classification permitted him to spend some time in America, during which he gave his testimony before the commission, ostensibly while he searched for a new ship. See 'Memorandum of conversation between Mr Craigie and Norman H. Davis', 31 Jan. 1921 (L.C., Davis Papers, box 9); and R. W. Flourney, 'Memorandum dealing with Lord Mayor O'Callaghan', 25 March 1921, and Fred K. Nielsen to Sec. of State, 29 March 1921 (L.C., Nielsen Papers, box 5). See McCartan, pp 215–16 and 221–23. For an appreciation of the work of the commission see Lincoln Colcord to W. J. M. A. Maloney, 17 April 1921 (N.Y.P.L., Maloney Collection, Maloney Papers, box 19). Frederick T. F. Dumont, the American Consul in Dublin, told the State Department that the commission could not be relied upon to present objective information, and that because the revolutionary activities were secret no knowledge of them could be effectively presented, only the British reactions to them. He also called attention to the facts that Senator Fletcher of Florida, one of the Committee of One Hundred, was likely to be influenced by his son-in-law Lionel Smith-Gordon, who directed the Sinn Féin land bank, and that in America Irish revolutionary interests had joined forces with anti-British oil interests. Dumont to Sec. of State, 12 Nov. 1920 and 28 Jan. 1921 (N.A., 841d.00/259 and –/314, rolls 217 and 218).

37. W. A. Neilson, president of Smith College, felt obliged to resign because he was convinced there would not be 'a fair distribution

of witnesses'. See Neilson to Villard, 30 Nov. 1920 (Harvard University Library, Villard Papers, bms Am 1321, vol. 1878); Charles Noble Gregory to Lord Bryce, 13 Jan. 1921, and Moorfield Storey to Bryce, 6 April 1921 (Bodl., Bryce Papers, vol. 14, fol. 69); and Senator John Sharp Williams to Demarest Lloyd, 18 Oct. 1920, and Lloyd to Williams, 22 Oct. 1920 (L.C., Williams Papers, box 53). *G.A.*, 2 Oct. 1920 and 9 April 1921. The testimony was also printed in the *Nation*, and at the request of L. Hollingsworth Wood a large number of copies was published, which Villard was unable to sell; indeed, by 1921 Villard was generally dissatisfied with the work and the attitude of the commission. See Villard to Wood, 20 and 26 Jan. and 25 March 1921, Wood to Villard, 21 Jan. 1921, and Villard to Norman Thomas, 29 March 1921 (Harvard University Library, Villard Papers, *Ibid.*). McCartan has suggested that these volumes were compiled by Dr Maloney with assistance from Dr Coyle. McCartan, pp 235–6.

38. Villard to George A. Dunning, 13 April 1921 (Harvard University Library, Villard Papers, bms Am 1323, vol. 1878); McCartan in fact called special attention to the success the reports did have in Europe. McCartan, pp 236–7. See also Albert Coyle to Art Ó Briain, 14 May 1921, and Ó Briain to de Valera, 31 March 1921 (N.L.I., Ó Briain Papers, MS. 8429). The commission was hard pressed to repay a loan of $10,000 to Dr Maloney and had fairly substantial printing costs. McCartan says that James O'Mara provided some of the money to meet publishing expenses. L. Hollingsworth Wood to Walsh, 18 and 21 May 1921 (N.Y.P.L., Walsh Papers, box 110).

39. O'Callaghan to American Red Cross, 16 Dec. 1920, and Farrand to O'Callaghan, 16 Dec. 1920 (N.A., 841d.48/5, roll 241). Various appeals to the American Red Cross during the autumn had been a source of concern to Sir Auckland Geddes and the Foreign Office, who regarded these efforts as motivated purely for the sake of propaganda. Geddes to F.O., 12 Nov. 1920, and minutes, and F.O. to Geddes, 11 Dec. 1920 (P.R.O., F.O. 371/4613). See Norman H. Davis to President, 15 Dec. 1920 (N.A., 841d.48/-a, roll 241). Memorandum by Sir Arthur Stanley (director of the joint committee of the British Red Cross and the Knights of St John of Jerusalem) to F.O., 29 Dec. 1920 (P.R.O., F.O. 317/4613); and American Red Cross to Mrs Golden, 30 Dec. 1920 (N.L.I., Golden Papers, MS. 13141, folder ii). Mrs Golden was in no way satisfied. Mrs Golden to American Red Cross, 1 Jan. 1921 (*Ibid.*) See Congressman James A. Gallivan to Bainbridge Colby, 14 Dec. 1920, and Alvey A. Adee (Acting Secretary of State) to Gallivan, 20 Dec. 1920 (N.A., 841d.48/-, roll 241); McCartan, p. 224; and *Irish World*, 1 Jan. 1921.

40. See McCartan, pp 223–7; *American Committee for Relief in Ireland and Irish White Cross, Report* (New York, 1922), pp 17, 48 and 51; and L. Hollingsworth Wood to James G. Douglas, 19

Dec. 1920, S. Graveson to B. Haughton, 29 Dec. 1920, and S.
Graveson to F. E. Pollard, 29 Dec. 1920 (Friends' Historical
Library, Dublin, Relief Work Papers, 1916–21). The executive
committee consisted of successful and prominent Irish-Americans:
chairman Judge Morgan J. O'Brien; treasurer John J. Pulleyn;
secretary Richard Campbell; and members Edward J. McPike,
James A. Healy, Thomas F. Ryan, Nicholas F. Brady, John D.
Ryan, Senator Thomas J. Walsh, Edward L. Doheny, James J.
Phelan, James A. Flaherty, Joseph C. Pellitier, Senator David I.
Walsh, Lawrence Godkin, John Quinn, Senator James D. Phelan,
Martin J. Gillen, Thomas J. Maloney, J. W. McConaughy, William
P. Larkin, L. Hollingsworth Wood and Bishop M. J. Gallagher.

41. The group was led by Clemens J. France and included R. Barclay
Spicer, former head of the Friends' Service Committee to Baltic
States, Oren B. Wilber, a dairy and creamery owner, William Price,
an architect, Philip W. Furnas, a housing expert who had served
two years with the Friends' Relief Unit in France, John C. Barker,
an agricultural reconstruction expert who had been with the
Friends' Relief Unit in France, Walter C. Longstreth, a lawyer and
settlement worker, and, as secretary, Samuel Duff McCoy, an
author and journalist who had served with the American Red
Cross. See American Committee for Relief in Ireland broadsheet,
30 Jan. 1921 (L.C., Walsh Papers, file B, box 190); and Richard
Campbell to Bainbridge Colby, 12 Jan. 1921 (N.A., 841d.48/3, roll
241). Furnas had earlier testified before the American Commission
on Conditions in Ireland; and in fact the British observed that
France was the brother of Senator Joseph I. France of Maryland,
'one of our most active enemies'. R. H. Hadow, 23 Feb. 1921,
minutes to American Committee for Relief in Ireland, 17 Feb.
1921 (P.R.O., F.O. 371/6542). See memorandum of conversation
with Samuel Duff McCoy and G. Howland Shaw, 21 April 1921
(N.A., 841d.48/35, roll 241); and H. Seymour to Sir Auckland
Geddes, 30 March 1921 (P.R.O., F.O. 371/5663). *American Com-
mittee for Relief in Ireland and Irish White Cross, Report*, pp 57–8;
Report of the Irish White Cross to 31st August, 1922, ed. W. J.
Williams (Dublin, 1922), pp 39–40; and minutes of meeting of the
Advisory Committee, 14 Feb. 1921 (Friends' Historical Library,
Dublin, Relief Work Papers, 1916–21).

42. Hoover to Sec. of State, 11 March 1921 (N.A., 841d.48/7, roll 214);
and Richard Campbell to Thomas J. Walsh, 25 Feb. 1921, and
Lucey to Morgan J. O'Brien, 25 March 1921 (L.C., Walsh Papers,
file B, box 190). See *Report of the Irish White Cross to 31st
August, 1922*, ed. W. J. Williams, pp 17–18. Work began as early
as January to publicise the need for relief work in Ireland, and in
this regard the hearings of the American Commission on Conditions in Ireland were important. Richard Campbell, although
anxious to get the work under way before the public were diverted
by other Irish-American organisations, told Senator Thomas J.

Walsh that funds were coming in almost unsolicited. Campbell to Walsh, 8 and 11 Jan. 1921 (L.C., Walsh Papers, file B, box 190). Harding to O'Brien, 26 March 1921, cited in *American Committee for Relief in Ireland and Irish White Cross, Report*, pp 6 and 38–9, and a letter of thanks from L. O'Neill (Lord Mayor of Dublin) to Harding, 29 March 1921 (N.A., 841d.48/17, roll 241). See also James J. Phelan to Senator Henry Cabot Lodge, 27 March 1921 (Massachusetts Historical Society, Lodge Papers, box H–Z); and 7 and 21 April 1921, *Hansard* 5 (Commons), cxl, cols 461–2, 465–6 and 2051–4.

43. *American Committee for Relief in Ireland and Irish White Cross, Report*, pp 40–7 and 50; and *The need for relief in Ireland* (New York, *c.* 1921). For a vivid description of fund-raising efforts in the United States see *White Cross News* (n.d.) (N.L.I., Moore Papers, MS. 10558). Even the Red Cross, which had earlier felt that conditions in Ireland did not warrant its intervention, contributed $100,000. Memorandum of conversation between Mr Persons and Dr Bicknell of the Red Cross and the 3rd Assistant Secretary of State, 28 March 1921 (N.A., 841d.48/19, roll 241). Despite the interest and participation of Irish and English Quakers, the committee was unable to elicit any support from the American Friends, who not only refused to participate in the project but also resented the specific mention of Quaker participants in the delegation sent to Ireland, with its implication that the delegation was in some way authorised by the American Friends' Service Committee. S. Graveson to Rufus M. Jones (chairman of the American Friends' Service Committee), 30 March 1921, and Jones to Graveson, 19 April 1921 (Friends' Historical Library, Dublin, Relief Work Papers, 1916–21); and Bishop Michael J. Gallagher to F. D. Frankhouse, 13 April 1921 (Chancery Archives, Archdiocese of Detroit, Bishop Gallagher Papers). Geddes to F.O., 5 May 1921 (P.R.O., F.O. 371/5663). See also S. D. McCoy, *Distress in Ireland* (New York, 1921); *The need for relief in Ireland*; and M. Curti, *American philanthropy abroad: a history* (New Brunswick, 1963), p. 302.

44. Memorandum of conversation with Samuel Duff McCoy and G. Howland Shaw, 21 April 1921, and memorandum on Irish relief by G. Howland Shaw for Sec. of State, 29 April 1921 (N.A., 841d.48/35 and –/38, roll 241); and F. T. F. Dumont to Sec. of State, 22 March 1921 (*Ibid.*, 841d.00/339, roll 218). Geddes to F.O., 5 May 1921 (P.R.O., F.O. 371/5663). Curzon wrote that the 'American proposal is in the main political in character, constitutes an unwarrantable interference with the Government of a foreign State, would be indignantly rejected had it been made in analogous circumstances to the American Government, and ought to be firmly though politely refused.' Curzon to Geddes, *c.* 9 May 1921 (*Ibid.*); C.P. 2921, Curzon to Cabinet, 'Ireland and America', 9 May 1921 (P.R.O., CAB. 24/123); C. 36/21(4), 10 May 1921 (P.R.O., CAB. 23/25).

45. 'Memorandum of interview with the British Ambassador', 23 May 1921 (L.C., Hughes Papers, file 76(b) Gt Brit., box 175); and Geddes to F.O., 25 May 1921, and minutes, and F.O. to Geddes, 6 June 1921 (P.R.O., F.O. 371/5663). Despite the government's decision to prohibit American relief operations in Ireland, the committee maintained Clemens J. France as its agent and sent money to James G. Douglas in instalments of from $35,000 to $55,000 three or four times a month; these remittances stopped from 8 July to 8 September, when they were resumed until 28 June 1922. *American Committee for Relief in Ireland and Irish White Cross, Report*, pp 39–40 and 45–6.

46. Dumont said that 2,000 bags of flour which had been sent for relief purposes had eventually been sold to a Cork baker. Dumont to Sec. of State, 22 March 1921 (N.A., 841d.00/339, roll 218). No doubt the department was not comforted with Shaw's information that Hoover had withdrawn his support and that Captain Lucey had resigned as director of the relief fund because of the growing anti-British tone of the proceedings. G. Howland Shaw to Sec. of State, 15 April 1921, and Harding to Sec. of State, 20 April 1921 (N.A., 841d.00/339 and –/392, roll 218). Wilbur J. Carr to Dumont, Mason Mitchell and William P. Kent, 11 April 1921 (*Ibid.*, 841d.48/22a, b, and c, roll 241). Dumont to Sec. of State, 23 April 1921 (*Ibid.*, 841d.00/351, roll 218), and 17 May 1921 (*Ibid.*, 841d.48/27, roll 241). To substantiate his argument that Ireland was more prosperous than before, Dumont cited the statistics of joint stock banks, post office savings and trustee savings, and he said that 1919 had seen the highest marriage rate recorded in Ireland.

47. Dumont to Sec. of State, 9 June 1921, and Hughes to Dumont, 11 July 1921 (*Ibid.*, 841d.00/381, roll 218). Dumont's allegations that the relief funds were being used for revolutionary purposes cannot be seriously refuted until more data is made available, especially about the operation and finances of the Dáil government. The fairly elaborate and detailed report published by the Irish White Cross Society a year and a half after the funds would have been most useful to the Irish Republic suggests that Dumont may have been unduly sceptical of the motives of people like Douglas and a bit indifferent to dislocation caused by the fighting. Of course, this is not to say that none of the money found its way into the hands of the revolutionaries or their dependants. See *Report of the Irish White Cross to 31st August, 1922*, ed. W. J. Williams, appendix D., pp 125–40.

48. 'Memorandum of interview with the British Ambassador', 23 June 1921 (L.C., Hughes Papers, file 76(a), Gt Brit., box 175). For State Department correspondence on the Anglo-Japanese Alliance see *Foreign relations, 1920*, ii, pp 679–86; and *Ibid., 1921*, ii, pp 313–19; for British correspondence see *Documents on British foreign policy, 1919–1939*, 1st series, xiv, pp 145–322.

49. See John W. Davis to Sec. of State, 27 and 30 Jan. 1920 (N.A.,

K

841.00/123 and –/125, roll 214); Director of Naval Intelligence to F.O., 30 Aug. 1920 (P.R.O., F.O. 371/4551); and Colonel A. C. Carter (Scotland Yard) to C. J. Phillips (Foreign Office), 17 Dec. 1920 (*Ibid.*, F.O. 371/4555). Sir Hamar Greenwood to Curzon, 2 June 1921 (*Ibid.*, F.O. 371/5655); and George Harvey (American Ambassador in London) to Sec. of State, 3 and 20 June 1921, and Hughes to Harvey, 18 June 1921 (N.A., 841d.00/360 and –/370, roll 218). See also Gloster Armstrong to Curzon, 10 June 1921 (P.R.O., F.O. 371/5655). British Embassy, Washington, to Hughes, 17 June 1921 (N.A., 841d.00/379 and –/2372, roll 218); and 'Memorandum of interview with the British Ambassador', 29 June and 28 July 1921 (L.C., Hughes Papers, file 76(a), Gt Brit., box 175). For outraged comments see *C.S.M.*, 18 June 1921.

50. See *N.Y.T.*, 23 Nov., 5 and 15 Dec. 1919; and Delegates of the Protestant Churches of Ireland, *Facts about Ireland for the consideration of American citizens* (New York, 1920). Both de Valera and the Protestant Friends of Ireland (a branch of the FOIF) repudiated the incident, but the damage had been done. *N.Y.T.*, 29 and 30 Dec. 1919. Irish-American nationalists did propose that the Coote mission be stopped by a libel suit against them on the basis of their charges of Sinn Féin atrocities. J. Grattan Mythen to Frank P. Walsh, 8 Jan. 1920 (N.Y.P.L., Walsh Papers, box 125). Moorfield Storey wrote to Lord Bryce that he approved of the Ulster delegation, but he thought that it was too clerical in composition and that people who could talk economics and politics would be more effective. Storey to Bryce, 22 Dec. 1919 (Bodl., Bryce Papers, vol. 10, fols 113–14).

51. See Lloyd and Smith to Senator John Sharp Williams, 9 April 1920, Smith to Williams, 10 May 1920, and Lloyd to Williams, 29 Jan. 1921 (L.C., Williams Papers, boxes 51, 52 and 53); Geddes to Curzon, bi-monthly consular reports, March–April 1920 (P.R.O., F.O. 371/4596); Denis McCarthy in O'Grady, pp 91–7; and *Sinn Féiner*, 19 March and 2 April 1921. Lloyd to Colby, 17 April 1920 (N.A., 841d.00/177, roll 215).

52. Loyal Coalition to Wilson, 3 June 1920 (L.C., Wilson Papers, file VI, no. 3926, box 559); Lloyd to Williams, 10 and 22 June 1921, and Williams to Lloyd, 13 June 1921 (L.C., Williams Papers, box 55). Lloyd and Smith to Wilson, 23 May 1920 (N.A., 841d.01/7, roll 224); Lloyd to Wilson, 30 June 1920 (Wilson Papers, file VI, no. 3926, box 559); Lloyd to Wilson, 21 Oct. 1920 (L.C. Tumulty Papers, box 4); and Lloyd to Williams, 8 and 22 Oct. 1920, and Williams to Lloyd, 18 Oct. 1920 (L.C., Williams Papers, box 53). June 1920, *Congressional Record, Appendix*, 66th Congress, 1st Session, vol. 59, pp 9349–50; and G. A. Dunning to O. G. Villard, 10 April 1921 (Harvard University Library, Villard Papers, bms Am 1323, vol. 1878). The Loyal Coalition was supported in its anti-Irish activities by several other American organisations—the Ulster League of North America, the Anti-Imperialist League, the

Loyal Orange Order, the British-American League, the Free-masons—although none of the others seemed to have the anti-Irish campaign as their sole purpose.

53. T. J. Rousseau to Senator Thomas J. Walsh, 22 July 1921 (L.C., Walsh Papers, file B, box 190). 13 Aug. 1919, *Congressional Record*, 66th Congress, 1st Session, vol. 58, p. 3852; 12 Dec. 1919, U.S. Congress, *To provide for the salaries of a minister and consuls to the Republic of Ireland*, pp 18–40; and 'Are you ready for the test?', an editorial advocating war with England for Irish independence, Chicago *Tribune*, 15 July 1919. Williams to Frank Moore, 20 June 1921, and Williams to F. W. Farr, 28 Oct. 1919 (L.C., Williams Papers, boxes 55 and 48). F. S. Fitzgerald, *This side of paradise* (1920; repr. New York, 1960), p. 210; and S. Lewis, *Babbitt* (1920; repr. London, 1965).

54. E. R. Turner, *Ireland and England* (New York, 1919). See also E. R. Turner, 'America and the Irish question', *World's Work*, xxxviii (Oct. 1919), pp 580–9; E. R. Turner, 'The Sinn Féin and the United States', *Ibid.*, xl (Oct. 1920), pp 544–9; D. T. O'Connell, *Edward Raymond Turner: apostle and apologist of reaction* (Washington, 1919); and O. Wister, *A straight deal or the ancient grudge* (New York, 1920), passim. Wister's book was violently denounced by Edward F. McSweeney in his pamphlet *The super-hyphenate—the Anglo-Saxon American* (n.p., n.d.) and by D. T. O'Connell in *Owen Wister, advocate of racial hatred* (Washington, 1920). See also M. J. O'Brien, *A hidden phase of American history, Ireland's part in America's struggle for liberty* (New York, 1919); and J. X. Regan, *Ireland and the Presidents of the United States* (Boston, 1921). H. S. Canby, *Education by violence* (New York, 1919), pp 57–66 and 78–82; M. Storey and M. J. Jordan, *Americans of Irish lineage: their duties and their aims* (Boston, n.d.); and four pamphlets by G. L. Fox: *Light on the Irish question* (New Haven, n.d.), *More light on the Irish question* (New Haven, n.d.), *Lest we forget how disloyal the Irish Sinn Féin Roman Catholics were and are* (New Haven, n.d.), and *Poisoning the wells* (New Haven, n.d.). R. C. Escouflaire, *Ireland an enemy of the Allies?* (New York, 1920); and R. Dawson, *Red terror and green* (London, 1920).

55. W. S. Sims, *The victory at sea* (Garden City, 1919), pp 83–5. Sims wrote: 'The members of this organization [Sinn Féin] were not only openly disloyal, they were openly pro-German. They were not even neutral; they were working day and night for a German victory, for in their misguided minds a German victory signified an Irish Republic.' Sims gave several examples of Irish 'Sinn Féiners' outnumbering and assaulting American sailors, and of Irish priests denouncing American naval officers.

56. E. F. McSweeney, *Ireland is an American question* (New York, 1919); *Ireland's part in the world's war* (Chicago, n.d.); *The truth about Ireland in the Great War: an analysis of Admiral Sims'*

unfair attack on the Irish people (Washington, 1919); *The Irish mess and an attack on the U.S. Navy* (Boston, 1919); and Daniel T. O'Connell (Director, Irish National Bureau) to Josephus Daniels (Secretary of the Navy), 1 Nov. 1919 (A.I.H.S., Cohalan Papers, drawer 2).

57. *C.S.M.*, 9 June 1921.

58. *G.A.*, 18 and 25 June and 2 July 1921; *Sinn Féiner*, 25 June 1921; James J. Grogan, circular letter, 28 June 1921 (N.Y.P.L., Walsh Papers, box 110); and John D. Moore to Harding, 8 June 1921, and Moore to Denby, 14 June 1921 (A.I.H.S., Cohalan Papers, drawer 3). Major Michael J. Kelly planned to greet Sims upon his return with an 'ironic' declaration containing a list of 1,000 Irish-American war dead. Support for Sims was created by the Allied Loyalty League and Frank A. Vanderlip, Casper Whitney, Hamilton Holt and Demarest Lloyd, who also had a delegation waiting for Sims at the pier in New York. The rector of Grace Methodist Episcopal Church in New York said: 'He stood on the bridge, with that immortal fleet which combed the North Sea for the cowardly assassins of the deep, while certain vociferous groups [the Irish] were, as he declares, giving aid and comfort to the butchers of Berlin.' *C.S.M.*, 10, 14, 21, 22 and 23 June 1921; *Lit. Dig.*, lxix, no. 13 (25 June 1921), pp 7–9 and 18.

59. 20 July 1921, *Congressional Record*, 67th Congress, 1st Session, vol. 61, p. 4114. The *Christian Science Monitor* said this was 'the first occasion when a member of the Irish bloc admitted without equivocation what had become apparent to other senators, namely, that that body and the country had reached the state of utter boredom and complete impatience with the perennial tirades on the Irish question'. *C.S.M.*, 21 July 1921. Senator David I. Walsh had come to a similar conclusion earlier that month, as he revealed privately to W. J. M. A. Maloney: 'For some reason or other, I feel that there has been a slump in American sentiment on the Irish question. I do not know how to account for it. It seems to me that it is time for us to move slowly and cautiously, and give serious thought to the cause for the present widespread indifference of the American people toward the Irish struggle.' Walsh to Maloney, 5 July 1921 (N.Y.P.L., Maloney Collection, Maloney Papers, box 11).

60. Storey to Bryce, 6 April 1921 (Bodl., Bryce Papers, vol. 10, fols 170–1).

Chapter 7
AMERICA AND THE FOUNDING OF THE IRISH
FREE STATE, 1921–1923
(pp 177–193)

1. For British sensitivity to American and dominion opinion in the drafting of new Irish Home Rule legislation in 1919 see cabinet minutes. War Cabinet 628(4), 7 Oct. 1919 (P.R.O., CAB. 23/12);

C.P. 56, 4 Nov. 1919, 'First report of the cabinet committee on the Irish question' (P.R.O., CAB. 24/92); and cabinet meeting 5/19(2), 11 Nov. 1919, cabinet meeting 12/19(10), 10 Dec. 1919, and cabinet meeting 16/19(9), 10 Dec. 1919 (P.R.O., CAB. 23/18).

2. *Sinn Féiner*, 9 July 1921; Sir Auckland Geddes to F.O., 29 Nov. 1921 (P.R.O., F.O. 371/5633); and *G.A.*, 26 Feb., 14 May, 2, 9 and 23 July, and 8 and 15 Oct. 1921. The Clan took great precautions to see that no uninvited members of the 'reorganised Clan' were able to disrupt their meeting. 'Secret letter to delegates to Clan convention in Boston on 4 July 1921', n.d. (N.L.I., Devoy Papers, box Misc.). The FOIF struggled to gain congressional support to make the British pay their war debts (or alternatively surrender Canada or the West Indies), to exempt American ships from paying tolls at the Panama Canal (a long-standing Irish-American grievance), and to discourage any compromise with the British at the Washington Naval Disarmament Conference. Diarmuid Lynch to members of the Senate, 9 Aug 1921 (L.C., Walsh Papers, file B, box 190); Thomas McGrath to Senator John Sharp Williams, 30 Oct. 1921 (L.C., Williams Papers, box 56); Lynch to FOIF branches, 13 Sept. 1921 (Catholic University of America Archives, Shahan Papers); and FOIF circular letter, 3 Dec. 1921 (N.Y.P.L., Walsh Papers, box 111).

3. See John McBarron to Senator Thomas J. Walsh, 24 Sept. 1921, and Butte, Montana, AARIR to Harding, 24 Sept. 1921 (L.C., Walsh Papers, file B, box 190). 15 July 1921 (H. Res. 150), *Congressional Record*, 67th Congress, 1st Session, vol. 61, p. 3917; and Miss MacSwiney to Cockran, 31 July 1921, and Cockran to Miss MacSwiney, 11 Aug. 1921 (N.Y.P.L., Cockran Papers, box 18). Senator LaFollette introduced a resolution in the Senate on 22 November which expressed the hope that the negotiations might end in peace for Britain and Ireland, but this resolution was worked out beforehand by several of the Irish-American leaders and politicians. 22 Nov. 1921 (S. Res. 173), *Congressional Record*, 67th Congress, 1st Session, vol. 61, p. 8117; Frank P. Walsh to Rev. Michael O'Flanagan, 15 Nov. 1921 (N.Y.P.L., Walsh Papers, box 111); and Basil M. Manly to Senator Thomas J. Walsh, 19 Nov. 1921 (L.C., Walsh Papers, file B, box 190). On the very day that the Treaty was signed Senator Thomas J. Walsh read to the Senate the resolution passed during the summer by the Dáil expressing gratitude to the people of the United States for their support for the first Dáil loan. 6 Dec. 1921, *Congressional Record*, 67th Congress, 2nd Session, vol. 62, p. 34; and 17 Aug. 1921, *Dáil Éireann rep. 1921–22*, pp 25–6.

4. Manly to Walsh, 7 July 1921, Walsh to J. H. Daly, 4 Oct. 1921, and Walsh to Joseph Scott, 19 Oct. 1921 (N.Y.P.L., Walsh Papers, boxes 110–11); Walsh to Art Ó Briain, 4 Oct. 1921 (N.L.I., Ó Briain Papers, MS. 8427); and Walsh to John McBarron, 1 Oct. 1921 (L.C., Walsh Papers, file B, box 190).

5. Bishop Gallagher to de Valera, 16 Aug. 1921, and John A. McGarry to de Valera, 16 Aug. 1921 (A.I.H.S., Cohalan Papers, drawer 3); Executive committee of the Irish White Cross Society to Senator Thomas J. Walsh, 27 Aug. 1921, and France to Richard Campbell, 2 Sept. 1921 (L.C., Walsh Papers, file B, box 190); and *American Committee for Relief in Ireland and Irish White Cross, Report*, pp 45–6.

6. Walsh to Joseph Scott, 19 Oct. 1921 (N.Y.P.L., Walsh Papers, box 111); 26 Aug. 1921, *Dáil Éireann rep. 1921–22*, pp 84–5; and 7 Jan. 1922, *Dáil Éireann treaty deb.*, pp 302–3.

7. Stephen M. O'Mara, circular letter, autumn 1921 (N.Y.P.L., Cockran Papers, box 17). See the British consular reports for growing concern about the reported use of money raised by Irish-American groups. Maurice Peterson to Curzon, 31 Aug. 1921 (P.R.O., F.O. 371/5633). As the bond-certificate drive appeared to get under way, the British Embassy grew increasingly anxious over the amount of money being sent to Ireland, although the Foreign Office itself seemed to feel that it was really too late to make any kind of meaningful protest to the United States government. Geddes to F.O., 7 Nov. 1921, and minutes (*Ibid.*). O'Mara to Barrett, 31 Oct. 1921 (N.Y.P.L., Cockran Papers, box 17).

8. Walsh to Patrick Lydon, 20 Oct. 1921 (N.Y.P.L., Walsh Papers, box 111); and 19 Dec. 1921, *Dáil Éireann treaty deb.*, p. 35. $30,000 were raised in Washington and $552,000 in Illinois; other areas brought the amount up to $622,720. 7 Jan. 1922, *Dáil Éireann treaty deb.*, pp 303 and 335; Downing in Fitz-Gerald, p. 221; and Lynch, p. 216.

9. Walsh to James B. McCavin, 12 Dec. 1921 (L.C., Walsh Papers, file B, box 190). The senator said much the same thing to several other people as well. For descriptions of the meeting see H. W. Nevinson, *Last changes, last chances* (London, 1928), pp 199–200; and Downing in Fitz-Gerald, p. 221. Boland later explained to the Dáil that he had made favourable statements when he heard that the Treaty had been signed because he was certain that the cabinet's minimum terms had been accepted; however, he spoke out against it when he read the terms himself. 7 Jan. 1922, *Dáil Éireann treaty deb.*, pp 334–5.

10. Cited in Tansill, p. 436. Doheny's satisfaction with the Treaty was noted by the British Embassy as early as 8 December when Geddes reported to the Foreign Office that he was attempting to take credit for creating the conditions which made it possible. Geddes to F.O., 8 Dec. 1921 (P.R.O., F.O. 371/5715). It was also observed that since the signing of the Treaty James Farrell, the president of the United States Steel Corporation, who was regarded as having 'strong Sinn Féin sympathies', spoke at a luncheon for Balfour.

11. 'Minutes of the national executive of the AARIR', 17 Dec. 1921 (N.L.I., Golden Papers, MS. 13141, folder v); Downing in Fitz-

Gerald, p. 221; and Walsh to Clemens J. France, 5 Jan. 1922
(N.Y.P.L., Walsh Papers, box 112).

12. 'Memorandum—why AARIR should be maintained', and Basil M.
Manly to Thomas W. Lyons (national secretary), 14 Dec. 1921
(*Ibid.*, box 111); and Downing in Fitz-Gerald, pp 221–2. See also
Thomas W. Lyons to Harding and members of Congress, 13 Feb.
1922 (L.C., Williams Papers, box 58). The members of the state
directorate who had been expelled for refusing to contribute to
the Irish Republic Defence Fund appealed to the national executive for reinstatement at the May conference, but the appeal was
rejected. See appeal of state directorate to the national executive,
AARIR, *c*. May 1922 (N.L.I., Devoy Papers, box Misc.); *N.Y.T.*,
14 Feb. 1922; and Thomas W. Lyons to Edward L. Doheny, 15
Feb. 1922 (N.L.I., Golden Papers, MS. 13141, folder v). Henceforth Doheny's money went to Sir Horace Plunkett and his
programmes.

13. Walsh to O'Mara, 17 March 1922, and Walsh to Harry Boland, 12
Feb. 1922 (N.Y.P.L., Walsh Papers, box 115); and Downing in
Fitz-Gerald, p. 222. Captain Monteith said that the organisation
had decreased from over a million members to almost nothing, and
that he was dismissed as an organiser. Monteith, pp 248–9. *Irish
World*, 10, 17 and 31 Dec. 1921, and 7 and 14 Jan. 1922.

14. Tansill, p. 437; *G.A.*, 10 Dec. 1921; and Lynch, pp 214–15. The
national convention of the FOIF was as much concerned with
drafting an anti-British foreign policy for the United States as it
was with the Anglo-Irish Treaty. Indirectly this was of some use
to the Irish cause inasmuch as when they attempted to organise
resistance in the Senate to the Four-Power Naval Treaty they
provoked Senator Williams to make another of his anti-Irish
speeches in the Senate. The reactions of both Williams's anglophile supporters and his anglophobe Irish-American opponents was
predictable, but it mercifully drew the attention of the Irish-
Americans away from the deteriorating events in Ireland and
towards a more satisfying target. See 14 and 15 March 1922,
Congressional Record, 67th Congress, 2nd Session, vol. 62, pp 3855
and 3907–10.

15. Splain in Fitz-Gerald, pp 253–4. See also *A contrast* (n.p., 1921).
G.A., 17, 24 and 31 Dec. 1921 and 21 Jan. 1922. The *Gaelic
American* argued that de Valera was a charlatan quibbling about
meaningless terms and that he had probably worked out the
dominion solution with Lloyd George during the summer but was
attempting now to escape the responsibility for it. Devoy to Collins,
16 Feb. 1922, cited in Tansill, pp 438–9; Cohalan to Matthew
Cummings, 13 March 1922 (A.I.H.S., Cohalan Papers, drawer 3);
and Cohalan to Daniel T. O'Connell, 13 March 1922 (*Ibid.*, drawer
1). *G.A.*, 4 and 18 March and 8 and 22 April 1922; and 'Declaration on the political situation in Ireland adopted by the national
council of the FOIF', 28 March 1922 (Catholic University of

America Archives, Shahan Papers). The FOIF declaration argued that 'The British soldiers can be got out of the country; the British controlled Police can be cleared out of the barracks; the economic and educational situation can be vastly improved. Then when the Irish people again decide upon absolute separation from England, a united Race abroad can swing world sentiment against a foreign invasion of Ireland. Thus the aim of our organization with regard to Ireland will be fulfilled.'

16. Monteith, pp 246–7; and France to W. J. M. A. Maloney, 20 Dec. 1921 (N.Y.P.L., Walsh Papers, box 112). By early February Congressman Rainey of Illinois introduced a resolution to appoint an ambassador to the Irish Free State, and shortly thereafter Sir Horace Plunkett noted in his diary conversations with several members of the executive committee about serious financial investment in Ireland; Frank P. Walsh was approached by one of the editors of *Bankers' Home Magazine* about the development of American banking interests in Ireland. 3 Feb. 1922 (H.J. Res. 265), *Congressional Record*, 67th Congress, 2nd Session, vol. 62, p. 2143; Plunkett diary, 8 Feb. 1922 (Plunkett Foundation, Plunkett Papers); and George A. Carroll to Walsh, 20 Dec. 1922 (N.Y.P.L., Walsh Papers, box 111).

17. France and Douglas to Morgan J. O'Brien and Richard Campbell, 19 Jan. 1922 (L.C., Walsh Papers, file B, box 190); France to Maloney, 19 Jan. 1922, and Douglas to John D. Ryan, 19 Jan. 1922 (N.Y.P.L., Maloney Collection, Maloney Papers, box 19). Both France and Douglas were convinced that relief money would be a decisive factor in either continuing guerrilla warfare or in building political stability, and not only did they outline these views to leading Irish-Americans but they also submitted proposals to Collins suggesting that the Irish government create an 'Industrial Finance Corporation', through the sale of $25,000,000 worth of bonds in the United States, in order to carry out employment-generating reconstruction on a scale well beyond the dimensions of the present relief operations. France to Collins, 13 Jan. 1922 (*Ibid.*). The implication of these assertions by France and Douglas served to reinforce the earlier conclusions of the American Consul in Dublin, F. T. F. Dumont, that the money from the American Committee for Relief in Ireland was assisting the Irish nationalists either to fight or to resist the British government. See Dumont to Sec. of State, 23 April 1921 (N.A., 841d.00/351, roll 218). When proposals were made in the Dáil to appropriate funds for relief to compensate for the shift in policy by the American committee, they were objected to by Boland and other members of the anti-Treaty party on the grounds that the American money should be used. 18 May 1922, *Dáil Éireann rep. 1921–22*, pp 446–55.

18. Plunkett diary, 8 Feb. 1922 (Plunkett Foundation, Plunkett Papers); and Monteith, pp 248–9.

19. Collins to O'Mara, 28 Feb. 1922, cited in Lavelle, p. 278; and

James G. Douglas to W. J. M. A. Maloney, 21 Jan. 1922
(N.Y.P.L., Maloney Collection, Maloney Papers, box 19). *Irish
World*, 25 March 1922; *G.A.*, 25 March 1922; and *N.Y.T.*, 18
March 1922. John J. Hearn, Francis J. Horgan, Joseph McGarrity,
Frank P. Walsh, Dennis O'Connor, Michael A. Kelly, Rev. Michael
R. Griffin and John F. Harrigan to Collins and de Valera, 13
March 1922 (N.Y.P.L., Walsh Papers, box 112).
20. Boland to Walsh, 28 Feb. 1922 (*Ibid.*); *Irish World*, 7 and 14 Jan.,
1 and 15 April and 6, 13 and 20 May 1922; *G.A.*, 25 March, 8 and
22 April and 6 May 1922. For descriptions of the tours of the two
delegations see Lavelle, pp 279–80 and 293–4; A. Marreco, *The
rebel countess: the life and times of Constance Markievicz*
(1967; repr. London, 1969), pp 269–76; J. Van Voris, *Constance
Markievicz: in the cause of Ireland* (Amherst, 1967), pp 310–12.
See also P. H. O'Dea to Devoy, 17 April 1922 (N.L.I., Devoy
Papers, box N–OL).
21. *G.A.*, 8 July 1922; and Quinn to Hyde, 15 July 1922, cited in Reid,
pp 527–8.
22. *G.A.*, 30 Sept. 1922; and Gloster Armstrong to Foreign Secretary,
11 Sept. 1922 (P.R.O., F.O. 371/7266). Archbishop Curley wrote
privately: 'It makes the heart of an Irishman bleed to see the
senseless stupidity of the De Valera people who seem to be bent on
murder and destruction and on nothing else.' Curley to Matthew
Cummings, 2 Feb. 1923, cited in Tansill, p. 440. The indignation of
Irish-American leaders was profound also, and they tended to
hold de Valera directly responsible for the conflict. For examples
see Cohalan to Bishop Gallagher, 19 July 1922, and Judge E. J.
Gavegan to Cohalan, 6 Aug. 1922 (A.I.H.S., Cohalan Papers,
drawer 3); and P. T. O'Sullivan to Cohalan, 15 Jan. 1923 (*Ibid.*,
drawer 2).
23. W. J. M. A. Maloney, 'Memorandum on his part in attempting to
reach a truce in August 1922' (N.Y.P.L., Maloney Collection,
Maloney Papers, box 20). Maloney and Father Magennis met with
General Mulcahy, Eóin Mac Néill, and other members of the
cabinet in Dublin on 24 August and later near Cork with Mary
MacSwiney and one of her brothers for the republicans, but they
were denied permission to consult with the republican commander-
in-chief, Rory O'Connor, who was being held in Mountjoy Prison.
The talks got no further. *G.A.*, 28 Oct. and 2 and 16 Dec. 1922;
and also Lynch, p. 215.
24. Murray to John F. Finerty, 18 July 1922, Finerty to Murray, 3
Aug. 1922, and Murray to Finerty, 10 Aug. 1922 (University of
Michigan Library, Finerty Papers, drawer 2, folder 6). *Irish World*,
15 and 29 July, 23 Sept. and 25 Nov. 1922 and 5 May 1923. Indeed,
the British Consul in New York felt that but for the *Irish World*,
de Valera would have little support in America. Gloster Armstrong
to Foreign Secretary, 2 Sept. 1922 (P.R.O., F.O. 371/7266). Draft
of circular letter, 21 Sept. 1922, Mrs Sheehy-Skeffington to Walsh,

31 Oct. 1922, and Walsh to Mrs Sheehy-Skeffington, 3 Nov. 1922 (N.Y.P.L., Walsh Papers, box 112); and Finerty to de Valera, 19 Feb. 1923 (University of Michigan Library, Finerty Papers, drawer 1, folder 7). De Valera to Joseph McGarrity, 10 Sept. 1922, cited in S. Cronin, 'The Fenian tradition', *Irish Times*, 25 April 1969. See also J. J. O'Kelly, *The case for upholding the Irish Republic* (New York, n.d.).

25. Bromage, pp 23 and 191–2; Irish Free State *v.* Guaranty Safe Deposit Company (1925), 212 N.Y.S. 421; (N.Y. Sup. Crt); Irish Free State *v.* Guaranty Safe Deposit Company (1927), 222 N.Y.S. 182 at p. 184 (N.Y. Sup. Crt); Irish Free State *v.* Guaranty Safe Deposit Company (1927), 222 N.Y.S. 182 at p. 202–3 (N.Y. Sup. Crt); reversed (1931), 251 N.Y.S. 104 (N.Y. Sup. Crt App. Div.); affirmed (1931), 257, N.Y. 618; 178 N.E. 819 (N.Y. Crt App.). De Valera appealed to his supporters in the United States for the returned funds, which he used to found the *Irish Press* in 1931. *G.A.*, and *Irish World*, especially Nov. 1925, May 1927, June 1931 and Nov. 1931. For illuminating comments about the cases see James Carroll to Judge Cohalan, 20 Jan. 1923 (A.I.H.S., Cohalan Papers, drawer 1); and John J. Hearn to John F. Finerty, 13 Dec. 1922, and Finerty to de Valera, 20 Jan. 1923 (University of Michigan Library, Finerty Papers, drawer 1). The Free State government was represented by a distinguished New York law firm and was defended in court by the former United States Ambassador to Great Britain and future presidential candidate, John W. Davis. The defendants, of whom there were several parties, were represented by a number of law firms whose lawyers included John F. Finerty, Frank P. Walsh, Martin Conboy, John T. Ryan and Michael Francis Doyle. Both the Finerty Papers and the Frank P. Walsh Papers have large valuable collections of documents dealing with the bond-certificate cases.

26. John McCann to Senator Thomas J. Walsh, 27 Nov. 1922, Walsh to McCann, 18 Dec. 1922, and Mrs Margaret Walsh to Walsh, 30 Jan. 1923 and 13 Feb. 1923 (L.C., Walsh Papers, Legislative file, box 272); and Manly to Frank P. Walsh, 14 Dec. 1922 (N.Y.P.L., Walsh Papers, box 112). See, for example, *Irish Legation Circular*, no. 1 (1 Jan. 1923); and Ginnell to de Valera, 6 Jan. 1923 (N.L.I., Ó Briain Papers, MS. 8422).

27. See Ginnell to de Valera, 6 and 19 Jan. and Feb. 1923, Ginnell to Art Ó Briain, 9 Feb. and 2 March 1923, Austin J. Ford (of the *Irish World*) to Art Ó Briain, 3 Jan. 1923, and 'Message from the AARIR to Ireland', *c.* 1 March 1923 (N.L.I., Ó Briain Papers, MSS 8422 and 8428); and *Irish Legation Circular*, no. 6 (12 April 1923). Finerty to Austin Stack, 21 Nov. 1922, John J. Hearn (national treasurer of AARIR) to Thomas W. Lyons, 24 March 1923, Henry E. Smithwick (Connecticut state president, AARIR) to Finerty, 2 April 1923, and John Larkin Hughes (New Jersey state president, AARIR) to Finerty, 5 April 1923 (University of

Michigan Library, Finerty Papers, drawer 1). The republican cause found some support in pamphlets and books. See R. Mason, *Rebel Ireland* (San Francisco, 1923); Rev. A. W. Allen, *Briefs for Irish independence* (Chicago, 1923); and J. Jones, *Eighteen months with the republicans in Ireland* (Brooklyn, 1921).

28. *Irish World*, 9 June 1923; and *G.A.*, 5 May and 16 June 1923. The *Gaelic American* was by 1923 devoting much more space to Anglo-American relations and the growing foreign policy of the Irish Free State than to the civil war. De Valera's mother appealed to the President for her son on the grounds that he was an 'American born Citizen'. Mrs Catherine T. Wheelwright to President Coolidge, 22 Sept. 1923 (N.A., 841d.00/618, box 4095).

29. Senator Thomas J. Walsh to Charles Evans Hughes, 22 Feb. 1924, Senator David I. Walsh to Hughes, 23 Feb. 1924, and Congressman Samuel Dickstein to Sec. of State, 4 April 1924 (N.A., 341D.1121 VALERA, EAMON DE /46–59, box 4095). 7 Jan. 1924 (H.J. Res. 1925, *Congressional Record*, 68th Congress, 1st Session, vol. 65, p. 679; Peter F. Tague to Willard DeLue, 24 March 1924 (N.L.I., DeLue Papers, MS. 8534); and Michael J. Kelly to New York state council AARIR officers, 8 April 1924 (N.L.I., Golden Papers, MS. 13141). Finerty to Colonel Robert Olds (American Red Cross, Paris), 24 Oct. 1923, and John Barton Payne (chairman, executive committee, national headquarters, American Red Cross, Washington) to Olds, 24 Oct. 1923 (University of Michigan Library, Finerty Papers, drawer 1).

30. Letters cited in Fitz-Gerald, pp 120–1. Sir Esmé Howard to Sec. of State, 24 June 1924, and Sec. of State to British Ambassador, 28 June 1924, 701.4111/487, and C. P. Slemp (secretary to the President) to Sec. of State, 7 Oct. 1924, 701.41d11/18, *Foreign relations, 1924*, ii, pp 246–8. The Irish-American nationalist organisations continued to function on a much-reduced scale for another decade. The AARIR eventually broke with de Valera when he entered the Free State Dáil in 1927. The FOIF survived into the 1930s, largely because of its interest in the bond-certificate litigation.

31. The failure until recently of Irish-American politicians in the years since the Second World War to find any support in Congress or from the American people for their resolutions protesting the partition of Northern Ireland illustrates this point. See Kinkead to Devoy, 13 Feb. 1927 (N.L.I., Devoy Papers, box J–L); and House to Cohalan, 1 Feb. 1934 (Yale University Library, House Papers, Cohalan, Daniel F.).

32. Lowell to Bryce, 23 Nov. 1921 (Bodl., Bryce Papers, vol. 8, fol. 147); Davis to Lloyd George, 7 Dec 1921, and the Orange, New Jersey, Rotary Club to George V, 9 Dec. 1921 (P.R.O., F.O. 371/5715); and 7 Jan. 1922, *Dáil Éireann treaty deb.*, p. 303.

33. Eliot to Bryce, 7 Jan. 1922 (Bodl., Bryce Papers, vol. 1, fol. 180). Eliot also expressed indignation at the 'foolishness' of some Irish-Americans who were encouraging the Dáil to reject the Treaty.

William Richie to Williams, 16 March 1922 (L.C., Williams Papers, box 58).

34. Newberry to Hughes, 5 July 1922, and Hughes to Newberry, 10 July 1922 (N.A., 841d.00/51, roll 219); Plunkett diary, 15 Jan. 1923 (Plunkett Foundation, Plunkett Papers). Plunkett was impressed with neither Harding nor his opinions on Ireland.

35. Memorandum of conversation between Senator Thomas J. Walsh and Secretary of State Hughes, 6 Oct. 1923 (N.A., 341D.1121 VALERA, EAMON DE /49, box 4095). This impatience was also revealed in the press. See New York *Herald*, 1 July and 9, 13, 23, 24 and 25 Aug. 1922; *C.S.M.*, 1 and 5 July and 22 and 26 Aug. 1922; and *Lit. Dig.*, lxxiv, no. 3 (15 July 1922), pp 8–9, and lxxv, no. 10 (9 Dec. 1922), pp 14–15.

36. Fox to J. St Loe Strachey, 12 Dec. 1921 (Beaverbrook Library, Strachey Papers, folder 3, 1919–21). A 'Scotch-Irishman' to Senator John Sharp Williams, 10 Dec. 1921 (L.C., Williams Papers, box 57).

37. A. Gerrie, *Ireland's woes and Britain's wiles* (Boston, 1922); C. S. Burr, *America's racial heritage: an account of the diffusion of ancestral stocks in the United States during three centuries of national expansion and a discussion of its significance* (New York, 1922), pp 16 and 221; and Grant, p. 59.

BIBLIOGRAPHY

SYNOPSIS

I. MANUSCRIPT SOURCES
   A. Great Britain
   B. Ireland
   C. United States

II. OFFICIAL PUBLICATIONS
   A. Great Britain
   B. Ireland
   C. United States

III. MEMOIRS, DIARIES, AND LETTERS

IV. PAMPHLETS AND CONTEMPORARY WRITINGS
   A. Pamphlets
   B. Contemporary Writings

V. NEWSPAPERS AND PERIODICALS
   A. Newspapers
   B. Periodicals

VI. LATER WORKS

I. MANUSCRIPT SOURCES

A. Great Britain

1. *London*
Beaverbrook Library
   Lloyd George Papers
   John St Loe Strachey Papers
British Museum (British Library)
   A. J. Balfour Papers
Plunkett Foundation
   Sir Horace Plunkett Papers

Public Record Office
  Cabinet Papers
    CAB. 1
    CAB. 21
    CAB. 23
    CAB. 24
    CAB. 27
    CAB. 37
    CAB. 41
Foreign Office Papers
  F.O. 371 (Dispatches, instructions, memoranda, and minutes relating
    to United States affairs)
  F.O. 800 (Private papers in the Foreign Office collection)
    –/23   Sir Francis Hyde Villiers
    –/83–6 and 112   Sir Edward Grey
    –/208–9 and 211   Lord Balfour
    –/223 and 225   Lord Reading
    –/241–2   Sir Cecil Spring Rice
2. *Oxford*
Bodleian Library
  Lord Bryce Papers
  Sir Matthew Nathan Papers

B. Ireland

Dublin
Friends' Historical Library
  Irish Relief Work Papers 1916–1921
National Library of Ireland
  Miss Ducibella Barton Papers
  Dáil Éireann Loan Papers
  Willard DeLue Papers
  John Devoy Papers
  George Gavan Duffy Papers
  Lawrence Ginnell Papers
  Peter Golden Papers
  Mrs Alice Stopford Green Papers
  Diarmuid Lynch Papers
  Colonel Maurice Moore Papers
  Moore–Devoy Papers
  Art Ó Briain Papers
  John Quinn Papers
  John Redmond Papers
Trinity College Library
  Canon James Owen Hannay Papers

C. United States

1. *Ann Arbor*
University of Michigan Library
  John F. Finerty Papers
2. *Boston*
Massachusetts Historical Society
  Henry Cabot Lodge Papers
3. *Cambridge*
Harvard University Library
  Walter Hines Page Papers
  Oswald Garrison Villard Papers
4. *Detroit*
Chancery Archives, Archdiocese of Detroit
  Bishop Michael J. Gallagher Papers
5. *Madison*
Wisconsin State Historical Society
  Charles McCarthy Papers
6. *New Haven*
Yale University Library
  E. M. House Papers
  Frank L. Polk Papers
  Sir William Wiseman Papers
7. *New York*
American Irish Historical Society
  Judge Daniel F. Cohalan Papers
New York Public Library
  William Bourke Cockran Papers
  W. J. M. A. Maloney Collection
    Joseph McGarrity Papers
    W. J. M. A. Maloney Papers
  Frank P. Walsh Papers
8. *Washington*
Catholic University of America Archives
  Fenian Materials
  Bishop Shahan Papers
Library of Congress
  William E. Borah Papers
  William Jennings Bryan Papers
  Bainbridge Colby Papers
  Norman A. Davis Papers
  Moreton Frewen Papers
  Charles Evans Hughes Papers
  Philander C. Knox Papers
  Robert Lansing Papers
  John Purroy Mitchel Papers
  Frederick K. Nielsen Papers
  Amos Pinchot Papers

Theodore Roosevelt Papers
Joseph P. Tumulty Papers
Thomas J. Walsh Papers
John Sharp Williams Papers
Woodrow Wilson Papers
National Archives
State Department Records

II. OFFICIAL PUBLICATIONS

A. Great Britain

Hansard, Parliamentary debates, 5th series (Commons) (London, [1909–])
Documents on British foreign policy, 1919–1939, 1st series, xiv (London, 1966)
Documents relative to the Sinn Féin movement, H.C. 1921 [Cmd 1108], xxix, 429

B. Ireland

Dáil Éireann, miontuarisc an chéad Dála, 1919–1921; minutes of the proceedings of the first parliament of the Republic of Ireland, 1919–1921, official record (Dublin, [1921])
Iris Dháil Éireann, tuairisg oifigiúil, diosbóireacht ar an gConnradh idir Éire agus Sasana do signigheadh i Lundain ar an 6adh lá de mhí na Nodlag 1921: official report, debate on the Treaty between Great Britain and Ireland signed in London on the 6th December 1921 (Dublin, [1922])
Dáil Éireann, tuairisg oifigiúil (official report) [1921–22] (Dublin, [1922])

C. United States

U.S. Congress
Congressional Record
House of Representatives, Committee on Foreign Affairs, *The Irish question,* Hearings on H.J. Res. 357 (House doc. no. 1832, 65th Congress, 3rd Session), 1919
House of Representatives, Committee on Foreign Affairs, Hearings on H. Res. 3404, *To provide for the salaries of a minister and consuls to the Republic of Ireland,* 66th Congress, 2nd Session, 1920
Senate, Committee on Foreign Relations, *Treaty of peace with Germany* (Senate doc. no. 106, 66th Congress, 1st Session), 1919
Senate, Subcommittee of the Senate Judiciary Committee, *Brewing and liquor interests and German propaganda,* Hearings pursuant to Senate Res. 307 (65th Congress, 2nd and 3rd Sessions), 1919
Senate, Subcommittee of the Senate Judiciary Committee, *Hearings*

on the National German–American Alliance, 65th Congress, 2nd Session, 1918
U.S. Commerce Department
  Bureau of the Census, *Thirteenth census of the United States taken in the year 1910* (Washington, 1911)
  Bureau of the Census, *Fourteenth census of the United States taken in the year 1920* (Washington, 1922)
U.S. State Department
  Foreign relations of the United States
  1916–1924 and *supplements*
  The Lansing papers, 1914–1920
  Paris Peace Conference, 1919

III. MEMOIRS, DIARIES, AND LETTERS

Baker, R. S., *American chronicle* (New York, 1945)
Bonsal, S., *Unfinished business* (Garden City, 1944)
Connolly, N., *The unbroken tradition* (New York, 1918)
Creel, G., *Rebel at large* (New York, 1947)
Devoy, J., *Recollections of an Irish rebel* (New York, 1929)
Devoy's post-bag, ed. W. O'Brien and D. Ryan, 2 vols (Dublin, 1948–53)
Egan, M. F., *Memoirs of a happy life* (London, 1924)
Emmet, T. A., *Incidents of my life* (New York, 1911)
Fingall, Countess of, *Seventy years young* (London, 1938)
Gaffney, T. St J., *Breaking the silence* (New York, 1930)
Gerard, J. W., *My four years in Germany* (New York, 1917)
Hobson, B., *Ireland yesterday and tomorrow* (Tralee, 1968)
The intimate papers of Colonel House, ed. C. Seymour, 4 vols (Boston, 1926)
Lansing, R., *The peace negotiations* (Boston, 1921)
Lansing, R., *War memoirs of Robert Lansing* (New York, 1935)
Le Caron, Major H., pseud. [T. M. Beach], *Twenty-five years in the secret service* (London, 1892)
Leslie, S., *American wonderland* (London, 1936)
Leslie, S., *Long shadows* (London, 1966)
Lloyd George, D., *War memoirs of David Lloyd George,* 6 vols (London, 1933)
Lynch, D., *The I.R.B. and the 1916 insurrection* (Cork, 1957)
MacBride, M. G., *A servant of the queen* (Dublin, 1950)
'Extracts from the papers of the late Dr Patrick McCartan', *Clogher Rec.,* v, no. 1 (1963), and v, no. 2 (1964)
McCartan, P., *With de Valera in America* (Dublin, 1932)
Miller, D. H., *The drafting of the covenant,* 2 vols (New York, 1928)
Monteith, R., *Casement's last adventure* (Dublin, 1953)
Mullen, P., *Come another day* (London, 1940)
Murray, A., *At close quarters* (London, 1946)
Nevinson, H. W., *Last changes, last chances* (London, 1928)

O'Leary, J. A., *My political trial and experiences* (New York, 1919)
The life and letters of Walter H. Page, ed. B. J. Hendrick, 3 vols
(London, 1922–26)
Percy, Lord E., *Some memories* (London, 1958)
The letters of Theodore Roosevelt, ed. E. Morison et al., 8 vols (Cambridge, 1954)
Sheehy-Skeffington, H., *Impressions of Sinn Féin in America* (Dublin, 1919)
Skinnider, M., *Doing my bit for Ireland* (New York, 1917)
Smith, Sir F. E., *My American visit* (London, 1918)
The letters and friendships of Sir Cecil Spring Rice, ed. S. Gwynn, 2 vols (London, 1929)
Diary of George Templeton Strong, ed. A. Nevins and M. Halsey (New York, 1952)
Tumulty, J., *Woodrow Wilson as I know him* (Garden City, 1921)
Vane, Sir F., *Agin the governments* (London, 1929)
Viereck, G. S., *Spreading germs of hate* (New York, 1930)
von Rintelen, F., *The dark invader* (London, 1933)
Willert, A., *The road to safety* (London, 1925)
Field-Marshal Sir Henry Wilson, ed. Sir C. E. Callwell, 2 vols (London, 1927)
A day of dedication: the essential writings of Woodrow Wilson, ed. A. Fried (New York, 1965)
Yeats, J. B., *Letters to his son, W. B. Yeats, and others*, ed. J. Hone (London, 1944)

IV. PAMPHLETS AND CONTEMPORARY WRITINGS

A. Pamphlets

Allen, Rev A. W., *Briefs for Irish independence* (Chicago, 1923)
America wake up (Chicago, n.d.)
American Commission on Irish Independence [F. P. Walsh and E. F. Dunne], *Report on conditions in Ireland with a demand for investigation by the Peace Conference* (Paris, 1919)
American opinion on the Irish question (New York, 1917)
American Truth Society, *The conquest of the United States* (New York, 1915)
America's appeal to Ireland (Chicago, n.d.)
Casement, Sir R., *The crime against Europe: a possible outcome of the war of 1914* (Philadelphia, 1915)
Cohalan, D. F., *Freedom of the seas* (New York, 1919)
Cohalan, D. F., *Statement of Hon. Daniel F. Cohalan* (n.p., 1919)
Connolly, J. A., *The still vexed Irish question* (n.p., n.d.)
Crawford, L., *The problem of Ulster* (New York, 1920)
Defeat to all Democrats (New York, 1919)
Delegates of the Protestant Churches of Ireland, *Facts about Ireland*

for the consideration of American citizens (New York, 1920)

Downing, R. F., *A report* (n.p., 1920)

Dunne, E. F., *What Dunne saw in Ireland* (New York, 1919)

The elements arrayed against the R.C. Irish (n.p., n.d.)

The case of the Erin's Hope Branch against the New York Municipal Council of the United Irish League of America (n.p., 1904)

FOIF committee on conventions, *To the men and women of the Irish race in America* (New York, 1918)

Fox, G. L., *Ireland and the Union* (New Haven, 1918)

Fox, G. L., *Lest we forget how disloyal the Irish Sinn Féin Roman Catholics were and are* (New Haven, n.d.)

Fox, G. L., *Light on the Irish question* (New Haven, n.d.)

Fox, G. L., *More light on the Irish question* (New Haven, n.d.)

Fox, G. L., *Poisoning the wells* (New Haven, n.d.)

Fox, G. L., *Sound truth about the Irish question* (New Haven, 1918)

Gallagher, Rt Rev. M. J., *Statement dealing with matters which arose out of the visit to the United States of America of the Hon. Éamon de Valera* (Detroit, 1921)

Ginnell, L., *Ireland's case for freedom* (Chicago, 1921)

Green, A. S., *The Irish Republican Army* (Washington, n.d.)

Hughes, K., *English atrocities in Ireland* (New York, 1920)

In darkest Ulster (New York, n.d.)

Ireland and British misrule: Lloyd George's insincerity (Washington, 1920)

Ireland under English intrigue (Washington, 1920)

Ireland's attitude on conscription (n.p., n.d.)

Ireland's part in the world's war (Chicago, n.d.)

The Irish mess and an attack on the U.S. Navy (Boston, 1919)

The League of Nations and the rights of small nations (New York, 1919)

The lion's share (New York, 1919)

McCormick, A., *The Black and Tans* (Chicago, n.d.)

McCormick, W., *Irish electors again proclaim the Republic* (Washington, 1920)

McCormick, W., *Irish republican arbitration courts* (Washington, 1920)

McCoy, S. D., *Distress in Ireland* (New York, 1921)

McGarigle, J. P., *The master mind* (Niagara Falls, n.d.)

McSweeney, E. F., *America first: dedicated to the teachers and students in the schools and colleges of America* (Boston, 1920)

McSweeney, E. F., *De-Americanizing young America: poisoning the sources of our national history and traditions* (Boston, 1920)

McSweeney, E. F., *Ireland is an American question* (New York, 1919)

MacSwiney, M., *The background of the Irish Republic* (Chicago, 1921)

Mahony, T. H., *Ireland and secession, an answer to Lloyd George* (New York, 1920)

Mahony, T. H., *Similarities between the American and Irish revolutions* (New York, 1921)

Maloney, W. J. M. A., *The recognised Irish Republic* (New York, 1920)

Mason, R., *Rebel Ireland* (San Francisco, 1923)

The need for relief in Ireland (New York, 1921)

O'Callaghan, K., *The Limerick curfew murders of March 7th, 1921* (Chicago, n.d.)

O'Connell, D. T., *Edward Raymond Turner: apostle and apologist of reaction* (Washington, 1919)

[O'Connor, T. P.], *Mr T. P. O'Connor, M.P., in Chicago* (n.p., n.d.)

Official documents from Ireland, including 'Ireland's case for independence' adopted by Dáil Éireann for presentation to the Peace Conference (New York, 1919)

O'Kelly, J. J., *The case for upholding the Irish Republic* (New York, n.d.)

O'Leary, J. A., *The fable of John Bull* (New York, 1916)

Oliver, F. S., *The Irish question, federation or secession* (New York, 1917)

O'Rahilly, The, *The secret history of the Irish Volunteers,* Tracts for the times, no. 3 (Dublin, 1915)

An Irish-American [S. O'Sheel], *The catechism of Balaam, Jr.* (New York, 1915)

[O'Sheel, S.], *A trip through headline land* (New York, 1915)

Pearse, P. H., *From a hermitage*, Bodenstown series, no. 2 (Dublin, 1915)

Pearse, P. H., *Ghosts,* Tracts for the times, no. 10 (Dublin, 1916)

Plunkett, Sir H., *A defence of the Convention* (Dublin, 1917)

The re-conquest of America (New York, 1919)

Revolution and co-operation (New York, 1919)

Russell, G., *Thoughts for a convention* (Dublin, 1917)

Storey, M., and M. J. Jordan, *Americans of Irish lineage: their duties and their aims* (Boston, n.d.)

That traitorous League of Nations (New York, 1919)

Torture and terror (Chicago, n.d.)

The truth about Ireland in the Great War: an analysis of Admiral Sims' unfair attack on the Irish people (Washington, 1919)

The United States has paid its debt to France (Chicago, n.d.)

Wallace, D. A., *The revelations of an American citizen in the British army* (New York, 1916)

We must recognize the Irish Republic (Los Angeles, n.d.)

Weigle, F., *Ireland as it is today* (n.p., 1920)

Yorke, Rev. P. C., *America and Ireland, an open letter to Mr Garrett W. McEnerty* [sic] (San Francisco, 1918)

B. Contemporary Writings

American Commission on Conditions in Ireland: interim report (Chicago, 1921)

American Committee for Relief in Ireland and Irish White Cross, Report (New York, 1922)

Baldwin, E. F., *The world war* (New York, 1914)

Barry, W., *The world's debate* (New York, 1917)

Beer, G. L., *The English-speaking peoples* (New York, 1917)

Bergin, J. J., *History of the Ancient Order of Hibernians* (Dublin, n.d.)

British versus German imperialism (New York, 1915)

Bullard, A., *The diplomacy of the Great War* (New York, 1916)

Burgess, J. W., *Political science and comparative constitutional law*, 2 vols (Boston, 1890)

Burr, C. S., *America's racial heritage: an account of the diffusion of ancestral stocks in the United States during three centuries of national expansion and a discussion of its significance* (New York, 1922)

Cambray, P. G., *Irish affairs and the Home Rule question* (London, 1911)

Campbell, J. H., *History of the Friendly Sons of St Patrick and of the Hibernian Society for the Relief of Emigrants from Ireland* (Philadelphia, 1892)

Canby, H. S., *Education by violence* (New York, 1919)

Clark, E. T., *Social studies of the war* (New York, 1919)

'Cosmos', *The basis of durable peace* (New York, 1917)

Creel, G., *Ireland's fight for freedom: setting forth the high lights of Irish history* (New York, 1919)

Creel, G., *The war, the world, and Wilson* (New York, 1920)

Daly, T. A., *The Friendly Sons of St Patrick* (Philadelphia, 1920)

Davitt, M., *The fall of feudalism in Ireland* (New York, 1904)

Dawson, R., *Red terror and green* (London, 1920)

Devoy, J., *The Irish Land League* (New York, 1882)

Dos Passos, J. R., *The Anglo-Saxon century and the unification of the English-speaking people* (New York, 1903)

Escouflaire, R. C., *Ireland an enemy of the Allies?* (New York, 1920)

Evidence on conditions in Ireland, ed. A. Coyle (Washington, 1921)

Fitzgerald, F. S., *This side of paradise* (1920; repr., New York, 1960)

Fitz-Gerald, W. G. (ed.), *The voice of Ireland* (Dublin, 1924)

Ford, P., 'The Irish vote in the pending presidential election', *North Atlantic Review*, cxlvii (1888)

Francis, P., *The poison in America's cup* (New York, 1919)

Gauss, C., *Why we went to war* (New York, 1918)

Gerrie, A., *Ireland's woes and Britain's wiles* (Boston, 1922)

Gleason, A., *Inside the British Isles* (New York, 1917)

Grant, M., *The passing of the great race* (New York, 1926)

Hackett, F., *Ireland: a study in nationalism* (New York, 1918)

Henry, R. M., *The evolution of Sinn Féin* (Dublin, 1920)

Hobson, B., *A short history of the Irish Volunteers* (Dublin, 1918)

Hosmer, J. K., *A short history of Anglo-Saxon freedom* (New York, 1890)

Hugins, R., *The possible peace* (New York, 1916)

Humphrey, S. K., *The racial prospect* (New York, 1920)

Irish Free State *v.* Guaranty Safe Deposit Company (1925), 212 N.Y.S. 421; (N.Y. Sup. Crt); (1927), 222 N.Y.S. 182 at pp 184 and 202–3 (N.Y. Sup. Crt); reversed (1931), 251 N.Y.S. 104 (N.Y. Sup. Crt App. Div.); affirmed (1931), 257 N.Y. 618; 178 N.E. 819 (N.Y. Crt App.)

Johnson, T. C., *The Irish tangle and a way out* (New York, 1920)

Jones, F. P., *History of the Sinn Féin movement and the Irish rebellion of 1916,* with an introduction by Judge J. W. Goff (New York, 1917)

Jones, J., *Eighteen months with the republicans in Ireland* (Brooklyn, 1921)

Joy, M., et al., *The Irish rebellion of 1916 and its martyrs* (New York, 1916)

Joyce, E. P., 'Recognition of Ireland, not war with Britain', *America,* 30 April 1921

Kilmer, J., *Poems, essays and letters,* ed. R. C. Holliday, 2 vols (New York, 1918)

Koester, F., *The lies of the Allies* (New York, 1916)

Lea, H., *The day of the Saxon* (1912; repr. New York, 1942)

Leslie, S., *The Irish issue in its American aspect* (London 1918)

Lewis, S., *Babbitt* (1920; repr. London, 1965)

MacDonagh, M., *The Irish at the front* (London, 1916)

MacDonagh, M., *The Irish on the Somme* (London, 1917)

McEnnis, J. T., *The Clan-na-Gael and the murder of Dr Cronin* (Chicago, 1889)

McGarrity, J., *Celtic moods and memories* (Dublin, 1938)

McGrath, T. F., *History of the Ancient Order of Hibernians* (Cleveland, 1898)

McGuire, J. K., *The King, the Kaiser and Irish freedom* (New York, 1915)

McGuire, J. K., *What could Germany do for Ireland?* (New York, 1916)

MacManus, S., *Ireland's case* (New York, 1917)

Mahan, A. T., *Retrospect & prospect: studies in international relations naval and political* (London, 1902)

Maloney, W. J. M. A., *The Irish issue* (New York, 1919)

O'Brien, M. J., *A hidden phase of American history, Ireland's part in America's struggle for liberty* (New York, 1919)

Regan, J. X., *Ireland and the Presidents of the United States* (Boston, 1921)

Regan, J. X., *What made Ireland Sinn Féin* (Boston, 1921)

Report of the Irish White Cross to 31st August 1922, ed. W. J. Williams (Dublin, 1922)

Roosevelt, T., *The foes of our own household* (New York, 1917)

Russell, G., H. Plunkett and J. Quinn, *The Irish Home-Rule Convention* (New York, 1917)

Sims, W. S., *The victory at sea* (Garden City, 1919)

Steiner, E. A., *The confession of a hyphenated American* (New York, 1916)

Steiner, E. A., *Nationalizing America* (New York, 1916)

Stimson, F. J., *Popular law-making* (New York, 1912)

Strother, F., *Fighting Germany's spies* (Garden City, 1918)

Szinnyey, S. I., pseud. [S. I. Stephen], *Neutrality* (Chicago, 1916)

Turner, E. R., 'America and the Irish question', *World's Work,* xxxviii (Oct. 1919)

Turner, E. R., *Ireland and England* (New York, 1919)

Turner, E. R., 'The Sinn Féin and the United States', *World's Work,* xl (Oct. 1920)

Walsh, F. P., 'Impressions of Ireland', *Nation,* cviii (7 June 1919)

Walsh, F. P., 'Ireland at truce', *Nation,* cxiii (12 Oct. 1921)

Walsh, J. C., *The invincible Irish* (New York, 1919)

The war from this side, 2 vols (Philadelphia, 1915)

Wilson, P. W., *The Irish case before the court of public opinion* (New York, 1920)

Wister, O., *A straight deal or the ancient grudge* (New York, 1920)

Woodberry, G. E., *Torch* (1905; repr. New York, 1920)

V. NEWSPAPERS AND PERIODICALS

A. Newspapers

Boston *Herald and Journal*

Brooklyn *Citizen*

Chicago *Tribune*

Christian Science Monitor (Boston)

Freeman's Journal (Dublin)

Gaelic American (New York)

Irish World (New York)

Masonic Observer

New York *American*

New York *Evening Mail*

New York *Herald*

New York *Nation*

New York *Sunday American*

New York *Times*

New York *World*

Newark *Ledger*

Philadelphia *Record*

The Times (London)

Wall Street Journal (New York)

Washington *Evening Star*

Washington *Post*

Washington *Times*

B. Periodicals

America
Bulletin of the Irish Progressive League (copy in N.L.I., Golden Papers, MS. 13141)
Irish Legation Circular
Leslie's Weekly
Literary Digest
Living Age
Nation
New Republic
North Atlantic Review
Sinn Féiner
World's Work

VI. LATER WORKS

Adler, S., *The isolationist impulse: its twentieth-century reaction* (New York, 1957)

Bailey, T. A., *Diplomatic history of the American people* (New York, 1940)

Bailey, T. A., *Woodrow Wilson and the great betrayal* (1945; repr. Chicago, 1963)

Bailey, T. A., *Woodrow Wilson and the lost peace* (1944; repr. Chicago, 1963)

Béaslaí, P., *Michael Collins and the making of a new Ireland,* 2 vols, (London, 1926)

Bowers, C. G., *Beveridge and the Progressive era* (Boston, 1932)

Bromage, M., *De Valera and the march of a nation* (London, 1956)

Brown, T. N., *Irish-American nationalism 1870–1890* (Philadelphia, 1966)

Cronin, S., 'The Fenian tradition', *Irish Times,* 22, 25 and 29 April 1969

Curti, M., *American philanthropy abroad: a history* (New Brunswick, 1963)

D'Arcy, W., *The Fenian movement in the United States 1858–1886* (Washington, 1947)

Digby, M., *Horace Plunkett: Anglo-American Irishman* (Oxford, 1949)

Donohoe, Sister J. M., *The Irish Catholic Benevolent Union* (Washington, 1953)

Duff, J. B., 'The Versailles Treaty and the Irish-Americans,' *Jn. Amer. Hist.,* lv (Dec. 1968)

Edwards, O. D., and F. Pyle (ed.), *1916: the Easter Rising* (London, 1968)

Fleming, D. F., *The treaty veto of the American Senate* (New York, 1930)

Fowler, W. B., *British-American relations, 1917–1918* (Princeton, 1969)

Fyfe, H., *T. P. O'Connor* (London, 1934)

Gelfand, L. E., *The inquiry: American preparations for peace, 1917–1919* (New Haven, 1963)

Gerson, L. L., *The hypenate in recent American politics and diplomacy* (Lawrence, 1964)

Gerson, L. L., *Woodrow Wilson and the rebirth of Poland* (New Haven, 1953)

Gibson, F. E., *The attitudes of the New York Irish towards state and national affairs 1848–1892* (New York, 1951)

Glynn, A., *High upon the gallows tree* (Tralee, 1967)

Gwynn, D., *De Valera* (London, 1933)

Gwynn, D., *The life and death of Roger Casement* (London, 1930)

Gwynn, D., *The life of John Redmond* (London, 1932)

Hachey, T. E., 'The Irish question: the British Foreign Office and the American political conventions of 1920', *Éire–Ireland*, iii, no. 3 (autumn, 1968)

Handlin, O., *Boston's immigrants* (1941; repr. Cambridge, 1959)

Harkness, D. W., *The restless dominion: the Irish Free State and the British Commonwealth of Nations, 1921–31* (New York, 1970)

Helbich, W. J., 'American liberals in the League of Nations controversy', *Public Opinion Quarterly*, xxxi, no. 4 (winter, 1967–68)

Higham, J., *Strangers in the land* (1955; repr. New York, 1963)

Hofstader, R., *Social Darwinism in America* (1944; repr. Boston, 1955)

Hyde, H. M., *Lord Reading* (London, 1967)

Jenkins, R., *Asquith* (London, 1964)

Lancaster, K. R., 'The Protestant churches and the fight for ratification of the Versailles Treaty', *Public Opinion Quarterly*, xxxi, no. 4 (winter 1967–68)

Larkin, E., *James Larkin, Irish labour leader, 1876–1947* (London, 1965)

Lavelle, P., *James O'Mara: a staunch Sinn-Féiner 1873–1948* (Dublin, 1961)

Leary, W. M., 'Woodrow Wilson, Irish Americans, and the election of 1916', *Jn. Amer. Hist.*, liv (June 1967)

Le Roux, L. N., *Patrick H. Pearse* (Dublin, 1932)

Le Roux, L. N., *Tom Clarke and the Irish freedom movement* (Dublin, 1936)

Levin, N. G., *Woodrow Wilson and world politics* (New York, 1968)

Link, A. S., *Wilson: campaigns for Progressivism and peace, 1916–1917* (Princeton, 1965)

Link, A. S., *Woodrow Wilson and the Progressive era 1910–1917* (New York, 1963)

Longford, Earl of, and T. P. O'Neill, *Éamon de Valera* (1970; repr. Boston, 1971)

Lyons, F. S. L., *The fall of Parnell 1890–91* (London, 1960)

Lyons, F. S. L., *The Irish Parliamentary Party* (London, 1951)

Lyons, F. S. L., *John Dillon: a biography* (London, 1968)

Macardle, D., *The Irish Republic: a documented chronicle of the Anglo-Irish conflict* (1937; repr. New York, 1965)

MacColl, R., *Roger Casement* (London, 1956)

McDowell, R. B., *The Irish Convention, 1917–18* (London, 1970)

McGurrin, J., *Bourke Cockran: a free lance in American politics* (New York, 1948)

McKenna, M. C., *Borah* (Ann Arbor, 1961)

MacManus, M. J., *Éamon de Valera: a biography* (1944; repr. Dublin, 1962)

Marreco, A., *The rebel countess: the life and times of Constance Markievicz* (1967; repr. London, 1969)

Martin, F. X. (ed.), *The Irish Volunteers, 1913–15* (Dublin, 1963)

Martin, F. X. (ed.), *Leaders and men of the Easter Rising: Dublin 1916* (London, 1967)

Maxwell, K. R., 'Irish-Americans and the fight for treaty ratification', *Public Opinion Quarterly*, xxxi, no. 4 (winter 1967–68)

Moody, T. W., 'Irish-American nationalism', *I.H.S.*, xv, no. 60 (Sept. 1967)

Moody, T. W., 'The New Departure in Irish politics, 1878–9' in H. A. Cronne, T. W. Moody and D. B. Quinn (ed.), *Essays . . . in honour of James Eadie Todd* (London, 1949)

Nowlan, K. B. (ed.), *The making of 1916: studies in the history of the Rising* (Dublin, 1969)

Noyes, A., *The accusing ghost of Roger Casement* (London, 1957)

O'Doherty, K., *Assignment America: de Valera's mission to the United States* (New York, 1957)

O'Grady, J. P. (ed.), *The immigrants' influence on Wilson's peace policies* (Lexington, 1967)

Osborn, G. C., *John Sharp Williams* (Baton Rouge, 1943)

Paine, A. B., *Thomas Nast, his period and his pictures* (New York, 1904)

Parmiter, G. de C., *Roger Casement* (London, 1936)

Parnell, J. H., *Charles Stewart Parnell* (New York, 1914)

Reid, B. L., *The man from New York: John Quinn and his friends* (New York, 1968)

Ryan, D., *The phoenix flame* (London, 1937)

Ryan, D., *Unique dictator, a study of Éamon de Valera* (London, 1936)

Schrier, A., *Ireland and the American emigration 1850–1900* (Minneapolis, 1958)

Shannon, W. V., *The American Irish* (New York, 1963)

Tansill, C. C., *America and the fight for Irish freedom 1866–1922* (New York, 1957)

These eventful years, the twentieth century in the making, 2 vols (London, 1924)

Tillman, S., *Anglo-American relations at the Paris Peace Conference of 1919* (Princeton, 1961)

Tucker, D. M., 'Some American responses to the Easter rebellion, 1916', *The Historian,* xxix (Aug. 1967)

Van Voris, J., *Constance Markievicz: in the cause of Ireland* (Amherst, 1967)

Vinson, J. C., *Thomas Nast, political cartoonist* (Athens, 1967)

Ward, A. J., 'America and the Irish problem, 1899–1921', *I.H.S.,* xvi, no. 61 (March 1968)

Ward, A. J., 'Frewen's Anglo-American campaign for federalism, 1911–21', *I.H.S.,* xv, no. 59 March 1967)

Ward, A. J., *Ireland and Anglo-American relations, 1899–1921* (London, 1969)

Wells, W. B., *The life of John Redmond* (New York, 1919)

Williams, T. D. (ed.), *Secret societies in Ireland* (Dublin, 1973)

Wittke, C., *The Irish in America* (Baton Rouge, 1956)

Young, K., *Arthur James Balfour* (London, 1963)

INDEX

Abbey Players, in US, 30
Adams, Edward L., 63
Addams, Jane, 163
Adler, Selig, 261n
Africa, 71, 73, 147
Ahern, Lt. Col. G.P., 129
Aiken, Frank, 186
Allied Loyalty League, 280n
America, 114, 125, 144
American Association for the Recognition of the Irish Republic, 5, 159-60, 166, 187, 197, 198; response to Admiral Sims, 174, 178; Anglo-Irish Treaty, 180-1, 183, 283n, 287n; Irish Civil War, 184-5
American Civil War *see* United States Civil War
American Commission on Conditions in Ireland, 162-3, 172, 198, 202, 206; hearings, 161, 164-5; reports, 164
American Commission on Irish Independence, 198, 202, 205, 206, 264n; in Paris, 131-2, 135-8, 255n, 256n; in Ireland, 133-4, 253-4n; senate hearings on peace treaty, 142-3, 259n; assists bond-certificate drive, 151, 153
American Commission to Negotiate Peace, 124, 131, 194, 200, 206; concerned with Irish affairs, 132, 135, 136, 138, 142, 255n
American Committee for Relief in Ireland, 162,

166-7, 175, 197, 198, 202, 275-7n; operations in Ireland, 167-8, 179, 284n
American Land League, 6
American National League, 6, 7
American Opinion, Irish question, 2-3, 9-10; home rule, 15, 19, 41; independence, 50; Ireland during the war, 93, 95, 97, 99, 117, 232n, 235-6n, 280n; Anglo-Irish truce, 177; recognition of Free State, 187, 192
American Rights Committee, 65
American Truth Society, 51, 103, 203
American Volunteer Fund, 32; American provisional committee, 32
Ancient Order of Hibernians, 6, 7, 27, 34, 230n; break with Redmond, 35, 38, 43, 48, 68, 216n; war crisis, 98, 106, 114; self-determination, 123, 146, 247n; bond-certificate drive, 151, 152
Austin, Walter I., 119
Austria, 47, 135
Austrian - Americanism, 146
Auxiliaries, 164
Anglo-American arbitration treaties, 9, 28, 29, 30, 192, 262n
Anglo-American relations, 10, 18, 20, 191, 203, 204, 206, 214,

287n; Casement, 77; during the war, 89, 90, 93, 94, 100; at peace conference, 123, 139; naval rivalry, 169, 192; threat of arms shipments, 170; native American desires, 172, 173; Anglo - Irish Treaty, 180
Anglo-Irish Treaty, 177, 179-80; disputes, 181, 183, 184, 188, 190, 195, 196, 201, 283n, 287; oath, 188
Anglo-Irish truce, 176, 177, 188
Anglo-Irish War (Irish War of Independence), 163-4, 166, 170, 196, 197, 198, 284n; State Department opinion, 268n
Anglo-Japanese Alliance, 169, 200
Anglo-Saxon superiority, 11, 12, 171
Anglophobia *see* anti-British sentiment
anti-American sentiment, 172
anti-British sentiment, 2, 10, 29, 40, 41, 42, 83, 102, 140, 144, 191, 198, 202, 203, 281n, 283n
anti-Catholic sentiment, 117, 139, 173, 191, 196, 213n
Anti-Imperialist League, 131, 278n
anti-Irish sentiment, 71, 105, 106, 117, 125, 130, 139, 149, 170, 173, 191, 196, 198, 206, 213n, 279n, 283n

and Versailles Treaty
Pearse, Patrick H., 30, 31, 50, 57, 59
Pellitier, Joseph C., 275n
Percy, Lord Eustace, 34, 44, 224n
Pershing, Gen. John J., 118, 119
Phelan, Sen. James D., 203, 242n, 275n; Casement resolution, 71, 75, 82; sends appeals to Wilson, 101, 105, 112; reply to Sen. Williams, 138, 261-2n; debate on Article X, 145-6
Philadelphia *Public Ledger*, 78, 113
Philadelphia *North American*, 37, 41
Phillips, W. Alison, 233n
Phillips, William, 129
Phoenix Park murders, 56
pickets, 154, 267n
Pillsbury, A. E., 41
Pinchot, Amos, 272n
Pittman, Sen. Key, 75, 76, 130, 226n; Pittman resolution, 75-6
Plunkett, George, Count, 131, 132, 133, 137, 138, 203, 270n
Plunkett, Sir Horace, 23, 24, 30, 40, 60, 61, 85, 117, 138, 200, 203, 241n; Balfour mission, 95, 97, 234n; Irish Convention, 99-100, 109-10, 235-6; Irish nurses for US Army, 118-19; moderate solution to Irish question, 129, 132; talks with American Committee for Relief in Ireland, 182-3, 284n
Poets' Meeting, New York, Central Park, 59, 66
Poindexter, Sen. Miles, 146
Poland, 92, 121, 127, 130, 139, 150, 190
Polk, Frank L., 204, 239n, 254; Kern resolution, 62, Casement appeals, 72, 73, 77, 82-3, 226n; 1916 relief efforts, 80; Gal-

lagher resolution, 125, 249n; prospects for Irish settlement, 129
Pomerene, Sen. Atlee, 76
Pond, Allen B., 130
population, Irish-American, 3, 208-9n
Preston, John W., 103
Price, William, 275n
pro-Ally sentiment, 41, 46, 82
pro-British sentiment, 48, 50, 81, 84, 171, 191, 198, 207
pro-German sentiment, among constitutional nationalists, 40, 41, 43; among revolutionary nationalists, 29, 46-7, 51-2, 67, 84, 104, 112, 146, 198, 202-3, 205, 279n
pro-Irish sentiment, 72, 89, 192, 198
Protestant Friends of Ireland, 278n
Protestantism, 71, 208n, 212n
Provisional Government, *see* Irish Free state government
Pulleyn, John J., 275n
Putnam, George Haven, 171

Queenstown, 104, 173, 174, 205
Quinn, John, 30, 65, 204, 275n; concern about home rule, 23, 24, 40, 213n, 217n; Casement, 35, 77, 78, 228n; moderate position during war, 90, 93, 95, 97, 99, 101, 103, 129, 233n; civil war, 184
Quincy, Josiah, 73

racial bias, native American, 10-13 passim, 21, 171, 191
Rainey, Cong. John W., 284n
Rankin, Cong. Jeanette, 105, 115, 128, 239n; Rankin resolution, 105
Ransdell, Sen. Joseph, 273n
Reading, Lord, 108, 109, 111, 200, 204, 241n, 244n, 251n

Red Cross, American, 165, 187, 274n, 276n; British, 165, 168; Irish, 165
Redmond, John, 74, 200, 204, 205, 214n, 216n; reunion of Irish Parliamentary Party, 7, 8; holds balance of power in House of Commons, 15, 17, 212n; praised for home rule progress, 20, 22, 27; control of Irish Volunteers, 32-5; loyalty to Empire in war, 36-46, 53; founds *Ireland*, 44-6; undercut by Rising, 56, 57, 64-8 passim, 222n, 231n; failure of home rule 1916, 70, 225n; need for relief, 79; assistance from US, 81, 87, 94-6, 101, 237n
Reed, Sen. James A., 16, 175
Regan, James J., 34, 216n
Regan, John X., 155
Reid, Whitelaw, 16
Reidy, James, 32, 248n
relief operations, 1921-2, 165-7, 170, 179, 182, 199, 225n, 228n; *see also* American Committee for Relief in Ireland, *and* Irish White Cross Society
religious bias, native American, 10-13, 21, 117, 171, 191
Repeal movement, 5, 11
Republican Party (US), attempts to win Irish-American support, 6, 17, 210n; 1916 election, 82-4; support Irish objectives in senate, 137, 139, 141-2, 249n, 262n; 1920 elections, 155, 159, 161-2, 268n
Republicans, anti-Treaty, *see* Anglo-Irish Treaty *and* Irish Civil War
Rice, Laurence J., 180
Riley, Judge Thomas P., 64
Rintelen, Captain Franz von, 49

alarmed by conscription crisis, 108-10; sends Baker to Ireland, 110-11, 241n; disapproves of McCarthy, 119; appealed to for action at peace conference, 121-3, 127-8, 247n, 248n; Gallagher resolution, 124-6, 249n; Metropolitan Opera House meeting, 128, 251-2n; meetings with Walsh, Dunne and Ryan, 132, 134-6, 253-4, 256n; lost support of Irish in League

fight, 139, 140, 142, 144-6, 153, 260n; appealed to by de Valera, 154
Winslow, Irving, 131
Wiseman, Sir William, 90, 108, 109, 111, 134, 144, 207, 241n, 254
Wister, Owen, 173
Women's International League, 164
Wood, L. Hollingsworth, 163, 274n, 275n
Woodberry, George Edward, 11
Woodenbridge, Redmond's speech at, 37,

47
Woolsey, L. H., 72, 226n
Wynne, Rev. John J., 234n

Yeats, John Butler, 30
Yeats, William Butler, 9, 204
Yorke, Rev. Peter F., 68, 160, 250n
Young, Kenneth, 232n
Yugoslavia, 130, 190

Zimmerman, Herr Arthur, 87